The Chinese Diaspora

The Why of Where
Series Editor: George J. Demko

Forthcoming:

Our Place in Time: A Cultural Geography of Popular Music
  by David J. Keeling

The Why of Where: Geography That Matters
  by George J. Demko

The Chinese Diaspora

Space, Place, Mobility, and Identity

Edited by Laurence J. C. Ma
and Carolyn Cartier

ROWMAN & LITTLEFIELD PUBLISHERS, INC.
Lanham • Boulder • New York • Oxford

ROWMAN & LITTLEFIELD PUBLISHERS, INC.

Published in the United States of America
by Rowman & Littlefield Publishers, Inc.
A Member of the Rowman & Littlefield Publishing Group
4720 Boston Way, Lanham, Maryland 20706
www.rowmanlittlefield.com

PO Box 317, Oxford, OX2 9RU, United Kingdom

British Library Cataloguing in Publication Information Available

Library of Congress Cataloging-in-Publication Data

The Chinese diaspora : space, place, mobility, and identity / edited by
Laurence J. C. Ma and Carolyn Cartier.
    p. cm. — (Why of where)
  ISBN 0-7425-1755-1 (cloth : alk. paper)—ISBN 0-7425-1756-X (pbk. :
alk. paper)
  1. Chinese—Foreign countries.   I. Ma, Laurence J. C., 1937– II.
Cartier, Carolyn L.   III. Series.
  DS732 .C5563 2003
  909'.04951—dc21

                                                                    2002151795

Printed in the United States of America

♾™ The paper used in this publication meets the minimum requirements of American
National Standard for Information Sciences—Permanence of Paper for Printed Library
Materials, ANSI/NISO Z39.48-1992.

Contents

Acknowledgments   vii

1   Space, Place, and Transnationalism in the Chinese Diaspora   1
      Laurence J. C. Ma

2   The Chinese Diaspora or the Migration of Chinese Peoples?   51
      Ronald Skeldon

Part I: Historical and Contemporary Diasporas

3   Diaspora and Social Restructuring in Postcolonial Malaysia   69
      Carolyn Cartier

4   Exclusion and Embeddedness: The Chinese in   97
      Thailand and Vietnam
      Jonathan Rigg

5   A Diaspora of Chinese Settlement in Latin America   117
      and the Caribbean
      Robert B. Kent

Part II: Hong Kong and Taiwan As Diasporic Homelands

6   Identity, Mobility, and the Making of the Chinese Diasporic
      Landscape in Hong Kong   141
      George C. S. Lin

7   Who Are the Taiwanese? Taiwan in the Chinese Diaspora   163
     Jack F. Williams

Part III: Ethnicity, Identity, and Diaspora As Home

8   Nation, Ethnicity, and Identity: Singapore and the
     Dynamics and Discourses of Chinese Migration   193
     Lily Kong and Brenda Yeoh

9   Ethnic Identity and Business Solidarity:
     Chinese Capitalism Revisited   221
     You-tien Hsing

10   Notions of Home among Diaspora Chinese in Germany   237
     Maggi W. H. Leung

Part IV: Migration and Settlements in North America

11   Chinese Americans: Immigration, Settlement,
     and Social Geography   261
     C. Cindy Fan

12   Community As Catalyst: The Chinese in Honolulu   293
     Sen-dou Chang

13   From Downtown Slums to Suburban Malls:
     Chinese Migration and Settlement in Canada   311
     David Chuenyan Lai

Part V: Transmigrants in Oceania

14   Chinese Immigrants and Transnationals in New Zealand:
     A Fortress Opened   339
     Manying Ip

15   New Middle-Class Chinese Settlers in Australia and the
     Spatial Transformation of Settlement in Sydney   359
     Chung-Tong Wu

16   Conclusion: Regions of Diaspora   379
     Carolyn Cartier

Index   391

About the Editors and Contributors   397

Acknowledgments

In the last three decades or so, geographical ideas and the work of human geographers have attracted increasing attention in cognate fields, especially history, anthropology, sociology, and economics. In China studies, there has been a distinctive "spatial turn" that has foregrounded the significance of space, place, and region in the analysis of historical, social, economic, and demographic issues. However, in the field of international migration research the mainstream paradigms have been more sociological and economic than geographical, despite the fact that migration is fundamentally place-based and characterized by spatial processes. Against this intellectual backdrop, this volume set as its main goal to feature the work of geographers and scholars with geographic perspectives on migration studies of Chinese overseas. The chapters in the volume also represent a diversity of geographical methods, including historical, hermeneutic, political, and economic approaches. We look forward to the book taking its place among recent studies of Chinese overseas, and to inspiring further work on geographical studies of migration.

We are grateful to all the contributing authors whose quick acceptance of our invitation to join the project convinced us of its merits. Several contributors were kind enough to rewrite or update their contributions following the release of new data or in response to new events. Whereas we are responsible for the scope of the book and selection of authors, the volume owes its initial origins to George Demko of the Department of Geography at Dartmouth College, who first suggested we do a book on the Chinese diaspora. We thank him for his foresight in identifying the rising scholarly interest in these subjects. We also thank assistant editor Alden Perkins, who gave meticulous attention to editorial matters and worked with us unfailingly in the final production of the volume. Xingli Zhang, doctoral candidate in International

Studies at the University of Southern California, assisted with the preparation of the index. Above all, we are grateful to Susan McEachern, our editor at Rowman and Littlefield, whose gracious encouragement and direct involvement in the evolution and production of the book made a substantial contribution to its quality and completion.

Laurence J. C. Ma
Carolyn Cartier

1

Space, Place, and Transnationalism in the Chinese Diaspora

Laurence J. C. Ma

Since the mid-1960s, the world has witnessed a dramatic increase in population mobility across international borders. From 1965 to 1990, the total migrant stock of the world grew from 75 to 120 million persons, involving almost all countries of the world (Zlotnik, 1998). The reasons for such an increased mobility are complex, ranging from the structural changes in developing countries, new immigration policies adopted by the leading Western nations, more efficient transportation and improved telecommunication technology that have compressed both time and space, a new international division of labor, increasing spatial fluidity of global capital, and the rise of flexible production and specialization in the global economy that allows smaller units of production to compete with multinational corporations (Harvey, 1989; Kritz, Lim and Zlotnik, 1992; Massey, 1998; Skeldon, 1997). Indeed, people everywhere have been on the move at such a large scale that it has been said that the contemporary world is in "the age of migration" (Castles and Miller, 1996).

Aside from a much greater volume, the social, economic and geographic patterns of international migration in the last three decades have differed significantly from those of earlier eras. Historic international migration was characterized by permanent, unidirectional, and onetime movement of people from one country to another often under economic, religious, or political duress at the places of origin. In some cases, the geographic uprootedness of migration meant the loss of homeland and the rupture of society as a consequence of oppression imposed on migrants by the authorities at places of origin, as typified by the movement of the Jews and African slaves. In other cases, migrants, voluntary as well as involuntary, worked under marginal conditions and suffered from social discrimination in host nations, such as the laborers recruited legally or shanghaied to work in the colonies of Western powers during the nineteenth century. In general, migrants tended to be spatially clustered in enclaves with little or no contact with the mainstream society, and their spatial and social interaction with their families back home was severely limited by the friction of distance.

The Chinese have been involved in international migration for centuries. In this introductory chapter, I divide the history of Chinese international migration into two broad periods to underscore the profound changes that have occurred since the 1960s. The circumstances surrounding overseas migration of the Chinese and the economic, geographic and social consequences in host societies prior to the 1960s were dramatically different from those in the post-1960s era. During the nineteenth and early twentieth centuries, Chinese migrants, primarily villagers from Guangdong and Fujian provinces in South China, went abroad as laborers, traders and farmers (Chen, 1940; Pan, 1999; Wang, 1991; Wickberg, 1994; Chen, 1999). However, in the last three decades, many Chinese have emigrated from Hong Kong, Taiwan and different parts of China and Southeast Asia. In the late 1980s and early 1990s, out-migration from Hong Kong was due largely to perceived political uncertainties associated with the return of Hong Kong to China in 1997. Likewise, emigration from Taiwan since the 1960s to a large extent has been attributable to political instability, paradoxically amidst economic prosperity, arising from fears of military intervention from mainland China. In both cases, income and employment are not the dominant reasons for emigration because Hong Kong and Taiwan have long achieved the status of newly industrialized nations where the economies have been prospering.[1] Re-migration of the Chinese from Southeast Asian nations to the United States, Canada, Australia and European countries since the 1960s has been due mainly to overt discrimination, hostility and sometimes violence against the Chinese. More recently, many recent Chinese transnational migrants are well-educated and relatively well-off businessmen or professionals. Still, the tragedies of "container migration" at the turn of the century demonstrate how Chinese migrants have diverse economic backgrounds. In response to technological, economic and immigration policy changes in Western societies, and spurred by the rise of the Asian economies and China's opening to the world economy in 1978, an unprecedented diversity of Chinese migrants have entered the global migration stream in the late twentieth and the beginning of the twenty-first centuries.

EXISTING THEORIES OF INTERNATIONAL MIGRATION

The nature of Chinese global migration since the 1960s raises important theoretical questions, since existing migration theories do not encompass the diverse experiences of the Chinese migrants abroad and are unable to account for the causes and consequences of their global movements. In the international migration literature, four major schools of thought have attempted to account for the causal processes of migration (Massey et al., 1994; Massey, 1999). First, neoclassical theories have focused on the factors of spatial imbalance in employment opportunities, regional wage differentials, expected income gaps for individuals or households, and changes in economic structure that cause economic disruption and leads to migration. Second and more recently, scholars of the new economics of migration have argued that international migration arises from the failures of the markets in the sending nations that threaten the material well-being of households and create barriers to their economic advancement. The third view relates to the thesis of people's desire to alleviate "relative deprivation," based on the assumption that migrants have a strong desire to improve their income so as to keep up with the Joneses in their community. Thus to reduce economic risks and to improve income, households send one or more family members of working age to foreign labor markets. Fourthly, the segmented labor market theory sees global migration as demand driven in advanced industrial societies where a two-sector economy exists that divides employment into a primary or advanced sector and a secondary sector. The primary sector uses skilled local labor while the secondary or informal sector employs low-skilled and low-wage workers who are often from overseas. Elements of each of these perspectives may be appropriate to informing the situation of Chinese migrants from different places and at different points in history, but no single perspective suitably frames the complexities of the diaspora.

In addition to these four schools of thought, scholars have used world systems theory, social capital theory, and the theory of cumulative causation to inform questions about migration, questions that extend beyond immediate economic factors to encompass the larger scale processes of the world economy in which migration events take place (Massey, 1999; Massey et al., 1994). World systems theory has provided perspectives on relations between core and peripheral economies, with more attention to the "global" and the "local," while perspectives on social capital and cumulative causation better inform the social and economic contexts of migration. Social capital theory has relevance for studying social relations among Chinese overseas for its emphasis on networks of relationships and how those relationships support economic activities, specifically, how social capital is convertible and may be translated into other forms of capital, especially financial capital. The theory of cumulative causation recognizes how migration events influence the social context of positive decisions about future migrations, and is suited to analysis of places where migration has been common over time. Migration from the coastal provinces of South China, the hearth of the Chinese diaspora, is in part cumulatively caused by the knowledge of numerous past migrations and their widespread effects. Still, these theoretical perspectives do not take into account the place-based qualities and spatial processes of Chinese diasporic migration (see Cartier, 2001).

TRANSMIGRATION, TRANSNATIONALISM AND DIASPORA

In an age of increasing globalization, greater spatial mobility has engendered a host of new migration phenomena across global space, including new settlement patterns and increased levels of spatial interaction between homeland and hostland, and among diverse places settled by global "tribes" (Kotkin, 1993). The old conceptions of international migration are simply incapable of capturing the essence of the rapidly changing nature of global migration, and new analytical frameworks are needed to understand the complex nature of new migrant geographies, social behaviors, economic activities and shifting cultural identities. To account for these new developments, two related conceptual frameworks have surfaced in the last two decades in the terms transmigration and diaspora. Inherently interdisciplinary, ideas about transmigration and diaspora encompass more dynamic, flexible, conceptually richer and more inclusive perspectives than the traditional conceptions of international migration. Transmigration and diaspora are among the most important constituent elements of the concept of transnationalism, and each has generated a vast amount of literature (see, for example, Bird et al., 1993; Clifford, 1997; Cohen, 1995, 1997; Fawcett and Carino, 1987; Hannerz, 1996; Hirst and Zeitlin, 1991; Kotkin, 1993; Olds et al., 1999; Pedersen et al., 1994; Schiller, Basch and Blanc-Szanton, 1992; Smith and Guarnizo, 1998; Van Hear, 1998; Vertovec and Cohen, 1999; Wang, 1997).

Transnationalism is a widely used concept and carries diverse meanings. Globalization of production and increasing spatial mobility due to more efficient transportation and communication have given rise to the characteristics of contemporary transnationalism. Schiller et al. (1992: 1–2) have conceptualized transnationalism as

> the process by which immigrants build social fields that link together their country of origin and their country of settlement. Immigrants who build such social fields are designated "transmigrants." Transmigrants develop and maintain multiple relations—familial, economic, social, organizational, religious, and political that span borders. Transmigrants take actions, make decisions, and feel concerns, and develop identities within social networks that connect them to two or more societies simultaneously.

This definition puts heavy emphasis on the process of creating transmigrants' "social fields" and sees transnationalism as a dynamic social process. While "social fields" are not precisely defined, they appear as a type of global space in which social, cultural, economic and political relations for a large group of people from a common place of origin are constituted and located. This space is transnational, i.e., it transcends the borders of nation-states without fundamentally undermining the meanings of nation-state powers. This is a space with contested cultural boundaries, flexible citizenship, and intensive flows of people, capital, subcontracted goods, technology and information, all tied directly or indirectly in their own ways with the transmigrants and their place-based social networks. It is the tension between the idea of diasporic individuals as creative and mobile agents and the continuing role of the nation-state in regulating the legal flows of people, capital and goods that suggests how we have to look beyond national borders to understand transnationalism and the formation of diasporas. This view is supported by Tölölyan (1991: 5) who argues that the power of the nation-state remains strong in a world where "diasporas are the exemplary communities of the transnational moment."

The word diaspora has been around for centuries and the world has been full of diasporas of different geographic origins and socioeconomic characteristics. Increasing spatial dispersal of transmigrants from different homelands in the last three decades has led to enhanced interest in the concept, rendering it a central idea in the study of transmigration. Indeed, as Skeldon's essay in this volume has noted, the term "diaspora" has been used so much lately that it has almost displaced the word "migration." He reminds us to pay attention to the diverse experiences of various Chinese migrant groups overseas and not to be carried away by the implicit meaning of uniformity embodied in the term "diaspora." To Skeldon, a Chinese diaspora exists, but it is made up of complex elements of migration. Similarly, Tölölyan (1996: 3) has observed that recent scholarly discourse on population dispersion has shifted its terminology preference to such an extent that the term "diasporas" has replaced such post-1960s names of communities of dispersion as exile groups, overseas communities and even ethnic and racial minorities.

In this introductory chapter, I propose that diasporas are best viewed geographically as complex and interrelated sets of places and spatial processes, created as a consequence of varied forms of transmigration and transnational economic activity. As Tölölyan (1991) has pointed out, diasporas are concerned with all of the forces and phenomena that constitute transnational movements, including the movements of capital, the introduction of alien cultures, the formation of plural societies, dual loyalties of populations, and multiple affiliations of transnational corporations. There have been intense scholarly interests in the intimate relationship between diaspora and transmigration, as can be seen from the growing number of papers on international migration in such established journals as *International Migration Review, Population and Development Review, International Migration* and *Asian and Pacific Migration Review*. In the last two decades, our understanding of transnationalism and global diasporas has been significantly enhanced by the publication of several new and more focused professional journals such as *Diaspora: A Journal of Transnational Studies* (since 1991), *Public Culture* (since 1988), *Transition* (since 1992), *Position: East Asia Cultures Critique* (since 1993) and *Sojourn* (since 1986). The way that scholarly discourse on dispersion has been redefined by and transformed into diaspora is truly remarkable. In the process of this conceptual shift, the negative characteristics of classic diasporas such as the loss of homeland, a collective memory of oppression and the gnawing desire for return have been suppressed, while the positive connotations of diasporas such as supermobility and flexible identities on the part of transmigrants as well as multiculturalism and transnational flows of capital have been elevated.

The growing literature on transmigration and diaspora has been produced substantially by anthropologists, sociologists, historians, geographers and literary critics. That migration, settlements of migrant communities and varied activities of migrants all occur in specific *places* is axiomatic, and that transmigration and globalization happen in and across *space* is indisputable. The thought patterns, actions and identities of transmigrants are shaped powerfully by experiences in their places of origin, travel and destination, which in turn are affected by their activities through remittances, investment and return visits to the homeland and by settlement formation, landscape modification, ethnic diversification and contribution to multiculturalism in the hostland.

In his recent analysis on the nature of diasporas, Gilroy (1994: 207) echoes the views of a number of leading scholars that diaspora is a new vocabulary that "registers the constitutive potency of *space, spatiality, distance, travel* and *itinerancy* in human sciences that had been premised upon time, temporality, fixity, rootedness and the sedentary" (emphases added). It is clear from this statement that diasporas are inherently geographic. However, despite such insights and the views that diasporas are "spaces of dispersal" (Kirshenblatt-Gimblett, 1994) and that a diasporic perspective "can direct the analysis of geographically dispersed institutions, identities, links, and flows" (McKeown, 1999: 307), the geographic character of diasporas has never been clearly articulated and specified, and the basic geographic concepts of space and place have rarely been foregrounded in the transmigration literature. Diasporas have been associated with "routes" and "travels" (Clifford, 1997) that treat ideas about space and place metaphorically. Cultural theorists have interpreted diasporas as "social form," "type of consciousness," "mode of cultural production" (Vertovec and Cohen, 1999: xvii–xx), and as deterritorialized cultural domain in the current age whose basic character is shaped powerfully by the flexible accumulation of capital (Ong and Nonini, 1997: 3–33). In these perspectives on diaspora, theories and realities of the geographical are only emergent and ultimately trapped in language that signifies the spatial but does not assess its meanings and empirical contexts. In such treatments, factors of space and place tend to be assumed unproblematically and without consideration for their inherent and acquired dynamic properties.

DIASPORIC SPACE

Diasporas are geographic expressions of human interaction across global space, and diasporic practices are always localized but not permanently fixed in particular places.[2] Yet this does not mean that diasporic events simply flow across space, as if, in Ohmae's terms (1990, 1995), we have a "borderless world." As Yeung (1998) and Lin (2000) have argued, the world is not really "borderless": the power of nation-states has not been usurped by regional and global forces, and geography is not irrelevant, as Ohmae, O'Brien (1992) and others would have us believe. Indeed the fundamental problem at the basis of such so-called "end of geography" accounts is the mistaken assumption that geography simply means location, instead of dynamic spatial and place-based processes. Whereas increasing globalization of production and capital and more efficient forms of transportation and communication have significantly reduced the friction of distance that has led to time-space compression, and although international boundaries may be more porous than before, geo-graphical space and territorial borders are far from being conquered and rendered less significant. To the contrary, it is the increasingly dynamic charac-ter of borders and border processes that makes transboundary studies interesting, and the increased movement of people, money and things that has made the transnational a compelling field of thought and scholarly analysis.

In this introductory chapter, I argue that there is a need to reconceptualize di-aspora from the perspectives of space and place, and that geographic frame-works of analysis have much to offer to our understanding of transnationalism and diaspora. I suggest that a diaspora can be a process, a group of people, a ge-ographic area and a spatial network. That diasporas are fundamentally geo-graphic is indeed embedded in the etymology of the word. Diaspora comes from the Greek verb *speiro* (to sow) and the preposition *dia* (over), and the an-cient Greeks used the word to mean essentially migration and colonization (Cohen, 1997: ix). Historically, the word connotes the loss of homeland, up-rootedness, expulsion, oppression, moral degradation, a collective memory of the homeland and a strong desire to return to it one day.[3] From this perspective, it is clear that the word diaspora represents a *process* of population dispersion in space, and a process full of emotional connotations. Over time, the word has been applied to the scattering and migration of other minority groups who have a common ancestral homeland, reside in several foreign areas, share a common culture, hold similar aspirations and beliefs, and maintain some kind of linkage with a homeland. The second category of meanings of diaspora refers to *groups of people* who have been dispersed from a common ancestral homeland and have settled in different places. The third meaning of diaspora emphasizes its regional significance. A diaspora has been defined as "the *area* outside Palestine settled by Jews" (*Webster's Third New International Dictionary*, 1971) and "*countries* collectively" (*Random House Webster's Unabridged Dictionary*, second edition, 1998) where Jews and other minority groups away from their homeland have settled.

Space and place are the primordial structural elements of diasporas, as groups of people must exist, function and interact in space and place. Spatial interaction is commonly manifested in terms of connectivity, exchange and spread of people, goods, ideas and information across networked space and among a number of places with varying degrees of intensity and directionality, and as such, diasporas are also *spatial networks,* with selected places serving as anchoring points. The spatial extent of networks as functional linkages of regional or transnational trade and transmigration can be specifically demarcated and materially grounded. Seen in this light, diasporas are functional spaces, characterized by the movement of people, capital, goods and information between homeland and hostland or among the places where a diasporic population has settled.[4] A diasporic *place* is a located context for spatial interaction, and various interconnected places give rise to a diasporic activity space. As an interrelated set of personal and business networks in which spatial interaction takes place, the areal extent of a diaspora changes constantly without permanently fixed physical boundaries. Diasporas are formed through spatial processes, each of them invariably containing one or more core places where a significant number of a dispersed people have settled, temporarily or permanently. Almost without exception, the original core is the ancestral homeland, real, imagined or aspired, and from which initial dispersal began. However, secondary cores may be formed over time in a diasporic space where a large number of migrants have stayed and from which secondary dispersal or re-migration may ensue. The original core can lose its leading position in diasporic activities, and its attractiveness to some transmigrants may wane if internal or external forces have altered its cultural, economic and ideological characters. In these ways, a diasporic core is neither permanently fixed in space nor spatially indivisible.

In the age of globalization, diasporas are what Castells (1996) has called the "spaces of flows" in which the flows are at once interstate and transstate and occur with far greater speed and frequency than during the pre-1960s era. Yet diasporic space is more than simply the space of capital flows and accumulation. Similarly, the space of flows is not the privileged domain of transnational corporations. Small businesses, individual traders, laborers and informal migrants have also taken advantage of the compression of space and time; the movements of people, family members, social ties and cultural values across diasporic space are just as important, if not more so, in the formation of local and regional societies and cultural contexts. Driven by different motives, diasporic individuals are constantly, to use Van Hear's (1998: 40) sparkling words, "moving out, coming in, going back, moving on" or "staying put." For the Chinese, diasporic spaces are not so much "ungrounded" and "deterritorialized" structures of economic domination across the Asia Pacific, as asserted by Ong and Nonini (1997: 20), as they are place-centered and network-based spaces with porous boundaries whose areal extents are changeable in association with intra-diasporic contexts and events. Thus the space of movement for the illegal migrants from Fujian province in South China would differ significantly not only in areal size, frequency of travel and temporal stability from that of a group of Hong Kong entrepreneurs in their global activity space, but also in terms of physical, political, cultural and psychological barriers that they encounter. Similarly, the diasporas of the Fujianese or the Hong Kong Chinese differ from that of a group of diasporans who have re-migrated from Indonesia to the Netherlands, or from Malaysia to Australia, New Zealand, Canada and the U.S. These Southeast Asian transmigrants have formed what Cartier has called "second wave diasporas" in her contribution to this volume (pp. 73–75). Within each activity space of a group of transmigrants with a similar lifepath are many individual activity spaces shaped by different life histories of the individuals. The activity space of each individual is created by the actor himself, often taking into consideration family needs, social networks available and the political and socioeconomic climates at the places of origin and destination.

DIASPORIC PLACES

Because of the way diasporic space is conceived here and the complex meanings of place as a geographic concept, a diaspora itself cannot be a "place." The reason lies in the fact that a diaspora is a space of places.[5] The idea of a space of places recognizes spatial structures and their formative political and economic processes and the importance of a set of places that are subject to and participate in, through various representative agents, both individual and institutional, such spatial dynamics. This perspective on place intersects with a large corpus of literature by geographers on the nature of place (cf. e.g., Massey, 1993, 1994, 1995; Pred, 1984; 1986; Relph, 1976, 1996; Tuan, 1977; Entrikin, 1991), which, since the 1970s, has attracted increasing attention from architects, urban and regional planners, anthropologists, sociologists and political economists (e.g. Norberg-Schulz, 1979; Zukin, 1992; Logan and Molotch, 1987). In general, earlier work on place tended to emphasize its phenomenological character, while more recent conceptualizations have considered the complexity of place formation in transformative cultural, political, and economic processes.

From the perspective of phenomenology, a place is more than simply a spatial container where people live or, in the absence of man, a part of nature. It is a locality of experience, meanings and feelings, constituted historically from social actions. Consider such places with human activities as a nation, region, city or village. Constituted sequentially in history with diverse cultural, social and environmental forces emanating from sources near and far that have converged locally, place provides a context within which the processes of social structuration are played out. A place consists of layers of cultural sediments that are bound, eroded and metamorphosed locally. It is a repository of meaning, positive or negative, for the residents where families strike roots and to which individuals are emotionally attached. Of particular importance to a transmigrant is his mother country, inspiring his initial patriotism, and his native place where he was born and raised and where his family has deep roots. A transmigrant's mother country or native place is the primordial starting point of his life that provides the most basic reference of orientation in his lifepath. This native place is a deep wellspring of lasting memories that cannot be easily erased. It is the quintessence of place and the ultimate home of a transmigrant, especially for one who spent their formative years in their native place.

It has been widely recognized in migration literature that social networks are crucial to a multiplicity of activities of transmigrants. In essence, however, migrants' social networks are based in geographic factors (*diyuan*). Social networks are largely place-based and place-nourished, including networks formed through consanguineous causes (*xueyuan*), which continue to remain strong in contemporary China, Taiwan, Hong Kong and overseas Chinese communities. Aside from consanguineous networks, there are other categories of social networks that are place-based and constituted by place-specific factors of network formation. A place is a social incubator that contains the basic ingredients of networking, including people with a shared experience, local culture, family ties, home, landed property, social clubs, schools, workplaces and a common language, all playing a role in binding individuals together and transforming them into kinsmen, co-villagers, neighbors, friends, classmates, alumni, colleagues and fellow club members. Capable of creating, instilling, cementing and reinforcing common feelings of a shared life, place provides a strong foundation through which various types of social networks can be structured, which in turn lead to personal trust and social ties and to a sense of camaraderie and group solidarity. Such feelings are greatly heightened for individuals who have moved to a foreign place from a common place of origin. However, place-based, social networks are not permanently fixed in space. As Tilly (1990: 84) has so cogently stated: "networks migrate; categories stay put; and networks create new networks." Nowhere is the power of such place-based social networks more evident than in the transnational businesses that span the space of the Chinese diaspora.

Although place-based, diasporic life is inherently diverse and contradictory. This is because people's experience with place, including home place, is not always positive. Tuan (1974: 4) used the term "topophilia" to refer to people's love of and attachment to a place, a term he defines as "the affective bond between people and place or setting." On the other hand, Relph (1996: 912) has reminded us that "our environmental experiences are not all pleasant. Even landscapes of persistent appeal can be the source of ugly and disturbing events." Unpleasant experience in a place can make the place repulsive, and in such a case people's overwhelming desire is to be somewhere else that is safe and secure and that offers a more attractive social and physical environment and more economic opportunities. Relph coined the term "topophobia" to encapsulate people's negative feelings of and unfriendly attitudes toward the places of fear, disgust, disappointment and disapproval. This is a highly useful concept for diaspora discourses to which we shall return.

Because of the powers of topophilia and topophobia, which frequently exist at the same place, a contemporary transnational migrant often suffers from the syndrome of spatial uncertainty. This uncertainty is never constant as places are always changing, contingent upon the socioeconomic, political and historical circumstances converging locally at a particular time. This means that the relative strengths of topophilia and topophobia wax and wane in a transmigrant's homeland as well as hostland in response to the shifting global, national and local forces of social formation. Although he may be physically at one place, his mind may be somewhere else. Feelings of *belonging to* and *longing for* a place do not always coincide, which can greatly torture him as he struggles with the questions of national and local cultural identity and with issues of nationalism, citizenship, nationality, patriotism, ethnicity, loyalty, cultural assimilation and social and spatial integration. Seen in this light, questions of personal or group identity are essentially questions of identity with one or more places. For one who is culturally sensitive or politically, ideologically or otherwise strongly attached to a home place, his physical and mental whereabouts are rarely spatially fixed. He is frequently psychologically pulled apart by feelings of in-betweenness.[6] He is rarely a complete person as his body and soul may be split, belonging simultaneously to two different places. As such, he is physically and emotionally sometimes here and sometimes there. He frequently questions who he is, who he wants to be, where he should be, and what to do with the contradictory feelings toward his homeland and hostland (and for a cosmopolitan diasporan, toward his multiple diasporic places as well).

CHINESE DIASPORAS

The contemporary surge in the amount of literature on the Chinese overseas (Pan, 1999; Sinn, 1998; Hsu and Serrie, 1998; Skeldon 1994; Pieke and Mallee, 1999; Benton and Pieke, 1998; Wang and Wang, 1998; Lever-Tracy, Ip and Tracy, 1996; Douw, Huang and Godley, 1999; Chiang, Chao and Hsu, 1998) reflects how the Chinese diaspora has fundamentally changed since the mid-1960s. In the following sections, I will compare and contrast the changing nature of the old Chinese diaspora, before the mid-1960s, with the conditions of the new diasporas in terms of population size, geographic distribution, varieties of migrants, their spatial interaction, settlement patterns and the vexing issues of citizenship and identity. As mentioned earlier, the current characteristics of the Chinese diasporas have been shaped by the political and economic developments in the homeland(s), by the discrimination against the Chinese in Southeast Asia, by the globalization of production and improved transportation, and by the changing immigration policies on the part of the United States, Canada, Australia, New Zealand and European countries.

Size and Geographic Distribution of the Chinese Overseas

It is almost impossible to ascertain the population size of the Chinese overseas because few nations have kept reliable statistics on them and because the term "Chinese overseas" is extremely difficult to define.[7] The problems of definition and enumeration can be seen clearly from Kent's discussion of the data on the Chinese in Latin America (this volume), and such problems have led to estimates that vary greatly. The most comprehensive tabulations on the global size of the Chinese overseas have been attempted by Chang (1968) for 1963, Poston and Yu (1990) for the early 1980s, and Poston, Mao and Yu (1994) for 1990. Relying mainly on the data gathered by the Commission on Overseas Chinese Affairs, a government agency of Taiwan, I have updated these estimates in comparative context. Table 1.1 shows the approximate size of the Chinese overseas in nations with 5,000 or more Chinese, in 1963, 1985 and 1997.[8] The spatial distribution of the Chinese overseas is shown in maps 1.1 and 1.2.

Table 1.1. Distribution of Chinese Overseas, circa 1963, 1985, and 1997

| | Total Population in 1997 (millions) (a) | No. of Chinese Overseas in 1997 (thousands) (b) | Chinese Overseas as % of Total Population (c) | Number of Chinese Overseas (thousands) | | Major Current Economic Activities (f) |
				c. 1985 (d)	c. 1963 (e)	
Asia	**2,382.6**	**25,515.0 (77.7%)**	**1.1**	**19,108.0**	**12,147.7**	
Indonesia	204.3	7,310.0	3.6	6,000.0	2,545.0	RT, LW, FA, FB
Thailand	60.1	6,358.0	10.6	5,000.0	3,799.0	RC, FB, MF, TX, FA
Malaysia	21.0	5,445.1	25.9	4,245.0	2,461.3	DG, RS, WR, EE
Singapore	3.5	2,311.3	66.0	1,953.9	1,302.5	ALL
Philippines	73.4	1,030.0	1.4	800.0	151.8	FB, RC, RT, TX
Vietnam	75.1	1,000.0	1.3	n/a	1,035.0	RS, FB, MF, FA
Burma	46.8	1,000.0	2.1	800.0	420.0	WR, DG, RS, TP, FA
Cambodia	11.2	300.0	2.7	n/a	260.0	RS, FB, MF, FA
Japan	126.1	234.3	0.2	80.0	46.9	RS, EE, WR, MP
India	969.7	167.8	0.0	130.0	53.2	LS, RS, WR, TO
Laos	5.1	160.0	3.1	n/a	24.3	WR, LW, TX
North Korea**	24.3	48.6	0.2	n/a	n/a	n/a
Brunei	0.3	45.3	15.1	44.3	21.8	RS, TO, EE, WR
Turkey	63.5	40.1	0.2	30.0	3.3	RS, SS, WR
Saudi Arabia	19.5	26.7	0.1	24.8	23.6	RS, WR, MP
Others (N = 15)	632.8	14.0	0.0	n/a	n/a	
North America	**297.8**	**3,643.0 (11.1%)**	**1.2**	**1,655.0**	**295.5**	
United States	267.7	2,723.0	1.0	1,315.0	237.3	RS, WR, EE, TX, FA, FB
Canada	30.1	920.0	3.1	340.0	58.2	RS, WR, TO, FA, TX, FB

continued

Table 1.1. Distribution of Chinese Overseas, circa 1963, 1985, and 1997 (continued)

	Total Population in 1997 (millions) (a)	No. of Chinese Overseas in 1997 (thousands) (b)	Chinese Overseas as % of Total Population (c)	Number of Chinese Overseas (thousands) c. 1985 (d)	Number of Chinese Overseas (thousands) c. 1963 (e)	Major Current Economic Activities (f)
Middle America	**160.1**	**274.2** (.08%)	**0.2**	**132.5**	**84.5**	
Panama	2.7	103.5	3.8	33.0	3.0	DG, WR, RS, TX, RC
Costa Rica	3.5	47.0	1.3	20.0	3.0	RS, WR, TO,TX, RC, FI
Jamaica	2.6	22.5	0.9	20.0	18.7	DG, RS, FA
Mexico	95.7	19.5	0.0	20.0	10.0	WR, RS, EE, TX
El Salvador	5.9	18.0	0.3	1.4	0.5	DG, RS, WR, TO, EE
Dominican Republic	8.2	17.8	0.2	5.5	1.1	RS, FA, EE
Guatemala	11.2	16.8	0.2	14.0	5.2	RS, DG, WR, FA
Trinidad & Tobago	1.3	9.0	0.7	9.4	12.0	DG, RS, FI, FA, MF
Cuba	11.1	6.0	0.0	7.0	31.0	RS
Belize	0.2	5.7	2.9	n/a	n/a	RS, RC, DG, MP, WR
Netherlands Antilles	0.2	5.5	2.8	2.2	n/a	DG, RS, WR, DL
Others (N = 6)	17.5	2.9	0.0	n/a	n/a	
South America	**324.2**	**821.5** (2.5%)	**0.3**	**257.9**	**54.0**	
Peru	24.4	540.2	2.2	80.0	30.0	RS, WR, FB, TP, FA
Brazil	160.3	127.7	0.1	85.0	6.8	DG, RS, WR, MF
Surinam	0.4	40.0	10.0	10.0	5.7	DG, RS, EE, FA, MF
Ecuador	12.0	35.0	0.3	12.8	4.2	RS, WR, TO, MF
Argentina	35.6	30.0	0.1	27.5	0.2	RS, DG, WR, EE, TO, FA, RC
Venezuela	22.6	12.7	0.1	14.0	2.6	RS, FA, DG, EE, TX
Bolivia	7.8	12.0	0.2	6.5	0.0	RS, WR, FA
Paraguay	5.1	8.6	0.2	7.0	0.0	WR, RS, FB, EE, MF

Guyana	0.8	6.5	0.8	6.0	n/a	DG, RS, EE, FA, MF
Others (N = 3)	55.2	8.8	0.0	9.1	4.5	
Europe	**590.2**	**1,937.9** (5.9%)	**0.3**	**580.2**	**20.2**	
Russia	147.3	1,000.0	0.7	n/a	1.2	WR, FA
United Kingdom	59.0	250.0	0.4	230.0	12.0	RS, DG, FB
France	58.6	225.0	0.4	210.0	2.0	RS, DG, EE
Netherlands	15.6	127.5	0.8	60.0	2.4	RS, DG, FB
Germany	80.0	102.8	0.1	30.0	0.8	RS, WR, DG
Italy	57.4	60.6	0.1	5.0	0.3	RS, DG, TO, WR
Austria	8.1	41.0	0.5	6.0	0.0	RS, WR, DG, FA
Spain	39.3	30.0	0.1	5.0	0.2	RS, DG, TO, WR
Belgium	10.2	23.0	0.2	14.4	0.3	RS, DG, FA
Switzerland	7.1	13.0	0.2	6.0	0.0	RS, WR, DG, EE
Sweden	8.9	12.8	0.1	9.0	0.0	RS, WR, DG
Czech Republic	10.3	12.0	0.1	n/a	0.1	TX, RS, WR
Hungary	10.2	10.3	0.1	n/a	n/a	RS, WR
Ireland	3.6	10.0	0.3	n/a	n/a	RS, DG, EE
Denmark	5.3	7.3	0.1	3.8	0.9	RS, DG, WR
Norway	4.4	5.2	0.1	1.0	0.0	RS, DG, WR, FA
Others (N = 6)	64.9	7.4	0.0	n/a	n/a	
Oceania	**28.7**	**528.2** (1.6%)	**1.8**	**207.4**	**34.6**	
Australia	18.5	372.0	2.0	160.0	19.8	WR, RS, FA, FC, TX, EE
New Zealand	3.6	111.3	3.1	23.0	9.5	WR, FA, RC, TX
French Polynesia	0.2	20.0	10.0	12.0	n/a	RS, WR
Fiji	0.8	10.0	1.3	4.7	5.0	DG, RS, TO
Papua-New Guinea	4.4	7.5	0.2	5.0	0.3	WR, RC, TO
Others (N = 6)	1.0	7.4	0.7	2.7	n/a	

continued

Table 1.1. Distribution of Chinese Overseas, circa 1963, 1985, and 1997 (continued)

	Total Population in 1997 (millions) (a)	No. of Chinese Overseas in 1997 (thousands) (b)	Chinese Overseas as % of Total Population (c)	Number of Chinese Overseas (thousands) c. 1985 (d)	Number of Chinese Overseas (thousands) c. 1963 (e)	Major Current Economic Activities (f)
Africa	**218.1**	**120.3** (0.4%)	**6.6**	**50.7**	**40.0**	
South Africa	42.5	31.0	0.1	9.7	5.1	WR, DG, RS, TP, TX, EE
Mauritius	1.1	30.0	2.7	15.0	23.0	DG, RS, TX
Madagascar	14.1	27.0	0.2	13.0	8.9	DG, RS, FA
Reunion	0.7	25.0	3.6	13.0	3.0	RT, DG
Nigeria	107.1	5.7	0.0	n/a	0.0	MF, WR
Others (N = 8)	52.6	1.6	0.0	n/a	n/a	
Total (N = 107)	**4,001.7**	**32,840.1** (100%)	**0.8**	**21,991.7**	**12,676.5**	

Notes: Countries with less than 5,000 Chinese overseas in 1997 are not included. DG: Selling daily goods and grocery. DL: Dry cleaning and laundrymat. EE: Electronics and electric goods. FA: Food processing and agribusiness. FB: Finance, insurance and banking. FI: Fishing. LS: Leather goods and shoe manufacturing. LW: Lumbering and wood processing. MF: Manufacturing. MP: Medicine and pharmaceuticals. RS: Restaurant. RT: Retail. TP: Transportation. WR: Wholesale and retail.

Sources:

(a) Population Reference Bureau, 1997 *World Population Data Sheet.*

(b) Commission on Overseas Chinese Affairs, Republic of China, *Overseas Chinese Economy Yearbook,* 1997.

(c) (b/a) x 100

(d) Commission on Overseas Chinese Affairs, Republic of China, *Overseas Chinese Economy Yearbook,* 1986.

(e) Sen-dou Chang, "The Distribution and Occupations of Overseas Chinese," *Geographical Review,* Vol. 58, No. 1, p. 99.

(f) Same as (a).

(g) *1998 Britannica Book of the Year,* p. 638. Chinese population for 1997 is based on 1989 ratio of 0.2%.

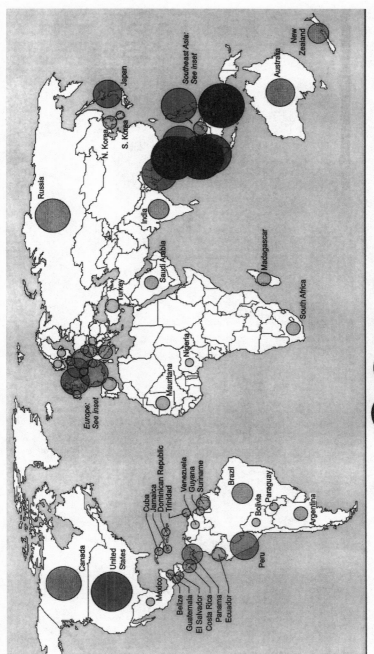

Map 1.1. World Distribution of Chinese Overseas (in thousands)

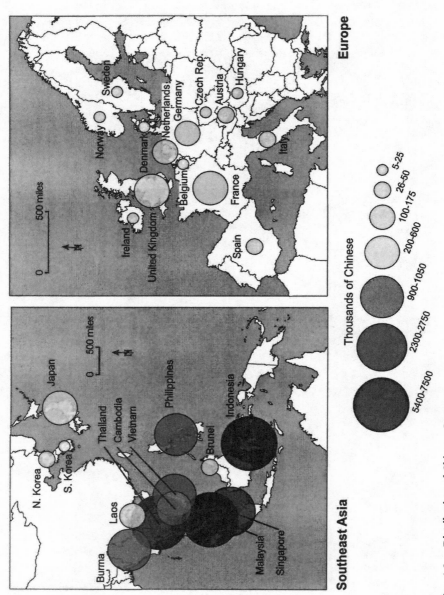

Southeast Asia

Japan

N. Korea
S. Korea

Thailand
Cambodia
Vietnam

Laos

Philippines

Brunei

Burma

Indonesia

Malaysia
Singapore

0   500 miles

N

Europe

Sweden

Norway

Netherlands
Germany
Czech Rep.
Austria
Hungary

Denmark

Belgium

Italy

Ireland
United Kingdom

France

Spain

0   500 miles

N

Thousands of Chinese

5-25

26-50

100-175

200-600

900-1050

2300-2750

5400-7500

Map 1.2.   Distribution of Chinese Overseas

Chinese communities are found in almost every country of the world. Their size and geographic distribution in the old diaspora revealed by Chang (1968) differ significantly from those of the new diasporic era in 1997. In terms of size, the global total increased from 12.7 million (including 3.2 million in Hong Kong) in 1963 to 32.8 million (excluding Hong Kong) in 1997. Although the vast majority of the Chinese overseas are still found in Southeast Asia, Asia's global share declined from 99.6 percent to 77.7 percent. On the other hand, Europe, North America and Oceania all gained substantially, due largely to the wars in Southeast Asia that sent many Chinese from Indochina to the Netherlands and France. Political instability in Hong Kong and Taiwan prompted a large number of people to move to Canada, the U.S., Australia and New Zealand. The relaxation of immigration policies in the U.S. and Canada in the 1960s and in Australia and New Zealand in the 1980s, combined with increased globalization of production and the end of China's international isolation beginning in 1978 also played a role in attracting the Chinese to these countries. The U.S., Canada, Australia and New Zealand have since become the most dynamic centers of transnational in-migration for the Chinese and these countries have played a key role in reshaping the spatial attributes and social characters of the new diasporas.

Spatial Attributes of the Chinese Diasporas

As networked systems of transnational interaction for the Chinese overseas, spatialities of the Chinese diasporas have been changing significantly, especially since the 1980s. The volumes and speed of the flows of people, goods, information and capital are far greater than before. Globalization of production and the fear of Chinese rule have made Hong Kong and Taiwan major actors in Chinese transmigration, substantially involved in the sending and receiving of transmigrants. The Chinese mainland is no longer the sole homeland of the Chinese abroad. In Southeast Asia, nations that once attracted millions of Chinese sojourners and setters have witnessed significant re-migration, a development that has expanded the areal extent of the Chinese diaspora, created new paths of transnational circulation of people and capital, and contributed to the diaspora's social heterogeneity. Thus instead of simple connection between a sending place in Guangdong or Fujian and a paired destination place in Southeast Asia before the 1960s, the patterns of spatial interaction today are multidirectional, based on multiple centers of origin and destination. Contemporary diasporic actors are also more footloose, less fixed in space and elusive in place attachment. This, however, is not to deny the fact that one-to-one place relationship still exists as in old days, as many migrants leaving a common place of origin still prefer to cluster in a common place of destination. Nonetheless, diversification of the places of origin has brought different types of transmigrants to new areas of settlement where their residential, social, economic and cultural characteristics differ markedly from those of their predecessors.

The new Chinese diaspora is far more complex and dynamic than the old one, always in a state of becoming and evolving in response to the changing conditions for emigration and immigration at the places of origin and destination while impacting both at the same time. The old diaspora in the nineteenth and early twentieth centuries, on the other hand, had a much simpler structure. The homeland was limited to the southeast provinces of Guangdong and Fujian with Hong Kong serving as the key point for transshipment and contact for migrants and foreign companies that organized their out-migration. From the rural villages in these two provinces, distinct native place-based streams of young and poorly educated male peasants ventured to the Nanyang (literally, "South Sea," meaning Southeast Asia) and the Americas as laborers, some with fixed-term contracts but others without, working in mines, plantations, farms and in railroad construction.

In the old diaspora, five major native-place and dialect groups of people accounted for almost all of the Chinese overseas: Cantonese from the counties near Canton, Hokkien from southern Fujian, Teochiu from Chaozhou and Shantou in Guangdong, Hainanese from Hainan Island, and Hakka from scattered hilly regions in northern Guangdong and southern Fujian. There was a remarkable degree of spatial coupling characterized by the fact that the places of origin and destination were often paired. Many migrants who were from a common region tended to settle in a common place of destination. For example, most of the Chinese in the Philippines were from Hokkien (Fujian), the majority of Chinese in Bangkok were from Teochiu (Chaozhou in Guangdong), most of the migrants in California were from Toishan (Taishan in Guangdong), and the Chinese in Korea were almost exclusively from Shandong. For those in Southeast Asia who chose not to return to China, their settlements were socially segmented and their economic activities tended to fall into neat occupational groups, differentiated again on the basis of native-place origin (Crissman, 1967). Colonial policies, thrift, diligence and social networks quickly rendered many of them "essential outsiders" in Southeast Asia (Chirot and Reid, 1997) where the social structure of their communities resembled that back home. Early laborers and traders in the old diaspora were not so much settlers who went abroad to sink roots as sojourners who ventured abroad to make some money because the economic conditions in China were in sad shapes as a consequence of repeated foreign invasions, domestic rebellions, regional armed conflicts and recurrent drought and flooding. Most of the Chinese overseas intended to return to their home villages after working a period of time overseas (Reid, 1996). Emotionally attached to their native place, many of them dreamed of returning to their home villages for retirement, much like falling leaves would naturally return to the roots of trees (*luoye guigen*) (Wang, 1994). At a time when ships were the only means of crossing the vast oceans and when the migrants were far from being rich, intra-diasporic interaction in the form of frequent home visits and transnational trade were rare.

Varieties of Chinese Diasporas

The Chinese diaspora has long been recognized as trade-based. Whereas this view is largely accurate for the pre-1960s diaspora and it continues to shed light today, the nature of trade for the Chinese overseas today differs greatly from that of the earlier periods (more analysis on this later). I argue that the post-1960s Chinese diasporic experiences are more than simply trade-based and that the term "Chinese diaspora" is best understood as a generic spatial phenomenon encompassing several constituent possibilities. For example, if one holds the view that the "Taiwanese" are ethnically and culturally Chinese but somehow are also different from the Chinese in China, then the suggested "Taiwanese diaspora" (see Williams' chapter in this volume for details) can be considered as a type of Chinese diaspora. In what follows, I present two other examples of Chinese diasporas with different spatial characteristics, economic activities, and other basic attributes: a cultural diaspora and a clandestine diaspora.

In his analysis of "Chineseness" and the future of traditional Chinese culture, Tu (1994) conceptualizes "cultural China" or the "Sinic world" as structured spatially into three "symbolic universes" analogous to cultural spheres, consisting of a core and peripheries that are continuously interacting with one another. The first universe includes mainland China, Taiwan, Hong Kong and Singapore, societies populated predominantly by ethnic Chinese. The second consists of Chinese overseas or members of the Chinese diaspora whose "Chineseness," emotional attachment to China and commitment to Chinese culture differs greatly. The third "universe" is formed by Chinese intellectuals abroad including non-Chinese intellectuals who are well informed about China and Chinese culture and who are particularly concerned about the essence and values of traditional Chinese culture and its role in the reconstruction of a future China as a "civilization-state" infused with (presumably Confucian) humanism rich in ethical-religious implications. The original cultural core was on the Chinese mainland that first emerged in the Wei River Valley, a tributary of the Yellow River, some four thousand years ago. But since the socialist revolution of 1949, a series of political movements on the mainland, some of them highly violent and destructive, had almost totally obliterated mainland China as the cultural center, leaving Taiwan, Hong Kong and Singapore as the preservers of China's cultural traditions in the first spatial/ cultural universe. Thus cultural China was effectively de-centered, rendering the periphery, including Taiwan, Hong Kong and Singapore, as the center of orthodox Chinese culture.

It should be noted that different types of diasporas exist for different types of transnational migrants, but all diasporas have common spatial characteristics, areas of experience with porous boundaries, specific places of encounter, and networks facilitating the movement of people, capital, goods and information. From this perspective, the Chinese cultural zones as conceived by Tu do not constitute the realities of diasporic experience and transformation because the zonal boundaries are rigid and static and because the patterns of inter-zonal flows of traditional Chinese culture (Tu's main concern) are tenuous at best.[9]

A more appropriate example that supports the view that there are different diasporas can be seen from the case of the illegal emigrants from Fujian Province. In June 1993, headlines broke out about the ship *Golden Venture* that carried 286 undocumented Chinese migrants and ran aground the coast of Queens in New York. Between the *Golden Venture* incident and the Dover container tragedy in 2000, in which over 50 migrants from Changle died from asphyxiation in a shipping container while crossing the English Channel, hardly a month went by without a news report on human smuggling from Fujian to the United States, Canada, Western Europe and Japan. Most illegal Chinese migrants have come from the surrounding areas of Fuzhou, the capital of Fujian since the 1990s, especially from towns and villages in Changle, Lianjiang and Fuqing counties.[10] Paying as much as US$70,000 to the smuggling ring leaders (known as "snakeheads") for passage to the U.S., Europe and elsewhere, they enter the U.S. either directly or by way of Hong Kong, Southeast Asia, Canada, Mexico, Eastern Europe, Central America or South America. They used to concentrate in New York City, working long hours in restaurants and sweatshops for two to three years just to pay off the debt that they had incurred for the passage. But in more recent years, they have also been concentrated in and around Washington, D.C., Baltimore, Boston, Los Angeles, Cleveland, Dayton, Houston, Denver, Toronto and Vancouver where they work in Chinese buffet restaurants run by Fujianese. Similar stories have been reported in Western European countries where the illegal migrants have originated from Fujian and Zhejiang, many by way of Eastern European states. These individuals travel by air, ship or over land, often stopping in transshipment places in different nations for days, weeks and even months at a time waiting for the opportune moment to make the next move before reaching their destinations. As the world of informal migrants is shaped by the spatialities of diaspora—places of origin, destination and transition, well connected spatial networks, routes of travel, and the movement of people and money (payments to smuggling organizers and remittances to families at home) across vast global space—it also represents a unique form of diaspora and geography in the ways that all of the social elements are clandestine, unpredictable and highly changeable. As such, the world of the illegal transmigrants can be appropriately conceptualized as a "clandestine diaspora."

Spatial Expansion of Diasporic Settlements

Significant changes have taken place in the settlement patterns of the post-1970s Chinese diasporas. Recent Chinese immigrants have carved out new spaces of settlement alternative to the traditional "Chinatowns." In the United States and Canada at least, early migrants tended to concentrate in Chinatowns as sojourners where they lived and worked, with little possibility of moving into better residential areas because of exclusionary legislation and unfriendly social environment (see Fan and Lai, this volume).[11] Initially Chinese communities were male "bachelor societies," but as some of the sojourners stayed and more migrants came after the mid-nineteenth century, Chinatowns gradually took form, due partially to the need for mutual support among the migrants and partly to social and racial constraints that limited their spatial integration with mainstream communities (Anderson, 1991; Lai, 1988; Lin, 1998; Wong, 1982). Located near downtown, Chinatowns were "spaces of difference" and "islands of externalities" that were created through the "mechanism of spatialization" developed by the mainstream society and that occupied the bottom of the spatial structure of a large city (Laguerre, 2000: 155). They were typically congested, where most of the residents were from lower social classes working in restaurants, small stores and sweatshops. Chinatowns, of course, continue to exist, but they tend to represent only one type of Chinese community that attracts mainly less well-off new migrants.

As shown in the chapters on the U.S., Canada, Australia and New Zealand in this volume, large numbers of Chinese transmigrants have arrived in these countries since the 1960s to take advantage of new immigration policies. These chapters reveal that the composition of the Chinese overseas has been significantly diversified in terms of place of origin, settlement patterns and socioeconomic characteristics. Aside from changes in immigration policy, the sudden surge of the Chinese in these nations is also a consequence of increasing globalization of capital and production and unstable political conditions in Hong Kong, Taiwan and Southeast Asia, as already noted above.

There is a tendency for the less well-off Chinese, including some illegal migrants and some from Indochina who arrived after the Vietnam War, to use Chinatowns as entrance points where they may choose to live and work for a period of time upon arrival. But those with skills and capital find the suburbs more attractive as places of residence. Many new Chinese communities have concentrated in suburban areas of such cities as New York, Los Angeles, San Francisco, Toronto and Vancouver. Unlike in traditional Chinatowns where people worked and lived in the same crowded enclave, new areas of suburban settlement are more dispersed where middle- to higher-middle-class residences are separate from people's businesses and where population and housing densities are much lower.

Since the 1970s, many new diasporic settlements have functioned as important business centers for Chinese transmigrants and their global enterprises. Ethnically, they belong to a category of urban space labeled by Laguerre (2000) as a "global ethnopolis," in which migrants maintain close economic ties with global, national and local actors and institutions that spatially represent one of the most distinct geographic expressions of the globalization of "Chinese capitalism," discussed below. In such new ethnic and economic places, the scope of the ethnic economy is at once diasporic and transnational, with high levels of ethnic ownership and co-ethnic labor participation. Many such areas have become enclaves of modern economy based on high-technology businesses, financial services, real estate and manufacturing, although traditional Chinese economic activities, especially restaurants and food services, are invariably present.

Called "ethnoburbs" (ethnic suburbs) and "global economic outposts" for the Chinese in the U.S. by Li (1998a, 1998b, 1999, 2000), places like Monterey Park, Rosemead, Hacienda Heights, Rowland Heights, and Alhambra in the San Gabriel Valley of Los Angeles County are suburban ethnic clusters with a high level of Chinese concentration who have recently arrived from Asia or moved out of the old Chinatown. Formed by recent immigrants from Taiwan, Hong Kong, the Chinese mainland, Vietnam, Cambodia and Laos, the ethnoburbs were still functionally attached to the Los Angeles Chinatown in the1980s but have since evolved into independent communities. As in Chinatowns, they are self-contained cities within cities. Today they are functionally diasporic ethnopolises with an active binational or multinational business orientation. Their workforce is characterized by high education, high wage, high skills, greater English proficiency, lower age structure and high levels of participation in local politics than the average Chinese population. However, they have retained some of the traditional characteristics of the Chinese ethnic economy such as the use of social networks and the reliance of personal trust in business. Relative to the Chinatowns, these new Chinese spaces are socially stratified and spatially differentiated to a much greater extent in terms of occupation, income and housing quality. In general, migrants from Taiwan and Hong Kong are doing considerably better than those from mainland Southeast Asia, with those from mainland China occupying a middle position. The new migrants in the ethnoburbs contrast sharply with the early sojourning laborers who were poor and poorly educated, worked on railroad construction, mines and plantations to eke out a meager living and who lived in inhospitable social environments and faced discrimination.

Diverse Diasporic Communities

Chinese diasporic communities display considerable internal subethnic diversity in population composition, spatial patterns, social structure and economic activities, even within the same country of settlement.[12] Such differences are due to the combined effect of global and local factors in the formation of place. Earlier in this chapter, I discussed the nature of place, emphasizing its humanistic aspects. Geographers have also demonstrated how "place" can make a difference in shaping the characteristic of localities (Massey, 1990; Massey and Jess, 1995; Warf, 1993; Cox and Mair, 1991). More geopolitical and geoeconomic in emphasis, this line of research does not assume that "place" has any causal power of its own independent of the processes of its social formation. Instead, place is seen as a social construct (Harvey, 1993) and a site at which power arises from the convergence of global, national and regional forces interacting with the local physical, historical, cultural, political and socioeconomic factors. In many instances, the same external forces will produce different effects in different localities because of different local conditions. These general place-based social relationships can readily be seen in the Chinese diaspora.

That place can make a difference in diasporic settlements has been documented by Zhou (1998), Tseng (1994) and Waldinger and Tseng (1992) in their studies of the Chinese communities in Los Angeles and New York City. In 1990, the Chinese communities in these cities were remarkably similar in the number of Chinese population (about a quarter of a million) and percentage of Chinese in the total metropolitan population (2.9 and 2.8). They had similar patterns of spatial expansion to the suburbs (to the San Gabriel Valley in Los Angeles and to Flushing and Sunset Park in New York). However, the demographic composition and ethnic economy of the Chinese in these cities differ greatly. In Los Angeles, the Chinese tend to be more educated and many of them live in middle- and high-class residential areas. Relative to New York, the ethnic economy of Los Angeles is characterized by professional services and high-tech businesses, a much larger number of

Chinese-owned firms, higher annual sales and better-paid employees, higher education and higher median household income. These differences are a consequence of a wide variety of factors, including the place of origin of the migrants (New York has more migrants from the Chinese mainland whereas Los Angeles has more from Taiwan), but it was the local contexts that really mattered. Zhou (1998) has ably evinced how geographic location of the cities, their histories of migration, local manufacturing and labor market structure, local transportation facilities, urban public services and capital market have all been consequential to the differences in the two cities' Chinese ethnic economies. While the Chinese areas in Los Angeles function as dynamic high-income centers oriented toward transnational trade, their counterparts in New York fall behind with a large number of the migrants, including illegal ones, working in low-skill and low-income jobs such as in the sweatshops of the garment industry and in restaurant kitchens.

In Canada, as in the U.S., the Chinese have come from different places with different backgrounds, and they tend to concentrate in a few large cities, especially Toronto and Vancouver, as Lai's contribution to this volume shows. Immigration policy changes since the 1970s spurred the arrival of the vast majority of migrants in Canada. Lai's data and maps show a remarkable temporal and spatial spread of the Chinese from British Columbia eastward. His population data indicate that the dual processes of spatial dispersal and local suburban concentration have taken place simultaneously among the Chinese in several Canadian cities, giving rise to new Chinatowns, new Chinese shopping centers and new areas of Chinese residential concentration. These patterns of spatial dispersal and local clustering are also independently confirmed by Wang (1999) and Lo and Wang (1997) for Toronto. They demonstrate that spatial clustering takes place along class lines and on the basis of the place of origin of the migrants. It occurs as part of the process of suburbanization because a large number of the new migrants are middle class or better who prefer to live away from the old Chinatowns, despite the fact that these neighborhoods have been undergoing significant redevelopment in recent years. These studies show clearly that the Chinese are far from being a homogenous group as perceived by many mainstream citizens. Relative to their predecessors in the pre-1960 era, the new migrants, many of them professionals, are more educated and economically much better off. As their numbers rise, traditional occupations such as restaurant and grocery businesses have declined in importance.

The activities of the Chinese have significantly affected the ethnic and economic landscapes of Canadian cities. In large cities such as Toronto and Vancouver, ethnic geographies have undergone a major transformation since the 1960s as a consequence of the influx of large numbers of Asians, especially Chinese (Ley, 1999). As the number of migrants from the United States and Europe, especially the United Kingdom, dwindled from 80 percent of the total in

1966 to only 30 percent in 1996, and as the inflow of domestic migrants to the cities declines, the effects of the Asians on the Canadian cities are further magnified. The presence of the Chinese in Vancouver has been particularly noteworthy: they accounted for 50 percent of all immigrants during the period 1991–1996, with 24 percent coming from Hong Kong alone, many of whom were fairly wealthy and admitted under the Entrepreneur Immigrant Program of 1984 (extended to include an Investor Program in 1989). Ley's work shows that the profile of migrants to Vancouver is quite unlike that of the migrants in Toronto and Montreal, characterized in particular by a disproportionately large number of the wealthiest classes of migrants from Hong Kong and Taiwan who were apprehensive about the political future of their homelands. Despite a distinctive presence, it should be noted that not all Chinese in Vancouver are rich. Ley's (1999: 12) data show that among the 21 ethnic groups in Vancouver in 1981–1991, the Chinese ranked 14th in personal income.

In New Zealand, as in North America, old Chinese migrants who began to arrive in 1866 from the villages around Guangzhou (Canton) used to live and work in spatially compact and socially homogeneous Chinese enclaves in such cities as Auckland, Wellington and Dunedin, as Ip's study in this volume explains. Since 1987, similar to the Chinese settlements in North America and Australia, new immigrants from Hong Kong, Taiwan, Malaysia, Singapore and China have opted to live in the suburbs of large cities. As in other countries, the Chinese tend to buy homes in certain preferred suburbs that have a good school system and easy accessibility. In New Zealand, perhaps because of the small size of the Chinese population, place of origin is not a factor in migrants' residential differentiation. The selection of housing area is more a function of socioeconomic ranking than provenance.

In Australia, Asian migrants have also increased rapidly, as Wu's chapter in this volume indicates. Settlers from Asia rose from 26.5 percent of the total number of migrants in 1981 to 44 percent in 1989. The introduction of the Business Migration Program in 1981 was followed by the arrival of tens of thousands of "new middle class" Chinese professionals and owners of small/medium enterprises from Hong Kong and Taiwan who brought to Australia a combined average total of A$14.8 million per year between 1982 and 1990 (Ip, Wu and Inglis, 1998: 80). As in North America, many Chinese migrants tend to move to the middle- and upper-middle-class suburbs of the large cities where the majority of them buy their own houses or apartments.

Chinese Business Networks and the Diasporic Entrepreneurs

The view that the Chinese diaspora is trade-based has been most systematically articulated by Cohen (1997). In his comprehensive examination and categorization of global diasporas, Cohen classifies the Chinese and Lebanese diasporas as "trade diasporas," in contrast to the original Jewish diaspora, the "victim diasporas" of the Africans and Armenians, the "labor and imperial diasporas of the Indians and British," and the "cultural diasporas" of the Caribbean states. Whereas his characterization of the "trade diaspora" is too narrow to capture the complexity of contemporary economic and social issues in the Chinese diaspora, the label does reflect the main feature of the Chinese diaspora in the earlier historical periods, especially one that existed prior to the mid-twentieth century. Although many Chinese overseas today remain petty traders as in the past, centuries of business experience have produced a significant number of highly successful capitalists in the Chinese diaspora, such as Chin Sophonpanish, Robert Kuok, Liem Sioe Liong, and Li Ka-Shing (Mackie, 1992a; Lim and Gosling, 1983). These Asian capitalists differ dramatically from earlier Chinese migrants in colonial Southeast Asia who were essentially trading minorities functioning as marginal middlemen.

Scholars have long recognized the important role of culture, especially social networks based on family and native-place ties, in the success of the Chinese in the business world and in the rise of "Chinese capitalism" in the age of globalization (Hamilton, 1991, 1996 and 1999; Kao, 1993; Redding, 1990; Weidenbaum and Highes, 1996). However, the view that Chinese capitalism is culturally shaped and ethnicity based is not without its challengers, and Hsing (this volume) has cautioned us not to essentialize Chinese entrepreneurial practices. Dirlik (1997) has argued against culturalist explanations in favor of a structural approach that sees the rise of Chinese capitalism as an integral part of the developments within global capitalism, which is marked by flexible production through transnational corporations. However, Dirlik concedes that the transnationalization of subcontracting practices associated with the new international division of labor does give rise to circumstances that favor the traditional Chinese business culture centered on medium- and small-scale production. Subcontracting practices have lent renewed significance to network-based organizational structure and production, and foregrounded the importance of personal relationships in business operations. As a result, the rise of the economic strength of the Asia Pacific region has led to suggestions that Western-style capitalism is becoming increasingly decentered through the processes of globalization (Berger, 1996).

It can be argued that the cultural/ethnic and the structural interpretations are not mutually exclusive and that global capitalism and Chinese capitalism are mutually influential, whether or not the latter is seen as separate from the former or as an integral part of it. It should be emphasized that a new class of capitalists consisting largely of owners of small-scale multinational firms has emerged in the major cities of the Chinese diaspora. Transnational Chinese firms differ significantly from their counterparts in the advanced industrial economies. Aside from being smaller in capitalization and firm size, their key characteristics include high spatial mobility of ownership and capital across diasporic space and heavy reliance on business trust and personal relationship embedded in common culture, place of origin and family ties. Cultural factors aside, the rise of Chinese capitalism is inseparable from the ability of Chinese entrepreneurs to respond quickly to the globalizing conditions of production. This would suggest that the rise of the Chinese business class cannot be understood through either the cultural or political economy (or human agency versus structure) explanation alone. Instead, these two perspectives are both valid in some respects and are not mutually exclusive.

In addition, it is important to note that contemporary Chinese capitalism is more than simply an enlarged version of traditional Chinese business culture centered on the family. Transnational production of Chinese diasporic capitalists has been reshaped in the last three decades into a hybrid form that incorporates both traditional *guanxi* (personal relations) networks and modern corporate culture. Lim (1983) has proposed a "convergence thesis" to account for the transformation of Chinese businesses overseas, arguing that the Chinese have always been highly adaptable to changing external environments and that as industrialization and modernization (and I would add, globalization) proceed, traditional and modern business cultures tend to converge.[13] This view has been echoed by Mackie (1992b) whose study of the large Chinese businesses in Southeast Asia shows that, whereas personal relationships are still very important and family ownership and control still dominant, there has been significant "corporatization" of Chinese businesses overseas relying increasingly on professional managers and credible and transparent managerial practices and on market mechanisms for production and business transaction. A significant number of family-owned businesses in Chinese diasporic locations have evolved into family-owned multinationals (Olds and Yeung, 1999; Van Den Bulcke and Zhang, 1995), and many such large businesses, structured as conglomerates and involved in a variety of business realms, are stock market-listed, with the owners holding majority shares. Among the best-known conglomerates are the Pico Group of Singapore, Cheung Kong Holdings of Hong Kong, the Lippo and Salim Groups of Indonesia, the Kuok Group of Malaysia, the Cojungco Group of the Phillippines, Charoen Pokphand and Bangkok Bank of Thailand, and the Formosa Plastic Group of Taiwan. Aside from professionalization of management, these firms have also relied on advanced modern technology for production, and business owners often send their children, who one day will succeed them, to top business schools in the West for advanced degree training. These firms have also widened the sources of development capital by approaching international financial markets instead of limiting their capital sources to family members and close friends. They have also strengthened their market power through inter-firm linkages with shared ownership and interlocking directorships in multiple firms.

However, there is also evidence pointing to how we should understand the ethnic factor by comparison to class alliances, especially in some parts of the world where Chinese-owned businesses play a major role in national economies. In Malaysia in the late twentieth century, for example, Chinese capitalists seemed to have transcended the ethnic factor, as class relations are becoming more important factors in business operations, as Cartier has noted in her chapter in this book. Using the transnational trade in mandarin oranges as an example, Cartier makes the insightful suggestion that network approach is better understood as a framework for the control over wholesale and retail trade of ethnic-identified commodities than as an organizational principle for firms among members of the same ethnicity.

Diminished importance of ethnic ties is also characteristic of Chinese transnational firms in the high-tech sector. Not only have large-scale overseas Chinese firms been reconfigured into modern business enterprises, many small firms have also adopted advanced Western technology so as to better compete in the global market, although the physical distance between the parent firm and its affiliates/subsidiaries tends to be shorter than that of large Western multinational firms (Huang, 1998). As in non-Chinese firms, profit is always the primary consideration in the location of Chinese transnational firms. In their recent study of the high-tech firms in Silicon Valley, California, and Hsinchu, Taiwan, Hsu and Saxenian (2000) have argued that the role of *guanxi* in transnational Chinese business interactions should not be overemphasized. They suggest that although ethnic networks and *guanxi* benefit transnational business and facilitate technological cross-fertilization, ethnic and personal ties do not determine the formation and operation of Chinese business networks in the high-tech industries. Market mechanisms, economic rationality, production process and technological requirements are just as important if not more so than *guanxi* networks in forging collaboration among transnational business firms.

The globalization of production has been accompanied by an increase in the flow of Chinese-owned capital in the diaspora. Fueled by the growing wealth of Singapore, Hong Kong and Taiwan since the 1960s, and the rapid expansion of the economy on the Chinese mainland (especially in the Pearl River Delta region and coastal Fujian) since the opening of China in 1978, transnational investments by Chinese entrepreneurs overseas have become the first or second most prominent source of foreign investment in such countries as China, Thailand, the Philippines and Vietnam. Chinese-owned capital flows so freely in the Chinese diaspora, and economic ties among these nations have become so close, that Kao (1993) has gone so far as to suggest that a de facto "Chinese commonwealth," or a fourth global economic power, has emerged which challenges the dominance of the U.S., Japan and Western Europe in the global economy.[14]

As stated earlier, the Chinese diaspora is an important "space of flow" of capital. In the last two decades, Chinese capital from small- and medium-sized businesses has been flowing rapidly among the constituting territories of the Chinese diaspora through preferential policies, transnational ethnic linkages and *guanxi* networks (Kaiser, Kirby and Fan, 1996; Kao, 1993; Kraar, 1994; Li, 1993; Li, 1998a; Tseng, 1999; Yeung, 2000). Consider the case of capital linkages between the Chinese businesses in Australia and mainland China. A recent study by Lever-Tracy and Ip (1996) on Chinese "multinational small firms" in Australia demonstrates that of 33 business owners surveyed, eight were from China, seven from Hong Kong, five from Malaysia, six from Taiwan, four from Singapore, and one each from Vietnam, Brunei and Papua New Guinea. The sources of their capital are not reported, but it would be reasonable to assume that many of the entrepreneurs, at least those from Hong Kong and Taiwan, brought their own money when they migrated to Australia, which they subsequently invested in China via Hong Kong. Whereas in the past the British colony was the main transfer port for Chinese laborers and transit center for the redistribution of remittances and family letters, Hong Kong today serves a critical role as the geographic node for the collection and (re)distribution of investment capital earmarked for China (Wang and Wong, 1997).

Intra-diasporic flows of capital are most evident in the shift of investment to mainland China from Hong Kong, Taiwan and Singapore (Bolt, 1996; Hsing, 1998; Leung, 1993; Lin, 1997; Lever-Tracy, Ip and Tracy, 1996). In response to significantly lower wages, rapidly expanding domestic markets on the Chinese mainland, and state policies encouraging foreign investment, a vast amount of Chinese overseas capital has flowed to China, in many cases through the mobilization of social networks (Ip, 1999), including "blood connection" and place ties (Hsing, 1996).[15] The impact of the infusion of overseas Chinese capital on the Chinese economy is well known and will not be discussed here (Huang, 1998; Lan, 1996; Sun, 1998). The chief motive for the influx of Chinese capital is profit, with sentimental reasons to make a contribution to the development of the investor's home place as a distant secondary factor. The opening of China has had a profound impact on the economy of Hong Kong and Taiwanese as well, as many of the labor-intensive manufacturing jobs have been shifted to the mainland, including the production of toys, shoes, electronics and jewelry. Hong Kong firms now employ more workers in Guangdong and Fujian Provinces than they do in Hong Kong itself, and the economy in the Pearl River Delta has been expanding to such an extent that Lin (1997) has assessed the "red capitalism" of the region. It is significant to note that the flow of capital was not one-way from overseas to China, as considerable amount of mainland capital has also been invested in other places, particularly in Hong Kong. By 1995, mainland investment in Hong Kong was estimated to have reached US$25 billion, an amount larger than that coming in from Hong Kong (Fung, 1996).

Spatial Mobility, Flexible Identity and Diaspora As Home

Aside from occupational differences, Chinese transmigrants from Hong Kong, Taiwan, China and countries in Southeast Asia since the 1960s differ dramatically from the pre-1960s sojourners, in spatial preferences, cultural identities and attachments to place. What is "Chinesenese" also differs among the Chinese in different places, even when comparing the experience of Chinese populations in the cosmopolitan port cities of Shanghai, Hong Kong, Singapore and San Francisco; differences in being Chinese in these cities points to the importance of place in shaping cultural identities and to the complexity of Chineseness (Wang, 1999). On the other hand, the relationship between spatial mobility and identity is highly controversial, as Lin's chapter in this book points out. But it is beyond doubt that increasing spatial mobility tends to facilitate locational linkages and connections while it simultaneously reduces the power of particular place attachment. Greater spatial mobility has also given rise to multiple and flexible personal identities that tend to change with shifting circumstances. Diasporic individuals, especially the first generation transmigrants in a new hostland, more frequently harbor a multitude of views about home, native place (*laojia* or *guxiang*), and fatherland or mother country (*zuguo*), which are either irrelevant to one's legal citizenship or only weakly tied to it. To better deal with the uncertainties and/or social alienation, real or perceived, in an adopted homeland and to more effectively negotiate the complex realities associated with being tangled in two or more cultures, countless diasporans have developed highly malleable multiple identities that they use as coping strategies. Diaspora consciousness, constituted both negatively and positively, is typically developed in relation to the consciousness of a prior home (Clifford, 1994: 311). Multiple identities are not a cluster of personal cultural traits with fixed forms that are permanently moored at any particular place. Instead, they are socially constructed and constantly becoming, each with a mix of ethnic, cultural, economic and political attributes. It is not unusual for a diasporan to activate one identity while suppressing others to deal with a particular issue or to achieve a specific goal, and different identities may be developed and activated at different places that intersect with one's lifepath.

One form of multiple identities is "flexible citizenship" found among many diasporic Chinese. Defined by Ong (1999: 6, 112) as "strategies and effects of mobile managers, technocrats, and professionals seeking to both circumvent *and* benefit from different nation-state regimes by selecting different sites for investments, work, and family relocation," flexible citizenship "refers to the cultural logics of capitalist accumulation, travel, and displacement that induce subjects to respond fluidly and opportunistically to changing political-economic conditions." The notions of flexibility and fluidity proposed by Ong can be used to dissect and understand the complex issues of home and homeland. In a related vein, Cartier (this volume) has suggested that contemporary transmigrants have "hybrid" and "situational" identities that are cosmopolitan in outlook and tied simultaneously to several places in different countries. Thus an extended family's diasporic lifepath might include several countries of residence. For example, many transnational subjects from Hong Kong and Taiwan maintain two or more homes. The male head of household may leave his wife and children in a second home in the United States, Canada or Australia and return to his homeland to work or make frequent business trips to China after experiencing the life of "reluctant exiles"—those who have found it difficult to establish a business or find suitable employment in the hostland (Skeldon, 1994; Schak, 1999). These diasporic homes are established essentially as a safety net for the sake of the children (especially for their education) and for the family in preparation for an eventual total abandonment of the homeland in the event of political instability in Hong Kong or Taiwan.

The fact that many diasporans hold two or more passports or legal residence documents and that they are equipped with multiple cultural identities raises serious questions about the meanings of citizenship, which normally demands a person to be loyal to his country of citizenship. In their study of the concepts of citizenship, Ip, Inglis and Wu (1997) argue that recent Asian migrants to Australia have instilled a new meaning in the term which they label "instrumental citizenship," i.e., citizenship acquired for practical business and "instrumental" purposes, which may or may not have much to do with loyalty to a country. A similar view is expressed by Chan and Chiang (1994: 356) who consider such multiple identities of the Chinese transmigrants as "strategies for structuring their relationships with the international business community, their family, society and state."

Diasporic individuals holding instrumental citizenship tend to travel frequently between two or more homes for business. As Manying Ip's (this volume) study of the Chinese in New Zealand has pointed out, frequent commuting is normal behavior undertaken to maintain intra-diasporic linkages and options. This type of spatial strategy represents a concrete manifestation of the traditional Chinese risk minimization perspective, "a smart hare has three burrows (*jiaotu san ku*)." However, frequent travel across the Pacific has given rise to a set of unique and unhealthy diasporic phenomena in recent years known as "astronauts (*taikongren*)" and "parachute kids" (Pe-Pua et al., 1996). The terms "astronauts (*taikongren*)" and "aerial flying men (*kongzhong feiren*)" refer to husbands who are constantly in the air flying between their diasporic homes and Hong Kong, Taiwan and China for business reasons, while "parachute kids" are children who live with their mother or relatives or who are living on their own in a diasporic home.[16] Problems of split families, extra-marital affairs, emotional stress and children with deviant behaviors are common in these diasporic and transnational families.

In contrast, many of Chinese diasporans who have settled in Canada, Australia and New Zealand under their immigrant investment programs, are not really economic migrants because profit is not the real reason for their transnational relocation. Instead, they are essentially voluntary political risk minimizers running away from the topophobia of a place of origin in the Chinese diaspora. In return for uprootedness from their homeland, these transmigrants are rewarded with a stable political milieu, a safe diasporic domicile, opportunities to work and live in an economically advanced and environmentally more attractive Western country, and with a quality education for their children without the stressful and highly competitive entrance examinations to high school and college that are deeply dreaded by students and parents alike in Taiwan and China.

For many diasporans, the notion of home is not automatically impregnated with the usual sense of place of belonging, as Leung's chapter in this volume on the Chinese in Germany has argued. For diasporic individuals, the concept of home possesses multiple meanings, ranging from a family dwelling to the country of origin. For many such individuals, especially those who are supermobile, the diaspora, or more specifically, selected diasporic cities, is (are) home(s). A diasporic home can be situated in a social environment devoid of local memories and nostalgia, and for many, indeed, it is nothing more than a dwelling for one's family. For those who are away from but strongly identified with the land, culture and destiny of their original home place or mother country, the sense of loss, separation and alienation resulting from living elsewhere can be acute. For such diasporic Chinese, "home" and "homeland" have different meanings. Home is where one is, a base of operation, a domicile neither temporary nor permanent, while homeland is either one's native place (*laojia*, literally, old home) or a place where one has lived and loved for an extended period of time before re-migration, places of emotional attachment. Many first-generation Chinese diasporans long for major improvements in the political and social conditions in their homeland, a hope that motivates them to sustain a keen interest in it, to teach their children about its language and culture, to maintain economic and social ties with it and to go back frequently. Besides making a distinction between home and homeland, these diasporans also easily distinguish China as a political space (nation-state) from China as a cultural place, and the love of the latter is not always accompanied by a corresponding love or support of the former. Given the current political, economic and environmental conditions in China, many Chinese diasporans have little hope for a fusion of home and homeland in the immediate future; nor do they see an affluent and modern China emerging any time soon basking in the kind of cultural splendor that the nation once enjoyed in the distant past.

Identity Formation and Living among Non-Chinese

Chinese overseas differ in their relationships with the host population as a consequence of historical factors at home and in hostland countries. A host state's policies toward ethnicity and ethnic relations strongly affect the lives of diasporic Chinese, a point made by Cartier's chapter in this volume. It is widely known that the Chinese in Indonesia have been discriminated against for decades. Violent outbreaks occurred in 1960, 1965, 1974 and 1998. The riots of 1965 across Indonesia were particularly violent, leaving half a million Chinese dead and prompting tens of thousands of ethnic Chinese to flee the nation. On the other hand, the Chinese in Malaysia have fared somewhat better amidst policies of Malaysianization that have favored the Malays in employment and education. While numerous Chinese have re-migrated from Malaysia to other diasporic places, Chinese Malaysians have established a basis for community and identity formation by demonstrating their historical roles in Malaysia's nation building, as Cartier (1993, 1997, 1998 and this volume) has demonstrated.

In North America, it is common knowledge that the Chinese in the nineteenth and early twentieth centuries were socially excluded by the mainstream society. The case of the Chinese in Hawaii, discussed by Chang in this volume, represents a significant exception. Chang demonstrates that the Chinese in Hawaii have meshed in harmony with other ethnic groups, due essentially to the early spatial dispersal of the Chinese migrants throughout the islands. His study represents a rare case that supports the melting pot thesis, which has largely been discredited because migrant groups have hardly "melted" into the social "pot" of the nation as expected.

However, social tension still exists in the contemporary era, even in nations that promote multiculturalism. The tension between the dominant group and Chinese migrants in some Vancouver neighborhoods is a case in point. A key issue that has caused ethnic conflict there arises from the construction of the "monster houses" by the wealthy Chinese from Hong Kong. Seen by locals as too large, too imposing and too ugly to fit the existing urban landscape, the "monster houses" replaced traditional houses in established neighborhoods and became a divisive social issue with strong racial overtones (Li, 1994); the Chinese demand for such housing also caused housing prices to skyrocket. In this case, the notion of "social exclusion" that Rigg has applied to the Chinese in Thailand (this volume) is not entirely applicable because the basis for the conflict in Vancouver lies in the migrants' affluence. But Wickberg's view (1994: 25) is quite accurate when he states that the conflict between the locals and the Chinese in North America arises in many cases from the perception that the Chinese have "overdone it" and that they are seen as "taking over" things that are considered by the locals as theirs.

Diasporization homogenizes as well as differentiates diasporic sentiments, and a place-based identity can be renegotiated in the process of transmigration. At the national level, a transmigrant's senses of national identity and nationalism can be heightened by globalization and by staying in a diasporic location other than his or her home place. In her study of the Chinese Singaporeans working in Beijing, Kong (1999a) discovered that feelings of "Singaporeaness" and rootedness in Singapore significantly strengthened after working in Beijing for a certain period of time. At the personal level, Chinese Singaporeans working in Beijing experienced complex negotiation and reconstruction of what they consider to be their Chineseness and diasporic identities, which suggests both the fluidity and enduring qualities of place-based identity (Kong, 1999b). It also lends strong support to the point made earlier in this chapter that place can make a difference—in this case, a change of place in the Chinese diaspora brings about identity reconsideration on the part of the diasporans.

Since China's initiation of economic reforms after 1978, the economy on the Chinese mainland has registered highly impressive gains and the international prestige of the nation has thus quickly risen. Such changes have engendered centripetal reactions on the part of many Chinese overseas. Not only have they invested heavily in China, many have also returned to their native places on the mainland to seek or reestablish ancestral and cultural roots (see Douw, Huang and Godley, 1999). In Southeast Asia too (Rigg, this volume), many individuals have sought to reclaim their Chinese identity or are showing renewed interest in their Chinese roots, after being forced to abandon them during the early post-colonial period when nationalism, fear of communism, and jealousy of the economic success of the Chinese resulted in anti-Chinese policies forcing adoption of citizenship and closing of Chinese schools and other cultural and political institutions. Even in Singapore, where three-quarters of the citizens are of Chinese descent, in the 1990s the state placed top priority on the formation of a Singaporean national identity and engaged in "submerging and subverting" Chineseness (see Kong and Yeoh, this volume). Instead, Chinese Singaporeans are rediscovering, revalorizing and revitalizing Chinese culture. Rising consciousness of Chineseness in the diaspora points to the fact that changes in the homeland can powerfully re-shape the views of the diasporans toward their homeland culture, and significantly alter their daily lives at the same time.

THEMES AND ORGANIZATION OF THE BOOK

The chapters of this volume present a number of geographic perspectives on the Chinese diaspora; all concern conceptual themes of space, place, transnational mobility and place-related identity. These four related themes are the basic components of the Chinese diaspora as a set of geographic events and processes, with space and place constituting the primordial con-ditions in which transnationalism, mobility, and identity formation are worked out, through travel, encounter, cultural practices and economic ac-tivities. Too often in the discourse on diaspora and transnationalism space and place are treated only locationally, or just metaphorically, without sus-tained treatment of diasporic places and spatial processes. In this chapter I have sought to distill the basic attributes and relationships of these geo-graphical concepts, as a foundation for situating our understanding of the Chinese diaspora. The Chinese diaspora, one of the great demographic sub-jects of the modern era, is also a fundamentally geographical subject whose analysis may be significantly enlivened through analysis of the emplaced conditions and experiences of diasporans. As Skeldon sets the stage in his critical examination of the subject, the popularity of the idea of diaspora has increased substantially, which has not always led to new insights about the complexity of diasporic experiences and instead has sometimes resulted in generalizing ideas about supposedly uniform or essentialized diasporic events—as if the Chinese around the world are a homogenous group. Geo-graphical perspectives demonstrate the diversity within the Chinese dias-pora, and hold the potential to provide greater understanding among and be-tween different population groups.

The three chapters in Part I provide a great deal of historical analysis on the Chinese overseas in Southeast Asia and Latin America, whose experiences dif-fer sharply from their counterparts elsewhere in the diaspora in the post-1960s era. The important role of the Chinese in a host country's social reconstruction is rarely publicly acknowledged, and Cartier's study of the Chinese role in Malaysia in their contribution to multiculturalism represents an exception. As an economically active minority, the social relationship of the Chinese with the mainstream population of a host country is complex and not always harmonious. Rigg's notions of "exclusion and embeddedness" neatly conceptualize two of the social realities that the Chinese in Thailand face. These two notions are also appropriate for our understanding of the Chinese in Malaysia and other Southeast Asian countries. Although we are less clear about how the recent Chinese migrants are doing in Latin America in this regard, Kent's chapter reveals that Chinatowns continue to be important for the Chinese in various Latin American countries and that associations based on the same surname and regional origin continue to be active.

In Part II, the important role of Hong Kong and Taiwan, peripheral islands off the coast of the Chinese mainland, as centers of the Chinese diaspora are examined by Lin and Williams. Although tiny in areal size, Hong Kong and Taiwan are major foci of intra-diasporic mobility, and domestic political and economic developments there raise serious questions regarding the future of the diaspora. In Part III, the complex issues of identity and identity formation at different geographic scales are elucidated in three studies on Singapore, China and Germany, respectively. Questions of identity have long been addressed by anthropologists, but the discussion often hovers "above the ground" without anchoring them in any space or place. On the other hand, the cause-and-effect relationship between identity and place in different geographic settings is by no means a simple relationship, as geographic diversity discourages the formulation of general principles. Much more empirical work is needed before a consensus can be reached regarding the interrelationships among place, transnationalism and identity. The contributions by Kong and Yeoh, Hsing, and Leung shed much light on such relationships.

Whereas Hong Kong and Taiwan have been the major sending areas of diasporic subjects, the U.S., Canada, Australia and New Zealand have been the leading recipients of Chinese transmigrants, including some from Southeast Asia, since the 1960s, as Fan, Chang, Lai, Ip, and Wu have demonstrated in their contributions in Part IV and Part V. Based in part on census data, their studies point to the important role the Chinese have played in the formation of Chinese spaces and places in non-Chinese settings and in their social and economic interactions with the mainstream populations. It is our hope that the studies of this volume will raise the level of consciousness of the importance of geographic perspectives among scholars interested in diasporas, especially the Chinese diaspora(s), and stimulate further research on the meanings of space, place, mobility and identity in the formation, functioning and change of diasporas.

NOTES

1. An exception to this argument is that the income gap is the main driving force prompting the informal migration of villagers from coastal Fujian to the advanced industrialized countries since the 1990s.

2. In his otherwise erudite dialectical exposition of the nature of global/local and spatial/place-based processes of social formation in the contemporary world, Dirlik (1999) criticizes the geographic literature for its preoccupation with the "social construction of space" while ignoring the importance of the "ecological" aspect of place, i.e., a place's "groundedness in topography." Although not specified, Dirlik uses the word "topography," which has entirely different meanings in geography, to mean a particular locality or a piece of sub-national territory with a porous boundary. He further argues that categories of social analysis such as capital, class and gender are place-based, which allows possibilities and contingencies. What needs to be pointed out here is that only one wing of human geography has focused on "the social construction of space" at the expense of place-based realities; there is certainly a vast amount of geographic literature on locality and place, as dynamic centers of transformation in their own right.

3. These characteristics are used by Safran (1991) to define diasporas. His formulation is based essentially on the "ideal type" of the Jewish diaspora. Whereas his definition encompasses the main features of traditional diasporas such as the Armenian, Maghrebi, Turkish, Palestinian, Cuban, Greek and the early Chinese diasporas, Safran fails to consider new diasporas that have emerged in the age of globalization and transmigration. Nor does his formulation specify the spatial structure of diasporas. It is mainly these two areas that I address in this introductory chapter.

4. This is not to exclude the possibilities that diasporic spaces may also be thought of in other terms, e.g., as symbolic space and the space of memory.

5. Taylor (2000) distinguishes space of places from space of flows in his call for the use of world-city network in the study of globalization. However, I view diasporas as both spaces of places and spaces of flows, without accepting the widely held assumption that the flows are free from the constraints of nation-states and other national, regional and global boundaries. After all, flows of all sorts are not aimless and omnipresent. They always go to preselected places and the spatial distribution is typically uneven. After all, capital only flows to places that it finds profitable, and people only migrate to places that they deem better. My view on the relationship between space and place does not conflict with that of Taylor, who takes the "spatial interactionist" position in seeing spaces of flows as interacting with spaces of places.

6. The use of "he" carries no gender implications in this discussion. For similar feelings about the elusiveness of home for female writers, see Hom (1999: 14–19).

7. There is a question concerning what is the appropriate term in English for the Chinese who are abroad. Historically, the term *huaqiao* (literally, sojourning Chinese) has been used by the Chinese government from the nineteenth century on to refer to Chinese citizens working or living abroad. This term, however, has also been widely used among the Chinese at home and abroad to refer to any Chinese living abroad re-

gardless of their citizenship. Wang (1992) has suggested that the term *huaqiao* be reserved for Chinese citizens abroad. In this introductory chapter, I use the term "Chinese overseas" in a generic sense to refer to all ethnic Chinese outside China, Hong Kong and Taiwan regardless of citizenship. This term is equivalent to *haiwai huaren* (Chinese living overseas) and *huayi* (Chinese descendent). We have not standardized the usage of these and other related terms in this volume where the contexts will determine the meaning of each term used.

8. This source is also heavily used by Poston and his colleagues, but it is not without its problems. One major drawback of this source is that it is not clear how the data are collected by the diplomatic or trade missions of the Taiwan government that the Commission relies on. Nor does it indicate what are the criteria for inclusion. Although the title of the publication uses the term *huaqiao*, it is clear that the data are not simply for the Chinese overseas nationals alone. The strength of the data lies in the fact they have been consistently collected since at least the early 1960s, and it is the only data set that covers the entire world. A check of the data against those in such sources as Lynn Pan's (1999) *The Encyclopedia of the Chinese Overseas* and Benton and Pieke's (1998) volume on *The Chinese in Europe* reveals that, with a few exceptions, the data in Table 1.1 are largely comparable and much more up-to-date. However, I question the reliability of the figures for Russia and Peru, which appear to be excessively large. It must be cautioned that the figures are approximates at best and should be seen merely as the possible sizes of the Chinese in different countries.

9. Since the publication of Tu's edited volume, traditional culture, particular Confucianism, has received renewed blessing from the state on the Chinese mainland. The second half of the 1990s witnessed a remarkable resurrection and rejuvenation of traditional Chinese culture on the mainland and in Southeast Asia, aided in part by several national and international conferences held in China with invited lectures from overseas, including Tu. The rebirth of Confucianism on the mainland no doubt was also fueled by the impressive economic performance and political stability of Singapore where Confucianism has taken on the role of *de facto* state ideology, thanks at least in part to strongman Lee Kuan Yew's promotion. The flows of traditional Chinese culture across zonal boundaries in the Sinic world and their impact on the nation-states and their peoples have not been substantially analyzed by scholars.

10. The reason for the Fujianese emigration is not poverty, as coastal Fujian is hardly poor by Chinese standards. The main driving force is to get rich quickly by going to the U.S. and Europe. See *The New York Times on the Web,* June 26, 2000; *The Washington Post Online,* December 30, 1999 and June 24, 2000. U.S. Immigration and Naturalization Service estimates that at least 100,000 Chinese are smuggled abroad each year, mostly from Fujian. See *Migration News (Internet Edition)* 7 (3), March 2000. For studies of the Fujian migrants in the United States, see Chin, 1999; Liang and Ye, 1999; Yuan, 1999.

11. It can be argued that race played an important role in the formation of Chinatowns. For a case study on the formation of Vancouver's Chinatown using such social construction approach, see Anderson (1991).

12. Examples of Chinese settlements in this section are drawn from geographic studies in the U.S., Canada, Australia and New Zealand and from the chapters in this

volume. I am not aware of any detailed geographic studies on the Chinese communities in Europe and elsewhere. For non-geographic studies of Chinese migration to Europe, see Pieke and Mallee (1999) and Benton and Pieke (1998).

13. It is not implied here that "Chinese capitalism" is bound to follow a linear path of transition to Western capitalism, which has been seen by some scholars as superior. What is underscored here is that Chinese business practices are adaptable to changing circumstances. "Chinese capitalism," or more appropriately, the overseas Chinese business practices, are not static and associated with a set of fixed cultural attributes, a theme that Hsing also emphasizes in her analysis of Chinese ethnic identity in this volume.

14. Whereas the term "Chinese commonwealth" is somewhat immature, there is indeed a strong feeling of camaraderie and a common desire for group solidarity among the Chinese entrepreneurs. This is evident from the First World Chinese Entrepreneurs Convention that attracted some 800 Chinese entrepreneurs from 35 countries to Singapore in 1991. Similar conferences have been held since then in Hong Kong and Taiwan.

15. Hong Kong has always been the largest source of capital flowing into China, exceeding that of any other nation by a large margin. In terms of the total amount of foreign capital actually used by China in 1996, official Chinese data show that US$20.85 billion came from Hong Kong, which accounts for nearly half of the total from all nations. It should be noted that some of the Hong Kong capital actually came from Taiwan. Excluding the amount counted in the Hong Kong total, Taiwan sent to China directly $3.48 billion in 1996, an amount comparable to that from Japan ($3.69 billion) and the U.S. ($3.44 billion) but larger than that from Singapore ($2.25 billion). See State Statistical Bureau, China (1997: 606–607). It is not clear from this source how much of the Hong Kong capital is from non-Chinese businesses but the amount is likely to be quite small.

16. *Taikongren* is a popular term among the Chinese because it could be playfully interpreted as a "man destitute of wife." The term "parachute kids" appears to have been coined to refer to the fact that many school-age children are airlifted from their old homes and dropped to an alien place about which they knew little in the beginning.

REFERENCES

Agnew, John A. and James S. Duncan, eds. 1989. *The Power of Place.* Boston: Unwin and Hyman.

Anderson, Kay J. 1991. *Vancouver's Chinatown: Racial Discourse in Canada, 1875–1980.* Montreal and Kingston: McGill-Queen's University Press.

Benton, Gregor and Frank N. Pieke. 1998. *The Chinese in Europe.* New York: St. Martin's Press.

Berger, Mark T. 1996. "Yellow Mythologies: The East Asian Miracle and Post–Cold War Capitalism," *Positions: East Asia Cultures Critique* 4 (1): 90–126.

Bird, Jon, Barry Curtis, Tim Putman, George Robertson and Lisa Tickner, eds. 1993. *Mapping the Future: Local Cultures, Global Change.* New York: Routledge.

Bolt, Paul J. 1996. "Looking to the Diaspora: The Overseas Chinese and China's Economic Development, 1978–1994," *Diaspora* 5 (3): 467–496.

Cartier, Carolyn L. 1993. "Creating Historic Open Space in Melaka," *Geographical Review* 83 (4): 359–373.

———. 1997. "The Dead, Space/Place, and Social Activism: Constructing the Nation-State in Historic Melaka," *Environment and Planning D: Society and Space* 15: 555–586.

———. 1998. "Preserving Bukit China: The Cultural Politics of Landscape Interpretation in Malaka's Chinese Cemetery," in Elizabeth Sinn, ed., *The Last Half Century of Chinese Overseas.* Hong Kong: University of Hong Kong Press, 65–80.

———. 2001. *Globalizing South China.* Oxford: Blackwell.

Castells, Manuel. 1996. *The Rise of the Network Society.* Cambridge, MA, and Oxford: Blackwell Publishers.

Castles, Stephen and Mark J. Miller. 1996. *The Age of Migration: International Population Movements in the Modern World.* London: Macmillan.

Chan, Kwok Bun and Clair Chiang See Ngoh. 1994. *Stepping Out: The Making of Chinese Entrepreneurs.* New York: Prentice-Hall.

Chang, Sen-dou. 1968. "The Distribution and Occupation of Overseas Chinese," *Geographical Review* 58 (1): 89–107.

Chen, Ta. 1940. *Emigrant Communities in South China.* New York: Institute of Pacific Relations.

Chen, Xiurong. 1999. "Migration Patterns of Chinese Overseas and the Ethnic Characteristics of Migrant Groups," *Dili yanjiu (Geographical Research)* 1: 45–52. (In Chinese).

Chiang, Nora Lan-hung, Chien-hsiung Chao and Jung-ch'ung Hsu. 1998. "Overseas Migration of Contemporary Chinese," *The Population of Taiwan and Related Phenomena: A Collection of Scholarly Confeence Papers.* Taipei: Population Association of the Republic of China, 63–94. (In Chinese).

Chin, Ko-lin. 1999. *Smuggled Chinese: Clandestine Immigration to the United States.* Philadelphia: Temple University Press.

Chirot, Daniel and Anthony Reid, eds. 1997. *Essential Outsiders: Chinese and Jews in the Modern Transformation of Southeast Asia and Central Europe.* Seattle and London: University of Washington Press.

Clifford, James. 1994. "Diasporas," *Cultural Anthropology* 9 (3): 302–338.

———. 1997. *Routes: Travel and Translation in the Late Twentieth Century.* Cambridge, MA: Harvard University Press.

Cohen, Robin. 1995. *The Cambridge Survey of World Migration.* New York: Cambridge University Press.

———. 1997. *Global Diasporas: An Introduction.* Seattle: University of Washington Press.

Commission on Overseas Chinese Affairs, Republic of China. 1986 and 1997. *Overseas Chinese Economy Yearbook (Huaqiao jingji nianjian).* Taipei: Commission on Overseas Chinese Affairs.

Cox, Kevin and Andrew Mair. 1991. "From Localised Social Structures to Localities As Agents," *Environment and Planning A* 23: 155–308.

Crissman, Lawrence W. 1967. "The Segmentary Structure of Urban Overseas Chinese Communities," *Man* 2 (2): 185–204.

Dirlik, Arif. 1997. "Critical Reflections on 'Chinese Capitalism' As Paradigm," *Identities* 3 (3): 303–330.

———. 1999. "Globalism and the Politics of Place," in Kris Olds, Peter Dicken, Philip F. Kelly, Lily Kong and Henry Wai-chung Yeung, *Globalisation and the Asia-Pacific: Contested Territories.* New York: Routledge, 39–56.

Douw, Leo, Cen Huang and Michael R. Godley, eds. 1999. *Qiaoxiang Ties: Interdisciplinary Approaches to 'Cultural Capitalism' in South China.* London and New York: Kegan Paul International.

Entrikin, J. Nicholas. 1991. *The Betweenness of Place: Towards a Geography of Modernity.* Baltimore, MD: Johns Hopkins University Press.

Fawcett, James T. and Benjamin V. Carino, eds. 1987. *Pacific Bridges: The New Immigration from Asia and the Pacific Islands.* New York: Center for Migration Studies.

Fung, K. C. 1996. "Mainland Chinese Investment in Hong Kong: How Much, Why, and So What?" *Journal of Asian Business* 12 (2): 21–39.

Gallagher, Winifred. 1993. *The Power of Place: How Our Surroundings Shape Our Thoughts, Emotions and Actions.* New York: Poseidon Press.

Gilroy, Paul. 1994. "Diaspora," *Paragraph* 17 (1): 207–212.

Guéhenno, Jean-Marie. 1995. *The End of the Nation-State.* Translated by Victoria Elliot. Minneapolis: University of Minnesota Press.

Hamilton, Gary G., ed. 1991. *Business Networks and Economic Development in East and Southeast Asia.* Hong Kong: University of Hong Kong, Centre of Asian Studies.

———. 1996. "Overseas Chinese Capitalism," in Wei-Ming Tu, ed., *Confucian Tradition in East Asian Modernity: Moral Education and Economic Culture in Japan and the Four Mini-Dragons.* Cambridge, MA: Harvard University Press, 329–400.

———, ed. 1999. *Cosmopolitan Capitalists: Hong Kong and the Chinese Diaspora at the End of the Twentieth Century.* Seattle: University of Washington Press.

Hannerz, Ulf. 1996. *Transnational Connections: Culture, People, Places.* New York: Routledge.

Harvey, David. 1989. *The Condition of Postmodernity.* London: Basil Blackwell.

———. 1993. "From Space to Place and Back Again," in Jon Bird et al., eds., *Mapping the Futures: Local Cultures, Global Change.* New York: Routledge, 3–29.

Hirst, Paul and Jonathan Zeitlin. 1991. "Flexible Specialization versus Post-Fordism: Theory, Evidence and Policy Implications," *Economy and Society* 20 (1): 1–56.

Hom, Sharon K., ed. 1999. *Chinese Women Traversing Diaspora: Memoirs, Essays, and Poetry.* New York: Garland Publishing, Inc.

Hsing, You-tien. 1996. "Blood Thicker than Water: Interpersonal Relations and Taiwanese Investment in Southern China," *Environment and Planning A* 28: 2241–2261.

———. 1998. *Making Capitalism in China: The Taiwan Connection.* New York and Oxford: Oxford University Press.

Hsu, Francis L. K. and Herdrick Serrie, eds. 1998. *The Overseas Chinese: Ethnicity in National Context.* New York: University Press of America.

Hsu, Jinn-Yuh and AnnaLee Saxenian. 2000. "The Limits of *Guanxi* Capitalism: Transnational Collaboration between Taiwan and the U.S.," *Environment and Planning A* 32 (11): 1991–2005.

Huang, Cen. 1998. "The Organization and Management of Chinese Transnational Enterprises in South China," *Issues and Studies* 34 (3): 51–70.

Huang, Yasheng. 1998. *FDI in China: An Asian Perspective.* Hong Kong: Chinese University of Hong Kong Press.

Ip, David. 1999. "Network As Capital: PRC Immigrant Entrepreneurs in Brisbane," in Yen-Fen Tseng, Cilla Bulbeck, Lan-Hung Nora Chiang and Jung-Chung His, eds., *Asian Migration: Pacific Rim Dynamics.* Taipei: Interdisciplinary Group for Australian Studies, National Taiwan University, 149–166.

Ip, David, Christine Inglis and Chung Tong Wu. 1997. "Concepts of Citizenship and Identity among Recent Asian Immigrants in Australia," *Asian and Pacific Migration Journal* 6 (3–4): 363–384.

Ip, David, Chung-Tong Wu and Christine Inglis. 1998. "Settlement Experiences of Taiwanese Immigrants in Australia," *Asian Studies Review* 22 (1): 79–97.

Kaiser, Stefan, David A. Kirby and Ying Fan. 1996. "Foreign Direct Investment in China: An Examination of the Literature," *Asia Pacific Business Review* 2 (3): 44–65.

Kao, John. 1993. "The Worldwide Web of Chinese Business," *Harvard Business Review* 71, March–April, 24–36.

Kirshenblatt-Gimblett, Barbara. 1994. "Spaces of dispersal," *Current Anthropology* 9 (3): 339–344.

Kong, Lily. 1999a. "Globalisation and Singaporean Transmigration: Re-Imagining and Negotiating National Identity," *Political Geography* 18 (15): 563–589.

———. 1999b. "Globalisation, Transmigration and the Renegotiation of Ethnic Identity," in Kris Olds, Peter Dicken, Philip F. Kelly, Linly Kong and Henry Wai-chung Yeung, eds., *Globalisation and the Asia-Pacific: Contested Territories.* New York: Routledge, 219–237.

Kotkin, Joel. 1993. *Tribes: How Race, Religion and Identity Determine Success in the New Global Economy.* New York: Random House.

Kraar, Louis. 1994. "The Overseas Chinese: Lessons from the World's Most Dynamic Capitalists," *Fortune* 130 (9): 91–114.

Kritz, Mary M, Lin Lean Lim and Hania Zlotnik, eds. 1992. *International Migration Systems: A Global Approach.* Oxford: Clarendon Press.

Laguerre, Michael S. 2000. *The Global Ethnopolis: Chinatown, Japantown and Manilatown in American Society.* New York: St. Martin's Press.

Lai, David Chuenyan. 1988. *Chinatowns: Towns within Cities in Canada.* Vancouver: University of British Columbia Press.

Lan, Ping. 1996. *Technology Transfer to China through Foreign Direct Investment.* Brookfield, VT: Ashgate.

Leung, C. K. 1993. "Personal Contacts, Subcontracting Linkages, and Development in the Hong Kong-Zhujiang Delta Region," *Annals of the Association of American Geographers* 83 (2): 272–302.

Lever-Tracy, Constance and David Ip. 1996. "Diaspora Capitalism and the Homeland: Australian Chinese Networks into China," *Diaspora* 5 (2): 239–273.

Lever-Tracy, Constance, David Ip and Noel Tracy. 1996. *The Chinese Diaspora and Mainland China: An Emerging Economy Synergy.* New York: St. Martin's Press.

Ley, David. 1999. "Myths and Meanings of Immigration and the Metropolis," *Canadian Geographer* 43 (1): 2–19.

Li, F. L. N. and A. M. Findlay. 1996. "Placing Identity: Interviews with Hong Kong Chinese Immigrants in Britain and Canada," *International Journal of Population Geography* 2: 361–377.

Li, Peter S. 1993. "Chinese Investment and Business in Canada: Ethnic Entrepreneurship Reconsidered," *Pacific Affairs* 66 (2): 219–243.

————. 1994. "Unneighbourly Houses or Unwelcome Chinese: The Social Construction of Race in the Battle over 'Monster Homes' in Vancouver, Canada," *International Journal of Comparative Race and Ethnic Studies* 1 (1): 14–33.

Li, Wei. 1998a. "Los Angeles's Chinese *Ethnoburb*: From Ethnic Service Center to Global Economy Outpost," *Urban Geography* 19 (6): 502–517.

————. 1998b. "Anatomy of a New Ethnic Settlement: The Chinese *Ethnoburb* in Los Angeles," *Urban Studies* 35 (3): 479–501.

————. 1999. "Building Ethnoburbia: The Emergence and Manifestation of the Chinese Ethnoburb in Los Angeles' San Gabriel Valley," *Journal of Asian American Studies* 2 (1): 1–28.

————. 2000. "*Ethnoburb* versus Chinatown: Two Types of Urban Ethnic Communities in Los Angeles," unpublished paper, Department of Geography, University of Connecticut.

Liang, Zai and Wenzhen Ye. 1999. "From Fujian to New York: Understanding the New Chinese Immigration," unpublished manuscript, Department of Sociology, Queens College, City University of New York.

Lim, Linda. 1983. "Chinese Economic Activity in Southeast Asia: An Introductory Review," in Linda Lim and L. C. Peter Gosling, eds., *The Chinese in Southeast Asia.* Ann Arbor, MI: Center for South and Southeast Asian Studies, University of Michigan.

Lim, Linda and L. A. Peter Gosling, eds. 1983. *The Chinese in Southeast Asia.* 2 vols. Ann Arbor, MI: Center for South and Southeast Asian Studies, University of Michigan.

Lin, George C. S. 1997. *Red Capitalism in South China: Growth and Development of the Pearl River Delta.* Vancouver: University of British Columbia Press.

————. 2000. "State, Capital, and Space in China in an Age of Volatile Globalization," *Environment and Planning A* 32: 455–471.

Lin, Jan. 1998. *Reconstructing Chinatown: Ethnic Enclave, Global Change.* Minneapolis: University or Minnesota Press.

Lo, Lucia and Shuguang Wang. 1997. "Settlement Patterns of Toronto's Chinese Immigrants: Convergence or Divergence?" *Canadian Journal of Regional Science* 20 (1–2): 49–72.

Logan, John R. and Harvey L. Molotch. 1987. *Urban Fortunes: The Political Economy of Place.* Berkeley: University of California Press.

Ma, Laurence J. C. and Biao Xiang. 1998. "Native Place, Migration and the Emergence of Peasant Enclaves in Beijing," *China Quarterly* 155: 546–581.

Mackie, J. A. C. 1992a. "Overseas Chinese Entrepreneurship," *Asian-Pacific Economic Literature*, May, 41–64.

———. 1992b. "Changing Patterns of Chinese Big Business in Southeast Asia," in Ruth McVey, ed., *Southeast Asian Capitalists.* Ithaca, NY: Southeast Asian Program, Cornell University.

Massey, Doreen. 1990. "Questions of Locality," *Geography* 78 (339), Part 2: 142–149.

———. 1993. "Power Geometry and a Progressive Sense of Place," in John Bird, Barry Curtis, Tim Putnam, George Robertson and Lisa Tickner, eds., *Mapping the Future: Local Cultures, Global Change.* London and New York: Routledge, 56–69.

———. 1994. *Space, Place, and Gender.* Minneapolis: University of Minnesota Press.

———. 1995. "The Conceptualization of Place," in Doreen Massey and Pat Jess, eds., *A Place in the World?: Places, Cultures and Globalization.* Oxford: Oxford University Press, 45–86.

Massey, Doreen and Pat Jess. 1995. *A Place in the World?: Places, Cultures and Globalization.* Oxford: Oxford University Press.

Massey, Douglas S. 1999. "International Migration at the Dawn of the Twentieth Century: The Role of the State," *Population and Development Review* 25 (2): 303–322.

———. 1998. *Worlds in Motion: Understanding International Migration at the End of the Millennium.* Oxford: Oxford University Press.

Massey, Douglas S., Joaquin Arango, Graeme Hugo, Ali Kouaouci, Adela Pellegrino and J. Edward Taylor. 1994. "An Evaluation of International Migration Theory: The North American Case," *Population and Development Review* 20 (4): 699–751.

McKeown, Adam. 1999. "Conceptualizing Chinese Diasporas, 1842 to 1949," *Journal of Asian Studies* 58 (2): 306–337.

Nonini, Donald M. and Aihwa Ong. 1997. "Chinese Transnationalism As an Alternative Modernity," in Aihwa Ong and Donald M. Nonini, eds., *Ungrounded Empires: The Cultural Politics of Modern Chinese Transnationalism.* New York: Routledge, 3–36.

Norberg-Schulz, Christian. 1979. *Genius Loci: Toward a Phenomenology of Architecture.* New York: Rizzoli.

O'Brien, Richard R. 1992. *Global Financial Integration: The End of Geography.* New York: Council on Foreign Relations Press.

Ohmae, Kenichi. 1990. *The Borderless World: Power and Strategy in the Interlinked Economy.* London: Collins.

———. 1995. *The End of Nation States: The Rise of Regional Economies.* London: Collins.

Olds, Kris and Henry Wai-chung Yeung. 1999. "(Re)shaping 'Chinese' Business Networks in a Globalising Era," *Environment and Planning D: Society and Space* 17: 535–555.

Olds, Kris, Peter Dicken, Philip F. Kelly, Lily Kong and Henry Wai-chung Yeung, eds. 1999. *Globalisation and the Asia-Pacific: Contested Territories.* New York: Routledge.

Ong, Aihwa. 1999. *Flexible Citizenship: The Cultural Logics of Transnationality.* Durham, NC: Duke University Press.

Ong, Aihwa and Donald M. Nonini, eds. 1997. *Ungrounded Empires: The Cultural Politics of Modern Chinese Transnationalism.* New York: Routledge.

Pan, Lynn, ed. 1999. *The Encyclopedia of the Chinese Overseas.* Cambridge, MA: Harvard University Press.

Pederson, Poul Ove, Arni Sverrisson and Meine Pieter van Dijk. 1994. *Flexible Specialization: The Dynamics of Small-Scale Industries in the South.* London: Intermediate Technology Publications.

Pe-Pua, Rogelia, Colleen Mitchell, Robyn Iredale and Stephen Castles. 1996. *Astronaut Families and Parachute Children: The Cycle of Migration between Hong Kong and Australia.* Canberra: Australian Government Publishing Service.

Pieke, Frank and Hein Mallee, eds. 1999. *Internal and International Migration: Chinese Perspectives.* Richmond, Surry: Curzon.

Poston, Dudley L. Jr. and Mei-yu Yu. 1990. "The Distribution of the Overseas Chinese in the Contemporary World," *International Migration Review* 24 (3): 480–508.

Poston, Dudley L. Jr., Michael Xinxiang Mao and Mei-yu Yu. 1994. "The Global Distribution of the Overseas Chinese around 1990," *Population and Development Review* 20 (3): 631–645.

Pred, Allan. 1984. "Place As Historically Contingent Process: Structuration and the Time-Geography of Becoming Places," *Annals of the Association of American Geographers* 74 (2): 279–297.

———. 1986. *Place, Practice, and Structure: Social and Spatial Transformation in Southern Sweden, 1750–1850.* Totowa, NJ: Barnes and Noble.

Redding, S. Gordon. 1990. *The Spirit of Chinese Capitalism.* New York: de Gruyter.

Reid, Anthony, ed. 1996. *Sojourners and Settlers: Histories of Southeast Asia and the Chinese.* St. Leonards, NSW: Allen and Unwin.

Relph, Edward. 1976. *Place and Placelessness.* London: Pion.

———. 1996. "Place," in Ian Douglas, Richard Huggett and Mike Robinson, eds., *Companion Encyclopedia of Geography: The Environment and Humankind.* London and New York: Routledge, 906–922.

Safran, William. 1991. "Diasporas in Modern Societies: Myths of Homeland and Return," *Diaspora* 1 (1): 83–99.

Schak, David. 1999. "Middle-Class Migration and Problems of Adjustment: Taiwanese Business Migrants in Brisbane," in *Asian Migration: Pacific Rim Dynamics.* Taipei: National Taiwan University, Interdisciplinary Group for Australian Studies, 117–148.

Schiller, Nina Glick, Linda Basch and Cristina Blanc-Szanton, eds. 1992. *Towards a Transnational Perspective on Migration: Race, Class, Ethnicity, and Nationalism Reconsidered.* New York: New York Academy of Sciences.

Sinn, Elizabeth, ed. 1998. *The Last Half Century of Chinese Overseas.* Hong Kong: University of Hong Kong Press.

Skeldon, Ronald, ed. 1994. *Reluctant Exiles? Migration from Hong Kong and the New Overseas Chinese.* Armonk, NY: M. E. Sharpe.

———. 1997. *Migration and Development: A Global Perspective.* Harlow, England: Addison Wesley Longman.

Smith, Michael Peter and Luis Edwardo Guarnizo, eds. 1998. *Transnationalism from Below*. New Brunswick, NJ: Transaction Publishers.

State Statistical Bureau, China. 1997. *China Statistical Yearbook, 1997*. Beijing: China Statistical Publishing House.

Sun, Haishun. 1998. *Foreign Investment and Economic Development in China: 1979–1996*. Brookfield, VT: Ashgate.

Taylor, Peter J. 2000. "Embedded Statism and the Social Sciences 2: Geographies (and Metageographies) in Globalization," *Environment and Planning A* 32: 1105–1114.

Tilly, Charles. 1990. "Transplanted Networks," in Virginia Yans-McLaughlin, ed., *Immigration Reconsidered: History, Sociology, and Politics*. New York: Oxford University Press, 79–95.

Tölölyan, Khachig. 1991. "The Nation-State and Its Others: In Lieu of a Preface," *Diaspora* 1 (1): 3–7.

———. 1996. "Rethinking Diaspora(s): Stateless Power in the Transnational Movement," *Diaspora* 5 (1): 3–36.

Tseng, Yen-Fen. 1994. "Chinese Ethnic Economy: San Gabriel Valley, Los Angeles County," *Journal of Urban Affairs* 16 (2): 169–189.

———. 1999. "The Mobility of People and Capital: Divergent Patterns of Taiwanese Capital-Linked Migration," in Yen-Fen Tseng, Chilla Bulbeck, Lan-Hung Nora Chiang and Jung-Chung Hsu, eds., *Asian Migration: Pacific Rim Dynamics*. Taipei: Interdisciplinary Group for Australian Studies, National Taiwan University, 49–68.

Tu, Wei-ming. 1994. "Cultural China: The Periphery As the Center," in Wei-ming Tu, ed., *The Living Tree: The Changing Meaning of Being Chinese Today*. Stanford, CA: Stanford University Press, 1–35.

Tuan, Yi-Fu. 1974. *Topophilia: A Study of Environmental Perception, Attitudes, and Values*. Englewood Cliffs, NJ: Prentice-Hall.

———. 1977. *Space and Place: The Perspective of Experience*. Minneapolis: University of Minnesota Press.

Van Den Bulcke, Daniel and Hai-yan Zhang. 1995. "Chinese Family-Owned Multinationals in the Philippines and the Internationalisation Process," in R. A. Brown, ed., *Chinese Business Enterprise in Asia*. New York: Routledge, 214–246.

Van Hear, Nicholas. 1998. *New Diasporas: The Mass Exodus, Dispersal and Regrouping of Migrant Communities*. Seattle: University of Washington Press.

Vertovec, Steven and Robin Cohen, eds. 1999. *Migration, Diasporas and Transnationalism*. Cheltenham, UK, and Northampton, MA: E. Elgar Publishing.

Waldinger, Roger and Yenfen Tseng. 1992. "Divergent Diasporas: The Chinese Communities in New York and Los Angeles Compared," *Revue Enropéenne des Migrations Internationales* 8 (3): 91–114.

Wang, Gungwu. 1991. *China and the Chinese Overseas*. Singapore: Times Academic Press.

———. 1992. "The Origins of Hua-Ch'iao," in Gungwu Wang, *Community and Nation: China, Southeast Asia and Australia*. St. Leonards, NSW: Allen and Unwin, 1–10.

———. 1993. "Migration and Its Enemies," in Bruce Mazlish and Ralph Buultjens, eds., *Conceptualizing Global History*. Boulder, CO: Westview Press, 131–151.

———. 1994 "Among Non-Chinese," in Wei-ming Tu, ed., *The Living Tree: The Changing Meaning of Being Chinese Today.* Stanford, CA: Stanford University Press, 127–147.

———. 1996. "Sojourning: The Chinese Experience in Southeast Asia," in Anthony Reid, ed., *Sojourners and Settlers: Histories of Southeast Asia and the Chinese.* St. Leonards, NSW: Allen and Unwin, 1–14.

———, ed. 1997. *Global History and Migration.* Boulder, CO: Westview Press.

Wang, Gungwu and Siu-lun Wong. 1997. *Hong Kong in the Asia-Pacific Region: Rising to the New Challenges.* Hong Kong: University of Hong Kong, Centre of Asian Studies.

———. 1999. "Chineseness: The Dilemmas of Place and Practice," in Gary G. Hamilton, ed., *Cosmopolitan Capitalists: Hong Kong and the Chinese Diaspora at the End of the 20th Century.* Seattle and London: University of Washington Press, 118–134.

Wang, Ling-chi. 1994. "Roots and the Changing Identities of the Chinese in the United States," in Wei-ming Tu, ed., *The Living Tree: The Changing Meaning of Being Chinese Today.* Stanford, CA: Stanford University Press, 185–212.

Wang, Ling-chi and Gungwu Wang. 1998. *The Chinese Diaspora: Selected Essays.* 2 vols. Singapore: Times Academic Press.

Wang, Shuguang. 1999. "Chinese Commercial Activities in the Toronto CMA: New Development Patterns and Impacts," *Canadian Geographer* 43 (1): 19–35.

Warf, Barney. 1993. "Postmodernism and the Localities Debate: Ontological Questions and Epistemological Implications," *Tijdschrif voor Economische en Sociale Geografie* 84 (3): 162–168.

Weidenbaum, Murray and Samuel Highes. 1996. *The Bamboo Network: How Expatriate Chinese Entrepreneurs Are Creating a New Economic Superpower in Asia.* New York: The Free Press.

Wickberg, Edgar. 1994. "The Chinese As Overseas Migrants," in Judith M. Brown and Rosemary Foot, eds., *Migration: The Asian Experience.* New York: St. Martin's Press, 12–37.

Wong, Bernard P. 1982. *Chinatown: Economic Adaptation and Ethnic Identity of the Chinese.* New York: Holt, Rhinehart and Winston.

Yeung, Henry Wai-chung. 1998. "Capital, State and Space: Contesting the Borderless World," *Transactions of the Institute of British Geographers NS* 23: 291–309.

———. 2000. "Embedded Foreign Affiliates in Transnational Business Networks: The Case of Hong Kong Firms in Southeast Asia," *Environment and Planning A* 32: 201–222.

Yuan, Patricia. 1999. "Recent Fujian Immigration in Southwestern Ohio," paper presented at the ISSCO Conference on the Chinese Diaspora in Latin America and the Caribbean, December 10–12, Havana, Cuba.

Zhou, Yu. 1998. "How Do Places Matter? A Comparative Study of Chinese Ethnic Economies in Los Angeles and New York City," *Urban Geography* 19 (6): 531–553.

Zlotnik, Hania. 1998. "International Migration 1965–96: An Overview," *Population and Development Review* 24 (3): 469–510.

Zukin, Sharon. 1992. *Landscapes of Power.* Berkeley: University of California Press.

2

The Chinese Diaspora or the Migration of Chinese Peoples?

Ronald Skeldon

OF DIASPORAS AND THE CHINESE

To say that the word "diaspora" has almost come to displace "migration" by those studying the international movements of peoples over the last decade is but a slight exaggeration. Recent work emphasizing "diaspora" in migration studies appears in studies by Cheng and Katz (1998), Cohen (1997), Van Hear (1998), Kotkin (1993), Chaliand and Rageau (1995) and distinctively in the journal *Diaspora: A Journal of Transnational Studies*. As the word literally means a scattering of peoples, the use of diaspora appears perfectly legitimate. Like so many popularized ideas, however, diaspora comes with "baggage," though one does not have to be a postmodernist to deconstruct its various meanings and their implications. Until its recent incorporation into the migration literature, its usage in the English language was primarily associated with the Jewish peoples who had been banished from their homeland and lived "in diaspora." Diaspora was also applied to other groups such as the Armenians or the Palestinians who had also been expelled from their homelands and lived scattered around the world. Peoples living in "exile" was thus an integral part of the concept of diaspora, together with the image of the migrant as victim.

To apply diaspora to a dynamic, entrepreneurial people such as the Chinese does not at first appear intuitively obvious. Only a tiny minority of the Chinese as a whole live outside China and, with the exception of the arguably fading aspirations of a Guomindang government-in-exile in Taiwan, they have not been expelled from their homeland. Also, as Taiwan was an inalienable part of China, whether they had ever been truly expelled from their homeland was a moot point. Nevertheless, diaspora has come to be associated with the movement of the Chinese, as the title of this volume well attests (see also the volumes edited by Wang and Wang, 1998). As these works have shown, the migrations of the nineteenth and early twentieth centuries produced a global network of overseas Chinese communities, concentrated in the Nanyang, or the countries of Southeast Asia, where Chinese settlement dates back "long before recorded history" (Reid, 1996: 17), but spreading to North, South and Central America as well as the Caribbean, southern Africa, Europe and Australasia. The Chinese truly were "scattered" around the world.

However, there was more to the idea of the Chinese diaspora than simply a scattering of peoples. Implicit in the concept of communities-in-exile is the assumption that peoples are not assimilated into the societies of destination: they retain their distinct identities ready for the day when they can return home. This fits well with the classic Chinese concept of migration that maintained the perspective that no self-respecting Chinese would leave home permanently but would travel as a "sojourner." From the point of view of the destination society, the sojourner does not wish, or is not allowed, to assimilate into that society. With the exposure of the myth of the American "melting pot," that the assimilation of migrants from different cultural backgrounds to some new American norm was not occurring, the term diaspora came to prominence. Perhaps the first use of the term applied to the Chinese in this context was in an article by Lyman originally published in the mid-1970s (Lyman, 1977). The designation "sojourner" dates from much earlier: the classic exposition on the sojourner by Siu dates to the early 1950s but he traces its roots back much earlier (Siu, 1952–53).

The idea of diasporas made up of communities of peoples who intend to return home raises interesting questions of identity and loyalty. Regular contacts with home communities have lent the concept of diaspora another dimension, that of transnational communities. The linkages within the migrant group across nations, that is between origin and destination(s), are seen as meaningful, if not more meaningful, than any linkages either between the migrants and the host society (and other migrant groups), or between the migrants and co-ethnics in the society of origin. Such a view fits with current ideas about the globalization of societies and economies and the erosion of the nation state as the fundamental community of our time. Transnational systems of circulation of migrants have created "ungrounded empires" (Ong and Nonini, 1997) for the Chinese that extend far beyond the territory of any single state.

Elsewhere, I have examined the concept of diaspora in the context of assimilationist and multicultural policies of destination countries, arguing that, as yet, diaspora communities offer little real challenge to the nation-state (Skeldon, 1998). Because the migration of the Chinese offers particular challenges, it is worthwhile here to consider their movements within the concept of diaspora, not only to elucidate the patterns of Chinese migration but also to reexamine the ideas implicit in diaspora. In the burgeoning field of Chinese and Chinese overseas studies, this chapter will attempt to review the most significant recent and not-so-recent research and identify lacunae in our knowledge. Rather than establishing a solid empirical base, a task well accomplished in other chapters of this book, I will seek to examine critically the whole idea of a Chinese diaspora within the context of concepts developed in population migration.

OF CHINESE AND CHINESE MIGRANT GROUPS

One of the consequences of according such importance to transnational linkages within the migrant groups in the concept of diaspora, as outlined above, is that the diaspora community is seen as fairly homogeneous. The ties within the migrant group that extend across states should be stronger than those across different groups within the state, either at origin, or especially at destination. That such conditions may not always, or even ever, hold has done little, thus far at least, to diminish the attraction of the idea of diaspora.

Information on international migration is constituted primarily with reference to nation-states. Thus, our data refer to the number of Mexicans in the United States, Pakistanis in the United Kingdom, Greeks in Australia and so on. While some national migrant groups are certainly more homogeneous than others, particular issues arise when the Chinese are considered as one group within a nation; the "Chinese diaspora" may imply a unity of migration patterns and conditions that is more apparent than real.

National identity assumes some commonly accepted criteria that make one national population distinct from another. The "idea" of the nation is, however, quite recent in history, dating from late-eighteenth-century Europe, and it is constantly changing (Hobsbawm, 1990). It is a concept that has been diffusing throughout the developing world as countries newly independent from colonial empires struggled to establish some kind of common identity from the often artificial creations of colonialism. The ideas of common nation identities, though, are diffusing alongside global forces and flows, including increasing migration, which are acting to erode national identities in favour of international values. China, never a colony, has nevertheless been profoundly affected by forces of modernization and by questions of national identity in the twentieth century. In the words of Lucien Pye, contemporary China is not so much a "civilization pretending to be a state but rather an empire claiming to be a nation-race" (cited in Dikotter, 1996: 599).

It is not, however, simply the "minority" peoples within China who need
to be brought within a common identity but also the Han peoples themselves.
Although they are of one racial group and come from a common Confucian
heritage with a virtually identical written script, there are significant differences among them in terms of spoken language, diet, and folk culture. Variously termed "ethnic groups," "sub-ethnic groups," "speech groups," or the
Chinese word "bang," the issue of ethnic divisions within the Han majority
remains one of the intriguing research questions within China and is of direct
relevance to the study of the Chinese diaspora. Wang (1988: 1) has argued,
somewhat enigmatically, that the Chinese have never had a concept of identity but only a "concept of Chineseness, of being Chinese and of becoming
un-Chinese." In terms of an identity based on place of origin, there is little between this broad sense of "Chineseness" and the local family unit to which an
individual belongs.

The critical questions as far as this chapter is concerned are the following:
first, whether there is a truly Chinese diaspora or whether there are a series
of separate diasporas based on specific place of origin of the groups concerned; second, whether any juxtaposing of the various Chinese groups with
non-Chinese peoples in overseas destinations has forged a new composite
sense of Chineseness; and third, whether the diaspora experience of the Chinese has forged new identities and, if so, whether these have expression in
the structure and function of the diaspora communities.

OF IDENTITIES, SETTLERS AND SOJOURNERS

In 1990, and excluding Hong Kong and Macau, it was estimated that there
were just over 30 million Chinese outside China and Taiwan (Poston, Mao
and Yu, 1994). A very significant proportion of that 30 million had, however,
been born in overseas destinations and belonged to families which had been
established overseas for several generations. Just over 85 percent of the Chinese overseas were in Asian countries in 1990 and were dominated by the
long-established communities in Indonesia, Thailand, Malaysia, Singapore
and the countries of Indo-China. The identity of the Southeast Asian Chinese
has already been the focus of much attention: for example, Cushman and
Wang (1988), Lim and Gosling (1983), Reid (1996) and Suryadinata (1997)
to name only the major overview studies. The minority status of Chinese in
all countries except Singapore in a region where China is one of the dominant
powers has lent a certain geopolitical cachet to the debate: whether the Chinese overseas see themselves primarily as Chinese or as citizens of the states
in which they live. If the former, do they then represent some kind of security

threat to their host societies? This complex issue is not central to the current discussion but suffice it to say here that there is little evidence of the Chinese overseas acting either as agents of Chinese expansionism or as active promoters of change back in China.

Whether the Chinese see themselves primarily as Chinese or as citizens of other countries appears a nonissue as they clearly can be both at the same time. Although the terms "Irish overseas" or "Scottish overseas" are not commonly used, the fact that citizens of the United States, Canada or Australia of Irish or Scottish descent are proud of their heritage and become misty-eyed on St. Patrick's or St. Andrew's night in no way detracts from their American, Canadian or Australian citizenship. Migrants of European descent were always seen to be settlers: the "Scottish emigrant," "the Irish settler," and so on. Yet, many of the European settlers did go home, as they continue to go home today. In the latter part of the nineteenth and the early twentieth centuries, the peak period of migration from across the Atlantic, about 20 percent of Scandinavians and just under 40 percent of English and Welsh returned home: between 40 and 50 percent of Italians returned during the early twentieth century (Baines, 1991: 39; see also Nugent, 1992: 35). During the time of free migration from China to North America before the imposition of the exclusion acts, the incidence of return for Chinese, at around 47 percent, was clearly comparable to that of Europeans (Chan, 1990: 38). The contrast between a Chinese sojourner system and a European settler system is thus oversimplified as there were European sojourners and Chinese settlers. Transnational circulation, as implied in the concept of diaspora, is an integral part of all international migration systems.

Today, large numbers of Americans, Canadians and Australians of European descent return to their countries of origin upon retirement and these settler societies have become important countries of emigration. For example, between 1947 and 1991, fully one-fifth of the 5.1 million settlers who arrived in Australia left. In addition, another 380,340 Australia-born left the country (Hugo, 1994: 43). One interesting indicator of the implications of this type of movement is that Australia pays, every year, more than $A22 million in pensions to British settlers to Australia alone—who have since left the country. Thus, the transnational linkages implied in the concept of diaspora have profound financial implications for countries of origin and destination. The fact that those European migrants had "double identities" did not appear to have prejudiced the emergence of strong independent states with identities in their own right.

Thus, the Europeans, too, were sojourners as well as settlers, just as the Chinese were settlers as well as sojourners. Of the 30 million Chinese overseas, as stressed above, the vast majority live in long-established communities in

Southeast Asia with, almost certainly, generally lower rates of return migration to China than those of European settlers to overseas destinations back to Europe. The principal reasons for this were the often disturbed political and economic conditions within China until the late 1970s and the relative poverty of China compared with overseas destinations.

There was return, nevertheless. Although emigration from China virtually ceased from 1949 until after the implementation of the reforms in 1979, the return of overseas Chinese was welcomed and encouraged, particularly when they faced persecution as in Indonesia in 1959–1960 and in 1967. It has been estimated that between 1949 and 1966 almost 500,000 overseas Chinese returned, some 94,000 in 1960 alone from Indonesia (Fitzgerald, 1972: 69), but this number represented less than 10 percent of the Chinese overseas at the time. That the Chinese migrants adapted to settlement at destinations in various ways will become more apparent below.

MIGRATION FROM CHINA

The above discussion draws attention to the fact that the transnational linkages of a Chinese diaspora may certainly have been no more, and were likely to have been less, than in European migratory flows. As mentioned, there was little migration from China for about 30 years between 1949 and 1979. The most significant outflows were to Hong Kong in 1960 and during the second half of the 1970s (Skeldon, 1986). Immediately after World War II there was little international migration of any of the Chinese peoples as few destinations were prepared to accept them. The settler societies of Australia, Canada and the United States only modified their immigration laws to accept Asians from the mid-1960s and the colonies that were soon to emerge as independent countries of Southeast Asia had essentially closed their borders to further Chinese migration. Those ethnic Chinese who could prove that they had been born on British-administered territory were an exception and this gave rise to a small but significant flow from the New Territories of Hong Kong to the United Kingdom (Watson, 1975). This flow, too, was gradually reduced after the passage of the 1962 Immigration Act of the United Kingdom.

By the 1970s, the United States, Canada and later Australia emerged as the principal destinations for the migration of the Chinese peoples (Skeldon, 1996). The movement began from the peripheral parts of China in the 1960s, from Hong Kong and Taiwan and, after the reforms of 1979, came to incorporate China itself. While the growth in the movement out of these Chinese areas is marked and the numbers quite significant, perhaps more notable is the fact that they are small compared with the base population of China itself.

However, any attempt to relate migration from China with the population of China is meaningless as the migrants come from a series of very small parts of that vast territory. One of the principal source areas in the western part of the Pearl River Delta in Guangdong Province is Siyi, or the four districts of Taishan, Kaiping, Xinhui and Enping. The population of the Siyi in the early 1990s was some 3.6 million, with about 1.8 million migrants and their descendants from that area living overseas and another 1.1 million in Hong Kong, Macau and Taiwan (data cited in Christiansen, forthcoming). In one part of Fujian Province, in Changle District, up to half of the population of particular villages is estimated to be living overseas, with, in the one extreme case of Houyu, an astonishing 80 percent of the population now living in New York and its environs (Hood, 1998: 33). Diasporas indeed, if on a local scale!

The regional origins of migration from China have long been recognized. The vast majority of migrants from China come from just three provinces in the south of the country, Guangdong, Fujian and Zhejiang, and from a relatively small number of areas within those provinces. The principal migrant groups from southwest to northeast along the coast are: Hainanese from the eastern part of Hainan Island; Cantonese or Yue-speaking peoples from around the Pearl River Delta: Teochiu (Chiu Chow or Chaozhou), or southern Min-speaking peoples from coastal areas of eastern Guangdong and the western border of Fujian; Hakka from inland areas of eastern Guangdong and southwestern Fujian; Hokkien, also a southern Min language, from coastal areas around Xiamen in Fujian; Hokchiu and Hokchia, northern Min-speaking peoples from areas around Fuzhou also in Fujian; and Wu dialect speakers of the areas around Wenzhou and Qingtian County in coastal Zhejiang. Of these language groups, only the Hokkien and Teochiu speak dialects of the same language, the others being mutually unintelligible. Even the Taishan dialect of the Cantonese of the Siyi can only be understood with difficulty by speakers of standard Cantonese.

In addition to these areas of origin must be added Hong Kong and Taiwan, which have dominated the more recent migration streams to North America and Australasia, particularly of business and investor migrants. While Hong Kong is predominantly Cantonese, and migration from mainland China to Taiwan has traditionally been dominated by migrants from Fujian, the ethnic composition of both areas is more complex, especially since the immigrations from China post-1949 (on Hong Kong see Guldin, 1997). Unfortunately, the data on movements from these two origins are rarely broken down by ethnicity and even the more detailed studies of Hong Kong emigrants (see Skeldon, 1994) contain little information on subgroups among Hong Kong migrants. The Shanghainese, for example, a small group compared to the total population of Hong Kong, accounting for 10 to 16 percent of the population, are known to have built up an extensive business network out of the city far more important than their mere numbers would suggest (Wong, 1988).

The predominance of Chinese emigrant origins in South China should not imply that no migration takes place or has taken place from other parts of China. There was a substantial movement of labour out of Shangdong, for example, to Europe to serve as auxiliaries during World War I, involving nearly 100,000 men (Summerskill, 1982), and from Shandong, Hebei and Henan to South Africa between 1904 and 1907 to work in the gold mines, involving over 60,000 men (Yap and Man, 1996: 111–135). Neither of these flows from northern provinces of China gave rise to long-term settlement and, with only a few exceptions, all the labourers were repatriated at the end of their contracts. This migration from northern China was in complete contrast to the movements from Zhejiang to Europe, and from Canton to South Africa, which gave rise to permanent communities. The Cantonese, in fact, showed little inclination to volunteer for work on the goldfields, showing why the recruiters turned to northern sources of supply. The northern Chinese and those from the Chinese heartland have not been part of any sustained Chinese diaspora although, in recent years, northerners from Heilongjiang have been moving into the Russian Far East and Mandarin-speaking students and technocrats from all parts of China have been going overseas as China joins the global community.

Although the actual situation can be exceedingly complex, certain flows from specific origins in China are often associated with specific destinations. The movement of ex-farmers from the New Territories of Hong Kong to the United Kingdom resulted in a pattern of concentration in the largest cities, and these migrants, given their trade of running Chinese restaurants and "takeaways," set up "branches all over" the country to serve a dispersed market (Baker, 1994). Over 40 percent of the movement towards Thailand was made up of Teochius and some 90 percent of rural Chinese in Cambodia came from that area. Hakka dominated the migration to western Sarawak and the domination of particular language groups to specific destinations was a characteristic of Chinese agricultural colonization throughout Southeast Asia (Hill, 1988: 125–126).

Until the mid-1960s the migration to North America, in its transitions of free immigration through exclusion, was dominated by Cantonese villagers from the western Pearl River Delta, most notably from the Siyi, and especially from Taishan, and from the Sanyi, or the three districts of Panyu, Nanhai and Shunde, plus the county of Zhongshan (see Lai, 1998; Ng, 1998). Included among the Cantonese were Hakka-speakers, also from the Pearl River Delta. The greater part of the recent illegal Chinese migration into the United States, perhaps some 200,000 in 1991–1993 alone, has been from one specific area of

Fujian, Changle County (Hood, 1998: 33). Unlike the movements to Southeast Asia, North America and Australasia, which were dominated by peoples from Guangdong and Fujian, migrants from Zhejiang, particularly from Qingtian and Wenzhou, went primarily to destinations in Europe.

Thus, the migration out of China has been made up of flows from highly localized origins to specific destinations that at first might not seem to fit easily with the idea of an overarching "Chinese diaspora." It is not simply in terms of origin that the diversity among Chinese migrants is to be found, but in occupation, too. From the Chinese coolie or laundryman of the nineteenth century to the entrepreneur promoting a special brand of Chinese capitalism of today, stereotypes have tended to characterize Chinese migration. That coolies, laundrymen and entrepreneurs were or are significant components of the migration flows is not in question but the composition of the flows was much more complex depending upon the type of migration, whether recruited as indentured servant or moving as a "free migrant," and the destination involved. While certainly the nature of the migration usually meant that the migrants moved through urban centres, many engaged in rural activities. Recruitment for plantations in Hawaii or Thailand, smallholder market gardening in Thailand and subsistence agriculturalists in Sabah were all important activities of Chinese overseas.

Again the ethnic dimension is important. The Teochiu appear to have pioneered the introduction of sugar cultivation in Thailand just as the Hainanese attempted to introduce a cotton plantation system into that country in the nineteenth century (Hafner, 1983: 34). The "ethnically homogeneous Chinese middleman group" in the Malayan Peninsula in more recent years was a Hokkien group (Landa, 1983), and Cantonese were pepper planters in Sibu district in Sarawak (Hill, 1988: 126).

One of the most ethnically diverse destinations of Chinese migration is Singapore and there the different dialect groups were associated with different occupations, specializations that were reinforced by their concentration in specific districts of the city (see Cheng, 1985: 89ff). There, in the early part of this century, the Hokkien dominated commerce and trade, the Teochiu "were more represented in agriculture than in commerce," and the Cantonese were famous for manufacturing furniture, leather goods, soya sauce, clock and watch repairing, tailoring, goldsmithry and jewellery. The Hakkas were involved in pawnbroking and in dealing in Chinese medicines and herbs as well as moving into the textile trade. The Hainanese dominated the coffee-shop trade and later catering and bakery businesses. Their relatively late arrival and isolation in Singapore led them to invest heavily in the education of the next generation, which saw a "rather high proportion of Hainanese academicians, graduates, professionals and prominent civil servants" in more recent years

(Cheng, 1985: 97). Road transport, including bicycle, motorcycle and the taxi business were dominated by Hokchias. Thus, in common with so many migrant groups around the world, place of origin becomes associated with occupational specialization. Migration is a critical factor in the segmentation of labour markets.

The existence of these distinct flows should not detract from the very real changes that have occurred in their volume and composition and in the nature of the communities of origin and destination over time. For example, the rise of Chinese nationalism from the beginning of this century and the later introduction of communism provided common ideological perspectives for all China; the gradual erosion of such perspectives under the reforms may see the reemergence of regionalism, as in other parts of the world experiencing the demise of socialism. Under communism, however, there was little migration out of China and its resurgence after the reforms of 1978 may both reinforce and be reinforced by that regionalism. Much depends upon what occurs in migrant destinations and there too significant and divergent changes have occurred.

THE CHINESE AS SETTLERS: THE HISTORICAL DIMENSION

Chinese migrants, as emphasized above, were not all sojourners: they became settlers and, depending upon the situation, assimilated to varying degrees with the indigenous populations. In some parts of Southeast Asia, Thailand and Cambodia, for example, that assimilation became virtually complete. In other areas, from the eighteenth century, an "intermediate" culture was created that was neither indigenous nor Chinese. Skinner (1996), in an exemplary analysis, examines this "creolization" of Chinese societies in three different contexts: Java, the Straits Settlements of the Malayan Peninsula, and the Philippines, in their Peranakan, Baba, and mestizo variants, respectively. While each of these three variants was descended from Hokkien migrant groups, the critical factors in whether intermediate societies were to emerge revolved around the nature of the host society and the barriers to assimilation. Even barriers themselves, however, did not necessarily determine the outcome. Where these were formidable as in the cases of more orthodox Islamic societies in Makasar, Aceh and Madura, Chinese might convert in order to obtain access to highly valued ends, essentially marriage partners, high social status, and economic opportunities (Skinner, 1996: 74). In these areas their children were assimilated into the local indigenous culture and no intermediate cultures emerged.

Significant changes in the nature of these intermediate societies occurred from the late nineteenth century. In the migration system the critical difference was the participation of increasing numbers of Chinese women, which led to ethnically "purer" Chinese groups, the *totok*. Space does not permit full consideration to be given to the sophistication of Skinner's analysis but from that time on, there became less need for Chinese migrants to assimilate into intermediate communities and tensions rose between the latter and the new *totok* groups. The policies of the dominant colonial power in each area were also specific to these migrant communities, as were the attitudes of the Chinese groups to the new nationalism emerging in China. In the Philippines the mestizo Chinese merged with indigenous groups to produce the new Filipino nationalism; in the Straits Settlements, the Baba were absorbed into broader Chinese communities; and in Java, only the Peranakan survived as an identifiable separate cultural group, very different from its Chinese origins and equally different from the *totok* Chinese.

The significance of Skinner's analysis for the theme of a Chinese diaspora is to reinforce the very different outcomes that can emerge from Chinese migration. Skinner's three cases all had a common origin in Hokkien settlement but because of a complex matrix of local, regional and global factors, generated three very different sets of outcomes. Adding other ethnic Chinese groups to the equation, whether Cantonese or Techiu, yet further complicates the picture.

THE "NEW" CHINESE SETTLERS

The inclusion of the "new" migrations from China from the 1970s onwards truly reveals the heterogeneous nature of the Chinese diaspora. The new migrant flows consist much more of the highly educated and of families than the old labour movements of the nineteenth and early twentieth centuries. Although there are large numbers of students going overseas to continue their studies in Canada, Australia, and the United States, the majority are ostensibly settlers. Within China, the recent migration appears to be mainly from traditional areas of outmovement in Guangdong, Fujian and Zhejiang Provinces. Hong Kong and Taiwan together with Southeast Asian countries are, however, among the major sources of the new migration, whose original ethnic origins are unknown. Whether that origin would be meaningful is also unknown as a Hong Kong or Singaporean identity may be of greater importance than a Shanghai or Hokkien origin. Also, the new migration out of Hong Kong is very different from the 1950s movement out of New Territories villages, for example.

Significant numbers of the settlers to North America and Australasia, however, appear to return home after establishing residence and/or citizenship in destination countries. The head of household only may return, leaving their families at the destination where the children are established in a school system less pressured than in Hong Kong, Singapore or Taiwan. These household heads may essentially commute across the Pacific at regular intervals creating transnational systems of circulation that give substance to the idea of diaspora as a transnational community. These household heads are the "astronauts," and in cases where both parents return to continue their work in origin areas, the children left at the destination are known as "parachute" kids (Skeldon, 1994; Pe-Pua et al., 1996).

The Chinese communities in North America, Australasia and in Europe have become increasingly heterogenous, divided by language, origin, political persuasion, class and legal status (Chen, 1992; Wong, 1987; Benton and Pieke, 1998). Yet within this heterogeneity new ethnicities and identities are being manufactured (Kwong, 1997). In the face of a new and hostile environment, no matter whether that hostility is real or perceived, common Chinese solidarity is emphasized. To the outsider the migrants, irrespective of background, are "all Chinese"; to the insider, a common Chinese front is in the best interests of self-protection. Thus, the commonality of "Chineseness" as a racial category, promoted by both outsiders and insiders for very different reasons, can obscure real and significant differences within the Chinese communities.

THE CHINESE DIASPORA IN CONTEXT

The Chinese migrants to Europe have been portrayed as the "first Europeans" (Christiansen, 1998) in the sense that they moved to Europe rather than to any single European state and seldom comprehended the differences among European nations. However, there were enough factions among them, and there were Chinese groups that had virtually no contact with others, so that it is difficult to see them as a single ethnic group. The communities in North America and Australasia similarly appear to be becoming increasingly heterogeneous. The direction of future change will depend to a large extent on the relative openness of all these communities to intermarriage. Changes equivalent to those observed by Skinner in the historical experience of Chinese communities in Southeast Asia can surely be expected in the destinations of Chinese migrants today. The outcomes are likely to be multiple depending upon factors internal to the Chinese migrant community, factors in the host community, and policies implemented by the host country. Multicultural policies, for example, may result in different outcomes from policies of a more assimilationist bent.

That there has been a Chinese diaspora in the sense of a spreading of Chinese peoples around the world is beyond doubt. The impact that this spreading has had, however, is various. Diaspora appears to imply some form of uniformity, of a single great wave of oriental peoples that may threaten other societies. That wave is made up of many separate and distinct parts. To include them all as if they were part of a single migration is extremely deceptive. Accepting the realities of the global migration system means becoming aware of the differences among and within migrant groups. For the Chinese, differences include those of background and place of origin, and differences that evolve in the destination areas themselves as people both are transformed by and transform their host societies. There has perhaps been a Chinese diaspora but, more meaningfully, there has been a varied and complex migration of Chinese peoples.

NOTE

Several of the ideas outlined in this chapter have received more extensive consideration in Ronald Skeldon, "The Dangers of Diaspora: Orientalism, the Nation-State and the Search for a New Geopolitical Order," in M. A. B. Siddique, ed., *International Migration into the 21st Century: Essays in Honour of Reginald Appleyard* (Cheltenham: Edward Elgar, 2001), 109–125.

REFERENCES

Baines, Dudley. 1991. *Emigration from Europe 1815–1930*. London: Macmillan.

Baker, Hugh D. R. 1994. "Branches All Over: The Hong Kong Chinese in the United Kingdom." In *Reluctant Exiles? Migration from Hong Kong and the New Overseas Chinese*, ed. Ronald Skeldon, 291–307. New York: M. E. Sharpe.

Benton, Gregor and Pieke, Frank N. (eds.). 1998. *The Chinese in Europe*. London: Macmillan.

Chaliand, Gerard and Rageau, Jean-Pierre. 1995. *The Penguin Atlas of Diasporas*. Harmondsworth: Viking Penguin.

Chan Sucheng. 1990. "European and Asian Immigration into the United States in Comparative Perspective." In *Immigration Reconsidered: History, Sociology and Politics*, ed. Virginia Yans-McLaughlin, 37–75. New York: Oxford University Press.

Chen Hsiang-Shui. 1992. *Chinatown No More: Taiwan Immigrants in Contemporary New York*. Ithaca: Cornell University Press.

Cheng Lim-Keak. 1985. *Social Change and the Chinese in Singapore*. Singapore: Singapore University Press.

Cheng, Lucie and Katz, Marian. 1998. "Migration and the Diaspora Communities." In *Culture and Society in the Asia-Pacific,* eds. Richard Maidment and Colin Mackerras, 65–87. London: Routledge.

Christiansen, Flemming. 1998. "Chinese Identity in Europe." In *The Chinese in Europe,* eds. Gregor Benton and Frank N. Pieke, 42–63. London: Macmillan.

———. Forthcoming. *Chinatown, Europe.* Richmond, Surrey: Curzon Press.

Cohen, Robin. 1997. *Global Diasporas: An Introduction.* London: UCL Press.

Cushman, Jennifer and Wang Gungwu (eds.). 1988. *Changing Identities of the Southeast Asian Chinese since World War II.* Hong Kong: Hong Kong University Press.

Dikotter, Frank. 1996. "Culture, 'Race' and Nation: The Formation of National Identity in Twentieth-Century China." *Journal of International Affairs* 49(2): 590–605.

Fitzgerald, Stephen. 1972. *China and the Overseas Chinese: A Study of Peking's Changing Policy, 1949–1970.* Cambridge: Cambridge University Press.

Guldin, Gregory E. 1997. "Hong Kong Ethnicity: Of Folk Models and Change." In *Hong Kong: The Anthropology of a Chinese Metropolis,* eds. Grant Evans and Maria Tam Siu-Mei, 25–50. Richmond, Surrey: Curzon.

Hafner, James A. 1983. "Market Gardening in Thailand: The Origins of an Ethnic Chinese Monopoly." In *The Chinese in Southeast Asia. Volume 1. Ethnicity and Economic Activity,* eds. Linda Y. C. Lim and L. A. Peter Gosling, 30–45. Singapore: Maruzen.

Hill, Ronald D. 1988. "Notes on Chinese Agricultural Colonization in Southeast Asia." *Erdkunde* 42: 123–135.

Hobsbawm, Eric J. 1990. *Nations and Nationalism since 1780.* Cambridge: Cambridge University Press.

Hood, Marlowe. 1998. "Fuzhou." In *The Encyclopedia of the Chinese Overseas,* ed. Lynn Pan, 33–35. Singapore: Archipelago Press.

Hugo, Graeme. 1994. *The Economic Implications of Emigration from Australia.* Canberra: Australian Government Publishing Service.

Kotkin, Joel. 1993. *Tribes: How Race, Religion and Identity Determine Success in the Global Community.* New York: Random House.

Kwong, Peter. 1997. *Forbidden Workers: Illegal Chinese Immigrants and American Labor.* New York: The New Press.

Lai, Him M. 1998. "The United States." In *The Encyclopedia of the Chinese Overseas,* ed. Lynn Pan, 261–273. Singapore: Archipelago Press.

Landa, Janet T. 1983. "The Political Economy of the Ethnically Homogeneous Chinese Middleman Group in Southeast Asia: Ethnicity and Entrepreneurship in a Plural Society." In *The Chinese in Southeast Asia. Volume 1. Ethnicity and Economic Activity,* eds. Linda Y. C. Lim and L. A. Peter Gosling, 86–116. Singapore: Maruzen.

Lim, Linda Y. C. and Gosling, L. A. Peter (eds.). 1983. *The Chinese in Southeast Asia.* Singapore: Maruzen, 2 volumes.

Lyman, Sanford M. 1977 "The Chinese Diaspora in America, 1850–1943." In *The Asian in North America,* ed. Sanford M. Lyman, 11–24. Santa Barbara: ABC-Clio Press.

Ng Wing Chung. 1998. "Canada." In *The Encyclopedia of the Chinese Overseas,* ed. Lynn Pan, 234–247. Singapore: Archipelago Press.

Nugent, Walter. 1992. *Crossings: The Great Transatlantic Migrations, 1870–1914.* Bloomington: Indiana University Press.

Ong, Aihwa and Nonini, Donald (eds.). 1997. *Ungrounded Empires: The Cultural Politics of Modern Chinese Transnationalism.* London: Routledge.

Pe-Pua, Rogelia, Mitchell, Coleen, Iredale, Robyn and Castles, Stephen. 1996. *Astronaut Families and Parachute Children: The Cycle of Migration between Hong Kong and Australia.* Canberra: Australian Government Publishing Service.

Poston, Dudley, Mao, Xinxiang Michael and Yu, Mei-Yu. 1994. "The Global Distribution of the Overseas Chinese around 1990." *Population and Development Review* 20(3): 631–645.

Reid, Anthony (ed.). 1996. *Sojourners and Settlers: Histories of Southeast Asia and the Chinese.* St. Leonards, NSW: Allen and Unwin.

Siu, Paul C. P. 1952–53. "The Sojourner." *The American Journal of Sociology* 58: 34–44.

Skeldon, Ronald. 1986. "Hong Kong and Its Hinterland: A Case of International Rural-to-Urban Migration." *Asian Geographer* 5(1): 1–24.

———. (ed.). 1994. *Reluctant Exiles? Migration from Hong Kong and the New Overseas Chinese.* New York: M. E. Sharpe.

———. 1996. "Migration from China." *Journal of International Affairs* 49(2): 434–455.

———. 1998. "From Multiculturalism to Diaspora: Changing Identities in the Context of Asian Migration." In *The Silent Debate: Asian Immigration and Racism in Canada,* eds. Eleanor Laquian, Aprodicio Laquian and Terry McGee, 213–226. Vancouver: Institute of Asian Research, University of British Columbia.

Skinner, G. William. 1996. "Creolized Chinese Societies in Southeast Asia." In *Sojourners and Settlers: Histories of Southeast Asia and the Chinese,* ed. Anthony Reid, 51–93. St. Leonards, NSW: Allen and Unwin.

Summerskill, Michael. 1982. *China on the Western Front.* London: Michael Summerskill.

Suryadinata, Leo (ed.). 1997. *Ethnic Chinese As Southeast Asians.* Singapore: Institute of Southeast Asian Studies.

Van Hear, Nicholas. 1998. *New Diasporas: The Mass Exodus, Dispersal and Regrouping of Migrant Communities.* London: UCL Press.

Wang, Gungwu. 1988. "The Study of Chinese Identities in Southeast Asia." In *Changing Identities of the Southeast Asian Chinese since World War II,* eds. Jennifer Cushman and Wang Gungwu, 1–21. Hong Kong: Hong Kong University Press.

Wang Ling-Chi and Wang Gungwu (eds.). 1998. *The Chinese Diaspora: Selected Essays.* Singapore: Times Academic Press, 2 volumes.

Watson, James L. 1975. *Emigration and the Chinese Lineage: The Mans in Hong Kong and London.* Berkeley: University of California Press.

Wong, Bernard. 1987. "The Chinese: New Immigrants in New York's Chinatown." In *New Immigrants in New York,* ed. Nancy Foner, 243–271. New York: Columbia University Press.

Wong, Siu-Lun. 1988. *Emigrant Entrepreneurs: Shanghai Industrialists in Hong Kong.* Hong Kong: Oxford University Press.

Yap, Melanie and Man, Dianne L. 1996. *Colour, Confusion and Concessions: The History of the Chinese in South Africa.* Hong Kong: Hong Kong University Press.

I

HISTORICAL AND CONTEMPORARY DIASPORAS

3

Diaspora and Social Restructuring in Postcolonial Malaysia

Carolyn Cartier

In February 1998, several months into the first year of the regional economic downturn that shattered the postwar run of rapid economic growth in Southeast Asia, the Malaysian government announced that it would adjust a 27-year-old policy favoring Malay ownership of domestic capital and allow Chinese or Indian businessmen to assume a larger share of corporate ownership (Pereira, 1998). In July 2000, one year into the recovery after the 1997–1999 regional downturn, Prime Minister Mahathir continued to "urge the Chinese community in the country to lend a helping hand to rebuild *Bumiputera* businesses affected by the recent economic turmoil in efforts to accelerate national prosperity" (BERNAMA, 2000). The apparent contrast between the situation of the Chinese community in Malaysia and the experience of the Chinese in Indonesia could not have been more striking: in September 1997 riots against Chinese in Indonesia underscored the state's fragile hold on the economy, while in Malaysia the state began to negotiate economic recovery by invoking the significance of the Chinese capitalist class and its fundamental role not only in economic development but the nation-building project at large. How the state's negotiation of the Chinese community in Malaysia has been a pivotal sphere of state-making and development planning in postcolonial society, interpreted through historical geographies of settlement patterns, economic activities, social organization, and cultural landscapes, and how Chinese identities have transformed in the process, are the subjects of this chapter.

Chinese migration to the Malay Peninsula and western Borneo, the lands that form the Malaysian nation-state, has substantially influenced the formation of both colonial Malaya and postcolonial Malaysian society. From the time of the British colonial period, Chinese migrants engaged in the full variety of economic activities. In the 1870s, a British colonial administrator in the Straits Settlements, J. D. Vaughan wrote, "The Chinese are everything" (Vaughan, 1992: 15). Chinese workers dominated the primary production economic activities of the colonial economy, the retail economy in the towns, and the wholesaling trade between the Nanyang and China. They provided the labor to open the tin mines and clear the forests for plantation agriculture. By the early twentieth century, Chinese communities had formed a variety of enduring social organizations, from clan and native place organizations to temples and schools, and, by the middle of the twentieth century, political parties. At independence, the dominance of Chinese participation in the economy became a politicized issue, and the postcolonial Malay-dominated government established special policies to enhance the position of Malays, known as the *Bumiputera,* especially through "affirmative action" policies in education, job opportunities, and capital ownership. Malaysian society reflects these kinds of policies and the country's political system based on state-defined racial groups, the impetus for which is arguably the size and distribution of the Chinese population and its central role in the economy. In Malaysia, economic geographies of the Chinese population, in diverse and changing ways, have driven basic political economic policy-making in the postcolonial Malaysian order.

POPULATION DISTRIBUTION, STATE-MAKING, AND THE NEW ECONOMIC POLICY

Among countries worldwide, Malaysia has the largest ethnic Chinese minority population by percentage of total population (Poston and Yu, 1990). Until the final quarter of the twentieth century, the Chinese population of Malaysia comprised over one-third of the total population of the country. Based on the 1991 census, the Chinese population had slipped to 28.1 percent of the total population, or 4.9 million of the total population of 18.4 million (PHCM, 1995), and in 2000 the Chinese population was 26 percent of the total population of 23.27 million (DOSM, 2001). The 1991 census also showed that the proportion of the population Chinese in peninsular or west Malaysia—where the Chinese population has historically been higher—began to decline from its historic highs, to 28.7 percent of the total (see table 3.1). The decline in the proportion of the Chinese population reflects the increase in size of the Malay population. During the middle of the twentieth century, the Malay population formed just under 50 percent of the total in peninsular Malaysia, and in response, the state urged a pro-natalist policy for Malays. The policy registered results, and by 1991, the proportion of the Malay population had increased to 58 percent (PHCM, 1995). By 2000, the proportion Malay increased to 65.1 percent of the total population (DOSM, 2001). The Indian population has also declined and now forms less than 10 percent of the total population. Birth rates in the Chinese and Indian communities continue to be lower than birthrates for Malays, which also reflects the higher percentages of urban residence among the Chinese and Indian populations.

By contrast to the patterns of the peninsula, the *Bumiputera* (sons of the soil) population, a term used by the state to designate Malays and indigenous population groups, has dominated the distribution in the Borneo states of Sabah and Sarawak. In 2000 *Bumiputeras* formed 80.5 percent of the population in Sabah and 72.9 percent of the population in Sarawak. In Sabah the proportion of the population Chinese is 13.2 percent, while in Sarawak the proportion of the population Chinese is more comparable to figures for the peninsula, at 26.7 percent (see table 3.2). The Borneo states are also different from the peninsula in that sizable Indian communities are absent from Sabah and Sarawak, which is a result of the specificity of migrant patterns during the colonial era. While *Bumiputeras* dominate the Borneo states, the population of those two states makes up only 20 percent of the national total (DOSM, 2001).

Historical differences in society and economy between the peninsula and the Borneo states are reflected in the state's development agenda: social processes of the peninsula, the region of the federal capital, widespread industrial development, and concentrated political and economic power, largely drive national policy decisions. The settlement patterns of the colonial period inscribed real differences in the Malayan economic landscape. Chinese and

Table 3.1. Population Distribution by Ethnic Group, Peninsular Malaysia, 1911–1991

Year	Chinese	Malay	Indian	Others
1991	28.7	58.2	9.4	2.9
1980	33.8	55.3	10.2	0.7
1970	35.8	52.7	10.7	0.8
1957	37.2	49.8	11.1	2.0
1947	38.4	49.5	10.8	1.3
1931	33.9	49.2	15.1	1.8
1921	29.4	54.0	15.1	1.5
1911	29.6	58.6	10.2	1.6

Sources: Malaysian Fertility and Family Survey, 1974; World Fertility Survey, First Country Report, 1977; Population and Housing Census of Malaysia, 1980, 1983; and Population and Housing Census of Malaysia, 1991, 1995.

Notes: The 1991 figures include only Malaysian citizens. In the 1991 census, Indonesians were classified "Others," whereas in previous censuses they were classified "Malays." Data from the 2000 census on total population of ethnic groups by region was not released at the time of this writing.

Table 3.2. Population Distribution by Ethnic Group in Sabah and Sarawak, 1960–2000

	Sabah		*Sarawak*	
Year	*Chinese*	*Bumiputera*	*Chinese*	*Bumiputera*
2000	13.2	80.5	26.7	72.9
1991	15.6	84.6	28.0	72.0
1980	16.2	83.8	29.5	70.5
1970	21.0	79.0	30.1	69.9
1960	23.0	77.0	30.8	69.2

Sources: Leete, 1996; *Demographic Transition* and *Population and Housing Census of Malaysia, 1991*, 1995; and DOSM, 2001.
Notes: The state uses the term *Bumiputera* to encompass Malays and indigenous communities, even as Malays are the focus of the system of special privileges and the state has historically compelled assimilation of indigenous peoples without self-determination. These *Bumiputera* figures include a small number of of persons of "Other" ethnic origin. Here, the non-Malaysian citizens in Sabah (465,000) and Sarawak (18,000) counted in the 1991 census have been included in the *Bumiputera* figures to make them consistent with the 1980 data.

Indian migrant populations dominated the colonial administrative towns, which were the main immigration ports and were concentrated on the west coast of the peninsula (Sidhu, 1976). The Chinese population also dominated entrepreneurial business activities in Malaya, and, at independence, Chinese entrepreneurs were the major economic force in society. The historic population settlement patterns are reflected in the contemporary population distribution. The six states in which Chinese comprise from 25 to over 45 percent of the total population are on the west coast, from north to south: Pulau Pinang (46.5), Perak (32), Selangor (30.7), Negeri Sembilan (25.6), Melaka (29.1), and Johor (35.4), across the causeway from Singapore (DOSM, 2001). The Malay population, by contrast, was largely rural and engaged in agricultural pursuits.[1] At the transition to independence, the new country's Malay leaders sought to rearrange the economic landscape, in large part by prioritizing the role of Malays in government and economy. Such policies led to restructuring the position of the Chinese community in society, and ultimately, the transformation of Chinese identities. As Heng Pek Koon (1988: 7) has characterized the historical situation, "The Chinese continued to enjoy virtual autonomy until the reins of power passed from the British Government to the Malay-dominated government of independent Malaya."

At independence, political parties constituted on the basis of the three main ethnic groups, the Malays, Chinese, and Indians, came together to form the National Front coalition. Its parties are the United Malays National Organization (UMNO), the Malaysian Chinese Association (MCA), and the Malaysian Indian Congress, in which the UMNO has been the de facto leader of the alliance. (Two major opposition parties have also been active, the Democratic Action Party (DAP), largely Chinese, and Parti Islam SeMalaysia.) Prompted in part by violent street protests after the 1969 federal elections, discussed below, the state, led by the UMNO, introduced the New Economic Policy, 1971–1990, to guide economic and social restructuring. The New Economic Policy (NEP) was explicitly designed to enhance the economic position of Malays, and ostensibly focused on poverty alleviation by providing educational and job opportunities to targeted populations, and land development schemes in rural Malay areas. The effects of the NEP began to even out the ethnic settlement landscape by encouraging Malays to migrate to urban areas for education, work, and housing. Although the primary justification for the NEP was the redistribution of wealth in society, the results were uneven, and by the 1980s data showed that "most of the benefits of the NEP went to the elite and middle class Malays" (Jesudason, 1989: 114).

As a result of the pro-Malay NEP, opportunities have decreased for non-Malays in public sector institutions, such as government employment and university education (see Means, 1991). The problems of uneven opportunities have fueled secondary migrations of Chinese in the final quarter of the twentieth century. Malaysian Chinese have emigrated in significant numbers to Australia, New Zealand, Singapore, Canada, England, the U.S., and other countries. Such "second wave" diasporas have created new patterns of mobility and established the basis for identity formations based on multiple countries and cultures.

SECOND WAVE DIASPORAS

While the Malaysian government does not make available statistical information on Chinese emigration from Malaysia in the postcolonial period, a number of trends in Chinese migration may be observed. First, among all ethnic groups, Chinese migrants have been leaving in the largest numbers (Hirschman, 1975; Sieh, 1988; Pillai, 1992; Pillai and Yusof, 1998). After 1957, Malaysia placed strict controls on immigration, but emigration proceeded with little state record and there have been no controls on the outflow of workers. It is believed that the events of 1969 propelled considerable Chinese migration, especially to Singapore (Hirschman, 1975: 45). Then and now, the profile of the Chinese emigrant is a skilled, relatively highly educated migrant seeking better educational and job opportunities abroad. The majority of migrants have been young men, but women are also leaving in significant numbers, at rates nearly comparable to men (Chan and Peng, 2000: 82). The 1985 recession "marked the first clear and consistent outflows of skilled and semi-skilled Malaysians to areas outside Southeast Asia" (Pillai and Yusof, 1998: 135), and subsequently at least 40,000 Malaysians emigrated to Australia, New Zealand, Canada, and the U.S. between 1983 and 1990, the majority of whom are assumed to be Chinese.

Limited data from the migrants' destination countries corroborate these estimates. Australia's 1996 census reported 76,359 Malaysian-born people who are "mostly Chinese" (DIMA, 1996: 1). Australia's 1986 census determined that at least 60 percent of Malaysian-born people in the country were Chinese; the percentage is only assumed to have increased in the late 1980s, since from 1986–1991, the Malaysian-born population in Australia increased 54 percent (DIMA, 1996: 2). During the next period, 1991–1996, the percentage of the population Malaysian-born increased only 6.5 percent. While these figures reflect the impacts of the recession, domestic political struggles in the late 1980s also worsened conditions for some Chinese in Malaysia. In 1987 the government detained over 100 people under the Internal Security Act, which allows the state to detain without trial persons it deems holding the potential to incite civil unrest. The Chinese leader of the DAP was detained for 18 months at this time, and *The Star,* the newspaper of the MCA, was closed for five months (see Means, 1991). In the United States, from 1980 to 1990 the number of Malaysian immigrants more than tripled, from 10,473 to 33,834 (Gibson and Lennon, 1999).

Labor sojourning migration to Japan and Taiwan is also reasonably common among working class Chinese men looking to enhance household income. Wages for jobs in construction work and other types of skilled and semiskilled work are higher in Japan and Taiwan than in Malaysia, where temporary jobs in construction are not well paid and tend to be dominated by migrant workers from even lower wage sending countries, typically Indonesia and Bangladesh. Donald M. Nonini's (1997) research on Malaysian Chinese transnational labor migrations has treated migrations as informed strategies, embedded in a wider constellation of opportunities and constraints. His examination of male Chinese migration for informal sector work in Taiwan and Japan has sketched how male labor migration operates as an economic opportunity and also as a kind of liberating form of resistance from job market constraints created under the NEP. By migrating to Taiwan and Japan, male Chinese workers experience travel and forms of social mobility—and at least the imaginations of class mobility—cosmopolitan activities of a sort that they have little access to within the social and economic constraints of Malaysian society. The opportunity to experience such alternative identity positions is often realized at the expense of these men's wives, whose domestic labor, in maintaining the household with absentee husbands, secures the men's mobility options. This potential spatial split of the household among working class Chinese—the localization of wives and the globalization of husbands—is a gendered expression of postcolonial Malaysian society under the NEP and its intersections with regional expressions of the international division of labor and uneven development.

DIASPORA AND CHANGING IDENTITY FORMATION

Diaspora has traditionally been understood as a one-way, two-country event, in which emigrants left a homeland for a new country of settlement, acculturation, and, ultimately, citizenship. Contemporary understandings of diaspora have shifted significantly, reflecting changes in migration opportunities and mobility patterns in association with changes in the world economy (Clifford, 1997; Castles and Miller, 1998; Ong, 1999). Postcolonial state policies affecting the Chinese in Malaysia, as elsewhere, have compelled people to consider more flexible lifepath strategies, including overseas education, employment and business ventures, and alternative domiciles. As a result, one extended family's disaporic lifepath might include several countries of residence. Concepts of Chinese identity in diasporic communities have also shifted. In an era of increasing globalization, opportunities for enhanced mobility and communications have transformed the possibilities of staying in contact with family members and communities in distant locations. Contemporary studies of diaspora and mobility widely agree that highly mobile people have "hybrid" and "situational" identities, in which they draw on values from multiple places and communities, and are simultaneously tied to different places in different countries (Massey and Jess, 1995; Clifford, 1997).

Tan Chee-beng (1983, 1988, 1999), in his significant body of work on the Chinese in Malaysia, has stressed the importance of understanding the complexities of Chinese identity, in diverse and located aspects of identity formation. Tan has emphasized how identity formation for Chinese people in Malaysia is differentiated through affiliation with diverse associations, including dialect groups and subgroups, educational and school ties, and churches and temples. In Tan's work, identities are also scaled, so that, for example, it is common to simultaneously maintain sentiments about one's schools and community, a national sensibility about belonging to the large group of Chinese Malaysians, and also global orientations about family ties to relatives in other countries. Such relatively cosmopolitan outlooks on identity sometimes contrast sharply with traditional or nationalistic ideas about identity formation based on the single scale position of the nation-state. This has certainly been the case in Malaysia, where the policies of the NEP have spilled over from the political and economic arenas not only to enhance the role of Malay culture in Malaysian postcolonial society but to also actively

diminish the significance of especially Chinese cultural forms. The marginalization of Chinese cultural practices was most systematically attempted
through the National Culture Policy, introduced in 1982. With this policy,
"Rather than defining Malaysian culture as an amalgam of many cultural
streams, Malay culture and language were taken as being appropriate for all
citizens, on the assumption that those of non-Malay cultural heritage should
either willingly accept Malay culture or perhaps be forced into assimilation
through active government programmes of cultural conversion" (Means,
1991: 133). On several fronts, national Chinese leadership successfully resisted the pro-Malay national culture policy, which is discussed below in a focused section, "The National Culture Debates." Despite the reality of heated
tensions among the different population groups, which are regularly fanned
by debates among political leaders, Malaysia lacks the history of violence that
has marked relations between majority populations and Chinese elsewhere in
the Southeast Asian region, especially in Indonesia and the Philippines.[2] Thus
one of the challenges of understanding the Chinese diaspora in Malaysia is
the set of historic relations between the different population groups, and how
the state has alternatively accommodated and constrained the activities of the
large Chinese population.

THE PIVOT OF DIASPORIC SETTLEMENT: MELAKA

The majority of Chinese overseas trace their ancestry to just two provinces in
China, Fujian and Guangdong. People with Fujian ancestry form the largest
proportion of the Chinese population in Indonesia, Malaysia, the Philippines,
and Singapore, whereas people from Guangdong Province, in the Zhujiang
Delta and Shantou areas, are larger groups in Thailand and Vietnam. Comparison of the patterns of population group distribution by dialect, in south
China and in Southeast Asia, confirms the historic ties between the two regions (see maps 3.1 and 3.2). The historic migrations between Fujian and
Guangdong Provinces and Southeast Asia were maritime voyages that bound
the ports of south China and the Nanyang into a regional trading system. In-
cipient trade journeys from China to the lands of Malay ecumene began over
two thousand years before the present era (Groenveldt, 1887; Wheatley, 1955,
1957). Little information exists to document these travels, but Chinese texts
recorded a wealth of exotic trade goods arriving from the Southeast Asian region in the first millennium C.E. (Wang, 1958, 1959; Wheatley, 1959). At the
pivot of the monsoon system that dominates the regional climatic regime
from India to Japan, the Malay Peninsula lay at the heart of the historic maritime trading networks, and mariners and merchants waited out the reversal

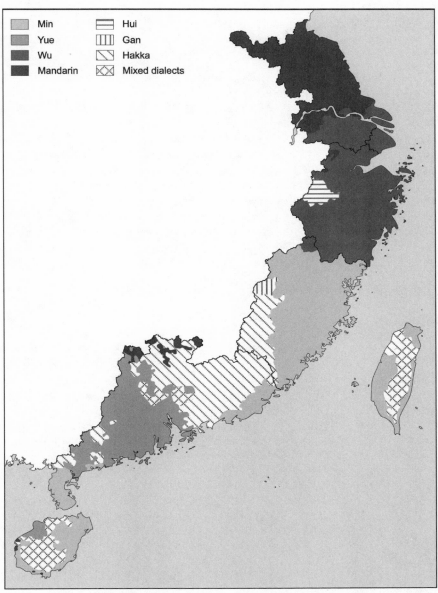

Map 3.1. Dialect Regions, Southern Costal China (Source: *Language Atlas of China*, 1988. Linework by Jane Sinclair.)

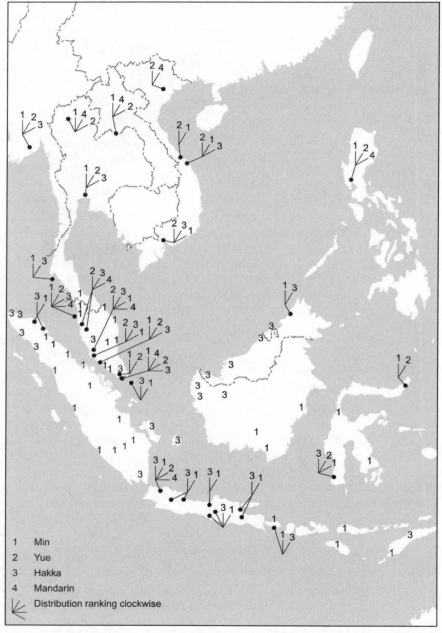

Map 3.2.   Chinese Overseas Populations in Southeast Asia by Dialect Group (Source: *Language Atlas of China*, **1988. Line work by Jane Sinclair.)** *Note*: **Limited data for the Philippines and mainland Southeast Asia.**

of the monsoon system at ports along the Strait of Malacca (Reid, 1993). Malaysia's Islamic origins are also the result of a diasporic history in the early mercantile period, when an Islamic trading diaspora moved through the Southeast Asian archipelagoes and established sultanates at key settlements (Marrison, 1951). The Melaka sultanate was the first one in the region, brought into existence circa 1402 (Sandhu and Wheatley, 1983). The Melaka sultanate established significant ties with China during the era of the Zheng He expeditions, 1405–1433, which enhanced its significance among regional ports (Reid, 1993: 205–206).

In many ways, the historical geography of the Chinese diaspora in Malaysia, through the period of the sultanate and the ensuing colonial eras, under the Portuguese, Dutch, and the British, is deeply intertwined with the development of Melaka. Melaka's economic importance attracted an Islamic sultanate, a diverse mercantile community, and European colonialists looking for established entrepôts through which to conduct the long-distance trade in Asian luxury goods and tropical cash crops. The Portuguese conquest of Melaka in 1511 ended the era of the Melaka sultanate, and yielded the first colonial outpost east of the Indian subcontinent. Holland's ascendance in Europe fueled the formation of the Dutch East India Company, whose emissaries took Melaka from the Portuguese in 1641. To promote economic activity, the Dutch encouraged Chinese trade and settlement (Purcell, 1967: 29). The first census of Melaka, taken in 1678, reported 852 Chinese residents out of a total population of 4,884. In 1750, during the later Dutch era, the Chinese population of Melaka was 2,161 out of 9,635, or 22 percent of the total (Braddell, 1861). By the second half of the eighteenth century, the British East India Company prevailed over its Dutch counterpart. In 1786 the British set up a trading base at the eastern entrance to the Strait of Malacca on the island of Pinang, which challenged Melaka's role in the Strait. Pinang's main settlement, Georgetown, flourished for a time and attracted a significant Chinese community. In 1819 colonial administrator Thomas Stamford Raffles founded Singapore, which grew to eclipse all other ports in the region, and a notable portion of the Chinese population from Melaka relocated there (Purcell, 1948: 70; Turnbull, 1983: 247). The British ultimately replaced the Dutch administration in Melaka in 1824, and in 1826 they formed a single administrative entity, the Straits Settlements, to jointly govern the three major ports of the peninsula. The formation of the Straits Settlements was a significant event that institutionalized a shared regional and cultural economy in the Strait. Its contemporary legacy endures in the "Straits Chinese" cultural complex, discussed below.

Large numbers of Chinese migrants to the Malay Peninsula began to arrive during the middle of the nineteenth century. The British encouraged labor migration, and especially sought men from south China where the "treaty ports" had just been opened to foreign trade by the Treaty of Nanjing, signed in 1842 between the British and China to conclude the Opium War. The Treaty of Nanjing established Hong Kong as a colony, and opened five ports to foreign trade and residence: Canton (Guangzhou), Amoy (Xiamen), Fuzhou, Ningbo, and Shanghai. The transport trade in labor migration soon became an important element of the treaty port mercantile economy, especially through Amoy, Canton, and Hong Kong. Hundreds of thousands of emigrants left China from these ports, and regular economic migration to Southeast Asia took place side by side with contracted or indentured labor migration. In the first decades of the treaty port system, Amoy, in Fujian Province, gained a reputation as the best place to fill a ship with Chinese laborers. Both Western and Chinese firms operated ship transport and migration services through Amoy, and by the early twentieth century upwards of 150,000–200,000 journeys to and from Amoy took place each year (*XHZ,* 1991: 15–30). As a result, people who speak the dialect of southern Fujian, southern Min, also known as Hokkien, form the largest Chinese dialect subgroups in Malaysia and Singapore (Cheng, 1985: 13–15; Tan, 2000: 38–41).

The early colonial economy in Malaya centered on mercantile trade in the ports of the Straits Settlements. Following the extension of British rule in 1874 into the Malay states of Negeri Sembilan, Selangor, and Perak, and 1888 into Pahang, Chinese immigration increased to about 150,000 annually through the end of the century, and to over 300,000 per year in the 1920s (Lee, 1989: 312). As the British increasingly gained control of the interior, the colonial economy evolved to develop resource extraction industries. Prospective Chinese miners and agriculturalists opened up the tin mines and cleared the forests to plant gambier, pepper, rubber, and, later, oil palm. Negri Sembilan, Selangor, and Pahang became centers of tin mining activity to the degree that a Chinese leader from Selangor, Yap Ah Loy, who made a fortune in tin mining, administered the settlement of early Kuala Lumpur and has been honored in postcolonial Malaysia as the founder of the capital (Carstens, 1988). In 1895 Melaka-born Tan Chay Yan planted the first rubber in Malaya, which ignited a "rubber boom" in Melaka that subsequently spread throughout the peninsula and dramatically transformed the landscape (Jackson, 1968: 218–219).

The high point of immigration passed in 1930. In 1933, with rising colonial concern for the sheer numbers of Chinese immigrants entering Malaya, the British colonial government implemented the Aliens Ordinance to limit Chinese immigration. But the Ordinance specified limitations only on male migrants, which led to increased numbers of Chinese female immigrants. The loophole was closed in 1938, after greater than 190,000 Chinese women entered British Malaya in just five years (Lee, 1989: 316). From the 1911 census, the ratio of Chinese men to women in peninsular Malaysia was 1,000 to 247, but by 1947 the ratio was 1,000 men to 833 women (Freedman, 1955: 392). Chinese women worked in a full range of labor opportunities, from domestic service to rubber tapping, tin mining, construction work, and prostitution. Chinese women working in tin mining especially increased through the early twentieth century: they comprised 36 percent of all Chinese tin miners by 1931, and fully 46 percent in 1947 during the Japanese occupation (Lai, 1986: 56). The increased numbers of female migrants contributed substantially to family formation and the evolution of settled Chinese communities.

THE "EMERGENCY" AND INDEPENDENCE

In the second half of the twentieth century the status of Chinese populations overseas transformed, both in China and abroad. China regarded Chinese abroad as "legally Chinese" until postcolonial state-making projects compelled new citizenship policies. Ideological ties between China and Chinese overseas sometimes threatened nascent nationalisms, and among the countries of Southeast Asia that became founding members of Association of Southeast Asian Nations,[3] Malaya was the one where the Communist movement threatened the stability of the state (Pye, 1956; Taylor, 1974).

The Malayan Communist Party (MCP) emerged by 1930, and despite its claims to pan-racial representation, MCP membership was predominantly Chinese. (Only in two Southeast Asian countries, Malaya and Thailand, was local communist membership largely Chinese.) The MCP began an armed guerilla struggle against the British after the Second World War. British troops put down the movement, labeled the "Malayan Emergency," but not completely until 1960. Because the MCP really had no constituency among the Malay population, the emerging leadership of the independent Malaysian state construed the movement as an example of the potential for problems stemming from the Chinese population. But neither did the majority of Chinese people find representation in the MCP, and ultimately the MCA became the legitimate and largest forum for political representation of Chinese people in Malaysia. The peninsular states became independent in 1957, and Sabah and Sarawak joined the Federation of Malaysia in 1963. Singapore also joined in 1963, but after two years of political tensions, and especially concern that Singapore's majority Chinese population would tip the balance of popular power in favor of the Chinese, Singapore was compelled to leave the Federation and became an independent country.

SOCIAL AND ECONOMIC RESTRUCTURING

In 1969, riots erupted in Kuala Lumpur after the federal election. Opposition candidates, many Chinese, won an unanticipated number of seats in parliament, and the complexities of the events reduced to interracial antagonisms, expressed in street violence, looting, and assaults. In response, the UMNO leadership called for new forms of national policy that would ensure the political economic power of Malays. The NEP was the primary result. Ever since, state promotion of special rights for Malays has found legitimacy in the memory of the 1969 postelection riots, and the Emergency (Oo, 1991; Crouch, 1992). In its implementation of the goals of the NEP, the postcolonial state has invoked the memory of these events to shape ethnic community formation and legitimize economic development plans.

The subsequent national economic plan, the Second Malaysia Plan, set forth the goal of restructuring "Malaysian society to correct economic imbalance, so as to reduce and eventually eliminate the identification of race with economic function" (Government of Malaysia, 1971: 1). On the eve of unveiling the NEP, Prime Minister Mahathir wrote, "Chinese business methods and the extent of their control of the economy of the country is such that competition between their community and other communities is quite impossible" (Mahathir, 1970: 56). The NEP prescribed explicit capital restructuring goals: *Bumiputera* ownership of total share capital should reach 30 percent by 1990 (from 2.4 percent in 1970), which made Chinese- and foreign-owned companies restructure their ownership. The NEP expanded the role of the state in the economy by institutionalizing a program providing Malays special terms for credit and business licenses and increased numbers of government contracts. The NEP also sought to transform settlement patterns by promoting urbanization of the new Malay capitalist class. From independence to 1991, the percentage of the urban Malay population nearly quadrupled, while that of the Indian population more than doubled (see table 3.3). Throughout, the Chinese population has remained the most urbanized ethnic group (figure 3.1).

Table 3.3. Proportion Urban by Ethnic Group, Penensu-
lar Malaysia, 1947–1991

Year	Chinese	Malay	Indian
1991	75.8	43.3	63.8
1980	56.1	25.1	40.9
1970	47.0	14.8	34.4
1957	44.7	11.3	30.6
1947	31.1	7.3	25.8

Sources: Saw, 1988 and *Population and Housing Census of Malaysia,*
1991, 1995.

Figure 3.1. Chinese New Year in Kuala Lumpur (Source: *Lat and His Lat Again . . . ,* 1983. Reproduced courtesy of Lat.)

How has the NEP affected the Chinese population? Recent research on the economic effects of the NEP shows that the total share capital held by Chinese business interests almost doubled during the NEP, from 22.8 percent in 1969 to 45.5 percent in 1990 (Gomez, 1999: 2). During the same period, *Bumiputera* share capital increased from 1.5 percent to 20.6 percent. Thus one of the main goals of the NEP—that the *Bumiputera* share of capital ownership should reach 30 percent—was not met, while the Chinese-held share increased. In response to these data, Edmund T. Gomez has raised two basic questions. How have Chinese interests managed to increase their capital share under the strictures of the NEP, which favored capital accumulation for Malays? Do the figures for Chinese share ownership reflect some advantages of "networked" Chinese business linkages? Network analysis has been a common contemporary approach in geographical research on Chinese business organization (e.g., Redding, 1993; Thrift and Olds, 1996; Yeung and Olds, 2000), and the network condition assumes that intra-ethnic business linkages promote favorable business opportunities.

By contrast to some expectations based on the network approach, "the rise of the most prominent Malaysian Chinese capitalists had little to do with intra-ethnic business networking, locally or abroad" (Gomez, 1999: 183). Moreover, "there is much evidence that the implementation of the NEP

divided Chinese capitalists more than unified them" (Gomez, 1999: 183). Instead, successful business operations managed by major Chinese capitalists
seemed to have largely transcended the ethnic factor. Several social conditions in Chinese Malaysian society support this argument. First, the strength
of group association based on dialect or clan has diminished in the late twentieth century. Second, Chinese community association based on class relations may be more important than factors of cultural association. In addition,
Chinese Malaysian businessmen have not forged substantial transnational
linkages with Chinese businessmen in other Asian countries.

Instead, corporate growth of Chinese-owned companies has depended significantly on basic growth-oriented business practices, such as raising finance
capital through the stock market, and strategic management of economic concessions awarded by the state. In regard to the latter strategy, the ability of
Chinese business elites to forge linkages with Malay political economic elites
has been a distinctive asset for large Chinese-owned companies (Gomez,
1999: 183–190). Thus in Malaysia, economic success for leading Chinese entrepreneurs has not depended on "networked Chinese capitalism," but rather
on interethnic linkages with Malay leaders. Such class alliances question the
significance of ethnic factors of economic organization in general, and suggest that in some cases contemporary network approaches have been based on
problematic assumptions about ethnic and racial homogeneity (rather than
class) as a basis for competitive economic organization.

Yet there are ethnic group-based responses to NEP economic policies. One
interesting case points to how the network approach should not be understood
so much as an organizational approach among members of the same ethnicity,
but rather as a framework for understanding control over wholesale and retail
trade of ethnic-identified commodities and provision of ethnic-identified services. The transnational trade in mandarin oranges is the case in point. Mandarin oranges are an important ritual foodstuff exchanged during the Chinese
New Year. They are imported to Malaysia from Guangdong Province, especially from areas in the Shantou hinterland, by ship via Hong Kong to Singapore, from where they are trucked in to the peninsula. Importation of mandarin
oranges has taken place through established commodity chains, managed by
fruit wholesaling networks whose members are practically all Chinese.

In 1985, several weeks before the Chinese New Year, the Malaysian government introduced measures to allow *Bumiputera* fruit wholesalers to import directly from China 80–90 percent of the total projected demand in mandarin oranges (Kuo, 1990: 12). The state simultaneously enforced measures prohibiting
import of fruit from "third countries," in this case, Singapore. Chinese fruit
traders and political leaders quickly perceived these measures as hostile acts designed to replace the traditional trade in mandarin oranges with a state-supported
Bumiputera monopoly. The government's logic was apparently based on the no-

tion that Chinese consumers would purchase the ritually important foodstuff no matter the conditions of the trade. However, news of the state's questionable preferential policy spread quickly, and consumers boycotted, purchasing no oranges that year or substituting regular oranges. Local small-scale produce retailers, the hawkers, also boycotted by not vending mandarins. The DAP encouraged the boycott, and the trade in mandarins collapsed (Kuo, 1990: 16).

Understanding the difference in the role of Chinese ethnicity between this type of economic activity, the fruit trade, and corporate conglomerate activity, discussed above, hinges on class differences produced under the NEP. While NEP policies resulted in increased household and corporate wealth for middle- and upper-class Malays, it was not as successful in raising standards of living for working class Malays and poor Malays, and especially small businessmen. The state's desire to intervene in the fruit trade was an attempt to create new opportunities for small-scale Malay businessmen. No doubt, the state reasoned that if *Bumiputera* fruit traders could gain supplies of the oranges directly from China, they could expand the trade into other commodities. But the commodity trade in mandarin oranges operated through well established transnational linkages largely among the subethnic Chinese group, the Teochew (Kuo, 1990: 18) (see table 3.4). The Teochew dialect group, at 11.3 percent of the Chinese population, is not the largest dialect group among Chinese Malaysians, but the dialect homeland of the group is the same as the major area of mandarin orange production—the northern coast of Guangdong in the Shantou area. The majority of Chinese fruit traders, in both Singapore and Malaysia, are Teochew. Thus in this case, both the geography of agricultural production for mandarin oranges and its transnational trade coincide with the geography of origin of the Teochew group and its historic diaspora in the Malay world. This case also underscores how the network concept of business organization is not specific to Chinese in general, but is rather appropriate in framing the geographies of some types of business activity.

Table 3.4.   Distribution of Chinese Population by
Subethnic Group, and Percentage of Subethnic
Groups Living in Urban Areas, 1991

	Percent of Total	Percent Urban
Hokkien	34.7	75.7
Hakka	23.5	72.4
Cantonese	18.3	82.7
Teochew	11.3	71.5
Foochow/Hokchiu	4.9	65.2
Hainanese	3.6	81.7
Other Chinese	3.8	66.3

Source: *Population and Housing Census of Malaysia,* 1991, 1995.
Note: "Other Chinese" includes Kwongsai, Henghua, Hokchia and
    others.

The controversy over the Mandarin orange trade was an economic example of a set of larger scale debates brewing in society over how to interpret the effects of the NEP. During the middle of the 1980s Malaysia faced a recession, and the state policy response included several economic development proposals whose social effects bore apparent anti-Chinese sentiment. The Bukit China controversy, over a state-led proposal to develop the site of Melaka's sacred Chinese burial ground, discussed below, also reflected the economic tensions of this era, as well as the national culture debates. In association with the implementation of the NEP, the state issued a series of policies aiming to define national culture, which, according to state definition, would be "based on the culture of the people indigenous to the region" (Carstens, 1999: 19). Thus the national culture policy preferred Malay culture as the basis for national culture. Debates ensued, and the larger Chinese community, led especially by political parties and school associations, worked to reassert meanings of Chinese culture and identity in society.

THE NATIONAL CULTURE DEBATES

By contrast to many other former colonial societies, in Malaysia, debates over postcolonial nationalism have not focused on the impacts of the colonial period. Instead, debates about the formation of national culture have revolved around race and ethnicity, and the accommodation of the Chinese and Indian diasporic populations in the postcolonial national order under Malay-dominated rule (see Carstens, 1988, 1999). The state first formulated a national culture policy in 1971, as part of a wider response to the events of 1969. Its implementation began to show substantial effects toward the end of the decade, and by the early 1980s Chinese institutions and community leaders had to organize to attempt to maintain basic spheres of Chinese cultural activity and institutions. Critical issues of the era were the establishment of a Chinese-language university, practice of the lion dance, and the historical recognition of Yap Ah Loy, founder of Kuala Lumpur.

At the turn of the 1970s, Chinese leaders in education were embroiled in controversy over the plan for a privately funded Chinese language university. The state ultimately forbade its establishment by law, even as by 1977 it had reduced non-Malay university admissions to less than 25 percent (Means, 1991: 60), and had already established an Islamic university. The Ministry of Education increasingly deemphasized English medium instruction in schools in favor of Malay medium, and spent its funds accordingly. Between 1971 and 1978 only 7 percent of state school funds for primary schools were used for Chinese schools even though Chinese primary schools enrolled more than 40 percent of all the primary students (Carstens, 1999: 37).[4] As a result of limited state support, the Chinese School Teachers Association and the Chinese School Committees Association organized to maintain Chinese language education. They have focused on providing Mandarin dialect education, which deemphasizes the use of regional Chinese dialects and serves to promote a national Chinese community identity based on a single language (Tan, 1988: 143).

National controversy over the lion dance erupted in 1979, when a Malaysian state official advised that "foreign" cultural practices, such as the Chinese lion dance, could not be accepted as part of Malaysian national culture (Kua, 1990: 11). Chinese organizations responded to the state challenge, and articulated the significance of the lion dance both among the Chinese community and in the larger context of Malaysian society. Media evaluations of the lion dance reported how the Prime Minister, upon his return from China, had been welcomed home by a lion dance troupe. Malaysian lion dance troupes also ranked among the first in the world in international lion dance competitions. In response to enhanced interest, Chinese associations increased practice of the lion dance. The redefinition of the lion dance came in spite of the fact that most members of lion dance troupes had been working class in origin (Carstens, 1999: 42). As Nonini (1997: 219) has explained, working-class Chinese enter the debates over cultural politics "in ways radically different from members of the urban Chinese middle classes who participate in the public sphere of antagonistic (if usually euephemized) polemics contesting the ethnic/racial and national identifications imposed by the Malaysian state." Widespread popularization of the lion dance, combined with its politicized notoriety, made it an enhanced symbol of Chinese identity in Malaysia during the 1990s and gave working-class Chinese a more prominent symbolic place in national culture.

State assault on Chinese cultural traditions took another turn in 1981, when the Ministry of Culture, Youth, and Sports announced that instead of Yap Ah Loy, a nineteenth-century Malay leader, Raja Abdullah, should be recognized as the founder of Kuala Lumpur (Carstens, 1988; 1999). In response, all the Chinese newspapers, plus *The Star,* associated with the MCA, ran long articles about Yap Ah Loy, explaining his important role in the early development of Kuala Lumpur. But this sleight of hand in state historic representation proceeded quickly: textbooks were rewritten, and in 1983 national school exams included a question about the founder of the capital. Still, the barrage of information on Yap Ah Loy left people newly aware of the identity of the historic founder of Kuala Lumpur, and the politicized ways in which landscapes and their histories are contested in postcolonial Malaysian society.

THE STRAITS CHINESE

During the national culture debates, an exhibition on "Baba Heritage" at the National Museum sparked further debate on Chinese identity in Malaysia. Some critics charged that highlighting Baba Chinese identity promoted Chinese integration into Malay society, rather than a multicultural approach to social organization (Kua, 1985). The hearth of Baba Chinese culture is Melaka, where a syncretic Chinese-Malay cultural form evolved early in the colonial era as Chinese men married local women and adopted aspects of Malay culture, including language, lifecycle rituals, dress, and foods. Chinese women later married into existing Baba families, and Baba Chinese culture has remained a distinctively Chinese subethnic identity with Chinese and Malay cultural roots. Baba Chinese are also tied by historical lineage to regional speech groups, especially Hokkien and also Cantonese, but identifying as a Baba often means choosing to speak a patois Malay. In the context of British Straits Settlements society, the Baba learned English and were British subjects, which allowed them to integrate into higher level social and economic positions in the colonial economy. Their local birth combined with complex identity positions—simultaneously Chinese, Malay, and English—distinguished the Baba from later Chinese migrants. The Straits Chinese cultural complex is the larger Chinese community of the British Straits Settlements, and had as its core the Baba Chinese (see Clammer, 1980; Tan, 1983, 1988). The position of the Baba and the Straits Chinese as relatively elite migrant groups faltered at independence, as the new political organization of society prioritized race-based identity formations based on primary ethnic groups, and in the case of the Chinese, speaking Mandarin. In contemporary society, Baba Chinese culture has gained new recognition, especially with the emergence of emphasis on local heritage, heritage organizations, and heritage tourism both for domestic and international visitors.

Straits Chinese Architecture

Malaysia and Singapore are centers of Straits Chinese style architecture, which is a fusion style amalgamating facade treatments of Western beaux-arts and neo-classical architecture with traditional Chinese building design (Kohl, 1984: 179–185). The most common building type in Straits Chinese style is the shophouse, which originated in southern China. The shophouse combines both commercial and residential space in the same structure: the shop faces the street on the ground floor and the dwelling area forms the rear and upper one or two stories of the structure. In addition to the use of classical facade treatments, decorative designs made from porcelain fragments, known as "broken bowl" work, also appear on shophouse facades and recall the historic maritime trade in Chinese porcelain. Straits Chinese shophouses proliferated in the British colonial Straits Settlements, and shopkeepers of all ethnic backgrounds set up business in shophouses (Piyadasa, 1993). Straits style shophouses were so common that their historic merits were not appreciated until they began to disappear from rapidly redeveloping urban landscapes in the 1970s and 1980s.

On a world scale, Straits Chinese style architecture exists only in Malaysia and Singapore, and to a much lesser degree in Xiamen, China, as a result of returned overseas Chinese who redeveloped central Xiamen in the 1920s and 1930s using the architectural designs of the Straits Settlements (Cartier, 2001a: 137). It has increasingly come under the protection of historic conservation programs, especially in Singapore (see Kong and Yeoh, 1994; Teo, 1994; Teo and Huang, 1995). Now conserved shophouses regularly appear painted in lively color combinations, reminiscent of renovated Victorians in San Francisco or historic buildings in the conservation districts of New Orleans. But in Malaysia the state has not prioritized conservation of the Straits Chinese shophouse (Cartier, 1996), and most conservation has taken place as a result of private and nongovernmental organization initiatives. Yet by the late 1990s, appreciation for the significance of the Straits Chinese architectural style had begun to increase. In 1999, Malaysian government heritage planners proposed Melaka town and the historic center of Pinang for World Heritage Site status, based on Georgetown's "more than 10,000 buildings of heritage value" and Melaka's "4,000 pre-war buildings" (Emmanuel, 1999). In both town centers, the shophouse is the common pre-war building type. Malaysian planners have been keen to rectify Malaysia's absence in the World Heritage Convention list, and now, in spite of the value system generated by the NEP, planners have responded to the potential of the heritage tourism economy and have begun to promote the built environment of the Chinese diaspora and the Straits Chinese (Cartier, 2001b).

Bukit China

The problems of the national culture debates and pro-Malay economic planning spurred by the NEP coalesced in the Bukit China incident in Melaka in 1984–1985. Bukit China, on the edge of central Melaka town, is the largest remaining traditional Chinese cemetery in the world. In the middle of the 1980s, real estate development proposals for the Bukit China site would have obliterated the burial ground and transformed the site for mixed-use commercial and residential properties, and, by one design, even a Chinese cultural theme park (Cartier, 1997). In response, an anti-development movement rose in Melaka, supported by the DAP and the MCA, and spread to the national level, ultimately influencing the state to cancel development plans. In the course of the movement, the anti-development groups based their preservation tactics on redefining concepts of place identity, which portrayed the hill as an unparalleled landscape of Malaysian national history.

The first indigenous Malay text, the *Sejarah Melayu* (Malay Annals), became one basis for redefining the meaning of the site for national culture. The *Sejarah Melayu* narrates the genealogical history of the Melaka sultanate, the fount of Islam in Malaysia, and describes an important diplomatic marriage between the reigning Melaka sultan and a daughter of the Chinese emperor (Brown, 1952: 90). The princess' entourage was "bidden to take up their abode at Bukit China: and the place goes by that name to this day" (Brown, 1952: 91). While Chinese textual sources do not corroborate the account in the *Sejarah Melayu* (Yeh, 1936: 76; Purcell, 1947: 119; Sandhu, 1983: 95), and scholars have considered it an apocryphal tale to explain the existence of a Chinese wife in the sultan's seraglio (Brown, 1952: 1–11; Sandhu and Wheatley, 1983: 497–498), the story of the Chinese princess is portrayed in a series of panels in the National Museum of History and Ethnography. In the ways that myths and legends serve societal interests, the story of the sultan and the Chinese princess established a vision of historic interracial community harmony in Melaka, and its place at the origins of the Malaysian nation. During the Bukit China development controversy, the national press repeated this story and many others about the importance of the Bukit China site in Malaysian history (see Cartier, 1993, 1997, 1998).

The construction of meaning about national culture in the landscape of Bukit China depended on the diffusion of knowledge about historic landscape events, which took place during preservation rallies and meetings, and through media reporting. One important statement, the Joint Memorandum of Melakan Graduates and Professionals to the Chief Minister of Melaka, explained the context of the development controversy and the goals of the Chinese community of Malaysia to preserve the hill as a cultural heritage monument of both the Chinese community and to Chinese-Malay relations in Malaysia. The document repeated the history of Bukit China, including the visits of Admiral Zheng He, the role of Bukit China narrated in the *Sejarah Melayu,* and the colonial constructions on the hill. It focused on the symbolism of Bukit China as "an intimate bond between the Chinese community and Malaysia," and explained how "amidst the communalist politics that has frequently clouded inter-community relations in this country, Bukit China serves as a reminder of the bond of friendship between the Malay and Chinese communities that already existed in the early days of the Melaka Sultanate" (*The Star,* 1984). The memorandum invoked Bukit China's nationalist and anticolonial symbolism, since it was "used by the Melaka Sultans . . . for attacking the Portuguese positions." Major news articles repeated these indigenous, immigrant, and colonial histories of landscape events, and in these ways and more, the preservation movement became a significant discursive enterprise, by demonstrating not only Bukit China's continuing cultural significance for the Chinese community, but its symbolism as the singular site in Malaysia to embody the history of the nation.

CONCLUSION

The contrast between the economic events of the 1980s—when the state was firmly engaged in pro-Malay economic and national culture policies that marginalized the Chinese community, and the 1990s, when the state apparently courted the Chinese community for the economic power of the Chinese capitalist class—may appear to represent a state policy change that would embrace the Chinese community. After twenty years of the NEP, the state has been able to claim widespread rise in standards of living, count a higher proportion of Malays in the country's national population, and the creation of a Malay urban middle class. Yet the state's rhetorical politics often serve diverse purposes in Malaysia and must be read in light of both domestic and international political opportunities. Calling on the Chinese community to support the domestic economy and Malay businesses through the regional economic downturn yields a positive international image for Malaysia by comparison to the troubles across the Strait in Indonesia. It does not mean that Malaysia will soon see the end of pro-Malay policies. What the call for Chinese support of domestic industries does invoke is the set of unstated relationships, identified by Gomez, among members of the Malaysian capitalist class at large. In this way, Prime Minister Mahathir's rhetoric does not signal an actual economic policy change but rather support for "business as usual" in the guise of a morsel of apparently more progressive politics.

The future for Chinese Malaysians will depend on securing dependable options for higher education and professional employment in Malaysian society. Although the NEP technically ended in 1990, its successor development strategy, "Vision 2020," a sweeping plan designed to vault Malaysia into developed country status by the year 2020, has trailed the pro-Malay elements of the NEP (Gomez and Jomo, 1997: 170, 177–178). Despite the problems of poor and working class Malaysians in general, the state's "Vision 2020" is a broad spectrum privatization scheme—Malaysia's equivalent of the global neoliberal platform—whose powers to redistribute wealth in society may be just as limited as the effects of the NEP. With the rise of standards of living across Asia and the Pacific, and increased global migration in general, and against the backdrop of continued NEP-related policies, Chinese emigration from Malaysia will continue and likely hasten. Understanding the size and destinations of the Chinese migration stream from Malaysia—the second wave diaspora—will emerge in the next era of global migration studies, as increased international migration will likely compel enhanced monitoring of transnational migration and mobility.

NOTES

1. The contemporary concentrations of Malay settlement by state also reflect these historic characteristics. Malays on the peninsula are most highly concentrated in the states to the east and furthest north, from north to south: Perlis (85.5%), Kedah (76.6%), Kelantan (95.0%), Terengganu (96.8%), Pahang (76.8%), and these states as a group are still less urbanized than the central west coast states (DOSM, 2001).

2. On the history of the Chinese in the Philippines and historic Chinese massacres in Manila, see Edgar Wickberg, 1965.

3. In 1967 the democratic market economies of Southeast Asia, Singapore, Malaysia, Indonesia, the Philippines, and Thailand, formed the Association of Southeast Asian Nations (ASEAN) to promote regional peace and security. ASEAN formed during the Vietnam War and at the height of the Cold War, as a partial counter to communist governments in the region.

4. In addition to enrollment of Chinese children in Chinese schools, some Malay and Indian families also enroll their students in Chinese-medium primary schools. Among non-Chinese families who select Chinese language schools, their reasons focus on perceived higher standards of education, and societal advantages of Chinese language ability.

REFERENCES

BERNAMA (Malaysian National News Agency). 2000. "Lend a Helping Hand to Bumis, PM Tells the Chinese Community," 16 July, http://www.lexis-nexis.com/universe.

Braddell, T. 1861. *Statistics of the British Possessions in the Straits of Malacca, with explanatory notes,* P. Pinang: Penang Gazette.

Brown, C. C. 1952. "*Sejarah Melayu,* or 'Malay Annals': A Translation of Raffles MS 18," *Journal of the Malayan Branch of the Royal Asiatic Society,* 25(2 and 3): 1–276.

Carstens, Sharon A. 1988. "From Myth to History: Yap Ah Loy and the Heroic Past of Chinese Malaysians," *Journal of Southeast Asian Studies,* 19(2): 185–207.

———. 1999. "Dancing Lions and Disappearing History: The National Culture Debates and Chinese Malaysian Culture," *Crossroads: An Interdisciplinary Journal of Southeast Asian Studies,* 13(1): 11–64.

Cartier Carolyn L. 1993. "Creating Historic Open Space in Melaka," *Geographical Review,* 83(4): 359–373.

———. 1996. "Conserving the Built Environment and Generating Heritage Tourism in Peninsular Malaysi," *Tourism Recreation Research,* 21(1): 45–53.

———. 1997. "The Dead, Space/Place, and Social Activism: Constructing the Nation-State in Historic Melaka," *Environment and Planning D: Society and Space,* 15(5): 555–586.

———. 1998. "Preserving *Bukit China:* A Cultural Politics of Landscape Interpretation in Melaka's Chinese Cemetery" in Elizabeth Sinn, ed., *The Last Half Century of the Chinese Overseas,* Hong Kong: University of Hong Kong Press, 65–89.

———. 2001a. *Globalizing South China,* Oxford: Blackwell.

———. 2001b. "Imaging Melaka's Global Heritage" in Peggy Teo, T. C. Chang, and Ho Kong Chong, eds., *Interconnected Worlds: Southeast Asian Tourism in the 21st Century,* Oxford: Elsevier Science, 193–212.

Castles, Stephen and Mark J. Miller. 1998. *The Age of Migration: International Population Movements in the Modern World,* New York: Guilford Press.

Chan, Kok Eng and Tey Nai Peng. 2000. "Demographic Processes and Changes" in Lee Kam Hing and Tan Chee-beng, eds., *The Chinese in Malaysia,* Oxford University Press, 71–93.

Cheng, Lim-Keak. 1985. *Social Change and the Chinese in Singapore: A Socio-economic Geography with Special Reference to Bang Structure,* Singapore: Singapore University Press.

Clammer, John R. 1979. "The Straits Chinese in Melaka" in K. S. Sandu and Paul Wheatley, eds., *Melaka: The Transformation of a Malay Capital,* vol. 2, Kuala Lumpur: Oxford University Press, 156–173.

———. 1980. *Straits Chinese Society: Studies in the Sociology of the Baba Communities of Malaysia and Singapore,* Singapore: Singapore University Press.

Clifford, James. 1997. *Routes: Travel and Translation in the Late Twentieth Century.* Cambridge, MA: Harvard University Press.

Crouch, Harold. 1992. "Authoritarian Trends, the UMNO Split and the Limits to State Power" in J. S. Kahn and F. L. K. Wah, eds., *Fragmented Vision: Culture and Politics in Contemporary Malaysia,* Honolulu: University of Hawaii Press, 21–43.

DIMA (Department of Immigration and Multicultural and Indigenous Affairs). 1996. *Malaysia-born People in Australia,* http://www.immi.gov.au/statistics/publications/community_profiles/MalaysiaNet.pdf. Dec. 2, 2001.

DOSM (Department of Statistics, Malaysia). 2001. "Census 2000: Key Summary Statistics by State, Malaysia" http://www.statistics.gov.my/English/pageDemo.htm., Dec. 2, 2000.

Duyvendak, J. J. L. 1939. "The True Dates of the Chinese Maritime Expeditions in the Early Fifteenth Century," *T'oung Pao,* 38(5): 341–412.

Emmanuel, M. 1999. "Striving for World Heritage Site Status," *New Straits Times* (Kuala Lumpur), 1 Aug., 12.

Fitzgerald, Stephen. 1972. *China and the Overseas Chinese: A Study of Peking's Changing Policy, 1949–1970,* Cambridge: Cambridge University Press.

Freedman, Maurice. 1955. "The Chinese in Southeast Asia" in Andrew W. Lind, ed., *Race Relations in World Perspective,* Honolulu: University of Hawaii Press, 388–411.

Gibson, Campell J. and Emily Lennon. 1999. *Historical Census of the Foreign-born Population of the United States: 1850–1990,* Population Division Working Paper No. 29, Washington, D.C.: U.S. Bureau of the Census.

Gomez, Edmund T. 1991. *Money Politics in the Barisan Nasional,* Kuala Lumpur: Forum.

———. 1999. *Chinese Business in Malaysia: Accumulation, Accommodation, and Ascendance,* Honolulu: University of Hawaii Press.

Gomez, Edmund T. and K. S. Jomo. 1997. *Malaysia's Political Economy: Politics, Patronage, and Profits,* Cambridge: Cambridge University Press.

Government of Malaysia. 1971. *Second Malaysia Plan, 1971–1975,* Kuala Lumpur: The Government Press.

Groenveldt, W. P. 1887. "Notes on the Malay Archipelago and Malacca," *Miscellaneous Papers Relating to Indo-China and the Indian Archipelago,* 2nd series, vol. 1, London: Trubner.

Heng, Pek Koon. 1988. *Chinese Politics in Malaysia: A History of the Malaysian Chinese Association,* Singapore: Oxford University Press.

Hirschman, Charles. 1975. "Migration from Peninsular Malaysia, 1957–1970," *The Malayan Economic Review,* 20(2): 38–54.

Jackson, James C. 1968. *Planters and Speculators: Chinese and European Agricultural Enterprise in Malaya, 1786–1921,* Kuala Lumpur: University of Malaya Press.

Jesudason, James V. 1989. *Ethnicity and the Economy: The State, Chinese Business, and Multinationals in Malaysia,* Singapore: Oxford University Press.

Kahn, Joel S. 1996. "Growth, Economic Transformation, Culture and the Middle Classes in Malaysia" in R. Robinson and D. S. G. Goodman (eds.), *The New Rich in Asia,* London and New York: Routledge, 49–79.

Kohl, David G. 1984. *Chinese Architecture in the Straits Settlements and Western Malaya: Temples, Kongsis and Houses,* Singapore: Heinemann.

Kong, Lily and Brenda S. A. Yeoh. 1994. "Urban Conservation in Singapore: A Survey of State Policies and Popular Attitudes," *Urban Studies,* 31(2): 247–266.

Kua, Kia Soong. 1985. *National Culture and Democracy,* Kuala Lumpur: The Malaysian Chinese Resource and Research Center.

———. 1990. *Malaysian Cultural Policy and Democracy,* Kuala Lumpur: The Malaysian Chinese Resource and Research Center.

Kuo, Eddie C. Y. 1990. *Ethnicity, Polity, and Economy: A Case Study of Mandarin Trade and the Chinese Connection,* Singapore: Working Papers No. 101, National University of Singapore, Dept. of Sociology.

Lai, Ah Eng. 1986. *Peasants, Proletarians, and Prostitutes: A Preliminary Investigation into the Work of Chinese Women in Colonial Malaya,* Singapore, Institute of Southeast Asian Studies, Research Notes and Discussion Papers, No. 59.

Lee, Sharon M. 1989. "Female Immigrants and Labor in Colonial Malaya: 1860–1947," *International Migration Review,* 23(2): 309–331.

Leete, Richard. 1996. *Malaysia's Demographic Transition: Rapid Development, Culture, and Politics.* Kuala Lumpur and New York: Oxford University Press.

Mahathir bin Mohamad. 1970. *The Malay Dilemma,* Singapore: D. Moore for Asia Pacific Press.

Marrison, G. E. 1951. "The Coming of Islam to the East Indies," *Journal of the Malayan Branch of the Royal Asiatic Society,* 24(1): 28–37.

Massey, Doreen and Pat Jess, eds. 1995. *A Place in the World?: Places, Cultures, and Globalization,* Milton Keynes: The Open University Press.

Means, Gordon. 1991. *Malaysian Politics: The Second Generation,* Singapore and New York: Oxford University Press.

Nonini, Donald M. 1997. "Shifting Identities, Positioned Imaginaries: Transnational Traversals and Reversals by Malaysian Chinese" in Aihwa Ong and Donald M. Nonini, eds., *Ungrounded Empires: The Cultural Politics of Modern Chinese Transnationalism,* London and New York: Routledge, 203–227.

Ong, Aihwa. 1999. *Flexible Citizenship: The Cultural Logics of Transnationality,* Durham: Duke University Press.

Oo, Yu Hock. 1991. *Ethnic Chameleon: Multiracial Politics in Malaysia,* Petaling Jaya: Pelanduk.

Pereira, Brendan. 1998. "KL to Allow Non-bumis Bigger Stake in Local Firms," *The Straits Times* (Singapore), 25 Feb., http://www.lexis-nexis.com/universe.

PHCM (Population and Housing Census of Malaysia, 1991). 1995. Kuala Lumpur: Jabatan Perangkaan, Malaysia

Pillai, Patrick. 1992. *People on the Move: An Overview of Recent Immigration and Emigration in Malaysia,* Kuala Lumpur: Institute of Strategic and International Studies.

Pillai, Patrick and Zainal Aznam Yusof. 1998. "Malaysia: Trends and Recent Developments in International Migration" in *Migration and Regional Economic Integration in Asia,* Paris: Organization for Economic Cooperation and Development, 133–143.

Piyadasa, R. 1993. "Early Transitional Facade Shophouses," *BusinessTimes* (Singapore), 16 Jan., 5.

Poston, Dudley L., Jr. and Mei-yu Yu. 1990. "The Distribution of the Overseas Chinese in the Contemporary World, " *International Migration Review* 24(3): 480–508.

Purcell, Victor. 1947. "Chinese Settlement in Melaka," *Journal of the Malayan Branch of the Royal Asiatic Society,* 20(1): 115–125.

———. 1948. *The Chinese in Malaya.* Oxford: Oxford University Press.

———. 1965. *The Chinese in Southeast Asia,* 2nd ed., London: Oxford University Press.

———. 1967. *The Chinese in Malaysia,* Kuala Lumpur: Oxford University Press.

Pye, Lucian W. 1956. *Guerilla Communism in Malaysia: Its Social and Political Meaning,* Princeton: Princeton University Press.

Redding, S. Gordon. 1993. *The Spirit of Chinese Capitalism,* Berlin: de Gruyter.

Reid, Anthony. 1993. *Southeast Asia in the Age of Commerce, 1450–1680,* vol. 2: *Expansion and Crisis,* New Haven: Yale University Press.

Sandhu, Kernial Singh. 1983. "Chinese Colonization in Melaka" in K. S. Sandhu and Paul Wheatley, eds., *Melaka: The Transformation of a Malay Capital,* vol. 2, Kuala Lumpur: Oxford University Press, 93–136.

Sandhu, Kernial Singh and Paul Wheatley. 1983. "The Historical Context" in K. S. Sandhu and P. Wheatley, eds., *Melaka: The Transformation of a Malay Capital,* vol. 2, Kuala Lumpur: Oxford University Press, 3–69.

Saw, Swee-Hock. 1988. *The Population of Peninsular Malaysia,* Singapore: National University Press of Singapore.

Sidhu, M. S. 1976. "Chinese Dominance of West Malaysian Towns, 1921–1970," *Geography,* 61(1): 17–33.

Sieh, Mei Ling. 1988. "Malaysian Workers in Singapore," *The Singapore Economic Review,* 33(1): 101–111.

Tan, Chee-beng. 1983. "Acculturation and the Chinese in Melaka: The Expression of Baba Identity Today" in L. A. Peter Gosling and Linda Y. C. Lim, eds., *The Chinese in Southeast Asia,* vol. 2, *Identity, Culture, and Politics,* Singapore: Maruzen Asia, 56–78.

———. 1988. *The Baba of Melaka: Culture and Identity of a Chinese Peranakan Community in Malaysia,* Petaling Jaya: Pelanduk.

———. 1999. "Socio-cultural Diversities and Identities" in Lee Kam Hing and Tan Chee-beng, eds., *The Chinese in Malaysia,* New York: Oxford University Press, 37–70.

Taylor, Jay. 1974. *China and Southeast Asia: Peking's Relations with Revolutionary Movements,* New York: Praeger.

Teo, Peggy. 1994. "Assessing Socio-cultural Impacts: The Case of Singapore," *Tourism Management,* 15(2): 126–136.

Teo, Peggy and Shirlena Huang. 1995. "Tourism and Heritage Conservation in Singapore," *Annals of Tourism Research,* 22(3): 589–615.

Thrift, N. and K. Olds. 1996. "Refiguring the Economic in Economic Geography," *Progress in Human Geography,* 20(3): 311–337.

Turnbull, C. M. 1983. "Melaka under British Colonial Rule" in K. S. Sandhu and P. Wheatley, eds., *Melaka: The Transformation of a Malay Capital,* vol. 1, Kuala Lumpur: Oxford University Press, 242–296.

Vaughn, J. D. 1992. *The Manners and Customs of the Chinese,* Singapore: Oxford University Press, reprint of the 1879 edition.

Wang, Gungwu. 1958. "The Nanhai Trade: A Study of the Early History of Chinese Trade in the South China Sea," *Journal of the Malayan Branch of the Royal Asiatic Society,* 31(2): 1–135.

———. 1959. *A Short History of the Nanyang Chinese,* Singapore: Donald Moore/Eastern Universities Press.

Wheatley, Paul. 1955. "The Malay Peninsula As Known to the Chinese of the Third Century, A.D.," *Journal of the Malayan Branch of the Royal Asiatic Society,* 28(1): 1–23.

———. 1957. "Possible References to the Malay Peninsula in the Annals of the Former Han," *Journal of the Malayan Branch of the Royal Asiatic Society,* 30(1): 115–121.

———. 1959. "Geographical Notes on Some Commodities Involved in Sung Maritime Trade," *Journal of the Malayan Branch of the Royal Asiatic Society,* 32(2): 1–140.

Wickberg, Edgar. 1965. *The Chinese in Philippine Life, 1850–1898,* New Haven: Yale University Press.

XHZ (Xiamen huaqiao zhi) (Annals of the Overseas Chinese from Xiamen). 1991. Xiamen: Lujiang chubanshe.

Yeh, H. F. 1936. "The Chinese of Malacca" in *Historical Guide of Malacca,* Malacca: Malacca Historical Society, Melaka, 71–83.

Yeung, Henry Wai-chung and Chris Olds. 2000. *The Globalization of Chinese Business Firms,* New York: St. Martin's.

4

Exclusion and Embeddedness:
The Chinese in Thailand and Vietnam

Jonathan Rigg

From nationalist perspectives, the Chinese communities in Southeast Asia are often portrayed as a "problem" or, at best, a challenge. Regarding the Chinese in the region, "the main themes," Douglas writes, "are problematic" (1997: 37), reflected in the tendency to talk in Indonesia of the *masalah cina*—the Chinese problem (see also Cribb, 1999: 21). The same is true in Vietnam since 1975 where, again, scholars are inclined to talk of the Chinese community representing a "problem" for the authorities (Tran, 1993: 3). Skinner (1957: 159–165) too earlier noted this perspective on the Chinese in Thailand, based in the developing spirit of Thai nationalism in the first two decades of the twentieth century. In this chapter, the objective is not to address the idea of the Chinese problem, or to examine the ways in which governments in the region have constructed the problem, but rather to discuss the ambivalent and ambiguous positions that Chinese communities occupy within the economies and societies of the different countries in the region. Particular concern will be paid to three linked issues: first, the role of the state in creating—and closing—for the Chinese their spaces for citizenship and economic activity; second, the shifting status of the Chinese in the area over time; and third, the idea that the Chinese have been an excluded community. The detailed discussion will primarily focus on the cases of Thailand and Vietnam.

The Chinese represent a significant proportion of the populations of the countries of Southeast Asia, ranging from a high of 77 percent in the case of Singapore—which is close to being a Chinese city-state—to 10 percent in Thailand, and a low of perhaps just 0.2 percent in the Laos People's Democratic Republic (see table 4.1). However, most estimates of the Chinese population in the region carry a disclaimer about the futility of attempting to count the ethnic Chinese, since "'who is Chinese" is increasingly understood through situated

Table 4.1. The Chinese in Southeast Asia: Comparison of Population and Economic Role (percentage of total)

	Population	Control of Economy
Burma/Myanmar	3.4	—
Cambodia	4.0	—
Indonesia	3.8	73
Laos	0.2	—
Malaysia	28	69
Philippines	1.3	50–60
Singapore	77	81
Thailand	10	81
Vietnam	1.4	—
South Vietnam, 1969	5	35–41

Sources: Lever-Tracy et al. 1996: 15 (Thailand); Rigg 1997; Tran 1993: 44 (Vietnam).
Note: Control of economy is based on share of listed firms by capitalization. All figures are estimates: the data on investment by ethnic group are generally poor, and ethnic Chinese businesses are often small scale and probably under-reported. In addition, counting the population "Chinese" is uncertain when citizenship is no longer a good guide to ethnic definition.

and complex contexts of citizenship, assimilation, and identity formation. In some countries, and particularly in Cambodia and Thailand, the Chinese have been extensively assimilated: they have taken local names, embraced Theravada Buddhism and, to a significant extent, ceased to exist as distinctive and separate communities. Thus in the context of contemporary societies, "Chineseness" is as much socially and politically constructed as it is a category of citizenship defined by ethnic difference. This means that a person's identification can vary through time and context, as Thai, Sino-Thai, or as a Chinese living in Thailand.[1] Indeed, shifts in identity affiliation may well vary through the course of a single day depending on the situation, such as with whom one interacts. Moreover, how a person sees him- or herself and how they are viewed by others do not necessarily coincide. While there has been a tendency to view Chinese identity as occupying an interstitial social space, it is more accurate to see the Chinese occupying multiple spaces of identity.[2] One of the outcomes of this kind of partial and fluid assimilation of the Chinese into societies of mainland Southeast Asia is that estimating the numbers of Chinese is an uncertain enterprise, more of a matter of interpretation than a demonstration of empirical fact. This is demonstrated in the wide variation in estimates for the number of Chinese living in Thailand (see table 4.2).

More important than the size of the Chinese populations living in the region is the role of Chinese communities in local and regional economies (see table 4.1). Despite the fact that the figures on this subject are even less reliable, few would dispute that the Chinese control a disproportionate share, relative to their population, of the economic activity in the region. This of course

Table 4.2.   Estimates of the Chinese Population of Thailand

Year	Total Population	Number Chinese	Percent Chinese
1955	20,480,000	2,315,000	11.3
1956	20,000,000	3,000,000	15
1960	26,257,911	2,670,000	10.2
1962	28,800,000	2,500,000	8.7

Sources: Skinner 1957: 183; Fisher 1966: 181; Purcell 1965: 3; Hunter 1966: 15.

is what makes their presence so problematic from political and nationalist perspectives. Prime Minister Mahathir Mohamad (1970: 60) of Malaysia, in his book *The Malay Dilemma,* suggested in response to the problems of economic inequalities that divide the Chinese and Malay populations in Malaysia that "Where necessary, laws must be promulgated in order to render effective whatever economic policy may be considered necessary [to deal with these inequalities]." He added: "Harsh punitive measures should be meted out to those who impede the elevation of the Malays to an equality with other races" (Mahathir, 1970: 60). The dilemma for the Chinese is also encapsulated in Cribb's assessment of the pattern of hostility and antagonism towards the Chinese in Indonesia:

> For some Indonesian Chinese, this situation has been tolerable: they could proceed with their economic activities and retain their Chinese-ness, even if this meant abdicating any broader role in Indonesian society and having to buy protection from the police, the military and the bureaucracy. For Indonesian Chinese who wanted to be part of the Indonesian nation, the result was a terrible feeling of being condemned to second-class citizenship, of having to endure discrimination and petty harassment on a daily basis without any hope of graduating eventually to a state of acceptance. (Cribb, 1999: 21)

In Indonesia, by contrast to Thailand, the state has not based citizenship on the concept of *jus soli;* Chinese born in Indonesia have not automatically become citizens of the country and have had to apply and pay for naturalized citizenship later in life. Still, the essence of the dilemma for the Chinese—if not its intensity—resonates with the situation in the other countries of the region.

THE CHINESE AND NATION BUILDING IN MAINLAND SOUTHEAST ASIA

Historically, the Chinese have had uneasy relationships with the ethnic and political mainstream societies of the countries in Southeast Asia. At the same time, these relationships have been both ambiguous and ambivalent. The

capitalist class among the Chinese communities has controlled, and continues to control, much of the economic activity of the region and yet this control has not brought commensurate power. As Wang Gungwu (in Blussé,
1991: 2) has put it, historically the Chinese were "merchants without empire" while today they have achieved "wealth without power." The possibilities of evolving economic and political roles of the Chinese in the region are
exemplified by the case of Thailand.

In historic Siam, a significant Chinese commercial community was present
in early-fourteenth-century Ayutthaya, the former capital. By the fifteenth
century, Chinese were being allocated "land" (status) through the *sakdi naa*
system, in the seventeenth century there was a community of several thousand Chinese in Ayutthaya, and by the early eighteenth century Chinese held
considerable political power within the machinery of government (Wyatt,
1982; Reid, 1997). Ayutthaya fell to invasion by the Burmese in the second
half of the eighteenth century, and the first king of the subsequent dynasty, the
current Chakri dynasty (of which the reigning King Bhumibol Adulyadej is
the ninth monarch), Rama I, was half Chinese and established the capital at
Bangkok. He married the daughter of the deposed King Taksin who was himself the son of a Chinese trader (Hamilton and Waters, 1997: 263). Throughout the first half of the nineteenth century the population of Bangkok was estimated to be over half Chinese, and it was not until the turn of the nineteenth
century that the Thai population approximated the numbers of Chinese in the
capital (Skinner, 1957: 81, 87). While the Chinese enjoyed considerable
power and prestige in the historic court at Ayutthaya, the modern migrations
of Chinese labor migrants in the nineteenth and early twentieth centuries
combined with the rise of nascent nationalism to lead to new stresses between
the Thai and the Chinese.

Anti-Chinese xenophobia surfaced as an explicit component of official discourse during the reign of King Vajiravudh (1910–1925), and subsequently
intensified during the first premiership of Field Marshal Phibun Songkhram
(1938–1944). From the mid-1930s until the end of World War II, the Thai
government sought to control Chinese immigration, expand state control of
the economy, and promote Thai business at the expense of Chinese (and to a
lesser extent foreign) interests. In the words of Phibun Songkhram's stock
slogan of 1938, the government promoted "a Thai economy for the Thai people" (Pasuk Phongpaichit and Baker, 1995: 118). However, while there is no
doubting the anti-Chinese rhetoric of this period, there is reason to question
the degree to which Chinese economic activity was affected. The Chinese
petty bourgeoisie may have had their activities curtailed, but Chinese capitalists found that, with some strategic alliance building, they could operate
largely without impediment (Hewison, 1989).

The ability of the Chinese to find a niche for themselves during periods of explicit state discrimination is perhaps best reflected during the War years (1941–1945). The Japanese *de facto* occupied Thailand from December 1941, and while the majority of Chinese in Thailand were anti-Japanese, reflecting Japan's wartime atrocities in China, many nonetheless cooperated with Japanese authorities in Thailand in order to avoid repression (Reynolds, 1997). At the same time, occupying Japanese forces realized that cooperation with the Chinese was highly desirable given their critical role in the Thai economy (Hewison, 1989: 72). Unlike in Singapore and Malaya, the Japanese followed a policy of constructive engagement with Thailand's Chinese community. Field Marshal Phibun Songkhram's government, for its part, clearly viewed the Chinese in a different light than the majority Thai population. For example, when the appalling conditions on the Burma-Siam railway became known, Phibun refused to recruit 13,000 additional Thai labourers to meet Japanese demands for labour and instead told the Japanese to employ Chinese "coolies." In response, in 1943 the Japanese turned to the Chinese Chamber of Commerce which, while cognisant of the horrific conditions, set about placing advertisements in the Chinese language press to entice workers out to the railway site at Kanchanaburi (Reynolds, 1997: 376–377). The Thai government was also worried that the Chinese were forming strategic economic alliances with the Japanese in order to gain economic advantage in the country. In such ways, the Chinese, on numerous occasions, were caught between the Japanese occupying forces and the Thai government. With the Japanese surrender in 1945, the Chinese "anticipated relief, not only from the forced cooperation with the Japanese, but also from Thai government 'oppression'" (Reynolds, 1997: 385). During the war years, the Chinese also established strategic alliances with influential Thai politicians in order to access preferential business opportunities, such as through state-granted licenses and permits, which began to afford some measure of protection against politically driven harassment and intimidation. That Chinese capitalists managed to strengthen their economic position during this difficult time is testament to the skill with which they negotiated their affairs. While the Chinese may have strengthened their economic position during the war, Ueda (2000: 187) argues that "The basic motive at this time was not a desire for economic gain, but the need for political protection: *fear,* not *greed,* to put it in blunt terms [emphasis original text]."

The Shifting Ground of the Chinese in Thailand

It has become common to treat Chinese transnational communities as diasporic social formations—"people with multiple allegiances to place" (Van

Hear, 1998: 4). For Van Hear, a diaspora is a population that must fulfill three minimal criteria:

> First, the population is dispersed from a homeland to two or more other territories. Second, the presence abroad is enduring, although exile is not necessarily permanent, but may include movement between homeland and new host. And third, there is some kind of exchange—social, economic, political or cultural— between and among the spatially separated populations comprising the diaspora. (Van Hear, 1998: 6)

Chinese communities in Southeast Asia fulfill Van Hear's criteria of diasporic populations. But characterizing the Chinese in this way can create the illusion that they occupy a fixed status in the countries where they reside. More interesting is the set of historical processes through which the Chinese have transformed from immigrant labourers, to pariah capitalists, to denizens—people who are not "foreign citizens . . . but also not naturalized citizens of the receiving country" (Hammar, 1990, quoted in Van Hear, 1998: 4)—and to citizens. While in some countries in the region the status of the Chinese as citizens is circumscribed in various ways, the overall historical trend has been one of integration. Clearly, however, this process is not fully played out, as in the case of Indonesia, and rarely can we talk of complete assimilation within the dominant culture. There are enduring elements of separation, some more visible than others, and there is also an important distinction to be drawn between forced and voluntary integration and assimilation. While terminology is important, and integration, acculturation, and assimilation have particular distinctions in meaning, the focus here is on historical processes of change. These historical processes have not been a series of unilinear events, and the experiences of the Chinese in Thailand and Vietnam show how, at certain times, such processes have been thrown into reverse:

> The story of the Chinese in Thailand is not one of economic or even ethnic continuity. Instead, it is a story of changes, of sudden transformations, of ethnic reconstructions, and of a succession of distinct groups of Chinese entrepreneurs. To tell the story of the Chinese in Thailand accurately is to tell the story of these discontinuities (Hamilton and Waters, 1997: 279).

In his well-known article "The Jews of the Orient," written in 1910, King Vajiravudh of Thailand portrayed the Chinese as a threat to his Kingdom. He noted their refusal to take Thai citizenship and their lack of loyalty and attachment to the country. He argued that they "keep on steadily draining the resources of the country of their temporary residence, like so many vampires who steadily suck dry an unfortunate victim's life-blood" (quoted in Pasuk Phongpaichit and Baker, 1995: 107). King Vajiravudh's statement highlights themes that have characterized relations between the Chinese and the Thai from the late nineteenth century: the sense of the Chinese as an alien community lacking in commitment to their country of residence, and their portrayal as parasites, exploiting the country and its people. As King Vajiravudh put it, "One is either a Chinaman or a Siamese; no one could be both at the same time" (Kasian Tejapira, 1997: 77). From this perspective, becoming Thai meant renouncing all things Chinese.

During World War II many Chinese in Thailand changed from being denizens, or long-term residents, to becoming citizens. This process was compelled by new government policies of discrimination toward the Chinese, in the context of the rise of state nationalism. The Phibun government introduced legislation from 1939 that discriminated against non-Thais in the business and political arenas. Kasian Tejapira argues that from this date, under the Field Marshal's xenophobic government, there occurred the "wholesale ethnicization of the Siamese polity as exclusively and monolithically Thai" (1997: 78). The response from the Chinese was to adopt Thai citizenship, take Thai names, and become Luuk Ciin or Sino-Thais (Hewison, 1989: 72). More often than not, they accepted the arrangements. However in some instances this was not possible. In 1941, the promulgation of royal decrees banned all non-Thais from living in six areas with military and defense sites, including three districts in the province of Nakhon Ratchasima, to the northeast of Bangkok, including the province encompassing the capital of the province, Khorat (Skinner, 1957: 270–271). Chinese entrepreneurs who had first moved from Bangkok to Korat in the 1930s largely either returned to Bangkok or left for Chiang Mai in the north, having had to sell or abandon nearly all they had built up. The ban lasted until 1945, and few returned it was lifted (Ueda, 2000).

Yet more than any other country in Southeast Asia, it has been widely observed that in Thailand the Chinese have assimilated into society. Indeed, "the social integration of the Chinese in Thailand is generally presented as a model of success in the Southeast Asian context" (Formoso, 1996: 245). In reality, the Thai government sought to control the Chinese community through the early twentieth century and in the process "effected a compromise of different and sometimes conflicting aims" (Skinner, 1957: 271). Thai government policy permitted Chinese business activity for the trade-off of accepting some forms of assimilation, such as adopting Thai names and attending government schools. Chinese have been able to apply for and attain naturalized citizenship, and Thailand-born children of ethnic Chinese became Thai citizens. These conditions are sometimes interpreted as meaning that the Chinese, pressurized by a nationalist and xenophobic government during the war and the immediate postwar years, decided to become invisible. More positive interpretations emphasize the inclusive and assimilating nature of Thai society, and particularly its basis in Theravadda Buddhism as creating a social medium of relative tolerance. In sum, a mixture of coercion, voluntary assimilation, and the inclusive character of Thai society allowed the Chinese to insinuate themselves into the Thai nation.

So, while Chinese consciousness is much reduced in contemporary Thailand, Chinese control of the modern sectors of the Thai economy remains supremely important. This is reflected in Ueda's study of ethnic Chinese entrepreneurs in the city of Nakhon Ratchasima (formerly Khorat). Almost 90 percent of the city's most influential businessmen are of Chinese descent, mostly Teochiu, but only three of the 41 entrepreneurs he interviewed were more at home speaking Chinese than Thai. The interviewees also maintained that Chinese business connections have little relevance in making one's way in contemporary business. Far more important than Chinese associations to second or third generation Sino-Thai businessmen are such nonethnic associations as the Chamber of Commerce and the Rotary Club. Ueda (2000: 177) expects that "the Chinese associations will fade away by the time social leadership passes to third-generation businessmen, who do not identify themselves strongly as Chinese." This leads to the conclusion that while commercial activities in Nakhon Ratchasima are overwhelmingly controlled by businessmen of Chinese descent, their cultural consciousness is no longer markedly Chinese.

But there is also some evidence to support the view that there has been a minor awakening of Chinese consciousness in Thailand during recent years. In Bangkok, for example, it has become fashionable to flaunt Chinese ancestry and to revive Chinese language and culture (Pravit Rojanaphruk, 1997). To some extent this is driven by economic opportunity, just as economic factors have been partially responsible for encouraging Chinese immigrants to embrace Thai culture. For example, when doing business in China in recent years, Sino-Thais use their Chinese surnames rather than their (adopted) Thai names. By learning Mandarin, Sino-Thais are responding to the demands of working in China just as much as they are rediscovering their ancestral origins (Vatikiotis, 1996: 22–23).[3] This is not to say, though, that in representing their ancestry these people have become more Chinese. They are not Hua Chiew (Overseas Chinese) or Khon Ciin (Chinese); they are Hua Ii (local) and Khon Cek or Luuk Ciin (Sino-Thai)—Thais of Chinese descent. As Vatikiotis has written:

Paradoxically, the ability of ethnic Chinese business people to revive their cultural roots rests on their long and successful record of assimilation in Thailand. Thailand's ethnic Chinese are secure and integrated; they have earned themselves prominence in business, and now increasingly in politics (1996: 23).

It is arguable that the internationalization of Southeast Asian economies has made life easier for ethnic Chinese business communities in the region. In the past, to ensure commercial success and even survival, it has been necessary in Thailand for entrepreneurs to form strategic links with national political elites (Montesano, 2000). But with increasing international economic activity, links with transnational firms are now often more important (see Yeung, 1999). It is this process, in broad terms, which has allowed the Chinese in the region to make the transition from the national to international stage. It has also encouraged greater mobility for the Chinese business class, and in the process encouraged shedding some of the baggage of nationalist history that served to diminish Chinese identity formation.

The Chinese in Vietnam

While the Thai experience, notwithstanding periods of xenophobia and anti-Chinese sentiment, has been one of successful integration and partial assimilation, the Chinese in Vietnam have faced much more concerted discrimination, culminating in the systematic mass expulsions of 1978–1979 during what was known internationally as the "boat people" crisis. The Vietnamese case not only offers a striking counterpoint to the experience of the Chinese in Thailand but also reemphasizes the degree to which the position of the Chinese can change, almost overnight. As Reid (1997: 61) has written with reference to the Chinese of northern Vietnam, "despite centuries of accommodation with the majority Vietnamese, this community was put under such pressure that almost all of its members had been forced to leave for China by April 1979" (see table 4.3). Since the victory of the Democratic Republic of Vietnam (DRV—former North Vietnam) over the Republic of Vietnam (RV—former South Vietnam), and the subsequent reunification of the country, the numbers of ethnic Chinese or Hoa in the country has decreased from 2.6% of the total population in 1976 to perhaps 1.5% in 1989 (see table 4.3). This represents a decline in numbers from 1,236,000 to 961,702 during a period when the population of the country overall was growing rapidly (Amer, 1996: 77). The decline of the ethnic Chinese population can only be understood in the context of Vietnamese government policies.

Table 4.3.   Chinese Population of Vietnam

	Population Chinese	Percent of Total	North	South
1943	466,000	2.1	—	—
1951	731,000	—	—	—
1960	—	—	174,000	—
1968	—	—	—	1,035,000
1970	—	—	208,000	2,000,000
1976	1,236,000	2.6	185,400	1,050,600
1979	935,000	1.8	187,400	771,000
1989	961,702	1.5	51,500	913,700

Sources: Tran 1993; Amer 1996; Reid 1997.
Note: As cautioned in the introduction to this chapter, figures for the numbers of Chinese in Southeast Asia are of doubtful accuracy. This applies equally to Vietnam. The numbers above are taken from various sources and should not be viewed as a coherent set of figures. They do, however, indicate general trends.

As in Thailand and elsewhere in the region, communities of ethnic Chinese have existed in Vietnam for hundreds of years. Even as Vietnam shares a border with China, the vast majority of Chinese migrants to Vietnam were mercantile traders, and, as characteristic of the diasporic Chinese in general during the historical period, left south China by boat. As a result, the largest settlement of Chinese in Vietnam concentrated in the main port and trade center of the country, Saigon, in the south, which was renamed Ho Chi Minh City in 1975. This long established Chinese community concentrated in a distinct area across the Saigon River from Saigon proper, known as Cholon (great market). Cholon has been one of the largest urban settlements in the Chinese diasporic world, and has repeatedly been described in the historic literature as not just a Chinatown, a Chinese district within a city, but "a Chinese town" or "a Chinese city" (e.g., De Poncins, 1957). During the French colonial period, estimates of the numbers of Chinese residents of the Saigon-Cholon area were upwards of half the total population. In 1887, for example, one estimate of Saigon's population counted 21,000 Chinese out of a total population of 33,000. The colonial census of 1911 reported a total of 293,000 Chinese in the whole of French Indochina: 156,000 in Cochin China, the region of southern Vietnam, 91,000 in Cambodia, 32,000 in Tonkin, the region of northern Vietnam, 7,000 in Annam, the central coast region, and 7,000 in Laos. Thus the majority of Chinese in Indochina were in southern Vietnam, and concentrated in Cholon. In 1913, the population of Saigon was 67,000, whereas the population of Cholon in 1914 was 181,000, of which at least 48 percent were Chinese (see Marsot, 1993: 92–96). Like Bangkok, Saigon was dominated by its Chinese population until after the turn of the century. Cholon became a district of the city of Saigon in 1932.

Cut off from China by geography, history, and politics, the Hoa population in southern Vietnam was both large and entrenched. Under the RV, the Chinese of the south tended to be aligned with the Guomindang and maintained ties with

Taiwan. In northern Vietnam by contrast, and under the government of the DRV, the Chinese population was comparatively rural and maintained closer connections with China and relations in Guangdong Province (Amer, 1991: 18).[4] This distinct political geography of the two major centers of Chinese population in Vietnam represented contradictory conditions for the new communist regime that would reunite the country in 1975. The Chinese urban population in the south played an important role in national trade and industry, but was less assimilated into Vietnamese society than the rural Chinese in the north.

After the communist victory in 1975 and reunification, the government of the Socialist Republic of Vietnam set about bringing private businesses in the former RV under state ownership and control. In September 1975 a program for the confiscation of the commercial and industrial assets of the so-styled compradore bourgeoisie was introduced (Amer, 1996: 80–81). The government in Hanoi was adamant that this—and other policies similarly designed to deconstruct the edifice of private business activity—were not anti-Chinese, but anticapitalist.[5] But since much of the commercial activity in the former South was controlled by the Hoa, the effects of the policies were to fall disproportionately on the shoulders of the ethnic Chinese population. For example, campaign XI launched on 11th September 1975 was aimed at identifying "speculators and economic monopolists," who would be arrested and their property confiscated in whole or in part. With the conclusion of the campaign, it was announced that 159 individuals had been so identified, of whom 117 were ethnic Chinese (Tran, 1993: 81).

The feeling that the government was engaged in a vendetta against the Chinese community in the country intensified from 1976 when the authorities ordered Chinese residents to register their citizenship. This forced Vietnamization of the ethnic Chinese had antecedents. In 1956 a series of decrees was passed in the Republic of Vietnam (the former South) by President Ngo Dinh Diem. Decree 48 declared all ethnic Chinese, if they were born in Vietnam, to be Vietnamese citizens. Those not born in the country were aliens. Decree 52 dictated that all ethnic Chinese citizens take Vietnamese names within six months, while decree 53 banned foreigners from eleven trades—all of which had formerly been controlled by ethnic Chinese (Tran, 1993: 29).[6] In the former Democratic Republic of Vietnam in the north, the communist government followed a similar strategy of ensuring that ethnic Chinese became Vietnamese citizens.[7]

State policies toward the Chinese took a more aggressive turn in 1978–1979. In 1978 ethnic Chinese began to be expelled from the Party and from all positions regarded as sensitive to national security. In addition, a state-orchestrated departure program for ethnic Chinese was instituted. In February 1979, Chinese forces attacked Vietnam and did not withdraw from the country until March of that year. The Chinese invasion further hardened the official position. In Amer's (1996: 88) view, "it was clear that [the] Vietnamese authorities were implementing a departure policy that was tantamount to expulsion of the remaining ethnic Chinese in the North." It is said that almost all ethnic Chinese in the north were expelled during this period between 1978 and 1979. As against the 174,000 Hoa recorded in the north in the 1960 census there were just over 50,000 remaining by the time of the 1989 census (see table 4.3). In 1979, the peak of the "boat people" crisis, 270,882 people left the country. Not all of these would have been ethnic Chinese, but most probably were. Chan and Dorais (1998: 287) estimate that up to 75 percent of the total who left during the years 1979–1981 were Chinese. Ethnic Vietnamese capitalists also sought to leave, since the capitalist class otherwise risked being sent to state "new economic zones" in rural areas (Tran, 1993: 84; 87). However while expulsion may have been the only option open to most ethnic Chinese in the north, the government of the SRV was in effect forcing people to make a choice. Either they could become full Vietnamese citizens and renounce any legal links with China, or they could leave the country. The category "Overseas Chinese," as Pelley (1998: 390) notes, "conspicuously disappeared from official discourse."

While China's invasion of Vietnam at the northern border brought anti-Chinese sentiment to a peak, it was just at this time that the government began to experiment with economic reform. In 1979 the Vietnam Communist Party recognized the country's growing economic problems—the industrial growth rate averaged 0.6 percent from 1976–1980 (Tran, 1993: 82)—and introduced selective reform measures for the next five-year plan, 1981–1985. Then in 1986 the government formally extended the process of reform through the umbrella policy of *doi moi* or economic renovation. The *doi moi* process proved that the state was willing to provide the Chinese capitalist class with far greater freedom to pursue their business activities. Indeed, it was not long after the 1979 episode that the authorities began to appreciate the central role that the Chinese could play in the reform process. In the first half of the 1980s, the government allowed the Chinese community greater economic opportunities, while memories of the border war with China led to continued monitoring of their political activities and international movement (see table 4.4). In 1986, less than a decade after enforcing the severe anti-Chinese policies, the government passed decree 256, giving the Chinese population of the country equal rights, at least as a discursive policy measure. Still, as compared to 1975, when the proportion of Chinese in trade and service occupations in Ho Chi Minh City was 70 percent, by 1988 Chinese firms in these sectors had been reduced to 24 percent (Tran, 1993: 87). New state policy measures promoting private business, including manufacturing enterprises, banks, and foreign investment, are leading to revival of Chinese businesses in Vietnam, but current information on the condition of the Chinese in Vietnam is remarkably scarce. This lack of knowledge reflects how the Chinese continue to be "socially excluded" from government and scholarly economic analyses in Vietnam under *doi moi*.

Table 4.4. The Ethnic Chinese and State Policies in Vietnam, 1975–present

	Economic Policies	*Political Policies Towards the Hoa*
1975–1978	State-led reconstruction; confiscation of property	Ethnic Chinese forcd to register their citizenship; Vietnamization
1978–1986	Beginings of economic reform	Expulsion of the ethnic Chinese from Party and sensitive positions; departure policy from the north
1986–present	Intensification of *doi moi*	Accommodation of ethnic Chinese within new climate of economic reform

RETHINKING "SOCIAL EXCLUSION" OF THE CHINESE IN SOUTHEAST ASIA

The foregoing discussion informs the broader set of issues concerning the concept of "social exclusion" and the ethnic Chinese in Southeast Asia. The perspective of social exclusion has especially emerged in analysis of ethnic minority groups in Europe, and characterizes the discourse of policy documents on this subject issued by the European Union (Levitas, 1996). While the idea of social exclusion defies simple definition (see Samers, 1998; de Haan and Maxwell, 1998), one common interpretation is ". . . the process through which individuals or groups are wholly or partially excluded from full participation in the society in which they live" (European Foundation, 1995, quoted in de Haan and Maxwell, 1998: 2). Social exclusion is also a spatial process, and geographical analysis of social exclusion has assessed exclusionary spaces and the ways those spaces are constituted (Sibley, 1998). Based on the experience of the Chinese in the Southeast Asian states, it is worthwhile to consider the application of the concept of social exclusion to the Chinese minority populations in the region. The point of departure is the position of the Chinese in Southeast Asia, in Reid's (1997: 34) terms, as "outsiders at the centre."

In the literature on Western countries, and particularly in the European context, the idea of social exclusion has become popularized as an alternative to more established related perspectives like poverty. Unlike poverty, which is typically assessed in association with income level, the perspective of social exclusion links deprivation and marginalization to conditions of employment and broader conditions of social organization and identity formation, especially the effects of nationalist ideologies, citizenship status, and state social policy implementation. The idea that social exclusion is the product of a failure to secure formal employment (Levitas, 1996: 8) does not seem to resonate with the case of the Chinese in Thailand and Vietnam and more generally in Southeast Asia. The Chinese are deeply embedded in the economies of the region to the degree that it has been extensively argued that without their presence the economies would collapse.[8] The linkage of social exclusion with poverty is also generally inappropriate to the case of the Chinese in Southeast Asia. It is the relationship between social inclusion, nationalism, citizenship, and state policy implementation toward ethnic groups that is relevant in interesting ways.

Among conditions of social exclusion, as formulated by Samers (1998) in his work on social exclusion and ethnic minorities in Europe, there are a number of conditions common to the experience of the Chinese in Southeast Asia (see table 4.5). This checklist of types of exclusion is divided into "material" and "discursive" exclusions. Especially material exclusions like inadequate access to social services, political participation, financial services, elite educational opportunities, and training for advanced employment have substantially affected Chinese communities at different times and in different countries in the region. The issue of discursive exclusions, or the ways in which institutions and institutional agents such as government, scholars, the media, and schools ignore or exclude minority groups by lack of attention in basic reporting and policy studies, has also characterized the experience of Chinese communities. This is distinctly the case in Vietnam, where basic news and media information on the status of the Chinese is rare. Even when Chinese in the region have local citizenship, and at least discursively defined equal rights, enforcement of equal rights is not reliably practiced, especially in the context of government employment, access to state services, and political participation. Citizenship too can be a complex condition, with different types of resident and citizenship status, which complicate matters of identity formation and societal participation. All of these conditions have spatial contexts, in defining where Chinese work and attend school, in what contexts they may be recognized, and where they may be welcome. Processes of social exclusion have certainly contributed to the formation of Chinatown enclaves, in Southeast Asia and in the wider world.

These conditions suggest that Southeast Asia is a region where the relative economic deprivation of the majority populations has created the political and social conditions for the social exclusion of the relatively affluent Chinese community.[9] So, while the social exclusion of the Chinese cannot be viewed as a function of poverty, instead it is correlated with their wealth by comparison to relatively lower incomes of the majority. In Europe, social exclusion among ethnic minorities is driven by destitution; in Southeast Asia it is propelled by affluence. This raises a further policy issue. Samers (1998: 139) notes that "to define a group or individual as 'socially excluded' (especially when policy intervention is envisioned) is to plan for their 'inclusion.'" For

Table 4.5. The Chinese As an Excluded Community

Applicability of characteristics of exclusion to the Chinese in Southeast Asia

Material exclusions	
Exclusion from a formal job	✗
Exclusion from social services	✓
Exclusion from adequate housing	✗
Exclusion from political (civic) participation	✓
Exclusion from adequate social contacts	✓
Financial exclusion (banking, access to loans)	✓
Exclusion from (prestigious and/or well-funded secondary) education	✓
Exclusion from employment training	✓
Exclusion from adequate consumption spaces	✗
Exclusion from recreation and leisure	✗
Discursive exclusions	
By academics (social invisibility in reports and surveys)	✗
By government officials and policy-makers	✗
By housing, social service and immigration authorities	✓
Exclusion by schools, universities, and other educational authorities	✓
Exclusion by the media	✓

Source: Adapted from Samers 1998.

this view to make sense in the case of the Chinese communities in Southeast Asia, it is necessary to turn it on its head: some governments in the region have promoted policies which have had the effect of recognizing the Chinese in order to perpetuate their exclusion. In both Europe and Southeast Asia, institutional processes occupy a central explanatory position in the creation of excluded communities.

Examination of social exclusion in regard to the Chinese in Southeast Asia offers a valuable counterpoint to the European literature on the topic. Writing from a European perspective, Levitas (1996: 19) has objected to the concept of social exclusion because it "places people either inside or outside mainstream society, synonymous with outside the labor market." Her key point is that just because people become integrated in the formal labor market it does not mean that they are no longer exploited.[10] This is also true for the Chinese, but once again for different reasons: the Chinese are integrated into the labor market, typically not as poorly paid workers, and yet they remain excluded. When Room argues the case for emphasis on social exclusion based on societal contexts in preference to poverty his justifications do strike a chord:

> The notion of poverty is primarily focused upon distributional issues: the lack of resources at the disposal of an individual or a household. In contrast, notions

such as social exclusion focus primarily on relational issues, in other words, in-adequate social participation, lack of social integration and lack of power (Room, 1995: 5).[11]

In one context, the Chinese in Southeast Asia are not socially excluded but rather they occupy a different social space by comparison to the majority. The Chinese in general are significant participants in the regional economy, whereas their participation in social institutions, in government, universities, and other places of national interest, is neither central nor guaranteed. This position of the Chinese, central in economic space, but marginal in social and national space, remains the problematic in both practical and conceptual terms. From a practical viewpoint, the challenge of incorporating the Chinese into the political mainstream remains particularly acute in countries like Viet-nam and Indonesia. From nationalist points of view, the conceptual challenge is how to demonstrate greater understanding about a community that is si-multaneously socially marginal and economically central.

NOTES

1. This point is illustrated in the current communal violence in Ambon, in In-donesia's eastern province of Maluku. There, second generation Bugis immigrants from South Sulawesi now find themselves alien people on the island of their birth, forced to flee because of their adherence to Islam. "I don't feel Bugis," says sixteen-year-old Nur Hasanah As'ad, "I feel like a Moluccan. I want to go back [to Ambon]" (Cohen and Murphy, 1999: 26).

2. In Indonesia, the Yogyakarta-based Peranakan Chinese business Kapitein Cina Tan Jing Sing was described as being "Cina wurung, Londa durung, Jawa tanggung" (no longer a Chinese, not yet a Dutchman, a half-baked Javanese) (Blussé, 1991: 5).

3. Lim and Gosling make much the same point but with reference to Southeast Asia as a whole when they argue that ". . . the hitherto bicultural Chinese of South-east Asia are suddenly reverting to open expressions of their original Sinic culture and flaunting rather than hiding their commercial success." They continue: "It is now not only socially acceptable but even socially and certainly economically desirable to be Chinese" (1997: 291).

4. Amer (1991: 25) also points out that when Vietnamese troops entered the Cholon district of Saigon on April 30, 1975, people widely displayed flags of China and portraits of Mao Ze-dong; this symbolic demonstration of interest in a commu-nist regime was not, however, the one the victorious Vietnamese would have wanted to see.

5. Pelley (1998: 390) writes about the pre-1975 period that in "DRV studies of the compradore bourgeoisie of the South . . . northern writers were interested in the Chi-nese as economic subjects, and not principally as ethnographic objects."

6. The eleven trades were: fishmonger and butcher; retailer of products in common use; coal and firewood merchants; dealer in petroleum products; second-hand goods dealer; textile and silk merchants handling less than 10,000 m; metal scrap dealer; cereal dealer; transporter of persons and merchandise by surface vehicle or boat; rice millers or processors; and commission agencies.

7. In spite of the apparent intent of these government policies to discriminate against the Chinese, Pelley (1998: 390) suggests that the absence of explicit mention of the Chinese in such DRV policies was "because there was such great uncertainty surrounding their legal and political status."

8. This perspective emerged during the anti-Chinese riots in Indonesia leading up to President Suharto's resignation in May 1998. Ueda also notes the comments of one elderly Sino-Thai businessman that when Chinese were prohibited from living in Korat in Northeast Thailand in 1941 the area suffered "economic paralysis and acute food shortages" (Ueda, 2000).

9. Labelling the majority population "relatively poor" and the Chinese as "relatively affluent" is clearly reductionist, disguising the heterogeneity that lies within the two groupings. However it is just this sort of poor/rich duality that propels government policies and public perceptions.

10. ". . . even if women, ethnic minorities and disabled people achieve equal opportunities within the labour market, it will still be the case that what 'integration' means is participation in a capitalist economy driven by profit and based upon exploitation" (Levitas, 1996: 18).

11. While Room may argue that poverty is about distributional rather than relational issues, it can be argued that this misrepresents at least some of the literature on poverty, which emphasises that poverty is indeed about relations between people.

REFERENCES

Amer, Ramses. 1991. *The Ethnic Chinese in Vietnam and Sino-Vietnamese Relations,* Kuala Lumpur: Forum.

———. 1996. "Vietnam's Policies and the Ethnic Chinese since 1975," *Sojourn* 11(1): 76–104.

Blussé, Leonard. 1991. "The Role of Indonesian Chinese in Shaping Modern Indonesian Life: A Conference in Retrospect," *Indonesia*: 1–11.

Brown, Ian. 1997. *Economic Change in South-East Asia, c.1830–1980,* Kuala Lumpur: Oxford University Press.

Chan, Kwok Bun and Louis-Jacques Dorais. 1998. "Family, Identity, and the Vietnamese Diaspora: The Quebec Experience," *Sojourn* 13(2): 285–308.

Cleary, Mark and Brian J. Shaw. 1994. "Ethnicity, Development and the New Economic Policy: The Experience of Malaysia, 1971–1990," *Pacific Viewpoint* 35(1): 83–107.

Cohen, Margot and Dan Murphy. 1999. "Swept Away: A Diaspora Is Turning Dangerous for South Sulawesi Migrants," *Far Eastern Economic Review* 8th April, pp. 26–29.

Cribb, Robert. 1999. "Indonesia's Chinese: The Genocide That Never Was," *NIASnytt* (Nordic Newsletter of Asian Studies) 1: 20–22.

de Haan, Arjan and Simon Maxwell. 1998. "Poverty and Social Exclusion in North and South," *IDS Bulletin* 29(1): 1–9.

De Poncins, Gontran, trans. by Bernard Frechtman. 1957. *From a Chinese City,* Garden City, NY: Doubleday.

Douglas, Stephen A. 1997. "Political Dynamics of the Diaspora: The Chinese in Southeast Asia," *Asian Journal of Political Science* 5(2): 37–48.

Fisher, Charles A. 1966. *South-East Asia: A Social, Economic and Political Geography,* London: Methuen.

Formoso, Bernard. 1996. "Chinese Temples and Philanthropic Associations in Thailand," *Journal of Southeast Asian Studies* 27(2): 245–260.

Hamilton, Gary G. and Tony Waters. 1997. "Ethnicity and Capitalist Development: The Changing Role of the Chinese in Thailand," in Daniel Chirot and Anthony Reid, eds., *Essential Outsiders: Chinese and Jews in the Modern Transformation of Southeast Asia and Central Europe,* Seattle: University of Washington Press, 258–284.

Hewison, Kevin. 1989. *Bankers and Bureaucrats: Capital and the Role of the State in Thailand,* Monograph series 34, New Haven: Yale University Southeast Asia Studies.

Hunter, Guy. 1966. *South-East Asia: Race, Culture and Nation,* London: Oxford University Press.

Kasian Tejapira. 1997. "Imagined Uncommunity: The *Lookjin* Middle Class and Thai Official Nationalism," in Daniel Chirot and Anthony Reid, eds., *Essential Outsiders: Chinese and Jews in the Modern Transformation of Southeast Asia and Central Europe,* Seattle: University of Washington Press, 75–98.

Lever-Tracy, Constance, David Ip, and Noel Tracy. 1996. *The Chinese Diaspora and Mainland China: An Emerging Economic Synergy,* Basingstoke: Macmillan.

Levitas, Ruth. 1996. "The Concept of Social Exclusion and the New Durkheimian Hegemony," *Critical Social Policy* 16(1): 5–20.

Lim, Linda Y. C. and L. A. Peter Gosling. 1997. "Strengths and Weaknesses of Minority Status for Southeast Asian Chinese at a Time of Economic Growth and Liberalization," in Daniel Chirot and Anthony Reid, eds., *Essential Outsiders: Chinese and Jews in the Modern Transformation of Southeast Asia and Central Europe,* Seattle: University of Washington Press, 285–317.

Mahathir, bin Mohamad. 1970. *The Malay Dilemma,* Kuala Lumpur: Federal Publications.

Marsot, Alain G. 1993. *The Chinese Community in Vietnam under the French,* New York: The Edwin Mellen Press.

Montesano, Michael J. 2000. "Market Society and the Origins of the New Thai Politics," in Ruth McVey, ed., *Money and Power in Provincial Thailand,* ed. Copenhagen: Nordic Institute of Asian Studies.

Pasuk Phongpaichit and Chris Baker. 1995. *Thailand: Economy and Politics,* Kuala Lumpur: Oxford University Press.

Pelley, Patricia. 1998. "'Barbarians' and 'Younger Brothers': The Remaking of Race in Postcolonial Vietnam," *Journal of Southeast Asian Studies* 29(2): 374–391.

Pravit Rojanaphruk. 1997. "Together Forever? What Does It Mean to Be Thai-Chinese in Today's Thailand?" *Bangkok Post* (Thailand), February 1, C1.

Purcell, Victor. 1965. *The Chinese in Southeast Asia,* London: Oxford University Press.

Reid, Anthony. 1997. "Entrepreneurial Minorities, Nationalism, and the State," in Daniel Chirot and Anthony Reid, eds., *Essential Outsiders: Chinese and Jews in the Modern Transformation of Southeast Asia and Central Europe,* Seattle: University of Washington Press, 33–71.

Reynolds, E. Bruce. 1997. "'International Orphans'—the Chinese in Thailand during World War II," *Journal of Southeast Asian Studies* 28(2): 365–388.

Rigg, Jonathan. 1997. *Southeast Asia: The Human Landscape of Modernization and Development,* London: Routledge.

Room, Graham. 1995. "Poverty and Social Exclusion: The New European Agenda for Policy and Research," in Graham Room, ed., *Beyond the Threshold: The Measurement and Analysis of Social Exclusion,* Bristol, UK: The Policy Press, 1–9.

Samers, Michael. 1998. "Immigration, 'Ethnic Minorities,' and 'Social Exclusion' in the European Union: A Critical Perspective," *Geoforum* 29(2): 123–144.

Sibley, David. 1998. "The Problematic Nature of Exclusion," *Geoforum* 29(2): 119–121.

Skinner, G. William. 1957. *Chinese Society in Thailand: An Analytical History,* Ithaca, NY: Cornell University Press.

Tran, Khanh. 1993. *The Ethnic Chinese and Economic Development in Vietnam,* Singapore: Institute of Southeast Asian Studies.

Ueda, Yoko. 2000. "The Entrepreneurs of Khorat," in Ruth McVey, ed., *Money and Power in Provincial Thailand,* Copenhagen: Nordic Institute of Asian Studies, 154–194.

Van Hear, Nicholas. 1998. *New Diasporas: The Mass Exodus, Dispersal and Regrouping of Migrant Communities,* London: UCL Press.

Vatikiotis, Michael. 1996. "Sino Chic," *Far Eastern Economic Review,* 11 January, 22–24.

Wyatt, David. 1982. *Thailand: A Short History,* New Haven: Yale University Press.

Yeung, Henry Wai-Chung. 1999. "The Internationalization of Ethnic Chinese Business Firms from Southeast Asia: Strategies, Processes and Competitive Advantage," *International Journal of Urban and Regional Research* 23(1): 103–127.

5

A Diaspora of Chinese Settlement in Latin America and the Caribbean

Robert B. Kent

HISTORICAL MIGRATION PATTERNS

Chinese immigration, albeit on a small scale, has figured in the migration history of Latin America and the Caribbean since the colonial period. During the colonial period, most Chinese probably entered the Spanish realm via Acapulco where the Spanish fleet landed on its annual trips between the Philippines and the New World. Small numbers of Chinese found their way to Mexico City and Lima, the vice-regal capitals of New Spain and Peru respectively. Although never numerous, their presence was significant enough to be recorded in an early population census of Lima at the beginning of the 1600s (Dobyns and Doughty, 1976: 118). Given Havana's role as the entrepôt between Spain's New World colonies and the metropolitan port of Cadiz in Spain, it is also likely that a small number of Chinese settled in that city as well during the early colonial period. In Brazil, Chinese immigration dates from the late colonial period, and in 1810 some 400 Chinese were brought to cultivate tea in the vicinity of Rio de Janeiro (Elias, 1970: 60).

Between the middle of the nineteenth century and the middle of the twentieth century, two distinct migration movements characterized Chinese immigration to Latin America and the Caribbean. The first involved the immigration of several hundred thousand laborers. Most of these arrived on long-term labor contracts during the last half of the nineteenth century. A second migration flow, involving "free" migrants, occurred after the turn of the century and ended during the decade of the Great Depression. The number of migrants during this period was far less, between 10,000 to 20,000. These migrants were mostly of working-class origins, and many were artisans and small-scale traders (Hu-DeHart, 1999: 254; Look Lai, 1999: 248).

The Caribbean Basin

A booming sugarcane economy in the Caribbean and the impending end of African slavery during the second half of the nineteenth century provided the impetus for the immigration of tens of thousands of Chinese between 1850 and 1900. In Cuba, sugarcane planters faced increasingly acute labor shortages after the middle of the nineteenth century, despite the continuation of the institution of slavery, which was not abolished on the island until 1886. The importation of contract Chinese laborers, or coolies, on long-term contracts, usually of 8 years, provided an attractive means of addressing this shortfall. In the quarter century between 1847 and 1874, some 125,000 Chinese reached Cuba where most worked as cane cutters and sugarcane mill laborers (Look Lai, 1999: 249).

A similar process occurred in several other Caribbean colonies, although the total number of Chinese migrants was considerably less. In the British colonies of the Caribbean, where slavery was abolished in 1834, the need to meet labor demands on sugarcane plantations brought a variety of labor importation schemes which included Chinese, East Asians, and others. The largest number of Chinese coolie laborers came to British Guiana (Guyana), where almost 15,000 arrived between 1850 and 1880. Far fewer Chinese workers arrived in other British colonies, just 2,700 in Trinidad, 1,200 in Jamaica, and less than 500 in British Honduras (Belize) (Look Lai, 1999: 249). In Surinam, a Dutch colony, about 2,700 Chinese coolies also destined for the sugarcane fields arrived during the same period (Look Lai, 1999: 249). These workers were recruited principally from southern Guangdong Province, among the Punti and Hakka, and specifically from the districts of Siyi, Sanyi, and Zhongshan (Look Lai, 1999: 249).

South America and Mexico

On the Latin American mainland, Chinese immigration followed the same general pattern but focused almost exclusively on Peru. Labor demands in Peru fueled migration of about 100,000 Chinese between 1850 and 1880 (He, 1990: 4–5). These coolies worked under long-term labor contracts similar to those in Cuba. The labor demands in Peru were more varied than in the Caribbean. Chinese laborers toiled initially mining guano deposits on the southern coast where many died, and then later on sugarcane plantations, in mines, and in railroad construction. The vast majority of these immigrants remained in coastal communities, although a few eventually found their way to the Andes and the tropical lowlands farther to the east.

Fewer Chinese immigrants went to Mexico and those who did went later than had been the case in Peru. In Mexico, most Chinese arrived in a 20- to 30-year period spanning the last decades of the nineteenth century and the first decades of the twentieth century. Small numbers of Chinese migrants arrived in the Pacific coastal ports of Mazatlán, Guaymas, and Ensenada in the 1880s and 1890s and established small communities in these cities (Curtis, 1995: 337). Many of these immigrants moved aggressively into small-scale retailing in settlements that were underserved or not served by the existing commercial network. These places included interior villages, railroad and mining towns, and agricultural service centers in the northern states of Sonora and Baja California del Norte (Hu-DeHart, 1999: 256). The more successful branched out into cottage industries producing shoes and clothing which were readily marketable in their retail establishments and some engaged in market gardening (Hu-DeHart, 1999: 256). The opening up of the Mexicali Valley just south of the U.S.-Mexico border to cotton cultivation after 1900 provided the impetus for the arrival of the greatest numbers of Chinese immigrants to Mexico. Agricultural labor contracts drew coolie labor and as many as 10,000 Chinese worked in the region by 1920 (Curtis, 1995: 338). Chinese population in Mexico peaked at about 25,000 around 1930. It then declined rapidly thereafter as the Depression fueled nationalistic sentiment among Mexicans and in some areas, most notably Sonora, the nationalization of Chinese businesses and the expulsion of Chinese nationals occurred. Conditions were more benign in the northern state of Baja California del Norte and a modest Chinese population and community survived and indeed even prospered there.

In most Caribbean colonies and Latin American countries Chinese populations tended to decline, or at best remain stable, in the decades after peak population numbers were reached. This is attributable to several factors. First, many Chinese, both coolies as well as the artisan and commercial migrants who came to the Americas later, came with the express intention of returning to southern China once they had amassed some capital. While many never succeeded in getting rich or even in accumulating a modest financial nest egg, some did return. In addition, most Chinese migrants, especially those who came as contract laborers, were male. There are only a few recorded instances of any appreciable numbers of female Chinese migrating during the coolie period. Some Chinese women did accompany male migrants during the later decades of free migration, but even then, they represented a comparatively small proportion of Chinese migrants, perhaps no more than 10 percent. In some instances, Chinese men did marry local women, and often they formed "free-unions" or common-law marriages. Lausent (1983: 103) has provided detailed documentation of this process in an agricultural valley on Peru's coast, just north of Lima during the late nineteenth century. Furthermore, remigration occurred from many of the early destinations of Chinese migrants. This was most commonly the case for those who came as part of the coolie movement. As early as the 1870s in the Caribbean, as many as 3,000 Chinese left British Guiana for neighboring colonies, especially Surinam and Trinidad

(Look Lai, 1999: 249). In the early decades of the twentieth century, Jamaica attracted additional Chinese from other Caribbean colonies. The economic boom in Panama driven by the building of the Panama Canal between 1904 and 1914 drew large numbers and many settled in the Caribbean port of Colón. In Mexico, the extreme xenophobia towards the Chinese community in Sonora in the 1920s and 1930s, as well as more attractive economic opportunities north of the border, led to the movement of many Chinese into the U.S. In South America the only appreciable Chinese population in a Spanish-speaking country was found in Peru, and re-migration from here appears to have been limited to small numbers of entrepreneurs who moved to urban centers in neighboring countries, often favoring the coastal cities in Ecuador and Chile.

Generally, the population geography of Chinese migrants in Latin America and the Caribbean before the middle of the twentieth century is well documented. Many scholarly studies provide detailed accounts of the immigration history of Chinese migrants, while a number of amateur historians have produced country-based studies on local Chinese communities. In contrast, the status of Chinese communities and the Chinese immigrant populations and their descendants during the last half of the twentieth century is poorly documented and not well understood.

Problems in the Enumeration and Identification of Chinese

Two of the principal difficulties in understanding the contemporary geography of the region's Chinese population are the identification of who precisely should be counted as "Chinese" and then their subsequent enumeration. Contrary to practice in the population censuses undertaken in the United States and Canada, in many Latin America and Caribbean countries national origin, language use, ethnicity, or race is often not tabulated. Often the only data that are enumerated which provide any clues for establishing the presence or magnitude of Chinese populations or communities are the numbers of foreign nationals.

Differences in the definition or conception of who precisely is "Chinese" confound efforts to count their numbers in Latin America and the Caribbean. Terminology is a problem. What are the appropriate terms for these people—Chinese, "overseas Chinese," Hispano-Chinese, or Anglo-Chinese? And assuming such groups can be identified, then who gets counted? Does one count only those Chinese who are foreign-born or foreign nationals? Or alternatively does one count all "overseas Chinese," a vague, poorly defined term which refers to Chinese originally from China, Taiwan, or other areas of Chinese settlement in Southeast Asia who may be native-born Chinese, naturalized Chinese, as well as the descendants of Chinese parents living abroad? In a few countries, notably Peru, such a broad definition could conceivably encompass hundreds of thousands of individuals, many of whom may have little or no inkling of their Chinese ancestry. Or alternatively, should only those with a strong cultural affinity with Chinese culture, say a functional knowledge of the Chinese language, be enumerated?

Peru provides a useful example of the difficulties of defining who is "Chinese" and who should be enumerated. The Peruvian census, similar to other censuses in Latin American countries, enumerates Chinese nationals and foreign-born Chinese. In Peru for instance, the Chinese population as recorded by the census of 1944 stood at 10,915 Chinese, while 40 years later, in 1981, the census enumerated just 2,700 Chinese (He, 1990: 6). At about the same time, in 1979, Taiwanese sources estimated a total of some 52,000 Chinese-Peruvians, of which about 13,000 were Chinese nationals (He, 1990: 7). Based on these estimates, as well as additional sources from the embassy of the People's Republic of China in Peru, He (1990: 7) estimated that the overseas Chinese population in Peru stood somewhere between 80,000 and 100,000 in the early 1990s. Other estimates suggest the nation's "Chinese" population is even greater. In her recent piece on Lima's Chinatown, the Peruvian anthropologist, Lausent-Herrera (1994: 319), who has studied the country's Chinese populations extensively, estimates a population of about 160,000. Much higher estimates come from Poston, Mao, and Yu's (1994) worldwide overview that places the number in Peru at 500,000 and the Commission on Overseas Chinese Affairs (1997) that estimates some 540,000 Chinese in Peru.

The racial makeup of the populations of some Latin American nations also works to diminish the distinctiveness of Asian populations and may hinder their enumeration. This is especially so with children of Chinese immigrants and mestizos, people of mixed indigenous and European parentage. Because the origin of the indigenous populations in the Americas can be traced to a series of population migrations across the Bering Strait, the racial characteristics of some indigenous peoples, as well as mestizos, can resemble Asians. Thus, olive skin colors or tones, little body and facial hair, black hair, and the frequent presence the epicanthic fold are racial characteristics that are common among large numbers of the population in some Latin American countries, especially those with a high proportion of indigenous peoples and mestizos.

Cultural affinity, a population characteristic which is difficult to measure, is largely ignored in most attempts to identify Chinese population numbers in Latin America and the Caribbean. Generally, Chinese immigrants and their children have acculturated quickly in local host societies and subsequent generations have assimilated into national populations. Often they hold only the most tenuous ties with Chinese culture and China. Knowledge and command of the Chinese language for instance is almost completely absent with the exception of those born in China or Taiwan (Look Lai 1999:

251). In Spanish-speaking countries, English rather than Chinese is usually the preferred second language for descendants of Chinese immigrants.

Contemporary Population Data Sources

Few data sources provide a comprehensive overview of the population geography of the Chinese in Latin America and the Caribbean since 1950. Nevertheless, benchmark estimates for various years in the 1960s and the 1990s are available from several sources and these provide a reasonable point of departure for understanding contemporary population geography of Chinese in the region.

The data reproduced in table 5.1 report two approximations of the Chinese population for the region for the 1960s drawn from three reputable secondary sources (Chang, 1968; Hu-DeHart, 1999; Look Lai, 1999). The most complete set of data is taken from Chang (1968) who provides a country by country overview of the overseas Chinese population worldwide at the beginning of the 1960s. Chang's data suggest that approximately 150,000 Chinese and their descendants lived in the region in the early 1960s. Unfortunately the specific sources for the data he reports for Latin American and Caribbean nations cannot be readily desegregated from his references. Some data clearly appear to be generalizations; hence neatly rounded estimates like 10,000 for Mexico and 30,000 for Peru, while others appear excruciatingly detailed. Consider for instance estimates like 4,171 for Ecuador or 152 for Uruguay.

The other data set for the 1960s, albeit somewhat incomplete, is derived from recent estimates published by Hu-DeHart (1999: 258) and Look Lai (1999: 252) in the *Encyclopedia of Overseas Chinese*. These data peg the Chinese population of the region at about 100,000 during the mid-1960s. In this case the quality of the data varies among the countries. The data for Latin American countries has been reported by Hu-DeHart, but these are based on Taiwanese estimates of overseas Chinese (Ho, 1967a; Ho, 1967b). These data appear to be more generalized and likely based on the estimates of local informants. Look Lai cites the data for the five Caribbean countries, Cuba, Guyana, Jamaica, Surinam, and Trinidad and Tobago in his study. He has drawn these almost exclusively from national population censuses or other local sources and considerable confidence can be placed in these numbers.

Contemporary estimates of the region's Chinese population published during the 1990s vary dramatically from those from the 1960s and are difficult to reconcile with the earlier data. Two of the most widely utilized contemporary sources on the region's Chinese population suggest that between 900,000 and 1.1 million Chinese and their descendants reside in Latin America and the Caribbean (see table 5.2).

Table 5.1. Estimates of Chinese Population in Latin America, ca. 1960

Countries	Early 1960s after Chang (1968)	Late 1960s after Encyclopedia of Overseas Chinese (1999)
Argentina	240	300
Aruba	486	
Belize		
Bolivia	35	50
Brazil	6,748	
Chile	2,950	2,000
Colombia	1,400	1,000
Costa Rica	3,000	
Cuba	31,039	11,834
Curacao	443	
Dominican Republic	1,060	1,000
Ecuador	4,171	4,200
El Salvador	515	500
French Guiana	308	
Guatemala	5,234	4,000
Guyana	5,000	4,074
Haiti	204	
Honduras	817	900
Jamaica	18,655	10,267
Mexico	10,000	10,000
Nicaragua	3,000	1,000
Panama	2,960	8,000
Paraguay	12	10
Peru	30,000	30,000
Surinam	5,700	5,339
Trinidad & Tobago	12,000	8,361
Uruguay	152	100
Venezuela	2,580	3,000
Other Countries		
TOTAL	148,709	105,935

Sources: Chang (1968: 99), Hu-Dehart (1999: 258), Look Lai (1999: 252).

Although not providing population estimates for all countries in the region, Poston, Mao, and Yu's (1994) widely cited paper dealing with worldwide patterns places the regional total at slightly over 900,000. The commonly utilized Taiwanese source (*Overseas Chinese Economy Yearbook,* 1997), which provides a snapshot of the Chinese population in each country where there is an appreciable number of Chinese, places the population in Latin America and the Caribbean at close to 1.1 million. This source provides data for all countries with the sole exception of French Guiana.

Table 5.2. Estimates of Chinese Population in Latin America and Caribbean, ca. 1990–2000

Countries	Poston et al. ca. 1990	Overseas Chinese Economy, 1997	Other Estimates	Best Guess Estimate, 2000
Argentina	20,000	30,000		10,000
Aruba		600		600
Belize		5,700	748[a]	750
Bolivia		12,000		3,000
Brazil	100,000	127,700	100,000[b]	30,000
Chile	13,000	4,300	2,000[c]	2,000
Colombia		4,000		1,500
Costa Rica	22,000	47,000	4,500[d]; 1,345[e]	5,000
Cuba	7,000	6,000	3,500[f]; 7,000[g]	3,500
Curacao		5,500[h]		1,000
Dominican Republic	6,500	17,800	10,000[i]	5,000
Ecuador	15,000	35,000		8,000
El Salvador		18,000	2,000[j]	2,000
French Guiana				
Guatemala	14,000	16,800		4,000
Guyana	6,000	6,500	1,800[k]; 1,338[l]	1,000
Haiti		6		
Honduras		1,200		500
Jamaica	20,000	22,500	5,372[m]	5,000
Mexico	20,000	19,500		15,000
Nicaragua		630		500
Panama	100,000	103,500	150,000[n]	25,000
Paraguay	7,000	8,600		2,000
Peru	500,000	540,000	80,000–100,000[o]; 160,000[p]	120,000
Surinam	10,000	40,000	3,048[q]	3,000
Trinidad & Tobago	8,000	9,000	4,313[r]; 5,279[s]	5,000
Uruguay		515		500
Venezuela	15,000	12,700		3,000
Other Countries	17,700			
TOTAL	901,200	1,095,051		256,850

Sources: Poston et al. (1994:637); Commission on Overseas Chinese Affairs (1997).
[a] Look Lai (1999: 252).
[b] Benavides (1999)
[c] Chou (1999)
[d] Grimes (1996)
[e] Leon Azofeila (1987: 361)
[f] Hongqiang (1999)
[g] Look Lai (1999: 252)
[h] This estimate is for the entire Netherlands Antillies
[i] Chao (1999)
[j] Quan (1999)
[k] Crawford (1989: 235)
[l] Look Lai (1999: 252)
[m] Look Lai (1999: 252)
[n] Mon P. (1998: 72)
[o] He (1990:7)
[p] Lausent-Herrera (1994: 319)
[q] Look Lai (1999: 252)
[r] Look Lai (1999: 252)
[s] Millet (1993: 37)

The incongruity between the population estimates of the 1960s and the 1990s is stark. If these population estimates are to be believed, Chinese population region-wide increased 700 to 800 percent during the 30-year period. An increase of this magnitude does not seem likely nor is there any credible explanation for it. The key difficulty with the population estimates for the late 1990s is that with the exception of Brazil and Panama, there is no evidence that the Chinese population in any country in the region has increased appreciably since the 1960s. Indeed in some instances, the situation is quite to the contrary.

Brazil is one of the few Latin American countries where there is evidence of an increase in the Chinese population during the last several decades. Benavides' (1999) unpublished study of the Chinese in São Paulo reports the movement of significant numbers of Chinese to Brazil when they fled the mainland from Shanghai at the end of the civil war in 1949 and then established themselves and their businesses in São Paulo. She notes an appreciable migratory flow from China to São Paulo in the last decade, suggesting that as many as 100,000 have immigrated to Brazil since 1990. However, Benavides provides no sources to substantiate this estimate.

Detailed country studies from the Caribbean suggest that Chinese population in at least five countries has declined steadily in the decades since the 1960s. The total numbers are not overwhelming, but the pattern is clear. Political independence, revolutionary movements, and nationalistic governments all played significant roles in the decline of Chinese communities in Guyana, Trinidad and Tobago, Surinam, Jamaica, and Cuba. The economic success of the Chinese in former British colonies propelled them firmly into the middle class by the time political independence became a reality during the decades of the 1960s and 1970s.

In Jamaica for instance, Chinese controlled the retail grocery trade, and were prominent in the civil service and professions. In the early 1960s they ranked among the best educated and wealthiest of Jamaicans (Kaplan, Blutstein, Johnston, and McMorris, 1976:102). The conflicts engendered in the country by differences in race and class immediately after independence in 1962 placed considerable pressure on many Chinese-Jamaicans, which led them to view their economic and social positions as precarious (Lee, 1998: 113). Some, especially among the more prosperous, opted to liquidate their business interests and migrate to Canada and the United States (Lee, 1998:113). Perhaps 5,000 Chinese-Jamaicans remained in the country at the end of the 1990s.

A similar process marked the events in Trinidad and Tobago, another former British colony that also became independent in 1962. Here too the Chinese had made considerable inroads in the commercial sector since their days as indentured coolie laborers on the islands. For example in the early 1970s, while the Chinese represented a scanty one percent of the total population, they represented about 10 percent of the nation's business elite. In addition, they were members of some of the islands' most exclusive social clubs, the Union Club, the Yacht Club, and the Country Club (Millett, 1993: 56). Black Power advocates viewed the Chinese as members of the nation's ruling elite, along with whites and "off-whites." In hopes of scotching any efforts to seize their businesses and property, some Chinese took out Trinidadian citizenship, while others chose to immigrate, again choosing Canada and the United States as preferred destinations (Millet, 1993: 57). The Chinese population dropped steadily from about 8,300 in 1960, to 7,950 in 1970, and to 5,300 in 1980 (Millet, 1993: 4). By the end of the twentieth century, the process of assimilation had diminished many of the distinctive social and economic traits of the Chinese population in Trinidad and Tobago, although it appears their numbers have not declined much below the levels present in the early 1980s.

On the South American mainland similar pressures and patterns occurred. In Guyana the Chinese population declined from 4,100 in 1960, to 3,400 in 1970, and to 1,800 in 1980 (Crawford, 1989: 235). An appreciable number of Chinese also concentrated in the Dutch colony of Surinam. When the colony became independent in 1975, becoming Suriname, many residents including those of Chinese origin opted for Dutch citizenship and emigrated. In the early 1990s, the Chinese population numbered around 8,000 and by the end of the decade is estimated to have declined to just 3,000 (Look Lai, 1999: 252).

In Cuba, the Communist revolution led by Fidel Castro in 1959 also brought a decrease in the nation's population of Chinese-Cubans. Chinese-Cubans apparently occupied a somewhat lower social and economic position than in other Caribbean countries. Look Lai (1999: 251) describes them as remaining in "a lower middle class sector." No doubt their commercial success had been held in check by the strong presence of American and Spanish business interests on the island, even after the country's independence in 1903. Nevertheless, by the 1950s, Chinese-Cubans had achieved considerable commercial success and they controlled some 3,500 small retail businesses—groceries, restaurants, laundries, and fruit and vegetable stands (Look Lai, 1999: 251). The revolution exerted tremendous pressure on private businesses, even small-scale operations that characterized the Chinese, nationalizing many and simply closing others. Like other upper and middle class Cubans, Chinese-Cubans abandoned the island in droves, with most emigrating to the United States, particularly south Florida and the New York metropolitan region. The population of Chinese-Cubans dropped from somewhere between 20,000 to 30,000 at the end of the 1950s to perhaps 5,000 to 6,000 at the end of the 1990s.

Furthermore, independent estimates for other countries rarely agree with the data from Poston, Mao, and Yu (1994) and the Commission on Overseas Chinese Affairs (1997). Usually these other sources estimate Chinese populations as considerably less numerous (see table 5.2). In Peru for example, Poston, Mao, and Yu estimate the Chinese population at 500,000, while the Commission on

Overseas Chinese Affairs pegs the number at 540,000 (see table 5.2). Benavides (1999) states that in addition to 25,000 Chinese nationals and 85,000 naturalized Chinese, the Chinese consulate in Peru asserts that 1.5 million Peruvians have a parent or grandparent born in China! While it may indeed be true that several hundred thousand Peruvians have some Chinese blood—perhaps 1/16th or 1/32nd—it is so miniscule that it is unlikely that most are even aware of it. Even if they were, would it be reasonable to call them "Chinese"? Other estimates for Peru suggest these numbers are grossly overstated. In the early 1990s, He (1990: 7) reviewed a variety of sources and estimated the total to stand between 80,000 and 100,000. Similarly, a recent piece on Lima's Chinatown by a Peruvian anthropologist, who has studied the country's Chinese community for many years, suggests that the number may stand at 160,000 (Lausent-Herrera, 1994: 319).

Although differing in magnitude, the data for the small Central American country of Costa Rica present a similar pattern. Poston, Mao, and Yu (1994) report some 22,000 Chinese and Chinese-Costa Ricans for early 1990s and the data from the *Overseas Chinese Economy Yearbook* (1997) places the number at, 47,000 (see table 5.2). In contrast, the Costa Rican census enumerated just 1,345 Chinese in 1984. This number included immigrants from China (87), Taiwan (1,219), and Hong Kong (39) (Leon Azofeila, 1987: 361). Another estimate pegs the number of Chinese-Cantonese speakers in the country at 4,500 (Grimes, 1996). But these estimates are not very satisfactory: the census figure ignores the Cantonese population which immigrated to the country over the last 100 years, while the final estimate ignores the Mandarin-speaking immigrants who have come from Taiwan in the last few decades.

With a plethora of wildly divergent estimates, what reasonable conclusions can be made about estimates of Chinese populations in Latin America and the Caribbean at the end of the twentieth century? It is clear that the population estimates published annually by the Commission on Overseas Chinese Affairs in its publication, the *Overseas Chinese Economy Yearbook,* and which are sometimes cited as authoritative, must be viewed with healthy skepticism. The sources for these data are not clear, and it is likely that in most countries Taiwanese diplomatic or economic envoys or local Taiwanese businessmen have provided these estimates. Unfortunately, the data for Latin American countries reported in Poston, Mao, and Yu's (1994) study in *Population and Development Review,* are no more reliable since these data have been drawn from the 1991 and 1992 editions of the *Overseas Chinese Economy Yearbook.*

Furthermore, many sources are silent or vague about who is considered Chinese and hence what is the specific Chinese population that is reported—i.e., are the estimates for Chinese nationals, naturalized Chinese, first generation descendants of Chinese origin, or anyone with any degree of Chinese heritage? National census organizations normally count only foreign nationals as Chinese, thus it is usually only the foreign born or first generation Chinese who may have established citizenship in Taiwan or China who will be included. Subsequent generations are lost in such efforts and disappear, at least statistically, into the broader national population.

In most national contexts, Chinese population estimates are unreliable. The data, almost without exception, represent rough estimates. However, when the estimates are based on the work of local scholars, with long-term experience with the Chinese community, considerable confidence may be placed in them. Thus, for example, the estimates suggested by Lausent-Herrera (1994) for Peru and those by Look Lai (1999: 252) for several Caribbean countries are supported by solid scholarly research and an intimate knowledge of the community.

A summary of the published estimates for Chinese population by country for the decade of the 1990s is presented in table 5.2. It includes the comprehensive data sets for the entire region published by Poston, Mao, and Yu (1994) and the Commission on Overseas Chinese Affairs (1997). In addition, other estimates and citations of the total population of Chinese from a variety of sources are also reported. With few exceptions there is no meaningful correspondence between the data reported in the two comprehensive data sets and that reported by other sources. In an effort to produce a more accurate picture of the Chinese regional population totals and Chinese population numbers by country, table 5.2 also reports the author's "best guess estimate, 2000." These estimates have been derived from a review of the available statistical data and estimates and supplemental information available on Chinese populations for each country. In the final analysis, however, these numbers represent only an informed estimate.

Geographic Patterns in the 1960s and 1990s

The geographic distribution of the region's Chinese population in the 1960s is portrayed in map 5.1. Chinese populations concentrated most heavily in the Caribbean and adjacent countries on the circum-Caribbean rim. Cuba, with over 30,000, dominated the region, but substantial concentrations of Chinese resided in Jamaica (18,000) and Trinidad and Tobago (12,000). Population totals ranged between 1,000 and 5,000 in most other Caribbean and circum-Caribbean nations. Beyond the Caribbean region, Chinese populations remained small. Peru and Mexico are notable exceptions, with 30,000 and 10,000 Chinese respectively. However, in the case of Peru, Chang's (1968) estimate seems too low, and a more reasonable estimate is probably closer to 100,000. With the exception of Peru, Chinese were conspicuous in their absence from most South American countries. At that time fewer than 7,000 lived in Brazil, an immense nation with a contemporary population of about 100 million. In the region's remaining nations and colonies, Chinese populations ranged from almost nil in Bolivia, Paraguay, and Uruguay, to as many as several thousand in Chile, Costa Rica, and Venezuela.

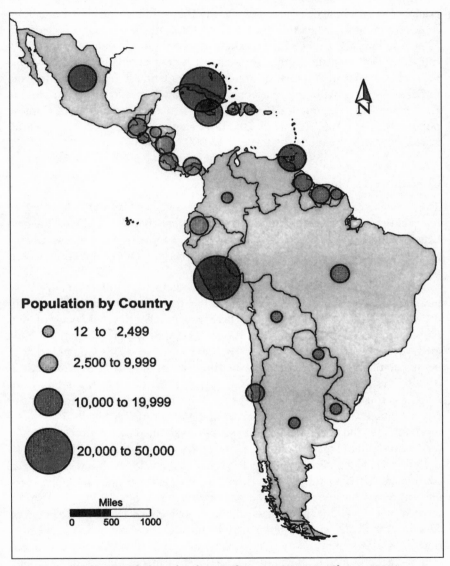

Population by Country

○ 12 to 2,499

○ 2,500 to 9,999

● 10,000 to 19,999

● 20,000 to 50,000

Miles

0   500   1000

Map 5.1.   Chinese Population of Latin America, 1960 (Source: Chang, 1968.)

The population distribution of the Chinese in the region experienced some notable changes between the 1960s and the 1990s. In the Caribbean and along South America's northeastern Caribbean coast, Chinese populations declined. Population numbers tended to remain fairly stable in Mexico and most Central American countries, although notable Chinese population growth seems to have occurred in Panama. In South America Chinese also appear to have remained stable, with modest population growth occurring in Argentina, Brazil, and Peru. Regionally, Peru hosts the greatest concentration of Chinese population, over 100,000, while Brazil, Panama, Mexico, and Argentina all have Chinese populations that exceed 10,000 (see map 5.2).

Chinatowns and the Chinese Communities

The Chinese communities in Latin America and the Caribbean have never reached the kind of residential concentrations that characterized North American cities like San Francisco, New York, or Vancouver. Nevertheless, Chinatowns flourished in a number of the Latin American cities, most typically in the national capitals.

In Cuba, Chinese gravitated to urban areas as their contracts on sugarcane plantations expired during the last part of the nineteenth century and the early decades of the twentieth century. Havana was the principal focus of that movement and Chinese congregated on the edge of the urban area in a marginal district known as the "Zanja" (Baker, 1997: 273). This Chinese district lay just to the west of the colonial core, in a part of the city known as El Centro. By the late 1940s, Havana's Chinese population is estimated to have stood at around 6,000 (Look Lai, 1999: 250), and most concentrated in the city's Chinatown. This area encompassed a number of city blocks, one major thoroughfare, and several small alleys and was defined by the streets of Zanja on the north, Salud on the south, Galiano on the east, and Escobar on the west.

Before the Cuban Revolution in 1959, the area bustled with a wide range of commercial activities run by Chinese and oriented to the country's Chinese population. Small businesses included laundries, retail shops selling food stuffs, three theaters including the somewhat infamous Shanghai Theater, nine hotels of "dubious moral character," gaming parlors, three Chinese pharmacies, and a variety of Chinese restaurants. Community institutions included two primary schools that provided bilingual instruction in Spanish and Mandarin, a Catholic Church, and two Buddhist temples (León and León, 1975: 7).

The commercial vitality of the area diminished dramatically after the Cuban Revolution, as did its population of Chinese. During the twentieth century, Cuba's Chinese had moved into a variety of urban service and retailing businesses and most were firmly entrenched in the middle and lower middle classes. The Cuban Revolution led to the nationalization of most

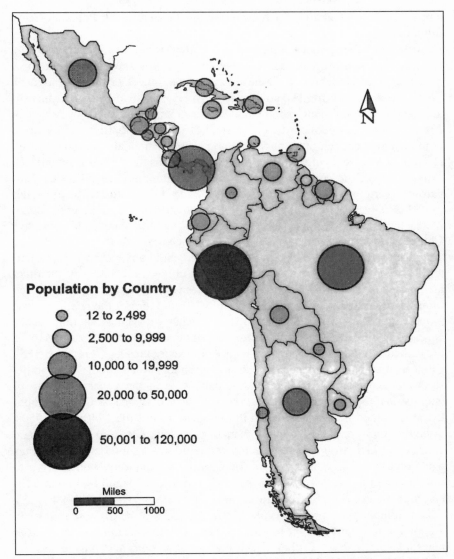

Population by Country

○ 12 to 2,499

○ 2,500 to 9,999

○ 10,000 to 19,999

○ 20,000 to 50,000

○ 50,001 to 120,000

Miles
0   500   1000

Map 5.2.   Chinese Population of Latin America, 2000 (Source: Table 5.2, last column)

small businesses and many of the island's Chinese fled Havana and abandoned its Chinatown. Nevertheless a small core population of Chinese did remain. At the end of the 1999 about 3,500 Chinese lived on the island, most in Havana, and a number were still resident in the Chinatown area. This group included about 250 holding Chinese passports resident in Cuba, about 400 Chinese immigrants who had become naturalized Cuban citizens, and about 2,700 Cubans of Chinese descent (Wang, 1999: Personal Communication).

Vestiges of the former Chinatown are evident today and there has been a concerted effort during the last few years of the 1990s to promote Chinatown as a tourist place. Thirteen Chinese associations, most originally based on family or regional affinities, still function in Havana's Chinatown or nearby, although many have few members. A Chinese language weekly newspaper, *Kwong Wah Po,* is published from a small office in the district and its circulation stands between 600 and 700 (Fung, 1999: Personal Communication). During the last years of the 1990s a group known as the *Grupo Promotor del Barrio Chino de la Habana* has been formed to attempt to revitalize the Chinatown district and promote it as a tourist venue. The revitalization effort has included a facelift of Calle Cuchillo, the district's principal commercial block. In addition, a small plaza for social and cultural events and a massive Chinese portico were constructed at the entrance to the district.

Chinatowns also flourished in Peru, Mexico, and Panama. A Chinese quarter began to develop in Peru's capital, Lima, in the last decades of the nineteenth century as the labor contracts of coolies who labored in agriculture and mines expired and many moved to the city. By the turn of the century, some 3,000 Chinese concentrated just outside of what was Lima's colonial urban core, a scant six to seven blocks from the principal plaza, the Plaza de Armas, the cathedral, and the presidential palace (Lausent-Herrera, 1994: 313, 316). Chinese merchants and social institutions concentrated along the parallel streets of Abancay, Ayacucho, and Andahuaylas in the general vicinity of what is now the central market (*Mercado Central*). The city's Chinese population remained firmly entrenched in this quarter until the 1940s and 1950s. Then the immigration of large numbers of rural migrants from the Andes and consequent increasing congestion and competition for land began to encourage Chinese to leave the quarter. The Chinese population began moving to middle- and upper-class suburban municipalities to the south like Pueblo Libre, San Isidro, San Borja, and La Molina (Lausent-Herrera, 1994: 318). Peru's military government (1968–1980) also viewed the Chinese quarter in a negative light and sought to enforce an aggressive health code and other measures that caused further out-migration of people and businesses. By early 1980s the city's Chinatown was a shadow of its former self with a local newsmagazine reporting that the "Chinese quarter is dead."

Within the last 15 years however, the Lima Chinatown has shown impressive signs of revitalization. This has been driven by increased investment in the quarter by Asian Japanese and Chinese capitalists as well as presence of appreciable numbers of illegal Chinese immigrants moving from China to the U.S. and Canada via Bolivia and Peru (Lausent-Herrera, 1994: 318-319).

At the end of the 1990s the municipal government of Lima made a concerted effort to transform the city's Chinatown. In 1997 the municipal authorities forced the removal of street vendors, which had clogged the district's streets since the 1960s. Its plan included creating a pedestrian mall along one city block in the core of the district, renovating sidewalks and streets, and adding a range of Chinese ornamentation to buildings creating a distinct sense of place. In a unique effort to link the renovations with Peru's Chinese immigrant history, the paving stones used as part of the street and sidewalk renovations are to be inscribed with the names of and surnames of Chinese who immigrated to Peru (Méndez Campos, 1999).

Despite the residential dispersion of most of Lima's Chinese population to middle- and upper-class suburbs of the city, its Chinatown still remains a center of Chinese culture and much commerce. Twelve Chinese associations operate in the neighborhood, most of which have existed for over one hundred years. Surprisingly, one was established as recently as 1997. Three Chinese newspapers, all apparently weeklies, and a newsmagazine are published in the barrio. The largest of these newspapers is the *Man Shing Pao*. It has a weekly press run of 2,000 and prints a total of twelve pages, four in Spanish and eight in Chinese. In addition, acupuncturist clinics, finger pressure massage salons, teahouses, import shops, and a plethora of Chinese restaurants occupy the ten to twelve square blocks of Lima's Chinatown (Méndez Campos, 1999).

Surprisingly, one of the most vibrant and well-defined Chinatowns in Latin America developed in Mexico. Contrary to the general pattern, this Chinatown evolved in a secondary urban center, the state capital of Baja California, Mexicali (Curtis, 1995). The city was founded at the beginning of the twentieth century when irrigation water opened the lower Colorado River Valley to cotton cultivation. Chinese coolies labored in the cotton fields, but many eventually moved into urban occupations in Mexicali. Their settlement, known locally as the "Chinesca," flourished during the 1920s and 1930s. During these years Chinese residence and commercial activity concentrated along a two-block strip along Avenida Juarez lying between Calle Azueta and Calle Morelos (Curtis, 1995: 344). Bunkhouses, shacks, and adobe dwellings housed the Chinese population that was almost exclusively male. Small businesses, including retail establishments selling foodstuffs and dry goods, restaurants, laundries, and others concentrated here as well as cultural institutions. Two Chinese theaters, a Masonic temple, a Chinese Methodist Church, a hospital, and a variety of Chinese benevolent societies, most notably the Consolidated Chinese Benevolent Society, which maintained a permanent structure, figured prominently among these institutions (Curtis, 1995: 344–345). Despite the expulsion of Chinese from Sonora in the 1930s and xenophobic government policies at the national level, the Chinese population in Mexicali persisted.

The Chinesca remains a clearly identifiable part of the urban fabric of Mexicali today, although greatly diminished in its commercial role and no longer a focus of residential settlement for the city's community of nearly 2,500 Chinese nationals and perhaps as many as 7,500 Mexican-Chinese (Curtis, 1995: 346). In the late 1980s Chinese merchants built a shopping center that encompassed an entire city block in the Chinesca. In addition to the shopping center, there are many other Chinese businesses, including nearly 20 restaurants, as well as social organizations located in the district. Assimilation and suburbanization have both dramatically affected the city's Chinese population, as most Chinese have taken up residence in middle-class suburbs with other Mexicans and moved their businesses to these neighborhoods as well (Curtis, 1995: 347).

A small concentration of Chinese population, perhaps barely qualifying as a Chinatown, is found in the national capital, Mexico City. This quarter carries the unofficial name of the "Barrio Chino" (the Chinese Barrio) and occupies a two-block section along Calle Dolores, in the center of the city near the Alameda Central (Sánchez-Crispin, 1999).

The critical role of the isthmus of Panama as a transshipment point since the colonial period undoubtedly gave rise to at least a small number of Chinese settling in Panama City since that time. However, the most significant growth of Chinese population dated from the building of the Panama Canal between 1904 and 1914. In Panama City, the capital, Chinese established businesses and residences in proximity to the public market (Mon P., 1998: 73). In addition to commercial activities, benevolent societies, specifically San Yap and Yun San Fa Yen, located here. An appreciable part of the Chinese population also appears to have been disbursed throughout Panama City's urban area. In the 1940s, when their population numbers are estimated to have been less than 3,000, they are reported to have so dominated the retail grocery trade ". . . that 'going to the Chino's' was synonymous with 'going to the grocery store'" (Biesanz and Biesanz, 1955: 102). In Panama City, the later decades of the twentieth century found Chinese abandoning the central city, combined with diminishing linguistic and cultural ties, and to some extent abandoning their emphasis on commerce and moving into professional occupations (Mon P., 1998: 73).

A secondary node of Chinese population also established itself in Colón, although it does not appear that a concentrated area of Chinese business and residence developed (Mon P., 1998: 73; Scarpaci, 1999: Personal Correspondence). In Colón the Chinese community focused largely on commercial activity and few Chinese engaged in professional occupations. In addition, the orientation there was strongly toward the English-speaking American community of the Canal Zone and many Chinese had a better command of English than Spanish (Mon P., 1998: 73).

CONCLUSION

The nations that comprise Latin America and the Caribbean are home to modest populations of Chinese and individuals of Chinese descent. All told, at the beginning of the new millennium, the total population of Chinese in the region is estimated to be about 250,000. Since the 1960s, the Chinese population of the region has shown modest growth. More significant has been the redistribution of the region's Chinese population during the last half of the twentieth century. In the Caribbean and circum-Caribbean, the Chinese population declined appreciably in several countries where large communities had previously existed. These declines were especially notable in Cuba, Jamaica, Guyana, and Trinidad and Tobago. On the other hand, Chinese populations grew in a few countries, most particularly Panama, Brazil, and Argentina. The Chinese population in Peru appears to have increased slightly in the last decades of the century, and the Chinese population in that country continues to be the largest in any single nation in the region.

The number of Chinese immigrants and the resident Chinese population in all Latin American and Caribbean nations has been small, and their percentage of the total population has rarely exceeded 1 percent. However, in some nations, especially in the Caribbean, their impact has far exceeded their limited numbers. In many of these small economies, Chinese filled key niches, especially in small-scale retailing. In Jamaica and Panama for instance, Chinese merchants controlled the local grocery trade in most urban centers. As subsequent generations assimilated, the descendants of early immigrants moved into professional occupations and government service in appreciable numbers.

While Chinese immigrants had the greatest impact in the economic sector, in some countries they were particularly numerous, like Peru, Cuba, and in some Caribbean nations modest Chinese influence can be seen in local culture and landscape. An appreciation of Chinese cuisine and food habits is especially notable. In Peru, hybrid Chinese dishes have become mainstream foods in local restaurants. For instance, a mixed rice, vegetable, and meat dish called *arroz chafu* is eaten in restaurants throughout the country. A range of other Chinese-inspired dishes are common in many Peruvian restaurants including wanton soup, fried wantons, and chicken with tamarind sauce. In the Lima telephone directory listings of Chinese restaurants occupy three of the five pages devoted to restaurants. It is estimated that there are over 2,000 Chinese restaurants, or *chifas,* as they are known nationally, in Peru (Anon., 1999: a2). In Cuba the Chinese presence has had some impact on the local cuisine. The cultivation of several common vegetables, notably string beans and cucumbers, as well as several trees, including the Chinese gunip-tree and the Chinese cinnamon-tree can be traced to their introduction by the Chinese (Guanche Pérez, 1999). In both Cuba and Puerto Rico the orange is commonly known as a *"china"* supposedly referring to the origin of the fruit. Chinese surnames, although not common, survive in appreciable numbers in several countries due to the patronymic naming practices and the preponderance of males among Chinese immigrants. This is probably most notable in Peru and Panama. However, the widespread acculturation of Chinese has meant that while Chinese surnames survive, first names are almost always of Spanish origin—José, Joaquin, or Alfredo for instance (Olien, 1973: 135–136). Indeed, because of assimilation it is probably not correct to speak of the region's Chinese population, but rather its Hispano-Chinese and Anglo-Chinese populations.

While significant Chinese immigration into Latin America in the future does not seem likely, except with the possible caveat of Brazil, there are two factors which will continue to bring some Chinese into the region. Latin America has become an intermediate staging area for illegal Chinese immigration into the U.S. and Canada. Although large numbers of Chinese have immigrated to the U.S. and Canada during the last 50 years, these immigration flows have favored those with wealth and education. As a consequence poorer and less educated Chinese have been drawn to countries in the hemisphere where the barriers to entry are low and from which they can attempt entry into the U.S. and Canada. Lausent-Herrera (1994: 318) has suggested that Peru and Bolivia may serve as intermediate stops for Chinese immigrants who subsequently move northward. There is considerable evidence that Panama has served as a key port of entry for Chinese immigrants whose ultimate goal was to reach the U.S. Recently the U.S. government accused Panamanian government officials of selling hundreds, perhaps even thousands of visas for up to $15,000 each to Chinese nationals who sought to enter the U.S. via Mexico (Marquis and Garvin, 1999). Northern Mexico, particularly Baja California and the Tijuana region has been used since the 1880s by smugglers as an entrepôt for illegal Chinese immigrants attempting entry into the U.S. (Proffitt, 1994: 267–268).

Taiwan's efforts to preserve official diplomatic relations with at least some nations in the world in the face of intense political and diplomatic pressure from China have contributed to a modest "ethnic" Chinese presence in a few Latin American and Caribbean countries. Taiwan's efforts have focused on small nations in Central America and the Caribbean that for a variety of reasons have never established diplomatic relations with China. Using a variety of economic incentives, Taiwan has sought to preserve its diplomatic relations with these nations. Direct government-to-government economic assistance has provided a key means of advancing Taiwan's political agenda (Cheng, 1992). Taiwan has also committed to providing a variety of funding to support regional development in Central America including financing most of a $300 million regional development loan to the Central American Bank for Regional Integration, and funding to rehabilitate the Inter-American Highway in Central America (EcoCentral, 1997). Taiwan's entrepreneurs have also moved into Central America, notably El Salvador and Costa Rica, where they have set up high-tech assembly facilities and other businesses employing local labor (EcoCentral, 1997; Quinones, 1998). However, it is unlikely these endeavors will result in any appreciable increase in Chinese population.

REFERENCES

Anon. 1999. "En todo el país existen más de dos mil chifas," *El Comercio* 15 August, A2.

Baker, Christopher P. 1997. *Cuba Handbook,* Chico, CA: Moon Publications.

Benavides, Maria A. 1999. "Chinese Immigrants in Brazil," unpublished manuscript.

Biesanz, John and Mavis Biesanz. 1955. *The People of Panama,* New York: Columbia University Press.

Chang, Sen-dou. 1968. "The Distribution and Occupations of Overseas Chinese," *Geographical Review,* 58(1): 89–107.

Chao, Alfonso Chiu. 1999. Personal communication with the director of *Kwong Wa Po.*, a local Chinese newspaper. December 8, Havana.

Cheng, Tuan Y. 1992. "Foreign Aid in ROC diplomacy," *Issues and Studies: A Journal of Chinese Studies and International Affairs,* 28(9): 67–84.

Chou, Diego L. 1999. "La imigración de los chinos a Chile, 1900–1930," paper presented at "Chinese Diaspora in Latin America and the Caribbean" conference, December 10–12, Havana, Cuba.

Commission on Overseas Chinese Affairs. 1997. *Overseas Chinese Economy Yearbook,* Taipei, Taiwan.

Crawford, Marlene Kwok. 1989. *Scenes from the History of the Chinese in Guyana,* Georgetown, Guyana.

Curtis, James R. 1995. "Mexicali's Chinatown," *Geographical Review,* 85(3): 335–348.

Dobyns, Henry F., and Paul L. Doughty. 1976. *Peru: A Cultural History,* New York: Oxford University Press.

EcoCentral: Central American Economy. 1997. "Taiwan Signs New Economic Accords with Central America," *EcoCentral: Central American Economy.* Information Access Company.

Elias, Jose Maria. 1970. "Introducao ao estudo da imigracao chinesa," *Anais do Museu Paulista,* 24: 55–100.

Fung, Abel Way Man. 1999. Personal Communication. Editor, *Kwong Wah Po.* Havana, Cuba, 9 December.

Grimes, Barbara, ed. 1996. *Ethnologue,* 13th ed. Summer Institute of Linguistics, http://www.sil.org/ethnologue/countries/Chin.html#CHN.

Guanche Pérez, Jesus. 1999. *The Chinese Presence in Cuba.* Havana: Grupo Promotor del Barrio Chino de la Habana.

He, Li. 1990. "Chinese Immigrants in Peru," *Ibero-Americana, Nordic Journal of Latin American Studies,* 20(2): 3–16.

Ho Ming Chung. 1967a. *Milu Huaqiao shouce* (The Manual of the Overseas Chinese in Peru), Taipei.

————. 1967b. *Nanmei guojioa ji Huaqiao shiye jianje* (Overseas Chinese Enterprises in South America), Taipei.

Hu-DeHart, Evelyn. 1999. "Spanish America," in Lynn Pan, ed., *The Encyclopedia of Chinese Overseas*, Cambridge, MA: Harvard University Press, 254–260.

Kaplan, Irving, Howard I. Blutstein, Kathryn Therese Johnston, and David S. Mc-Morris. 1976. *Area Handbook for Jamaica*, Washington, D.C.: GPO.

Lausent, Isabelle. 1983. *Pequeña propiedad, poder y economia de mercado: Arcos, valle de Chancay*, Lima: Instituto de Estudios Peruanos y Instituto Frances de Estudios Andinos.

Lausent-Herrera, Isabelle. 1994. "Lima: au coeur de la ville, le quartier chinois," *Problèmes de Amérique Latine*, 14: 311–319.

Lee, Russell. 1998. "The Chinese Retail Grocery Trade in Jamaica," in Wang Ling-chi and Wang Gungwu *The Chinese Diaspora: Selected Essays, Volume II*, Singapore: Times Academic Press, 112–130.

Leon Azofeila, Moises Guillermo. 1987. *Chinese Immigrants on the Atlantic Coast of Costa Rica: The Economic Adaptation of an Asian Minority in a Pluralistic Society*, unpublished Ph.D. dissertation, Tulane University.

León, Julio A. and René León, 1975. *Requiem por el Chinatown de la Habana*, United States: s.n.

Look Lai, Walton. 1999. "The Caribbean," in Lynn Pan, ed., *The Encyclopedia of Chinese Overseas*, Cambridge, MA: Harvard University Press, 248–253.

Marquis, Christopher and Glenn Garvin. 1999. "U.S. Accuses Panama of Running Visa Scam," *Akron Beacon Journal*, 2 September, A15.

Méndez Campos, Marco. 1999. "El barrio Chino renueva sus pistas y veredas y cambia de ornamentación," *El Comercio* (Lima, Peru), 15 August, A2.

Millett, Trevor M. 1993. *The Chinese in Trinidad*, Port of Spain, Trinidad: An Inprint Publication.

Mon P., Ramon Arturo. 1998. "The Latest Wave of Chinese Immigration in Panama, 1985–1992: Legal Entry and Adaptation Problems," in Wang Ling-chi and Wang Gungwu, ed., *The Chinese Diaspora: Selected Essays, Volume II*, Singapore: Times Academic Press, 72–77.

Olein, Michael D. 1973. *Latin Americans: Contemporary Peoples and Their Cultural Traditions*, New York: Holt, Rinehart, and Winston.

Poston, Dudley L., Jr., Michael Xinxiang Mao, and Mei-Yu Yu. 1994. "The Global Distribution of the Overseas Chinese around 1990," *Population and Development Review*, 20(3): 631–645.

Proffitt, T. D., III. 1994. *Tijuana: The History of a Mexican Metropolis*. San Diego, CA: San Diego State University.

Quan, Adan. 1999. "Chinese in El Salvador," paper presented at "Chinese Diaspora in Latin American and the Caribbean," December 10–12, Havana, Cuba.

Quinones, Sam. 1998. "Central American Tiger," *World Trade Magazine*, 11(3): 36–38.

Sánchez-Crispin, Alvaro. 1999. Personal Correspondence, 20 September.

Scarpaci, Joseph L. 1999. Personal Correspondence, 17 September.

Wang, Hongqiang. 1999. Personal Communication. First Secretary, Chinese Embassy, Havana, Cuba. 9 December.

II

HONG KONG AND TAIWAN AS DIASPORIC HOMELANDS

6

Identity, Mobility, and the Making of the Chinese Diasporic Landscape in Hong Kong

George C. S. Lin

One of the most important issues brought out in recent debates over globalization and transnationalism has been the changing interrelationship between identity and mobility of international migrants. Whereas one major line of inquiry in migration studies has focused on how migrants of different social, spatial, and gender identities have different interpretations of places and therefore have made migration decisions differently, a recent alternative intellectual current is to see identity as being embedded in mobility rather than locality. This new interpretation has been derived in part from the ongoing processes of globalization through which diaspora capitalists are believed to have developed an independent "third culture" (Featherstone, 1990) and given rise to dislocated "global tribes" (Kotkin, 1993) that transcend their places of origin and settlement. The transnational movement of the Chinese has been used as a prime example to illustrate this reinterpreted relationship between identity and mobility.

In the literature on Chinese diaspora, there is an established tradition to document the importance of place-based identity in social organization, network building, and residential segregation of Chinese overseas (Wang, 1991; Wickberg, 1994; Skinner, 1957; Coughlin, 1960; Lim and Gosling, 1983; Hamilton, 1977; Cheng, 1985; Honig, 1996). Early Chinese immigrants in Southeast Asia and North America were socially organized on the basis of voluntary associations such as *huiguan* (clan or place association) and *tongxianghui* (same native-place association). These organizations are based on locality (same native place), kinship (same surname), and dialect which played a major role not only in the initial settlement of the Chinese immigrants but also the formation of business networks (Woon, 1989; Faure and Siu, 1995; Sinn, 1997). Recent research on transnationalism, discussed by Ma in the introductory chapter of this volume,[1] shows that Chinese diasporans have managed to build effective transnational business networks that stretch from their place of origin (*jia-xiang* or *laojia*) to their place of settlement (Lever-Tracy, Ip, and Tracy, 1996; Smart and Smart, 1998), and thus meet the challenges of globalization (Woon, 1990; Liu, 1998). In some cases, "old linkages" based on place of origin, kinship, and dialect have been remade into "new business networks" (Ma, this volume; Leung, 1993; Yang, 1994; Mitchell, 1995; Hsing, 1997; Lin, 1997; Yeung, 1998). These studies suggest that processes of globalization have not undermined the role of place-based identity in the transnational movement of people and capital. On the contrary, globalization has in diverse contexts propelled a return to the local and reinforced "primordial attachments" that are instrumental to the global mobility of the Chinese and the formation of diasporas as spatial systems and networks (Geertz, 1973: 259; Kearney, 1995: 548; Liu, 1998: 608; Cartier, 1997, 1998).

The importance of understanding place-based identities in facilitating the spatial mobility of diasporic Chinese stands in contrast with a competing interpretation that has centered on the notions of deterritorialization, dislocation, and displacement. Citing the work of David Harvey (1989) on flexible strategies of accumulation and time-space compression, some researchers working on Chinese transnationalism have argued that, as a result of deterritorialization and spatial displacement, identities are no longer tied to cultural or national space and mobility is not shaped by place-based identity. Some even contend that it is the other way around. Liu (1997), for instance, argues that the integration of China into the global economy has opened up great opportunities for Chinese nationals to travel at home and abroad. Increased mobility, particularly the ease of international travel, has been a crucial means by which new cultural knowledge is gained, new spatial images and meanings are generated, and new cultural or national identities are formed. In a similar manner, Mayfair Yang (1997) highlighted the effect of transnational mass media in transcending local boundaries and suggested that increased mobility has become the means through which the social reproduction of cultural and national identities is carried out.

These viewpoints are summarized bluntly by Ong and Nonini (1997) who maintain that the identities of Chinese transnationalists are "diaspora based rather than land-based" (Ong and Nonini, 1997: 326). Identity is reinterpreted "as a politics rather than as an inheritance, as fluidity rather than fixity, as based on mobility rather than locality, and as the playing out of these oppositions across the world" (Ong and Nonini, 1997: 327). In this perspective, identity is not an identifiable symbol shared among members of bounded communities. Identity formation is understood as ongoing processes of construction, negotiation, and transformation. Instead of being an independent force capable of shaping mobility, identity is described as being embedded in and constantly reworked through mobility (Lowenthal, 1985; Silvey and Lawson, 1999).

These competing interpretations point to the complex nature of the issues at stake and raise questions important to the understanding of the interrelationship between identity and mobility. In what ways is identity formation a place-based or placeless phenomenon? How are identity and mobility interrelated? What are the geographical implications of the interplay between them? How has the changing relationship between identity and mobility shaped the geography of the Chinese diaspora? This chapter attempts to engage in the ongoing discussions by presenting data on Hong Kong immigration and settlements in an ethno-linguistic framework.

With its central position in the global movement of Chinese people, Hong Kong represents an important case for analyzing issues concerning the complex interrelationship between identity and mobility. Based on an analysis of historical and spatial data, this study attempts to investigate the changing relationship between identity and mobility concerning Chinese migration to and from Hong Kong. The purposes are to identify the forces propelling high mobility of Chinese people to and from Hong Kong and to uncover the diasporic landscape created by the Hong Kong settlers with diverse ethno-linguistic backgrounds and identities.

DATA AND METHODOLOGY

Before the case of Hong Kong is analyzed and presented, several important concepts require clarification. The diverse meanings of "overseas Chinese," "Chinese diaspora," and "Chinese sojourners" have been widely discussed and debated (Wang, 1991; Wang and Wong, 1997; Clifford, 1994; Helmreich, 1992; Cohen, 1997; Skeldon, 1994). In this study, the term "Chinese diaspora" is used to describe the historical migration out of mainland China. The term "Chinese overseas" is used to include ethnic Chinese living outside the People's Republic of China and Taiwan. Hong Kong and Macao were not considered to be part of the PRC before 1997 and 1999 respectively (Poston, Mao, and Yu, 1994: 631). For the term "mobility," this study follows the earlier work of Zelinsky (1971) and Skeldon (1990) and sees it as a concept to signify all types of population movement. No distinction is made between long-term and short-term or temporary and permanent population movement. The emphasis in this chapter is on international or cross-border movement of the Chinese. Finally, I use the term "identity" to refer to how people regard themselves and are regarded by others. The Chinese equivalent of the term is *rentong* which literally means "to identify that which is the same" (Wang, 1991: 216). Identity has multiple levels and is changeable depending on various circumstances, including forms of national identity, cultural identity, ethnic identity, and class identity. For the Chinese diaspora, shared social identities can be based on the same surname, occupation, political faction, language/dialect, or place of origin. This study focuses on native-place identity, which has been generally considered an important element of sub-ethnic identity (Wang, 1991; Cohen, 1968; Sparks, 1976; Blake, 1981; Honig, 1996; Guldin, 1997).

Analysis of native-place identities among the Hong Kong population is not an easy task. In the Hong Kong census reports, native place is indicated by place of birth, place of origin, and/or the usual language spoken at home. These three different indices should be taken with caution although they are closely interrelated and have sometimes been used interchangeably. For instance, the place of origin, known as *jiguan* in Chinese, refers to the ancestral home of a Chinese migrant and may not be the same as the place of birth. One could be born in Hong Kong but his/her place of origin could be somewhere else on the Chinese mainland. In a similar manner, the usual language spoken at home may or may not be consistent with the place of birth and place of origin. It is not uncommon for immigrants whose place of birth and place of origin is Shanghai or Fujian to speak Cantonese at home because their children insist on speaking Cantonese. The discrepancy between the three indicators should be small at the early stage of migration when immigrants first arrived in Hong Kong and should increase as time goes on. Which one, then, is the most appropriate approximation of the native place of the population? Typically, place of origin is the leading pivot of identity for migrants. However, this index is not unproblematic in the current situation. To many people who were born in Hong Kong and speak the local language (Cantonese), having a place of origin in Shanghai or Fujian does not necessarily give them a meaningful identity.

This study follows the existing studies on Chinese (sub)ethnicity and uses the usual language spoken at home as an approximate indicator of native place. The analysis is based on the census conducted in 1961 and 1996. The 1961 census, the first census conducted in Hong Kong after World War II, is the earliest census that can reveal the spatial distribution of the Hong Kong population. It captures the massive influx of migrants fleeing the Chinese mainland when the Communists were taking over the nation in 1949. The 1996 census, on the other hand, provides the most updated systematic data available. It is acknowledged that the usual language spoken at home is not a perfect indicator of native place. It should be noted, however, that in 1981 the Hong Kong government ended inquiry on place of origin and retained only the usual languages spoken at home in the census. Choosing the usual languages spoken at home as an indicator allows not only a comparative assessment of the changing situations over time but also a better reference with the existing literature on Chinese (sub)ethnicity. Moreover, the discrepancy between usual language spoken at home and place of origin or place of birth should be small for 1961 when the settlement of immigrants from the mainland was at an early stage.

The balance of this chapter has three parts. It begins with an integrated historical and geographical perspective about Hong Kong as a place of origin and destination for the Chinese diaspora. This is followed by an analysis of the changing spatial distribution of the Hong Kong population according to their different ethno-linguistic backgrounds. The last part links the case of Hong Kong with the transnationalism literature and addresses the implications of this case study.

RELUCTANT EXILES OR VOLUNTARY MULTINATIONALS?

From its inception, Hong Kong has been a society predominantly made up of immigrants. An overwhelming majority of the Hong Kong population has come from China's mainland, particularly Guangdong Province. When the British first occupied Hong Kong in 1841, there were only a few thousand people there. Population had grown quickly after the territory was ceded to Britain in 1842 and most of the population influx had been immigrants. When the first population census was conducted in 1881, only 3,668 people, or 4 percent of those who responded to the survey, considered Hong Kong their home. Over 95 percent of the population were from Guangdong Province (Hong Kong, Registrar General's Office, 1881: 4). One hundred years later, the dominance of immigrants in Hong Kong's population has remained unchanged although the total population increased substantially from 113,462 in 1881 to 4.98 million in 1981. In the 1981 census, people who considered Hong Kong their place of origin accounted for less than 3 percent of the total. An overwhelming majority (95 percent) of people were from the mainland, particularly Guangdong Province (86 percent).

Chinese immigration into Hong Kong has not been a simple onetime and one-way movement. There had been much migration back and forth across the border between Hong Kong and the mainland up to 1984, when effective border control was put in place by both sides for political considerations.[2] Large-scale immigration from the mainland often took place when China suffered from natural catastrophes, wars, and domestic turmoil. This pattern of migration has given rise to the notion that the Hong Kong population is substantially made up of "refugees" or "exiles" from the mainland (Skeldon, 1994: 8). Prior to 1997, Hong Kong under British rule had indeed functioned as a major receiving point for Chinese out-migration.

Not only has Hong Kong been a major destination for emigrants from the mainland, it has also been a major place of origin of Chinese moving to Southeast Asia, Europe, and North America. In the early twentieth century when Chinese immigration to the English-speaking countries was effectively restricted by government policies, Hong Kong served as a transshipment point for Chinese emigrants going to Southeast Asia. After the 1960s when the U.S. and commonwealth countries relaxed their limitation on Chinese immigrants, Hong Kong became one of the main sources of immigrants to North America, Australia, and New Zealand. Figure 6.1 depicts the growth of out-migration since 1970 using the data based on "place of last permanent residence." The volume of out-migration from Hong Kong was not significant during the 1970s, possibly because the takeoff of this newly industrializing economy had created a favorable social and economic environment at home. When compared with the Chinese of the mainland, Taiwan, and Southeast Asia, however, Hong Kong people were among the first to take advantage of the relaxation of control over immigration in the U.S., Canada, and Australia (Skeldon, 1994: 29). In two decades, for instance, an estimated 90,548 Chinese immigrants entering the U.S. were from Hong Kong, which exceeded the number of immigrants from China's mainland and Taiwan combined (44,421). The rapid upsurge of emigration took place after the Sino-British Joint Declaration was signed in 1984. It took about two years for the political event to manifest in emigration. After 1986, the volume of emigrants shot up quite dramatically and reached its climax in 1994. The main destination of Hong Kong emigrants was Canada, followed by the United States and Australia.

Hong Kong remained the main source of Chinese immigrants to Canada and Australia until the mid-1990s, when immigrants from the mainland increased. As for the U.S., Hong Kong used to be a main source of Chinese immigrants in the 1960s and the 1970s. Since the 1980s, however, Hong Kong has lost its leading position possibly because immigration policies in Canada and Australia have been more liberal than those in the U.S. Until recently, Hong Kong indeed functioned as a main source out-migration to the English-speaking countries (Pan, 1999; Skeldon, 1994).

The wave of Hong Kong emigration in the last decade was driven primarily by a fear of political instability caused by the transfer of Hong Kong from Britain to Chinese rule in 1997. Out-migration from Hong Kong bears significant resemblance to the movement of people who fled their homeland before the Communists took over China in 1949. Whereas early Chinese migrants in Hong Kong were known as "refugees" or "exiles," recent out-migrants from

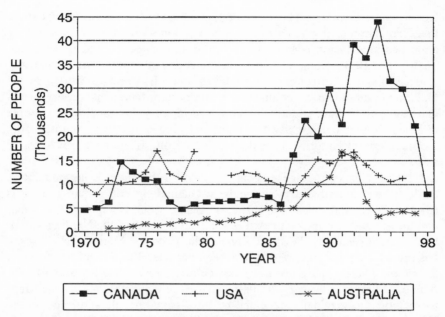

Figure 6.1. Hong Kong's Emigration by Major Destinations, 1970–1998 (Sources: Skelton [1994, 28]; OECD [1998, 288]; U.S. Department of Justice, INS [1991, 50; 1997, 30; 1999, 28]; Citizenship and Immigration Canada [1999, digital data].)

Hong Kong have been called "reluctant exiles" abroad (Skeldon, 1994: 8). Implied in this notion is the idea that Hong Kong people were forced to move by undesirable social and political changes in their homeland. This interpretation has stood in contrast with a different view that takes a more sanguine perspective. Known as "diaspora capitalism" or "Chinese transnationalism" (see Lever-Tracy, Ip, and Tracy, 1996; Ong and Nonini, 1997; Smart and Smart, 1998; Mitchell, 1995; Zhou, 1998; and Li, 1998), these alternative perspectives see the Chinese leaving Hong Kong as active players in the world economy capable of creating "global tribes" (Kotkin, 1993) and "global ethnoscapes" (Appadurai, 1991) that stretch from their homeland to the host countries.

The Hong Kong people, past and present, have demonstrated a spatial mobility significantly greater than their counterparts on the mainland and in Taiwan. Indeed, great spatial mobility, adaptability, and flexibility have been identified by many anthropologists and sociologists as important characteristics of the "Hong Kong man" or "Hongkongese" (Baker, 1983; Wong, 1986; Lau and Kuan, 1988; Wang and Wong, 1997; Evans and Tam, 1997). The factors contributing to the great spatial mobility of the Hong

Kong people are many. They include the gateway location of the city state, its colonial connections and frequent interaction with the English-speaking countries, possession of necessary capital and/or technological skills that qualify the Hong Kong people to be independent immigrants, and traditional linkages with those ethnic Chinese who had already settled in the U.S. and commonwealth countries. One important factor that deserves special attention is the distinctive place-based identity that most of the people of Hong Kong had originally developed in China before they migrated from the mainland to Hong Kong and later from Hong Kong to North America and Australia.

Like the diasporic Chinese generally, most of the Hong Kong population came from southern China, particularly Guangdong and Fujian Provinces (Faure, Hayes, and Birch, 1984; Ng and Baker, 1983; Johnson, 1996). Geographically, this is a region known as Lingnan or south of the Nanling Mountains, which separates the Pearl River Delta from the Yangzi Delta region. Historically, the Lingnan region had been peripheral to the culture cores of the nation. The Yangshao and Longshan cultures, the two earliest and most influential Chinese cultures, were both centered in the distant north. The Lingnan region was originally inhabited by the Nanyue people and ruled by the Nanyue Kingdom (203–111 B.C.). The region was forcibly incorporated into the Qin empire during the southern expansion of the dynasty. This military invasion was followed by a mass migration of people from the north to subjugate the local people. Most of the migrants from the north were "not the cream of the crop but deportees, criminals, and escapees" who were sent to the south because it was used "as an oubliette for China's undesirables" (Lary, 1996: 8). Eventually, the Nanyue people were sinicized by the Chinese from the north. However, they have maintained their own spoken languages and a way of life significantly different from the population elsewhere in the nation. Cantonese speakers in Guangdong Province, for instance, made up less than 4 percent of the total Chinese population. This is in contrast with the Mandarin speakers who have accounted for over 64 percent of the entire nation (Wurm and Li, 1987: A1). Despite their popularity in Hong Kong and the overseas Chinese communities, Cantonese food and opera are a distinct minority in the country. This marginal cultural and ethnographic identity, combined with the peripheral location of the region, has given rise to a great sensitivity to social and political change in the heartland of the nation and a tradition of sojourning or "refugee mentality." This special ethno-linguistic identity of the southern Chinese also explains why the diaspora Chinese including those in Hong Kong have often demonstrated a strong emotional attachment more to their native place or their ancestral home in southern China than to a vague and apathetic national entity like "China."

Ethno-linguistic status is only one aspect of the place-based identity of the Hong Kong people who came from southern China. Other aspects that have significant mobility implications include easy access to countries overseas and a strong tradition of doing business and international trade. Although the Lingnan region is far from the culture cores of the nation in the north, it has enjoyed an externally oriented location characterized by its geographic proximity and easy accessibility to Europe, Southeast Asia, and many countries overseas. For this reason, Guangzhou (Canton) was one of the earliest port cities to become established in the south even before Shanghai and many other port cities were developed on the eastern coast (Lin, 1997: 63). Guangzhou was also China's first port city reached by Europeans, the Portuguese in 1516, and by the Americans in 1784. When the China coast was closed in 1757 for defense reasons, Guangzhou was the only port city that remained open for trading with the outside world. In the recent past, when the Maoist ideology of anti-commercialism was sweeping across China, Guangzhou was selected as the site to host the biannual national export fairs in the early 1970s, a function that continues to exist today. Whereas Guangzhou has been the key city with strong business linkages with overseas places, the tradition of international trade has also been strong in the Lingnan region in general (Cartier, 2001). This distinct place-based identity with business and overseas orientations has undoubtedly found its way to Hong Kong and shaped the spirit of entrepreneurship of the people, whose places of origins are primarily in southern China. This special identity is one of the root-causes of transnationalism which has characterized the migrants from Hong Kong who have played an active role in the formation of the Chinese "global tribes."

THE MAKING OF THE DIASPORIC LANDSCAPE

The importance of place-based identity in shaping the mobility of the Hong Kong people has been highlighted in the existing literature (Baker, 1983; Pan, 1991; Wong, 1992; Skeldon, 1994; Cohen, 1997; Mathews and Lui, 2001). Yet studies of the dynamics of identify formation and its relations with social and spatial mobility of the Hongkongers have tended to focus on processes with little attention paid to geographical patterns (Skinner, 1957; Sparks, 1976; Blake, 1981; Guldin, 1997; Mathews and Lui, 2001). Without necessary knowledge about key geographical patterns of migration and settlements, however, it becomes ambiguous and elusive to describe and interpret the sophisticated processes of identity formation and its cause-effect relationships with mobility, both socially and geographically. Analyses of Hong Kong identity has concentrated on the special characteristics of the "Hong Kong man" or "Hongkongese" as a uniform group of people different from either the Chinese on the mainland or westerners. The following section examines the spatial distribution of different speech groups in Hong Kong as a means to explore how place-based identity has shaped the geography of Chinese diaspora in the territory.

To assess the spatial implications of native-place identity, the chapter next presents systematic census data on major speech groups in Hong Kong for 1961 and 1996. The 1961 census identified a total of seven ethno-linguistic groups. It is not surprising that Cantonese speakers accounted for the majority (79 percent) of the total population. Most of the Cantonese speakers were either born in Hong Kong or immigrated from the central or western part of Guangdong. The second largest speech group was known locally as the Hoklo, who speak dialects belonging to the Min linguistic group and account for about 6 percent of the total population. The geographic origins of the Hoklo are primarily in the coastal areas of southern China, including the Chaozhou area in eastern Guangdong, the Leizhou Peninsula in western Guangdong, the Xiamen-Zhangzhou area in eastern Fujian, Hainan Island, and Taiwan. The "boat people," locally known as the Tanka, were also included in the Hoklo group. It should be noted that the term Hoklo has never been used by people of this linguistic group to refer to themselves. Just as the term *guailou* has been used by the local people to refer to westerners, Hoklo is a product of Cantonese chauvinism, a term created by the Cantonese to identify a group of minority people who are not considered part of them (Sparks, 1976; Guldin, 1997). It is probably for this reason that the Census Department has since 1991 abandoned the term and changed it into two more specific and "neutral" categories of Chaozhou and Fujian people. The next largest group was the Kejia (Hakka) group, which accounted for about 5 percent. Kejia literally means "guest" or "visitor"; the Kejia people in Hong Kong were originally from Bao'an County across the border and have traditionally lived in the mountainous areas of the New Territories (Ng and Baker, 1983; Faure, Hayes, and Birch, 1984; Johnson, 1996). Other linguistic groups included the Siyi group (essentially a branch of the Cantonese), the Shanghainese, Mandarin, and English speakers.

The spatial distribution of the major speech groups in Hong Kong is mapped and displayed in Figures 6.2a and 6.2b, using standard deviation as a means of analysis. Among the seven speech groups, the Cantonese is the only one that demonstrated a relatively even distribution across the territory. This can be illustrated by its coefficient of variance (0.21), which is the smallest among the seven groups. As a dominant ethno-linguistic group,

Cantonese speakers represented the majority of the population in almost all districts in 1961. They were especially visible in the downtown areas such as Central, Wan Chai on Hong Kong Island, and Yau Ma Tei in Kowloon. There were three noticeable exceptions, however. In the three districts of the Peak, Sai Kung, and Tai Po, the proportion of Cantonese speakers was abnormally low. The Peak has traditionally been one of the most prestigious residential areas in Hong Kong, reserved for the elite until the 1970s. Considering the colonial history of Hong Kong, it is understandable that local Cantonese speakers were unable to "monopolize" the privilege of living in the Peak and had to share the locale with other elite groups such as the English-speaking people and the Shanghainese. The other two exceptional areas (Sai Kung and Tai Po) are both located in the less-developed New Territories and are occupied primarily by the Kejia people, who traditionally have been connected with agricultural activities (Cohen, 1968; Blake, 1981).

In sharp contrast to the even distribution of the Cantonese, the English-speaking population had high representation in a few selected areas, namely the Peak, Mid-Levels and Pok Fu Lam, and the South, all prestigious locales on Hong Kong Island. The uneven distribution of the English-speaking population is demonstrated by its coefficient of variance (2.40), which is the highest among the seven speech groups. While the English-speaking people were concentrated in a few selected places on Hong Kong Island, they accounted for a very small proportion in most places in the New Territories. Apparently, the English-speaking population did not seem to be interested in living in the less developed New Territories, which was leased to Britain in 1898 for 99 years. The only area in the New Territories that showed high representation of English speakers was a locale known as Kamtin, which served as the British garrison at the time. In a similar manner but for a different reason, the Shanghainese were more visible in several selected areas, particularly Tsuen Wan, Tsim Sha Tsui, the Peak, and North Point. The selected residential preference of the Shanghainese has to be understood against the historical context. Historically, most of the Shanghainese immigrated to Hong Kong around 1949 to flee the Communist takeover of the mainland. A significant proportion of Shanghainese immigrants were industrial entrepreneurs who brought with them capital and technology (Wong, 1988). Many of the Shanghai industrialists had set up textile factories in Tsuen Wan and North Point where cheap land and labor as well as good transport infrastructure were readily available for development (Wong, 1988; Hayes, 1993; Johnson, 1996). Some of the elite Shanghainese who brought with them sizable capital had taken up residence in such prestigious areas as the Peak and Tsim Sha Tsui.

152   *George C. S. Lin*

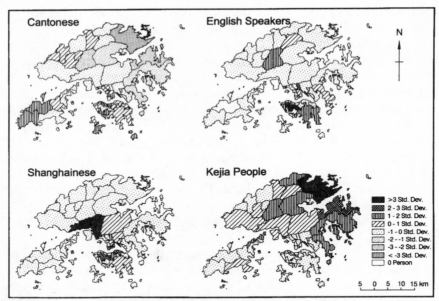

Figure 6.2a. Spatial Distribution of Major Speech-groups in Hong Kong,1961 (Source: Hong Kong, Census and Statistics Department, 1962: 40–42.)

While the English and Shanghainese had occupied most of the prestigious and urbanized locales on Hong Kong Island, the indigenous Kejia people were largely found in the countryside of the New Territories. They were hardly visible in either Hong Kong or Kowloon but they had a large representation in nearly all districts in the New Territories. In the border region (the North) and some fishing areas of the east (Taipo and Sai Kung), the Kejia people had a share of the local population higher than any other speech group.

The other three speech groups, namely the Hoklo, Siyi, and Mandarin, simply filled the gaps between the elite English-speaking population and the Shanghainese on the one end and the indigenous Kejia people on the other. The Hoklo, which included the boat people (Tanka) and those originated from Fujian and Chaozhou, had significant representation in Kwun Tong, Kowloon City, and the northern part of Lamma Island. Among the districts on Hong Kong Island, only two places (North Point and the Western District) displayed a concentration of the Hoklo population. The Western District has traditionally been the area where the Chaozhou people clustered to engage in the Nam-Pak-Hong wholesale business of such commodities as rice, Chinese herbs, salt fish, and dry groceries (Leeming, 1977: 46). North Point, on the other hand, is located on the immediate outskirts of the commercial center (Causeway Bay) and has long been favored by the Fujian immigrants. In a similar manner, the Siyi people tended to be clustered in a few locales in western Kowloon particularly in Sham Shui Po. The Mandarin speakers, who came from either the mainland or Taiwan and had the smallest share of the population in most of the districts, were spatially dispersed. The only area that showed a high visibility of the Mandarin speakers was Kwun Tong, a new town developed as a part of the resettlement program initiated in the mid-1950s to accommodate the influx of new migrants from the mainland.[3] In a nutshell, the geography of (sub)ethnicity in Hong Kong in 1961 was characterized by a spatial polarization of the elite Cantonese, Shanghainese, and English-speakers on the one end and the indigenous Kejia people on the other. The areas lying between the two ends were selectively taken by other speech groups, who managed to find their ways in a society clearly divided into different classes and in a space segregated according to native-place identity.

The diasporic landscape as identified above has experienced significant transformation over the last three decades since 1961. Figures 6.3a and 6.3b display the spatial distribution of major speech groups according to the most recent census conducted in 1996. A comparison of the data gathered in 1961 and 1996 reveals a clear trend of homogenization. This trend can be illustrated by the increased popularity of Cantonese speakers whose share rose from 78 percent in 1961 to 88 percent in 1996. Geographically, Cantonese speakers

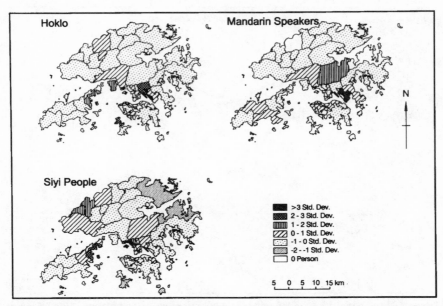

Figure 6.2b. Spatial Distribution of Major Speech-groups in Hong Kong,1961 (Source: Hong Kong, Census and Statistics Department, 1962: 40–42.)

dominate nearly all districts except the Peak; its coefficient of variance dropped from 0.21 in 1961 to 0.15 in 1996. In a similar manner, the English-speaking population had increased proportionally from 1.2 percent in 1961 to 2 percent in 1996 and its coefficient variance declined from 2.4 to 1.58. Mandarin speakers have also become slightly more popular as their share of the population rose from 0.9 to 1.1 percent. By comparison, other minority ethno-linguistic groups such as the Chaozhou, Fujian, Siyi, and Kejia have shown a reduction in their shares of the total population. The coefficients of variance for these minority groups have slightly increased, however, suggesting that these people are now concentrated in fewer locales, while the Cantonese group has consolidated its dominance in the territory at the cost of other minority speech groups.

Although the general population has been homogenized linguistically and socially, the legacy of the diasporic landscape developed earlier has remained visible. The English-speaking population, for instance, still enjoys the privilege of living in the Peak and the South including Repulse Bay and Stanley. The locational preference of the Shanghainese towards Tsim Sha Tsui, Tsuen Wan, the Peak, and North Point remains noticeable in the map for 1996. For the Kejia people, the prime location of residence is still the New Territories

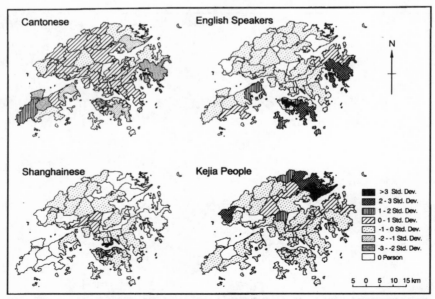

Figure 6.3a. Spatial Distribution of Major Speech-groups in Hong Kong, 1996 (Source: Compiled from digital data provided by Hong Kong, Census and Statistics Department, 1999.)

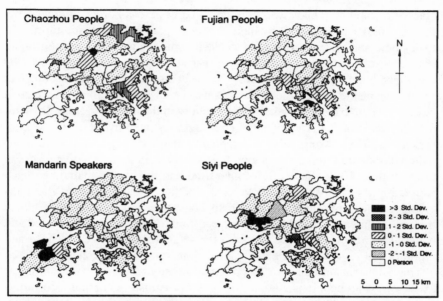

Figure 6.3b. **Spatial Distribution of Major Speech-groups in Hong Kong, 1996 (Source: Compiled from digital data provided by Hong Kong, Census and Statistics Department, 1999.)**

except that their share of the total population has been reduced and that they are now visible in fewer places than before. In a similar manner, the Fujian and Chaozhou people have displayed a spatial pattern consistent with the one for the Hoklo as identified earlier for 1961. Those from Fujian tended to be concentrated in North Point and the Chaozhou people are largely found in the Western District of Hong Kong Island and Kwun Tong and Kowloon City in Kowloon. The ongoing homogenization process, therefore, has not completely wiped out the contour of the diasporic landscape that was developed earlier on the basis of ethno-linguistic identity.

CONCLUSION

Hong Kong as a hub of international migration for the Chinese has been subject to the growing influence of both the Chinese mainland and the English-speaking world. With its colonial connections and strategic location, Hong Kong has served as both a major place of origin and destination for the Chinese going overseas. The remarkable tendency for the Hong Kong people to move internationally, due in part to their "refugee mentality," has existed ever since the colonial enclave was formed. Whereas cross-border migration before the 1970s was spurred by natural catastrophes and domestic turmoil in their homeland, recent emigration to North America and the commonwealth countries was triggered primarily by a fear of political instability caused by the impending transfer of Hong Kong from British to Chinese rule. The great sensitivity of the Hong Kong people toward social and economic change is closely related to their marginal ethnic identity in the nation. In a similar manner, the remarkable entrepreneurial spirit demonstrated by the diaspora capitalists from Hong Kong today is inseparable from the commercial and international trade tradition that has long been established in their native places in South China. While the nature of data used and the macro-spatial approach adopted in this study do not allow an evaluation of the contention that individual Chinese migrants were able to constitute and transform identities through global mobility, this study instead foregrounds a more grounded and material approach for future work on the relationship between identity and mobility and its spatial and geographical contexts in Hong Kong.

The persistent influence of place-based identity in the global mobility of the Hong Kong people is evident not only in the historical patterns of international migration but also in the diasporic landscape evolved in Hong Kong over the past century. The mixture of immigrants from various parts of the mainland resulted in an uneven diasporic landscape in Hong Kong in the early 1960s. Whereas the central and prestigious locales were monopolized by the elite English, Shanghainese, and Cantonese speakers, most of the indigenous Kejia people were relegated to the peripheral areas in the New Territories. The intermediate locales were occupied by other minority speech groups such as those who came from Fujian Province or the Chaozhou region in eastern Guangdong. The public housing program of the 1960s and new town development of the 1970s stirred up the "melting pot" and significantly facilitated the homogenization of Hong Kong citizens. However, the legacy of the diasporic landscape created earlier has remained visible.

The case of Hong Kong suggests the complex nature and multiple facets of interrelationship between identity and mobility in Chinese migration. Literature on transnationalism has strongly suggested that Chinese diaspora capitalists, as active agents of globalization, have been able to constitute, negotiate, and transform their identities through the capital's global mobility (Ong and Nonini 1997; Lever-Tracy, Ip, and Tracy 1996; Smart and Smart 1998). But the increased global mobility of diasporans and capital has not been devoid of the effect of place-based identity, despite ongoing processes of deterritorization and displacement. As this study has demonstrated, the great mobility of the Chinese in Hong Kong and the diasporic landscape they have created therein have been shaped by place-based ethno-linguistic identities.

Other empirical studies have also revealed that much of Hong Kong's capital investment in the Pearl River Delta has actually taken place in the home towns of Hong Kong's investors (Vogel, 1989: 176; Lin, 1997: 174). On the other edge of the Pacific, Chinese diaspora capitalists from Hong Kong, Taiwan, and Southeast Asia have established "bamboo networks" on the basis of place-based ethnic identities (Mitchell, 1995; Zhou, 1998; Li, 1998). The global mobility of Chinese diasporans is thus not simply an independent process through which identities are formed and transformed. Rather, increased global mobility of the Chinese has been based on and facilitated by pre-existing, place-specific identities. The case of Hong Kong further illustrates the persistent importance of locality in social and landscape formation in the era of globalization.

NOTES

1. The concept of transnationalism has been criticized as too restrictive because social fields that cross national boundaries can be constructed and maintained without emigration. See Smart and Smart (1998: 106).

2. The border between Hong Kong and China's mainland was closed in 1953. However, cross-border migration continued and illegal immigrants who made their way to Hong Kong Island and Kowloon were tolerated under the "touchbase rule" or "reached base rule." This rule was abandoned after September 1980 in the face of massive influx of illegal immigrants from the mainland after China's opening up. It was only after the Sino-British Joint Declaration was signed in 1984 that Hong Kong and the mainland worked together to set up effective border control to dam illegal migration.

3. Kwun Tong was the first industrial town developed by the Hong Kong government in the mid-1950s to accommodate excessive immigrants from mainland China. This development was triggered in part by a devastating fire which took place in slums in Shek Kip Mei on Christmas Eve in 1953. For a detailed discussion, see Lai and Dwyer (1965), Leeming (1977), Castells, Goh, and Kwok (1990), and Yeh (1990).

REFERENCES

Appadurai, Arjun. 1991. "Global Ethnoscapes: Notes and Queries for a Transnational Anthropology," in Richard Fox, ed., *Recapturing Anthropology: Working in the Present,* Santa Fe, NM: School of American Research Press, 191–210.

Baker, H. 1983. "Life in the Cities: The Emergence of Hong Kong Man," *The China Quarterly,* 95: 469–79.

Blake, C. Fred. 1981. *Ethnic Groups and Social Change in a Chinese Market Town,* Honolulu: University of Hawaii Press.

Cartier, Carolyn L. 1997. "The Dead, Place/Space, and Social Activism: Constructing the Nationscape in Historic Melaka," *Environment and Planning D: Society and Space,* 15(5): 555–86

———. 1998. "Preserving Bukit China: The Cultural Politics of Landscape Interpretation in Melaka's Chinese Cemetery," in Elizabeth Sinn, ed., *The Last Half Century of Chinese Overseas,* Hong Kong: Hong Kong University Press, 65–80.

———. 2001. *Globalizing South China,* Oxford: Blackwell.

Castells, M., L. Goh, and R.Y.W. Kwok. 1990. *The Shek Kip Mei Syndrome: Economic Development and Public Housing in Hong Kong and Singapore,* London: Pion.

Cheng, Lim-Keak. 1985. *Social Change and the Chinese in Singapore: A Social Economic Geography with Special Reference to Bang Structure,* Singapore: Singapore University Press.

Clifford, James. 1994. "Diaspora," *Cultural Anthropology,* 9(3): 306.

Cohen, Myron L. 1968. "The Hakka or 'Guest People': Dialect As a Sociocultural Variable in Southeast Asia," *Ethnohistory,* 15(3): 237–92.

Cohen, Robin. 1997. "Diaspora, the Nation-State, and Globalization," in Wang Gungwu, ed., *Global History and Migrations,* Boulder, CO: Westview, 117–44.

Coughlin, Richard. J. 1960. *Double Identity: The Chinese in Modern Thailand,* Hong Kong: Hong Kong University Press.

Evans, G., and M. Tam. 1997. "Introduction: The Anthropology of Contemporary Hong Kong," in G. Evans and M. Tam, eds., *Hong Kong: The Anthropology of a Chinese Metropolis,* Surrey, UK: Curzon, 1–24.

Faure, David, and Helen F. Siu, eds. 1995. *Down to Earth: The Territorial Bond in South China,* Stanford: Stanford University Press.

Faure, David, James Hayes, and Alan Birch, eds. 1984. *From Village to City: Studies in the Traditional Roots of Hong Kong Society,* Hong Kong: Centre of Asian Studies, University of Hong Kong.

Featherstone, Mike. 1990. "Global Culture: An Introduction," *Theory, Culture, and Society,* 7(2/3): 1–14.

Geertz, Clifford. 1973. *The Interpretation of Cultures,* New York: Basic Books.

Guldin, G. E. 1997. "Hong Kong Ethnicity: Of Folk Models and Change," in G. Evans and M. Tam, eds., *Hong Kong: The Anthropology of a Chinese Metropolis,* Surrey, UK: Curzon, 25–50.

Hamilton, Gary. G. 1977. "Ethnicity and Regionalism: Some Factors Influencing Chinese Identities in Southeast Asia," *Ethnicity,* 4: 347–51.

Harvey, David. 1989. *The Condition of Postmodernity: An Enquiry into the Origins of Cultural Change,* Oxford: Blackwell.

Hayes, James. 1993. *Tsuen Wan: Growth of a New Town and Its People,* Hong Kong: Oxford University Press.

Helmreich, Stefan. 1992. "Kinship, Nation, and Paul Gilroy's Concept of Diaspora." *Diaspora* 2 (2): 243–49.

Hong Kong, Census and Statistics Department. 1962. *Report of the Census 1961,* Hong Kong: Government Press.

———. 1969. *Hong Kong Statistics 1947–1967,* Hong Kong: Government Press.

————. 1982. *Hong Kong 1981 Census, Main Report,* Hong Kong: Government Press.

————. 1997. *1996 Population By-Census: Main Tables,* Hong Kong: Government Press.

Hong Kong, Registrar General's Office. 1881. *Hong Kong Census of 1881,* Hong Kong: Government Document.

————. 1901. *Report on the Census of the Colony for 1901,* Hong Kong: Government Document.

Honig, Emily. 1996. "Native Place and the Making of Chinese Ethnicity," in Gail Hershatter et al., eds., *Remapping China: Fissures in Historical Terrain,* Stanford: Stanford University Press, 143–55.

Hsing, You-tien 1997. *Making Capitalism in China: The Taiwan Connection,* New York: Oxford University Press.

Johnson, Graham E. 1996. "Tsuen Wan: From Hakka Enclave to Post-industrial City," *China Perspectives,* 8:20–26.

Kearney, M. 1995. "The Local and the Global: The Anthropology of Globalization and Transnationalism," *Annual Review of Anthropology,* 24: 547–65.

Kotkin, Joel. 1993. *Tribes: How Race, Religion, and Identity Determine Success in the New Global Economy,* New York: Random House.

Lai, David C. Y. and Dennis J. Dwyer. 1965. "Kwuntong, Hong Kong: A Study of Industrial Planning." *Town Planning Review* 35: 299–310.

Lary, Diana. 1996. "The Tomb of the King of Nanyue—The Contemporary Agenda of History: Scholarship and Identity," *Modern China,* 22(1): 3–27.

Lau, S. K., and H. C. Kuan. 1988. *The Ethos of the Hong Kong Chinese,* Hong Kong: Chinese University Press.

Leeming, Frank. 1977. *Street Studies in Hong Kong: Localities in a Chinese City,* Hong Kong: Oxford University Press.

Leung, C. K. 1993. "Personal Contacts, Subcontracting Linkages, and Development in the Hong Kong-Zhujiang Delta Region," *Annals of the Association of American Geographers,* 42(4): 403–21.

Lever-Tracy, Constance, David Ip, and Noel Tracy. 1996. *The Chinese Diaspora and Mainland China: An Emerging Economic Synergy,* New York: St. Martin's.

Li, Wei. 1998. "Anatomy of a New Ethnic Settlement: The Chinese Ethnoburb in Los Angeles," *Urban Studies,* 35(3): 479–501.

Lim, Linda Y. C., and L. A. Peter Gosling, eds. 1983. *The Chinese in Southeast Asia. Vol. 2: Identity, Culture and Politics,* Singapore: Maruzen Asia.

Lin, George C. S. 1997. *Red Capitalism in South China: Growth and Development of the Pearl River Delta,* Vancouver: University of British Columbia Press.

Liu, Hong. 1998. "Old Linkages, New Networks: The Globalization of Overseas Chinese Voluntary Associations and Its Implications," *The China Quarterly,* 155: 582–609.

Liu, Xin. 1997. "Space, Mobility, and Flexibility: Chinese Villagers and Scholars Negotiate Power at Home and Abroad," in Aihwa Ong and Donald M. Nonini, eds., *Ungrounded Empires: The Cultural Politics of Modern Chinese Transnationalism,* New York: Routledge, 91–114.

Lowenthal, D. 1985. "Mobility and Identity in the Island Pacific: A Critique," *Pacific Viewpoint,* 26: 280–315.

Mathews, Gordon, and Tai-lok Lui. 2001. *Consuming Hong Kong,* Hong Kong: Hong Kong University Press.

Mitchell, Katharyne. 1995. "Flexible Circulation in the Pacific Rim: Capitalisms in Cultural Context," *Economic Geography,* 71(4): 364–82.

Ng, Peter Y. L., and Hugh D.R. Baker 1983.. *New Peace County: A Chinese Gazetteer of the Hong Kong Region,* Hong Kong: Hong Kong University Press.

OECD (Organization for Economic Co-operation and Development), 1998. *Trends in International Migration,* Paris, France.

Ong, Aihwa, and Donald M. Nonini. 1997. "Afterword: Toward a Cultural Politics of Diaspora and Transnationalism," in Aihwa Ong and Donald M. Nonini, eds., *Ungrounded Empires: The Cultural Politics of Modern Chinese Transnationalism,* New York: Routledge, 323–332.

Pan, Lynn. 1991. *Sons of the Yellow Emperor: The Story of the Overseas Chinese,* London: Michelin House.

———. 1999. *The Encyclopedia of the Chinese Overseas,* Cambridge, MA: Harvard University Press.

Poston, Dudley L., Michael X. Mao, and Mei-Yu Yu,1994. "The Global Distribution of the Overseas Chinese around 1990," *Population and Development Review,* 20(3): 631–45.

Silvey, Rachel, and Victoria Lawson. 1999. "Placing the Migrant," *Annals of the Association of American Geographers,* 89(1): 121–32.

Sinn, Elizabeth. 1997. "Xin Xi Guxiang: A Study of Regional Associations As a Bonding Mechanism in the Chinese Diaspora, The Hong Kong Experience," *Modern Asian Studies,* 31(2): 375–97.

Skeldon, Ronald. 1990. *Population Mobility in Developing Countries: A Reinterpretation,* London: Belhaven Press.

———, ed. 1994. *Reluctant Exiles? Migration from Hong Kong and the New Overseas Chinese,* Hong Kong: Hong Kong University Press.

Skinner, G. William. 1957. *Chinese Society in Thailand: An Analytical History,* Ithaca, NY: Cornell University Press.

Smart, Alan, and Josephine Smart. 1998. "Transnational Social Networks and Negotiated Identities in Interactions between Hong Kong and China," in Michael. P. Smith and Luis E. Guarnizo, eds., *Transnationalism from Below,* New Brunswick, NJ: Transaction Publishers, 103–29.

Sparks, D. W. 1976. "The Teochiu: Ethnicity in Urban Hong Kong," *Journal of the Hong Kong Branch of the Royal Asiatic Society,* 16: 25–56.

U.S. Department of Justice, Immigration and Naturalization Service. 1991. *1990 Statistical Yearbook of the Immigration and Naturalization Service,* Washington, D.C.

———. 1997. *1995 Statistical Yearbook of the Immigration and Naturalization Service,* Washington, D.C.

———. 1999. *1996 Statistical Yearbook of the Immigration and Naturalization Service,* Washington, D.C.

Vogel, Ezra. 1989. *One Step Ahead in China: Guangdong under Reform,* Cambridge, MA: Harvard University Press.

Wang, Gungwu. 1991. *China and the Chinese Overseas,* Singapore: Times Academic Press.

Wang, Gungwu. and Siu-lun Wong., eds. 1997. *Hong Kong in the Asia-Pacific Region: Rising to the New Challenge,* Hong Kong: Centre of Asian Studies, The University of Hong Kong.

Wickberg, Edgar. 1994. "The Chinese As Overseas Migrants," in Judith M. Brown and Rosemary Foot, eds., *Migration: The Asian Experience,* New York: St. Martin's, 12–37.

Wong, Siu-lun. 1986. "Modernization and Chinese Culture in Hong Kong," *The China Quarterly,* 106: 306–25.

———. 1988. *Immigrant Entrepreneurs: Shanghai Industrialists in Hong Kong,* Hong Kong: Oxford University Press.

———. 1992. "Emigration and Stability in Hong Kong," *Asian Survey,* 32(10): 918–33.

Woon, Yuen-fong. 1989. "Social Change and Continuity in South China: Overseas Chinese and the Guan Lineage of Kaiping County, 1949–87," *The China Quarterly,* 118: 324–44.

———. 1990. "International Links and the Socioeconomic Development of Rural China: An Emigrant Community in Guangdong," *Modern China* 16(2): 139–72.

Wurm, S. A., and Rong Li., eds. 1987. *Language Atlas of China,* Hong Kong: Longman.

Yang, Mayfair Mei-hui. 1994. *Gifts, Favors, and Banquests: The Art of Social Relationships in China,* Ithaca, NY: Cornell University Press.

———. 1997. "Mass Media and Transnational Subjectivity in Shanghai: Notes on (Re)cosmopolitanism in a Chinese Metropolis," in Aihwa Ong and Donald M. Nonini, eds. *Ungrounded Empires: The Cultural Politics of Modern Chinese Transnationalism,* New York: Routledge, 287–322.

Yeh, Anthony G. O. 1990. "Public and Private Partnership in Urban Redevelopment in Hong Kong." *Third World Planning Review* 12 (4): 361–83.

Yeung, Henry, and Wai-Chung. 1998. *Transnational Corporations and Business Networks: Hong Kong Firms in the ASEAN Region,* New York: Routledge.

Zelinsky, Wilbur. 1971. The Hypothesis of the Mobility Transition," *Geographical Review,* 61(2): 219–49.

Zhou, Yu. 1998. "Beyond Ethnic Enclaves: Location Strategies of Chinese Producer Service Firms in Los Angeles," *Economic Geography,* 74(3): 228–51.

7

Who Are the Taiwanese?
Taiwan in the Chinese Diaspora

Jack F. Williams

The island of Taiwan has played a special role in the Chinese diaspora, serving as both a receiver of immigrants from the Chinese mainland and a sender of emigrants abroad. In a manner of speaking, Taiwan has been an outlier of the Chinese polity as well as a way station, a kind of funnel, for the Chinese diaspora. A key question in this process is to what degree Taiwan has been or is truly part of China? Although commonly viewed today as part of "Greater China," that ambiguously defined realm in which Chinese people and culture dominate, the true extent of Taiwan's historical integration with the mainland is hotly debated by scholars and others worldwide (e.g. Pan, 1999: 14–17). Taiwan has seen successive waves of immigration in its history—aboriginals from Southeast Asia, various Chinese subgroups from the mainland, plus foreign colonial rulers who have come and gone. All have left their imprint and contributed to the ambiguity of who "Taiwanese" are, even though in the post–World War II era that term has come to signify, in political terms, a very specific group of people on Taiwan. In addition to the island's complex sequent occupancy and cultural and political history, the Taiwanese diaspora, the major out-migration of "Taiwanese" abroad, developed mostly as a one-way flow, although there have been significant returns in the wake of reforms in Taiwan since 1987. Who, then, are the people of Taiwan, who really are the "Taiwanese," and what role have they played in the Chinese diaspora, both within and outside of Taiwan?

THE DIASPORA TO TAIWAN

From the earliest known times Taiwan has had migrants moving to the island, but the real settlement of the island is a much more recent phenomenon, dating primarily from the seventeenth century onward. Although the focus of this book is on the post–World War II era of the Chinese diaspora, it is impossible to understand the complexities of Taiwan's experience in the last half of the twentieth century without knowing something of the island's historic in-migration before 1945.

Origins of the "Taiwanese"

In simplest terms, one could state that the Taiwanese are the people who were born and live on the island of Taiwan, just as the Javanese are from Java or the Haitians from Haiti. But in Taiwan's case, "Taiwanese" has come to have special meaning. Taiwan's population of over 22 million today is defined in terms of four main ethnic groups: aborigines, two groups of "Taiwanese" Chinese, and mainlander Chinese, each with their own ethnicity, history, and political identity.

Aborigines

The aborigines are the true original settlers or "natives" of the island. These people consist of nine major tribes (the largest being the Ami, Atayal, and Paiwan), descendants of settlers believed to have come to Taiwan 12,000–15,000 years ago from southern China and Southeast Asia and classified by anthropologists as Austronesians.

The Chinese have had many names over the centuries for the aborigines, some derogatory. In the pre-1945 era, the most polite name was the *shan-ti jen*[1] (mountain people), referring to their primary location within Taiwan at that time. The plains aborigines had been largely assimilated to Chinese by intermarriage and acculturation. After 1945 the aborigines became the *shan-pao* (mountain compatriots), by an exiled Republic of China (ROC) government eager to court political support. Today, in the liberalized climate of Taiwan, the politically correct term for the aborigines is *yuan-chu min* (original settlers), reflecting the heightened political consciousness of Taiwan's pluralistic society. The reality is that this group, by whatever name, numbering officially about 380,000 in 1997 (less than two percent of Taiwan's population), has always had a marginal role in Taiwan's economy, society, and politics (although now they are nearly evenly split in location between the plains and mountains) (*Republic of China Yearbook 1998:* 26–33).

Taiwanese

The Taiwanese are politically defined as Han Chinese who were born on the island before 1945 or their offspring (Ahern and Gates, 1981). Collectively, they are referred to as *pen-ti jen* (people from this land) or *pen-sheng jen* (people from this province). They consist of two distinct subgroups, however. The smaller group is the *Hakka,* constituting about 12 percent of Taiwan's population today. The Hakka (or *kechia,* guest families), are found in Guangdong, Fujian and other provinces of the south. Engaging in fishing and trading in coastal areas, some Hakka migrated to the Pescadores (Penghu) Islands off the southwest coast of Taiwan and then eventually settled into small enclaves on Taiwan itself starting as early as 1000 A.D., but most went to Taiwan within the last 300 years. The Hakka on Taiwan came particularly from Jiaying, Huizhou, Chaozhou, and Tingzhou Prefectures in Guangdong (map 7.1). The Hakka language is a distinctive dialect (or group of dialects) of Chinese.

The largest group of Taiwanese, accounting for about 71 percent of the total contemporary population, belongs to the southern Min dialect group, concentrated in the area of southern Fujian Province. This group, also known as the *Hoklo,* emigrated to Taiwan starting primarily in the seventeenth century and was the majority group throughout the Qing period (1644–1911). Most of the Hoklo came from Quanzhou and Zhangzhou Prefectures in Fujian. The Hoklo speak *Min-nan hua,* or southern Min, the same dialect still found in Fujian, but typically referred to on Taiwan today

Map 7.1.   General Source Areas and Settlement Destinations of Hokkien and Hakka Migrants to Taiwan

as (imprecisely) the "Taiwanese" dialect or language. Most Hakka learned to speak Min-nan hua in order to survive and succeed on Taiwan. Both Hoklo and Hakka were forced to learn Mandarin Chinese (known on Taiwan as *kuo-yu,* or national language) after 1945 by the Kuomintang (KMT) government.

For the sake of simplicity, and for political differentiation, the Hakka and Hoklo have been lumped together in post-1945 Taiwan as the collective "Taiwanese," to distinguish them as the "native" Chinese of Taiwan as opposed to the more recent Han Chinese immigrants (the "mainlanders") of the postwar era. This classification of the "Taiwanese," which has both ethnic and political overtones, was a creation of the mainlander-run ROC government, but was accepted and even embraced by most Hakka/Hoklo Taiwanese in the harsh political climate of post-1945 Taiwan.

Mainlanders

The Mainlanders are those Han Chinese who moved from the mainland to Taiwan between 1945, when Taiwan was returned to the ROC government after 50 years of Japanese colonial rule, and 1949, when the ROC government fled to Taiwan after losing the civil war with the Communists on the mainland and established its government-in-exile. Known on Taiwan also as the *wai-sheng jen* (people from outside the province), the mainlanders, accounting for roughly 15 percent of the population today, came from many provinces and thus contributed to the pluralization of the Han Chinese population on Taiwan. These latest arrivals consisted of government officials and their families, industrialists and their dependents, and a sizeable number of military troops.

Cut off from the mainland by the embargo on relations between Taiwan and the mainland from 1949 onward, the mainlanders still regarded themselves as natives of their respective home provinces, not as Taiwanese. Taiwan was merely a temporary abode, a refuge, until such time as the ROC government could carry out its pledge to retake the mainland and oust the Communist government in Beijing (Peking).[2] Over the years, the mainlanders produced offspring, but even though born on Taiwan, or having gone to Taiwan as children with their refugee parents, these people were still regarded as mainlanders, identified by the home provinces of their father.[3] This identification has prevailed in spite of the fact that many of these mainlanders learned the Taiwanese language (the southern Min dialect), many have intermarried with Taiwanese (some, especially servicemen, even with aborigines), and in recent years have had a weakening sense of identification with the mainland and their parents' ancestral sites.

Early Settlement and Movement within Taiwan

Prior to the Japanese era (1895–1945), the Hoklo were pushed out of the mainland, just as were the Hakka, by economic hardship and political turmoil, and drawn to Taiwan by economic opportunity.[4] These are the classic circumstances of migration around the world and throughout history. In the case of Taiwan, the relatively late incorporation of the island into the Chinese state and the difficulties of maritime navigation from the mainland to the island tended to suppress immigration. Until the brief period of Dutch rule (1621–1661) there were few Chinese living on Taiwan. The Dutch encouraged immigration, as part of their process of trying to settle and develop the southwest plain around the area of Tainan, but their rule was too brief to accomplish much. Their main impact was to put Taiwan on the map and lay the foundations for later agricultural development in the southwest. Dutch rule was followed by the brief period of Ming loyalist Chinese control under the Cheng (Zheng) family (1661–1683), after which the island fell to the Manchus and their Qing dynastic rule (1644–1911). Taiwan's population at the time of Qing acquisition (1683) has been estimated at about 100,000 aborigines (half plains settlers, half mountain dwellers), and slightly fewer Chinese, for a tiny total population of roughly 200,000. The Chinese were concentrated on rice and sugar farms in the Tainan area, while the plains aborigines were spread thinly all along the western coastal plain, living on horticulture and deer hunting (Shepherd, 1993: 14). The next two centuries consisted of a complex process of continued Chinese immigration (in spite of early efforts by the Qing to restrict immigration), with movement of the Chinese out of their enclave in the southwest of the island to gradually fill up most of the west coast plain. In the process the aborigines were pushed out of the best lands and exploited by ruthless Chinese.

Shepherd's study of the Taiwan frontier identifies six major characteristics of Chinese migration from the mainland to Taiwan from the Qing dynasty up to the Japanese era (Shepherd, 1993: 311–316). First, migration was initially a quest for economic livelihood, with intentions to return to the mainland; later the migration evolved into a permanent relocation as migrants saw less and less need or desire to return. Second, most of the migrants were male. Only later did women and families follow, but males still outnumbered women for a long period, adding to the ingredients for lawlessness and social instability. Third, the Han migrants came from all classes and occupational backgrounds. Fourth, the settlers tended to locate in ethnic and clan enclaves on Taiwan, determined by their origin and ethnicity on the mainland. Thus evolved a clearly mappable mosaic pattern of settlement by the time of the Japanese era that reflected many of the cultural and economic characteristics of the settlers (map 7.2). Habitats on Taiwan were closely correlated with the occupations of the migrants in their native prefectures on the mainland. For example, "Ch'uan-chou had the least agricultural land, and its population, crowded onto a long, jagged coast, supplemented agriculture with handicraft production, trade, fishing . . . Thus, Ch'uan-chou migrants were attracted to the coastal cities and markets that organized Taiwan's commerce . . ." (Shepherd, 1993: 313). These characteristics of the Taiwan coast were similar to the coastal conditions of southern Fujian around Ch'uan-chou (Quanzhou). Fifth, social ties reinforced native-place ties and subethnicity. In other words, migrants preferred to be with kin and fellow villagers whenever possible. Sixth, migrants brought with them traditions of violence and self-defense common to the coastal areas of southeast China.

Throughout most of their history, the Hoklo and Hakka were anything but homogeneous or peaceful in their dealings with each other. Lamley (1981: 282–318) notes that the Hakka tended to have relative solidarity among themselves, being historically an embattled minority both on the mainland and on Taiwan, while the Hoklo experienced extreme disunity and divisiveness. (One is tempted to seek some correlation between this historic pattern and the fractious political climate on Taiwan today!) Subethnic dialects were common in both groups, and reinforced by relative isolation in premodern Taiwan. Feuds, organized fighting, banditry, and uprisings among the Hoklo and between Hoklo and Hakka were frequent during the 200 years of Qing rule. In spite of Qing efforts to limit immigration, and the unstable conditions on Taiwan, the population of the island reached an estimated two million by 1811, and added another million by 1895, when the Japanese took over. Indeed, the inability of the Hoklo and Hakka to stand up successfully to foreign invaders and colonizers (especially the Japanese) may have derived in part from their long-standing rivalry and hostility toward each other. In May, 1895 there was a short-lived, but ill-organized, effort to declare an independent Republic of Taiwan by the literati of the island, involving both Hakka and Hoklo. Even if the Hoklo and Hakka had been fully united, there was little chance of holding off the far superior Japanese forces as they took over Taiwan.

The degree to which the Qing government exercised effective rule over Taiwan in that critical period of 1683–1895, when Taiwan was nominally part of the Chinese empire, is an important element of the argument for proponents of Taiwan independence today. They maintain that Qing rule was weak and unable to maintain social order on the island. They also claim that Qing authorities were not really even interested in the island until foreign colonial predators (French, Japanese, Americans) started casting covetous eyes on the island in the latter half of the nineteenth century as the carving up of China proceeded. Some

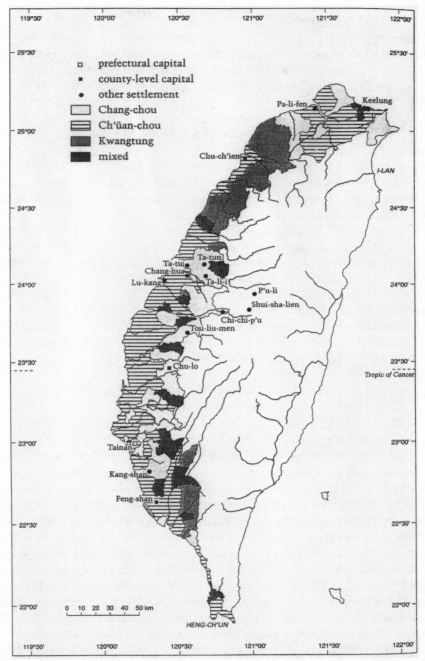

Map 7.2. Distribution of Population by Local of Origin, Taiwan, 1926. (Reprinted from
Statecraft and Political Economy on the Taiwan Frontier, 1600—1800, p. 314, by John Robert
Shepherd. © 1993 by the Board of Trustees of the Leland Stanford Junior University.)

historians disagree. Shepherd (1993: 21), for example, claims that Qing authorities were, in fact, following a rationally calculated policy of indirect control and quarantine. Ineffective or not, in the eyes of many Taiwanese one form of colonial rule (Manchu) was replaced by another (Japanese).

THE JAPANESE ERA (1895–1945)

In the end, the Japanese won out in the competition for Taiwan at the height of the worldwide colonial era. At war with China in 1894, Japan emerged victorious and the subsequent Treaty of Shimonoseki between China and Japan yielded Taiwan to Japan as a colonial territory.

As a result, mainland immigration to Taiwan virtually came to a halt, and was replaced by immigration of Japanese colonial administrators, military forces, and settlers, all determined to make a success of Japan's first foreign colony and show the world that Japan could contend with world colonial powers. At the peak of the Japanese presence on Taiwan in 1945, there were just over 107,000 Japanese living in Taipei (out of a total Taipei population of 335,000), with lesser numbers widely scattered around the island (Yeh, 2000). Although all of these Japanese eventually were repatriated after World War II, the Japanese left behind a remarkable legacy.[5]

Economy

The Japanese established a classic colonial economy that focused on exploitation of local resources for the benefit of Japan. Yet, in the process they advanced Taiwan economically, so that at the start of World War II Taiwan was far ahead of almost all regions of the mainland in economic development. This reality contributed directly to the bad relationship that developed between Taiwanese and mainlanders after 1945 (when the mainlanders viewed with jealousy the relative well-being and sophistication of the Taiwanese, who reciprocated with contempt for the "country bumpkin" character of many mainlanders). The Japanese greatly expanded the agricultural economy, which included rice and sugar cane as the cornerstone of the system, plus tropical fruits, lumbering, fishing, and other activities. In the process, vast tracts of land were opened up and Taiwanese were encouraged to settle them, including active settlement for the first time of the narrow east coast valley of Taiwan. Much of this newly opened land, however, was turned over to Japanese colonial companies that established sugar plantations and laid the foundation for what was later to become a key monopoly of the post-1945 ROC government operations on the island—the Taiwan Sugar Corporation (Williams, 1980).

The agricultural expansion was generally at the expense of the aborigines, who were ruthlessly suppressed and treated even worse than the Hoklo and Hakka by Chinese settlers before 1895. Thus as the Japanese expanded their control and utilization of the island, settlement and agricultural production penetrated further and further into the lower slopes and foothills of the mountainous interior of the island at the expense of the aborigines.

The Japanese also established the island's first railroad system, modern roads, and communications systems, and built up the island's cities, especially Taipei as the colonial capital in the north (founded on a small Chinese provincial center) and Kaohsiung as the chief port (and later industrial center) in the southwest. Japanese administrators and dependents lived primarily in Taipei, of necessity and desire, with relatively small numbers of Japanese scattered over the rest of the island. Again, this was a classic colonial settlement pattern found throughout the world, and one that was repeated after 1945 when the mainlander ROC government took over Taiwan. Urban centers thus took on a distinctly Japanese appearance, filtered through a Japanese interpretation of nineteenth century European/Western architecture and city planning in their efforts to imitate the West. Nowhere was this truer than in Taipei, where important architectural remnants of the Japanese era still stand today.

Culture and Society

The Japanese also had a profound impact on the culture and society of the Taiwanese. The colonial government had every intention of converting Taiwan into a permanent part of the empire. By the 1930s, this included a heightened effort to "Japanize" all the people of Taiwan, by requiring Japanese language education and use (and the suppression of Taiwanese and other Chinese dialects), the adoption of Japanese names for people and places, and the imposition of Japanese culture (food, music, house styles, art, religion). It is remarkable how many aspects of Japanese culture not only survived but also continued to thrive in post-1945 Taiwan. The Taiwanese culture today, half a century later, still shows the clear imprint of Japan, in food tastes, architecture, music, language, and other areas. Japanese is the second most widely studied and spoken foreign language in Taiwan (after English), and many parents still opt to send their children to Japan for university studies, rather than to the U.S.[6] Taiwan is a favored site for Japanese tourists, and parts of Taipei have a distinctly "Tokyo" look to them. Japan still maintains strong economic ties with Taiwan and, although officially recognizes the People's Republic of China (PRC), is very supportive of Taiwan in all other ways. In this regard, Japanese colonialism was similar to British colonial rule, in terms of the long-lasting impact. Yet, one might argue that the close ties between Taiwan and Japan and the enduring elements of Japanese culture might not have been so durable had the mainlander ROC government behaved differently in Taiwan after 1945. In effect, the mainlanders drove some Taiwanese to romanticize the Japanese era and to make it seem better in their memories than it really was, because of the harsh treatment at the hands of the ROC government in those first decades of mainland rule. One can discern this, for example, in talking with older Taiwanese who were born and at least partially educated during the Japanese era, and who often speak better Japanese than Mandarin. Regardless, the reality is that 50 years of Japanese rule further transformed the Taiwanese and made them even more different from the mainlander Chinese culture and political system, providing one more plank in the platform for the Taiwan independence movement.

Politics and Government

Japanese colonial rule was anything but democratic. In the classic colonial fashion, the Japanese were harsh, even ruthless, toward those who opposed their rule. Natives who welcomed, or at least accepted and tried to work accommodatingly with Japanese rule survived and even prospered. Large numbers of Taiwanese did so, partly because of their limited sense of national identity (Yeh, 2000). They accepted that they were of Chinese ethnic and cultural heritage, yet so weakly tied into the mainland system during the previous 200 years of Qing rule that it was relatively easy to accept Japanese rule. Moreover, no one had asked them if they wanted to be part of the Japanese empire, and they could not foresee any likelihood of return to China, certainly not in their lifetimes, and hence they did what they could to survive. Japanese administration, in its efficiency and harshness, brought to a virtual end the internal feuding and instability that had plagued Taiwan during the previous two centuries. While linguistic and other differences between Hakka and Hoklo did not disappear, those differences became less and less important as the native Taiwanese tried simply to get along and have their families prosper under the Japanese. Thus, in a sense, one of the most important contributions of the Japanese to Taiwan's development was an inadvertent one, i.e., helping to forge the beginnings of a "Taiwanese" consciousness, making the Hakka and Hoklo see themselves more as members of a majority group, the "natives" of the island, and with commonalities of interests that outweighed the linguistic and other differences that had divided them in the past.

Another important development of the Japanese era was the beginning of what might be called the "Taiwanese diaspora," i.e., the movement of Taiwanese out of Taiwan to other places. Immigration from the Chinese mainland had all but ceased during the half century of Japanese colonial rule. In its place, migration mainly consisted of a two-way flow of Japanese to and from Taiwan, and Taiwanese going to Japan to study, work, and some to stay permanently. By 1940 there were 22,000 Taiwanese resident in Japan (Yeh, 2000: 10). The primary motive was to seek economic advancement for oneself and one's family by learning from the colonial power; many Asians, including the Taiwanese, in the early twentieth century at least, saw Japan as a model. Some of the migrants to Japan were also political revolutionaries who had independence or other political ambitions for Taiwan. Regardless, the foundations of a Taiwanese expatriate population in Japan were established, a group that would grow in numbers after 1945 and play an important role in the Taiwan independence movement.

In any event, the relative ease of Japanese rule in Taiwan (as opposed, for example, to the vicious occupation of Korea that still poisons relations between Japan and Korea to this day), had another unforeseen consequence: it contributed to the perception by the mainlander government that the Taiwanese had collaborated with the Japanese enemy and contributed to the Japanese depredations on the mainland during the Second World War. (Taiwanese men, for example, were conscripted into the Japanese imperial army.) Thus, the Taiwanese could not be trusted after restoration of ROC rule in 1945, their loyalty to China was questioned, and the ROC government believed it had to do everything in its power to "sinify" the Taiwanese and restore their "Chineseness." In this paranoid distortion of reality, the ROC government laid the foundation for the tragedy of post-1945 Taiwan, whose painful consequences have troubled the island ever since and may never completely heal.[7]

THE REPUBLIC OF CHINA ON TAIWAN

The ROC government recovered Taiwan in 1945, but did not fully retreat to the island until losing the civil war with the Communists in 1949. That four-year period was one of deteriorating relations between mainlanders and Taiwanese. To start with, the mainlanders stripped the island of foods, industrial goods, and other wealth that could be used in the fight against the Communists on the mainland. Preoccupied with that life-and-death struggle, the ROC government had little time for administration of Taiwan, and thus conditions on the island rapidly worsened. The breakdown of society led to the tragic revolt of February 28, 1947 (the infamous "2-28 Incident") and subsequent March massacre of the Taiwanese leadership by ROC forces, determined to stamp out all traces of real or potential opposition to Kuomintang rule. When the ROC established a government-in-exile in 1949, martial law was imposed and a Leninist police state set up that was not very different in form, politically, from the one imposed by the Communists on the mainland after 1949. To be sure, however, from 1957 to 1976 China was a true totalitarian state, which was not really the case in Taiwan.

Thus, the post-1945 era consists of two distinct parts, divided by the watershed year of 1987 when martial law was finally ended. During these two sub-eras, both overshadowed by the ongoing determination of the PRC to recover political control of Taiwan, vast changes swept the island. Particularly important for the purpose of this study have been the changing character of Taiwan society, the relationships between the various peoples of Taiwan, and the emergence of the "New Taiwanese."

Martial Law Era (1949–1987): New Migration Patterns

During the roughly 40 years of martial law, a harsh authoritarian political system held an iron grip on Taiwan and suppressed all political dissent under one-party rule by the Kuomintang (KMT). As in the Japanese era, most Taiwanese had no choice but simply to try to survive. Those who could not stomach KMT rule were either thrown into prison (many sent to Green Island off the east coast of Taiwan, which became the main political prison site during this era, and now is being turned into a historical tourism site), or left Taiwan in what was to become the greatest wave of the Taiwanese diaspora.

Resumed Immigration from the Mainland

Perhaps the most striking and immediate impact of the return of ROC rule was the resumption of immigration of Chinese from the mainland, with the arrival of over half a million ROC government leaders, military forces, and accompanying dependents. Seen as "carpetbaggers" by Taiwanese nationalists, these mainlanders settled primarily in the Taipei region, and initially in the newly vacated Japanese homes and buildings. It is easy to see how the Taiwanese made the analogy of one colonial master being replaced by another. Relatively few mainlanders located elsewhere on the island, except as key military or civilian administrators, with dependents, such as the managers of the Taiwan Sugar Corporation plantations or other mainland-owned businesses, or mayors of towns and cities. This geographical distribution of Taiwanese versus mainlanders remains remarkably true to this day, with a majority of mainlanders and their descendants still concentrated in the Taipei metro region. One of the major impacts of the new mainlander population was to introduce a new cosmopolitanism to the island, especially the Taipei region, in terms of many Chinese dialect groups from all over the mainland, along with the various cuisines and other cultural customs of those groups.[8]

This phase of new migration from the mainland was short-lived, of course, stopping abruptly in 1949 when the PRC was established on the mainland. A complete break in contact of almost any kind between Taiwan and the mainland continued for the next several decades, as part of the ROC government's "Three Noes" Policy, the cornerstone of its attitude toward the mainland government: "no contact, no negotiation, no compromise."

Resumption of the Taiwanese Diaspora

As the harshness of mainlander rule deepened through the 1950s and 1960s, the Taiwanese diaspora resumed. Many Taiwanese fled the island in the late 1940s, especially right after the 2-28 Incident in 1947. But far more emigrated from Taiwan in an indirect way, as students going abroad to study. Most students went to the United States, which became the principal protector of Taiwan under the Mutual Defense Treaty signed with the ROC in 1954; others went to Japan, and lesser numbers to European countries, such as West Germany. Most young Taiwanese were forced to endure the indoctrination by the KMT education system through high school and then undergraduate college training in Taiwan. Males were required to perform two years of compulsory military service either before or after college study (this policy continues to this day). Graduate study abroad also attracted large numbers of men and women postgraduates, many of whom simply stayed abroad. Mixed motives were involved, including desires for better paying jobs and professional opportunities, reluctance to return to the authoritarian society of Taiwan, and in some cases fear of being imprisoned for political activism abroad.

One could characterize the attitude of most Taiwanese in that period, until the mid-1980s, as one of quiet resignation, or acquiescence, to the political system, as long as their families continued to prosper. It took great courage to openly dissent. The minority unwilling to live under such a system either went to prison or fled the island. Thus, the great diaspora of Taiwanese to America, Europe, and Japan unfolded, creating large and increasingly powerful blocs of expatriate Taiwanese. A substantial number of Taiwanese overseas fanned the flames of Taiwanese nationalism under many splinter groups arguing for Taiwan's independence from both the ROC and the PRC.[9] To some of these Taiwanese, it was like a badge of honor to be on the ROC government's "black list," which prevented political activists from returning to Taiwan for nearly 40 years.

It is ironic that the very actions of the mainlanders, through the ROC government and the single-party rule of the KMT, worked directly counter to the goal of creating a sense of Chinese—not Taiwanese—identity in the minds of the majority Taiwanese. Efforts to suppress Taiwanese language and culture, not to mention dissent of any kind, and to promote mainland Chinese culture and Mandarin Chinese as the official language, in an oppressive and heavy-handed way, was short-sighted, in that it drove many Taiwanese toward increased belief in the need for the Taiwanese to have their own nation-state and distinctive identity, completely apart from the mainland. If the mainlanders had welcomed the Taiwanese right from the start in 1945, as true compatriots, accepted their cultural and linguistic differences, treated them with friendship and equality, and brought them directly into the political process, the post-1945 history of Taiwan almost certainly would have been much different and the risks of separatism to a unified China greatly reduced from what they are today. But the ROC government of that era was completely incapable of such a progressive and magnanimous vision of China, just as the Communists on the mainland were equally incapable (and appear to still be, in light of their dogmatic and heavy-handed position about reunification).

Hence, the Taiwanese diaspora. This study is not the place to go into great detail about the Taiwanese experience in the U.S. (or elsewhere), but a few pertinent characteristics are noteworthy. The exact numbers of how many Taiwanese went abroad and still live abroad are impossible to determine. In total, however, there are undoubtedly several hundred thousand Taiwanese living outside of Taiwan today, the majority of these in the United States. Ng has done perhaps the best job of trying to document the numbers of Taiwanese in the U.S. and their economic, social, and other characteristics. Ng (Ng, 1998: 15ff) discerns three distinct periods of Taiwanese immigration in the post-1945 era. From 1945–1965 a small number of students came to the U.S. for graduate studies, joining the mostly Cantonese Chinese already in the U.S. In addition, a limited number of spouses of American military personnel who had been stationed in Taiwan arrived. Most of these immigrants ended up in professional-class occupations, living in the major metropolitan regions of the West and East coasts, plus some in the Midwest. The period from 1965–1979 was shaped by the new Immigration Act of 1965, which increased the quota of Chinese immigrants to 20,000, and established preferences for family members and those with skills needed in the U.S. Many Taiwanese were able to enter the U.S. under these provisions. After 1979 and up to the present, the establishment of diplomatic ties with the PRC resulted in dividing the U.S. annual quota of 20,000 Chinese between China and Taiwan, which made it more difficult for Taiwanese trying to relocate or travel. In 1982 the U.S. gave Taiwan its own quota of 20,000, but these numbers were increasingly dwarfed by much greater immigration of mainland Chinese. As table 7.1 shows, immigrants from Taiwan during the ten years, 1984–1994, averaged

Table 7.1.   Immigrants from Taiwan, Hong Kong, China, and Singapore Admitted to United States, by Region and Country of Birth, Fiscal Years 1984–1994

	Taiwan	Hong Kong	China	Singapore
1984	12,478	5,465	23,363	377
1985	14,895	5,171	24,787	460
1986	13,424	5,021	25,106	480
1987	11,931	4,706	25,841	469
1988	9,670	8,546	28,717	492
1989	13,974	9,740	32,272	566
1990	15,151	9,393	31,815	620
1991	13,274	10,427	33,025	535
1992	16,344	10,452	38,907	774
1993	14,329	9,161	65,578	798
1994	10,032	7,731	53,985	542

Source: U.S. Immigration and Naturalization Service. 1996. *Statistical Yearbook of the Immigration and Naturalization Service, 1994,* Table 3; Ng (1998: 140).

perhaps 12,000 a year, while mainlanders numbered several times that amount. In just 1996 alone, for example, 42,000 mainlanders immigrated to the U.S., while the number from Taiwan was 13,000, and from Hong Kong, 8,000 (Gilley, 1998). People from Taiwan tend to be heavily concentrated in professional and executive occupations, while mainlanders are found more evenly distributed throughout the occupational classes (table 7.2).

Table 7.2.   Immigrants Admitted by Major Occupation Group and Region and Selected Country of Birth: Fiscal Year 1994

	Taiwan	Hong Kong	China
Occupation			
Professional specialty and technical	1,636	872	7,272
Executive, administrative, and managerial	1,273	969	2,993
Sales	165	125	729
Administrative support	506	580	1,721
Precision production, craft, and repair	37	174	676
Operator, fabricator, and laborer	57	92	2,159
Farming, forestry, and fishing	43	2	2,248
Service	231	244	3,664
No occupation or not reported	6,084	4,673	32,523
Total	10,032	7,731	53, 985

Source: U.S. Immigration and Naturalization Service. 1996. *Statistical Yearbook of the Immigration and Naturalization Service, 1994,* Table 21; Ng (1998: 143).

It should be noted, of course, that a minority of the migrants from Taiwan in this era were actually mainlanders or descendants of mainlanders, drawn to the U.S. for many of the same reasons as the native Taiwanese. U.S. immigration statistics do not differentiate among immigrants from Taiwan on the basis of their ethnicity or home province. Hence, it is impossible to determine any breakdown in the numbers. One could surmise, however, that economic and educational factors played a much greater role in mainlander emigration from Taiwan than political factors, compared to the ethnic Taiwanese.

Internal Migration

A third trend in this martial law era involved internal migration within Taiwan, with profound consequences. An irony of this era is that while a political stranglehold continued in Taiwan, the government provided an optimum environment for economic growth under an increasingly private enterprise system, in marked contrast with the PRC. Commonly referred to as the "economic miracle" that transformed Taiwan into one of the "Newly Industrialized Countries" (or "Economies," as the PRC prefers them to be called), or "Asian Tigers," this complex process involved massive industrialization and urbanization that made Taiwan look increasingly like modern Japan by the 1980s and 1990s.[10] Millions of Taiwanese migrated out of the countryside and small towns to move to the cities, especially Taipei and to a lesser extent Kaohsiung, Taichung, and others, in response to rapid increases in job opportunities. Cultural characteristics, such as ethnicity, clan affiliations, and original home location in Taiwan, played critical roles in where these migrants settled in Taipei and other places, repeating to some extent practices evidenced in earlier migration from the mainland to Taiwan in the island's pre-Japanese history.[11] It was not uncommon, though, for urban families to retain some rural roots, with part of the family in urban centers and part back home on the farm, with movement in both directions over the course of the year. The small size of Taiwan contributed to the ease of this two-way flow.

The Hakka of Taipei provide one interesting example of domestic migration (Chang, 1998). The Hakka first migrated from the mainland to settle in Taoyuan, Hsinchu, or Miaoli Counties some 300 years ago. By the time they came to Taipei, starting in the nineteenth century, the city center was already occupied by Hoklo, so the Hakka established homes in the suburbs outside the city gates. Neighborhoods, such as Hulin Street in Sungshan District, Konan Street in Kuting District, Tunghua Street in Taan District, and a few others became areas of high concentration of Hakka. This pattern persisted through the Japanese era and continues remarkably strong today. Taipei's population now is about 15 percent

Hakka as a whole, some 300,000–400,000 people, with much higher concentrations in the older districts, such as Tunghua Street.

Regardless of where the Taiwanese settled in this migration process, it meant leaving behind their rural backgrounds and small town practices, and having to develop new living and work habits. This is the classic rural-to-urban migration process that has occurred in countless countries around the world in the past half century. Taiwan does differ, however, in the exceptionally rapid progress of its economic transformation, so that social change has also occurred at an accelerated rate. While a good part of that change has been adjustment to living in crowded urban environments, with pollution, terrible traffic, and all the other problems associated with overly rapid urbanization, the Taiwanese migrants have also had to contend with the changing political realities both inside and outside of Taiwan, changes that have brought both increased hope and opportunities for all the people of Taiwan but also increased stress and uncertainty.

Post-Martial Law Era (1987–Present)

By the 1980s, the ROC government realized that continued economic success, and hence the military strength and ability to keep the PRC at arm's length, required that the Taiwanese be given a greater role in the political system, a process started by then-President Chiang Ching-kuo. Simultaneously, the growing well-to-do middle class of Taiwanese was increasingly dissatisfied with just a rising standard of living. Their demands led to the dramatic and swift transformation of the political system starting in the mid-1980s, with the end to martial law in 1987, the accession of Lee Teng-hui, a Taiwanese Hakka (albeit member of the KMT) to the presidency, the legalization of opposition political parties, most importantly the founding of the Democratic Progressive Party (DPP), removal of most restrictions on freedom of the press, assembly, and dissent, and other reforms. In less than 10 years, Taiwan became one of the great success stories of political modernization, following on the heels of its already remarkable record in economic development.[12]

For the Taiwanese this has been a mixed blessing. On the one hand, they have been able to field their own candidates, either through the DPP or other parties that have emerged, for offices from the local to the highest national level. The KMT, in turn, has seen a steady diminution in its political power and support. Exiled Taiwanese have been free to return, and a gradual "Taiwanization" of the political system has unfolded. The idea of Taiwan's independence is openly debated in public. All change comes with costs, however. The internal costs have consisted of rising social problems, including crime, corruption, divorce, and others.

The greatest cost, however, arguably has been an increasingly complex and dangerous relationship with the PRC. Until the mid-1980s, the mainland was willing to be patient with the ROC government about the matter of reunification, because the government was firmly under KMT control and the one policy both sides in the still-unfinished Chinese civil war agreed upon was that Taiwan was a province of China, just temporarily not under the control of the mainland. The Taiwan independence activists were seen as an isolated, impotent minority in exile, with no real chance of coming to power. Now, all that has changed. For one thing, the ROC's "Three Noes" became the "Three Maybes," in the sense that Taiwan, of necessity for its economic survival, began having contact, compromise, and negotiation with the mainland, to establish flourishing trade, investment, tourism, and other relations.[13] It has been mainly a one-way flow, from Taiwan to the mainland, with relatively little flow in the opposite direction, and ostensibly always through third parties (especially through Hong Kong) to try to maintain the fiction that the ROC and PRC were not having official face-to-face dealings.

Statistical evidence demonstrates the huge economic links that have been created with the mainland (Cheng, 2001). Two-way trade between Taiwan and China in the year 2000 came to US$32 billion, accounting for 11 percent of Taiwan's total exports. The surplus with the mainland is what continues to give Taiwan a total trade surplus. Estimates of Taiwan investment in the mainland range from $40–$100 billion as of mid-2001, making Taiwan the fourth largest investor in China. Taiwan investment is especially heavy now in the Shanghai area. Some 50,000 Taiwan companies are now invested in the mainland to some degree and employ millions of mainland workers. Taiwan companies now account for 60 percent of China's information technology exports, and less than half of Taiwan's information technology products are now made in Taiwan itself. Every day, some 10,000 Taiwanese business people enter the PRC. In other words, economic integration of Taiwan and China is well underway. These links have become massive: in late 2001 the administration of Chen Shui-bian formally called for the establishment of direct transport and other links with China, and significant easing of restrictions on Taiwan investment as a way to spur continued economic growth in the face of a worldwide recession ("EDAC Recommendations," 2001). In other words, the "Three Noes" are now a dead policy.

Yet, at the same time, political reunification seems a long way off. Taiwan has basically three options facing it: the status quo, reunification, or independence, although some argue that the last two are not realistic options at this time. Most of the public in Taiwan are in favor of the status quo for the immediate future (although no island-wide full referendum on this issue has ever been carried out). The government's Mainland Affairs Council (MAC) takes regular polls of public attitudes. In a poll taken in July 2001, the results were: 32.1 percent wanted to defer the choice between independence and unification until a later date; 10.2 percent liked the idea of declaring Taiwan's independence at a later date; 16.7 percent expressed preference for unification with the mainland at a later date; and 21.5 percent hoped that things would not change ("MAC Poll," 2001).

The position of the political parties is more diffuse, as the number of parties has increased in recent years. The KMT, seemingly crumbling from within because of weak leadership and internal corruption, has witnessed several splinter parties sheer off. The New Party (NP) was the first, in 1993, and most openly pro-reunification. It has failed to find a real voice, however, and has very little Taiwanese support. The People First Party (PFP) came into being in 2000, under James Soong, the renegade former KMT member and Taiwan governor. It also supports reunification but is less open about pushing it too strongly. Reunification is nominally still supported by the KMT but only under its terms and in the future when the mainland adopts a fully democratic system. The Taiwan Solidarity Union (TSU) was founded in 2001 with the aid of Lee Teng-hui (former President and Chair of the KMT). This fledgling party is for "constructive engagement" with the mainland, but Lee has become increasingly outspoken since leaving office (and being kicked out of the KMT as a "traitor") and shown increasing public support for the DPP cause. The DPP began its existence in 1986 on a strong independence plank, for declaration of an independent Republic of Taiwan (or perhaps "Formosa," the old name for the island), but this stand has been diluted greatly in recent years as the real implications of such an action have become clearer to all concerned. The PRC has been consistently unequivocal that an outright declaration of independence would be a provocation that it could not complacently accept. Hence, now the DPP under Chen Shui-bian is also arguing for the status quo, but with the proviso that someday Taiwan must be ruled by the Taiwanese for the Taiwanese, in a multiparty, pluralistic democratic system, and that the Taiwanese (here meaning all the people of Taiwan) should have the right to decide if they want to be a part of the PRC or not. Taiwan has thus moved far, from a starkly divided pre-1987 political system to a multiparty system. The future is murky and fraught with the danger of conflict with the mainland. As Arthur Waldron (1998) has stated, "Two sovereign states in the Chinese cultural world, with no reason to fight and every reason to get along, have huge differences between them in system and legitimacy."

New Migration Patterns

In the reform era, migration has also taken on new dimensions. In regard to immigration, the most prominent pattern has been the increased return of

Taiwanese from abroad. Many of the Taiwanese who went into exile for political reasons have returned, to participate in the new political process, the
economic boom, and to become part of their native culture again. Far fewer
Taiwanese have the desire or need to permanently relocate abroad, whether to
the United States or elsewhere, although out-migration certainly has not
ceased. Millions of Taiwan residents travel abroad each year as tourists and
business and professional people, to China, Southeast Asia, Europe, Japan,
the U.S., and elsewhere. Organized Taiwanese tour groups are now almost as
ubiquitous in world tourist haunts as Japanese tour groups.

Very few Taiwanese have become involved with *qiaoxiang* (emigrant communities) on the mainland. Unlike many of the mainlanders on Taiwan, or the
Chinese in Southeast Asia, the overwhelming majority of native Taiwanese
(Hoklo and Hakka) have been physically, politically, and culturally separated
from the mainland and their ancestral homes in Fujian and Guangdong for so
long that their sense of kinship and village ties are weak, at best. Many Taiwanese have traveled to the mainland in the post-1987 reform era to visit their
ancestral home sites, but mostly out of curiosity, the way many American
tourists visit their family ancestral homes in Europe, say, rather than out of a
deep sense of ethnic ties. Rarely do these Taiwan visitors have any desire to
reestablish residency on the mainland, although many are business people, as
already noted, who do invest in manufacturing infrastructure to take advantage of cheaper labor and operating costs.

To what degree Taiwan's aborigines have participated in international migration is extremely difficult to determine, as the data are not readily available. Undoubtedly, some aborigines have succeeded in joining the flow, but
the numbers probably are relatively insignificant. Other immigration to Taiwan in recent years has consisted of significant numbers of migrant workers
(labor migration), a consequence of Taiwan's booming economy and the rising gap in wealth between Taiwan and some other Asian countries. As of
1997, there were just under 250,000 legal "foreign workers," as the government calls them (with an uncertain number of additional illegal workers) in
Taiwan (*ROC Yearbook 1998:* 345). Most are employed in manufacturing,
plus construction, followed by services (e.g., maids, nursing, caretakers).
Most come from Thailand, followed by the Philippines. Strictly regulated,
these workers are supposed to leave after a certain period, but complete control of these migrants proves difficult, as other rich Asian states with foreign
workers (e.g., Hong Kong, Japan, Singapore) also have discovered. Interest-
ingly, limited immigration from the mainland resumed, starting in the early
1990s, with spousal reunions and cross-strait marriages (especially with
Taiwan-resident mainlanders), plus very limited labor migration (Williams,
1994: 235). This process is very tightly controlled and unlikely to amount to

much in the immediate future, but it has important long-range implications in terms of Taiwan-PRC relations. In addition, indeterminate numbers of illegal Min-nan speakers from Fujian are known to be working in low-wage jobs in Taiwan.

Yams, Taro, and Peanuts: The "New Taiwanese"

Into this equation has been projected the concept of the "New Taiwanese." The idea has been gestating in Taiwan for at least ten years, but President Lee gave it full public exposure and backing in the final days of the Taipei mayoral election of December 1998, when a KMT candidate (Ma Ying-jeou) narrowly defeated a DPP candidate (Chen Shui-bian) who was thought by many to be a certain winner (Schubert, 1999). On the one hand, the term, "New Taiwanese," is an attempt to conceptualize a demographic reality of modern Taiwan. The fact is, most of the people living in Taiwan today were born there, regardless of where their parents came from. Thus, by extension, the "Taiwanese" today truly are simply the people born and residing on the island of Taiwan. Thus, the term, "New Taiwanese," was being promoted by Lee and others as a way of encouraging all the people of Taiwan to put aside ethnic, political, and other differences, to stop seeing themselves as "Yams" (a local term for Taiwanese) or "Taro" (a local term for Mainlanders), and instead to think of themselves as a community of people with common interests and a common destiny, faced with a formidable opponent on the other side of the Taiwan Strait (Chung, 1999). If Taiwan is to maintain its status quo, for however long it takes the mainland to reform its own internal system to the level demanded by Taiwan for serious consideration of possible reunification, then all the people of Taiwan need to unite together, the argument continues. The current President, Chen Shui-bian, has urged people to forget about yams and taro and everyone on the island to regard themselves as "peanuts," another widely grown crop on the island that easily takes root and thus aptly symbolizes the desired unity of the island's people. The "indigenization" of Taiwan's people, and development of their identity, is still very much an incomplete process, however, as evidenced by a survey conducted by the ROC's Mainland Affairs Council in October 1998, in which 38 percent of Taiwan's population felt they were Taiwanese rather than Chinese, while 12 percent regarded themselves as Chinese rather than Taiwanese, and the remaining 45 percent embraced a dual identity ("Elusive Answers," 2000). Thus, the idea of the "New Taiwanese" is still far from a reality.

A subtheme of the "New Taiwanese" is the emergence of increased identity consciousness among both the aborigines and the Hakka, and increased unwillingness on their part to accept relatively sublimated roles in Taiwan.

The aborigines are increasingly integrating into Taiwan's modern society, partly as a result of the government's Living Guidance Plan for Aborigines Residing in Cities (*ROC Yearbook 1998:* 32). Various other programs help the aborigines to maintain their native languages, culture, and customs, yet at the same time to become active participants in modern society. However, it is difficult to maintain traditions and become assimilated at the same time. It is not uncommon on Taiwan now for aboriginal youths to speak better Mandarin or Taiwanese than their native language. Still, acute social problems, such as alcoholism, unemployment, and adolescent prostitution, are still widespread among the aborigines. The ideal of the aborigines maintaining pure, traditional lifestyles in the mountains of Taiwan is increasingly an illusion.[14]

For the Hakka, the 2000 presidential campaign highlighted the differences that still exist between them and the Hoklo majority in the Taiwanese community. Many Hakka voters went for one of the former KMT candidates (Soong, who ran outside the KMT), rather than the DPP candidate (Chen) heavily favored by most Hoklo, because of still unresolved resentments over being a minority discriminated against by the larger majority (the Hoklo). Many Hakka fear the eventual disappearance of the Hakka language, and hence their cultural identity, now that the Taiwanese Hoklo are in control of the government and the Taiwanese language (the Min dialect of the Hoklo) is perceived as gaining increased usage. It is a matter of dispute whether the Hoklo language is increasing or declining. It appears to be increasing in political discourse, in schools, and in the media, while declining in other ways as mixed families and Taipei migrants, especially younger people, adopt Mandarin Chinese as their everyday language. Anyway, many Hakka have ambivalent feelings: while few want reunification under the PRC, many worry about how to preserve their distinctive identity within the new Taiwan (Kiang, 1992). Thus, one can now see many publications by the Hakka community, web page sites, and other activities, all designed to rally the Hakka and promote their cause.

It is clear that Taiwan has to develop a society and political system that provide full participation and equality for all groups, that cultivate a true sense of a "national" (i.e., island-wide Taiwanese) identity, while still preserving the distinctiveness of each group. As many multicultural states around the world have experienced, however, this is an extremely difficult goal to achieve. It is even more difficult for Taiwan, given that most of the world's nations do not recognize it as a sovereign nation.

Taiwan and the PRC

Not surprisingly, the PRC views the emergence of this concept of the "New Taiwanese" and its active promotion by the ROC government and the various political parties as a highly dangerous development for China's national interest. The larger issue, from the perspective of the Beijing government, is the viability of China as a nation-state and the political integrity of all the pieces of the Chinese empire. If Taiwan is allowed to go its own way, explicitly or even implicitly, the risks increase greatly for separatism in Tibet, Xinjiang, and other peripheral regions of the country. The 9-11 terrorist events in the U.S. and the worldwide fallout from that have reinforced this fear in China (hence, China's ready willingness to join the U.S.-led effort to crack down on "terrorists," which to China equates with "separatists," or "splittists" as China also calls them). Taiwan thus has to live with the harsh reality of PRC policies toward Taiwan. Hence, the grave danger that the island faces as the mainland increases its economic, and military, buildup. These geopolitical realities have caused most of the proponents for Taiwan independence to temper their public declarations, if not their innermost thoughts, about Taiwan's future.

In March 2000, Taiwan had a presidential election that not only dramatically advanced the democratic process in Taiwan, but also brought to the forefront the internal debate about independence, and the major ethnic and political differences between the then two dominant political parties, the KMT and DPP. Chen Shui-bian, the DPP candidate, won, to the surprise of many, primarily because the KMT vote was split between two other candidates and because, some observers contend, strong verbal threats from the PRC government just before the election swayed some Taiwanese voters to go over to the DPP side. Although Chen won, it was only with 39.4 percent of the vote and a narrow margin, with the KMT still dominant in the legislature. Hence, the Chen administration was plagued with legislative gridlock and numerous political blunders based on inexperience and the immaturity of Taiwan's fledgling democracy. Immediately upon winning the election, Chen adopted a conciliatory stance toward the PRC, offering to visit the mainland and talk with the PRC leaders. The main stumbling block, however, remains the same: Chen is unwilling to publicly proclaim there is only "one China," but is willing to discuss the issue with Beijing, while Beijing requires a public endorsement from Taiwan of "one China," without any ambiguous qualifications about what "one China" means, before any talks can begin. By his second year in office, Chen went even further in moving to a centrist position not all that different from the KMT, with what has been described as his "One If and Five Noes Policy," namely, that if the PRC would renounce the use of force, then Taiwan would maintain the status quo by not declaring independence, not changing the national title from the current Republic of China, not changing the constitution, not carrying out a referendum on independence, and not abolishing the KMT-developed Guidelines for National Unification (Sicherman, 2001). The PRC has maintained a stony silence and refused to deal with the Chen government at all. Observers thought that Beijing was waiting for the December 2001 legislative elections, hoping that the KMT, in alliance with the other splinter parties (NP and PFP) might rally and gain greater strength in the legislature. Beijing might also be waiting for the 2004 presidential election, with the hope that Chen and the DPP would be defeated. Regardless, the impasse between the two sides continues into its second half-century and the Chinese civil war remains without final closure.

One could argue that the principal hurdle facing all political parties on Taiwan today is how to convince the leaders in Beijing that it is also in the best interests of the PRC to maintain the status quo. At the present time, neither side in the dispute is ready internally, in terms of political and social development, to deal rationally and equitably with this extremely sensitive issue. The PRC is rapidly evolving, just as is Taiwan. Leaders still imbued with the harsh divisions of the Cold War and the past still influence policy in both the PRC and ROC. Hence, the argument goes, the immediate future is not the time to push for complete reunification. Now is the time for moderates on both sides to stand back and let nature take its course without forcing the issue one way or the other. It is possible that some sort of reunification short of full political ties may be achievable in the coming decades. For now, anyway, the question of who are the "Taiwanese" still cannot be fully answered. Perhaps sometime in the twenty-first century a final answer will emerge.

NOTES

1. For romanization of Chinese names in this chapter, the Wade-Giles system is used for places and persons on Taiwan; for mainland names the pinyin system is used. These two systems, officially used by the governments concerned, are a reflection of the political divisions between the two sides.

2. As part of their perceived "duty" to preserve China's traditional Confucian culture from the hated Communists, the ROC brought with it to Taiwan a vast collection of priceless art treasures, originally salvaged and protected over the preceding years during the long war with Japan and then the resumed civil war. These art objects were later enshrined in a magnificent new Palace Museum constructed in the northern suburbs of Taipei, and arguably one of the top Chinese art museums in the world today. The Museum also served the purpose, from the government's viewpoint, of helping to educate the native Taiwanese about their cultural heritage.

3. Since 1992, identity cards issued to every citizen on Taiwan no longer carry the "native place" information, i.e., the place of birth of one's father.

4. For a very useful collection of essays by a variety of Taiwan scholars on the historical and spatial development of Taiwan, see Knapp (1980). Ahern and Gates (1981) is also an excellent collection of anthropologically focused studies by some of the leading anthropologists in Taiwan studies. Meskill (1979) presents a fascinating in-depth analysis of one of the great Taiwanese families during the course of the Qing period.

5. There is a rich literature on the Japanese era in Taiwan. Davidson (1903) is one the best first-hand sources for that critical period of late Qing/early Japanese occupation. Also recommended are: Barclay (1954), Ho (1966), Tsurumi (1977), and Kerr (1974).

6. Japan has reemerged in recent decades as a desired locale for education, especially at the university level, for students from many countries, including the PRC, repeating a role that Japan had in the pre–World War II era.

7. Japan also occupied another part of China before World War II, namely, Manchuria, in 1931, established a puppet government there under Emperor Puyi and renamed the area "Manchukuo." That endeavor, however, was different in almost all respects from their rule in Taiwan, except insofar as the Japanese hoped it would also be a permanent occupation. See, for example, Spence, 1990.

8. One positive consequence of this was eventually to turn Taipei into one of the great culinary centers of the world for both Chinese and Japanese cuisines.

9. As a notable example, the International Committee for Human Rights in Taiwan published the *Taiwan Communique,* and distributed this revolutionary periodical several times a year through its branches in Europe, Canada, and the U.S. After 1987, the Committee was able to set up an office in Taiwan as well and continues its work, now transformed into promoting Taiwan's continued independence from PRC control and the issue of outright independence.

10. Among the many studies on Taiwan's economic development, particularly recommended are: Ho (1978); Bain (1993); Gold (1986); Kuo, Ranis, and Fei (1981); and Liu (1987).

11. See, for example: various chapters in Ahern and Gates (1981); Gallin (1966).

12. The political reformation of Taiwan has been intensively examined in a number of studies. See, particularly: Tien (1989); Tucker (1994); and Lai, Myers, and Wei (1991). Lai et al. provide a more recent contrast with the earlier study by Kerr (1974), long considered a classic because of its scholarship and first-hand reporting on the tragic events in Taiwan from 1945–1947.

13. Much of this interchange with the mainland has been conducted through two semi-governmental agencies created by the two sides to give the illusion that Taiwan was not dealing directly with the PRC: the Straits Exchange Foundation (SEF) for Taiwan, and the Association for Relations Across the Taiwan Straits (ARATS) for the mainland. See: Williams (1994).

14. The diminished position of the aborigines over the centuries, and beginning resurgence in recent years, have interesting parallels with the experience of the Native Americans (American "Indians") in North America, and reflect in a broader sense the struggles of countless minority aboriginal peoples found in many countries of the world, such as Australia.

REFERENCES

Ahern, Emily Martin and Hill Gates, eds. 1981. *The Anthropology of Taiwanese Society,* Stanford: Stanford University Press.

Bain, Irene. 1993. *Agricultural Reform in Taiwan: From Here to Modernity?* Hong Kong: The Chinese University Press.

Barclay, George W. 1954. *Colonial Development and Population in Taiwan,* Princeton: Princeton University Press.

Chang, Chiung-fang. 1998. "Home Is Where the Heart Is: The Hakka 'Guests' of Tunghua Street," *Sinorama,* May: 50–61.

Cheng, Allen T. 2001. "The United States of China," *Asiaweek,* July 6: 19–26.

Chung, Oscar. 1999. "Neither Yam Nor Taro," *Free China Review,* February: 6–13.

Davidson, James W. 1903. *The Island of Formosa: Historical View from 1430 to 1900,* New York: Macmillan.

"EDAC Recommendations to Be Implemented." 2001. *Taipei Journal,* August 31: 7.

"Elusive Answers to Ethnic Issues," *Taipei Journal,* March 4, 2000: 7.

Gallin, Bernard. 1966. *Hsin Hsing, Taiwan: A Chinese Village in Change,* Berkeley: University of California Press.

Gilley, Bruce. 1998. "Character Building: Beijing and Taipei Fight for Young Minds in the U.S.," *Far Eastern Economic Review,* October 29: 26–27.

Gold, Thomas B. 1986. *State and Society in the Taiwan Miracle,* Armonk, NY, and London: M. E. Sharpe.

Ho, Samuel P. S. 1978. *Economic Development of Taiwan, 1860–1970,* New Haven and London: Yale University Press.

Ho, Yhi-min. 1966. *Agricultural Development of Taiwan, 1903–1960,* Nashville: Vanderbilt University Press.

Kerr, George H. 1974. *Formosa: Licensed Revolution and the Home Rule Movement, 1895–1945,* Honolulu: The University Press of Hawaii.

Kiang, Clyde. 1992. *The Hakka Odyssey and Their Taiwan Homeland,* Elgin, PA: Allegheny Press.

Knapp, Ronald G., ed. 1980. *China's Island Frontier: Studies in the Historical Geography of Taiwan,* Honolulu: The University Press of Hawaii.

Kuo, Shirley W. Y., Gustav Ranis, and John C. H. Fei. 1981. *The Taiwan Success Story: Rapid Growth with Improved Distribution in the Republic of China, 1952–1979,* Boulder: Westview Press.

Lai, Tse-han, Ramon H. Myers, and Wei Wou. 1991. *A Tragic Beginning: The Taiwan Uprising of February 28, 1947,* Stanford: Stanford University Press.

Lamley, Harry J. 1981. "Subethnic Rivalry in the Ch'ing Period," in Emily Martin Ahern and Hill Gates, eds., *The Anthropology of Taiwanese Society,* Stanford: Stanford University Press, 241–281.

Liu, Alan P. L. 1987. *Phoenix and the Lame Lion: Modernization in Taiwan and Mainland China, 1950–1980,* Stanford: Hoover Institution Press.

"MAC Poll Shows Support for Status Quo," *Taipei Journal,* July 27: 5.

Meskill, Johanna Menzel. 1979. *A Chinese Pioneer Family: The Lins of Wu-feng, Taiwan, 1729–1895,* Princeton: Princeton University Press.

Ng, Franklin. 1998, *The Taiwanese Americans,* Westport, CT, and London: Greenwood Press.

Pan, Lynn, ed. 1999. *The Encyclopedia of the Chinese Overseas,* Cambridge, MA: Harvard University Press.

Republic of China Yearbook 1998, Taipei: Government Information Office.

Schubert, Gunter. 1999. "The New Taiwanese: A Look at Taiwan's National Identity," *Topics* (Taipei American Chamber of Commerce), May: 43–45.

Shepherd, John Robert. 1993. *Statecraft and Political Economy on the Taiwan Frontier,* Stanford: Stanford University Press.

Sicherman, Harvey. 2001. "Taiwan's Chen Shui-Bian: A President's Progress," *Foreign Policy Research Institute* (fpri@fpri.org), May 11.

Spence, Jonathan. 1990. *The Search for Modern China,* New York: W. W. Norton.

Tien, Hung-mao. 1989. *The Great Transition: Political and Social Change in the Republic of China,* Stanford: Hoover Institution Press.

Tsurumi, E. Patricia. 1977. *Japanese Colonial Education in Taiwan, 1895–1945,* Cambridge, MA: Harvard University Press.

Tucker, Nancy Bernkopf. 1994. *Taiwan, Hong Kong, and the United States, 1945–1992: Uncertain Friendships,* New York: Twayne Publishers.

U.S. Immigration and Naturalization Service. 1996. *Statistical Yearbook of the Immigration and Naturalization Service, 1994,* Washington, D.C.: U.S. Department of Justice, Immigration and Naturalization Service.

Wachman, Alan M. 1994. *Taiwan: National Identity and Democratization,* Armonk, NY, and London: M. E. Sharpe.

Waldron, Arthur. 1998. "Conflicting Realities," *Free China Review,* September: 42–44.

Williams, Jack F. 1980. "Sugar: The Sweetener in Taiwan's Development," in Ronald G. Knapp, ed., *China's Island Frontier: Studies in the Historical Geography of Taiwan,* Honolulu: The University Press of Hawaii, 219–251.

———. 1994. "China and Taiwan," in Denis Dwyer, ed., *China: The Next Decades,* New York: John Wiley and Sons, 222–242.

Yeh, Chienwei. 2000. *Colonial Taipei: A Family Caught in Japanese Time and Space,* unpublished Ph.D. dissertation, Canberra: Australian National University.

ETHNICITY, IDENTITY, AND DIASPORA AS HOME

8

Nation, Ethnicity, and Identity: Singapore and the Dynamics and Discourses of Chinese Migration

Lily Kong and Brenda Yeoh

Singapore, a multiracial city-state, comprises about 77.3 percent Chinese, 14.1 percent Malay, 7.3 percent Indians and 1.3 percent "Others" (using official categories) (*Yearbook of Statistics,* 1996). This balance is primarily the outcome of nineteenth- and early-twentieth-century movements, which saw especially the translocation of Chinese and Indians from south China and India respectively to what was then Malaya (including present-day Malaysia and Singapore). Our focus in this chapter is on the Chinese population in Singapore, and their renegotiations of identity, particularly in the face of Singapore's establishment as an independent state in 1965, and the concomitant state-led efforts at nation building and emphasis on national identity construction. We take the reader through the years of independence to the most recent historical moment in which Chinese Singaporeans are now returning as transmigrant workers to China amid state calls for regionalization. They in turn are confronted by transnational contexts in which they renegotiate their ethnic identities yet again.

Our chapter begins by painting the backdrop of nineteenth-century Singapore as quintessential product of overlapping diasporas, an alternative perspective to the more standard account of Singapore as a creation of British colonialism. In particular, we highlight the dynamics of Chinese diasporic encounters in a colonial city where they quickly assumed the position of the majority "race," gained considerable foothold in the economy as "guest-workers" and entrepreneurs, but otherwise sank shallow roots in a place where social and political power remained in the hands of the British. We then proceed to our main focus on the post-independence years, when the end of colonial rule corresponded with a disruption to old patterns of transnational migration, introduced new discourses of nation building and national identity construction, and attempts were made to shape people's attachment to place. In particular, we examine state policies towards the Chinese in Singapore in the post-independence decades. We begin with those which sought to submerge and subvert ethnic identity to the "larger" purposes of nation building and national identity construction. Second, we examine subsequent policies and plans which seemed to recreate and reclaim Chinese links and identity. Throughout, we show how everyday practices among the Chinese sometimes reflect and reinforce state policies to privilege multiracial, national perspectives, but at other times, openly proclaim the strength of Chinese ties or quietly contest efforts to subdue such ties.

NINETEENTH CENTURY SINGAPORE: PRODUCT OF DIASPORAS

Singapore is a child of diaspora. Its history embodies many of the tensions of blood and belonging that the concept evokes. Singapore testifies to the difficulties of creating a modern nation-state on a model inherited from Europe in a region where history mocks the nation-state's claims to cultural and linguistic exclusiveness. The post-colonial experience of Singapore has been dominated by the attempts of the state—an artifact of British rule—to surmount these constraints and to create a national community bounded by a common culture and a sense of place, and bonded by individual allegiance. (Harper, 1997: 261)

As "a child of diaspora" in the nineteenth and earlier half of the twentieth centuries, Singapore was a polyglot migrant world constituted by streams of immigrants from China, India, the Malay archipelago, and other far-flung places, and dominated by a small European imperial diaspora. By the last quarter of the nineteenth century, Singapore had rapidly consolidated its position as the premier entrepôt and trading center in the Far East. The rapidly expanding economy, coupled with a liberal open door policy on immigration, drew ever-increasing numbers of immigrants. With only about 10,000 people on the island in 1824 (five years after Stamford Raffles established Singapore as a British trading post), the total population grew past the 100,000 mark not long after the first extensive census in 1871, and took only another two decades for the population to double and pass the 200,000 mark in 1901. The next doubling was in the 1930s and in the immediate postwar era, the population size reached one million. On the eve of independence in the early 1960s, the people of the newly conceived city-state numbered about one and a half million. As a component of population dynamics, migrational surplus outweighed natural increase which was in fact negative prior to 1921. Not only were mortality rates (the main killers being malaria, tuberculosis and beri-beri) extremely high up to the early twentieth century, the sex ratio among Chinese and Indian immigrants was highly imbalanced (with about three men to every woman in the early twentieth century), thus resulting in low fertility rates. Natural increase did not replace migrational surplus as the dominant contributor to population growth until some time after 1957.

As Demaine (1984: 29) argues in the context of Southeast Asia, labor migration was strongly encouraged as the European colonial powers sought to introduce immigrants from outside colonized territories in order to fill specific occupational niches unpopular with the indigenous population. In a port city such as Singapore, entrepôt trade and the development of the port economy was dependent on a continuous stream of immigrants to supply sufficient cheap labor. Migration gave colonial Singapore a distinctively plural character in the Furnivallian sense of a society with

> different sections of the community living side by side, but separately, within the same political unit . . . Each group holds by its own religion, its own culture and language, its own ideas and ways. As individuals they meet, but only in the market place, in buying and selling . . . Even in the economic sphere there is a division of labor along racial lines. Natives, Chinese, Indians and Europeans all have different functions, and within each major group, subsections have particular occupations. (Furnivall, 1948: 304–305)

Each immigrant group was accorded a specific place in Singapore's social and economic landscape. The European population, which never expanded beyond about one to two percent of the population, were the governing and mercantile elite, possessing socioeconomic and political power disproportionate to their numbers. Indian immigrants, making up about eight percent of the population at the turn of the century, arrived in Singapore mainly as traders and laborers although some came as garrison troops, camp followers and transmarine convicts (Turnbull, 1977: 37). They were particularly conspicuous in textile and piece-goods, wholesaling and retailing, and money lending as well as workers around the port and railway. Most were south Indian Tamils although Sikhs, Punjabis, Gujeratis, Bengalis and Parsis also numbered among them. The small local Malay population was also soon augmented by immigrants from Malacca, Sumatra, Java, the Riau archipelago and other eastern islands and these became boatmen, fishermen, wood cutters, carpenters, policemen, watchmen, office "boys," drivers and house servants (Turnbull, 1977: 37; Roff, 1964: 77). At the turn of the century, they accounted for about 15 percent of the total population. Among the much smaller minority groups, the Arabs and Jews were of note as wealthy merchants and landowners, while the Armenian and Japanese communities, though small, also found a place in Singapore's cosmopolitan landscape.

The Chinese were by far the most dominant ethnic group in numerical terms, accounting for 63 percent of the total population by 1881. The Chinese immigrants hailed mainly from the provinces of Guangdong and Fujian in southeast China and comprised five major *bang* or dialect groups: Hokkien, Teochew, Cantonese, Hakka and Hylam (Hainanese). Spanning a wide range of occupational niches including merchants, shopkeepers, agriculturalists, artisans and manual laborers of all sorts, they brought with them an entire array of organizations such as clan and dialect associations, trade guilds, temples dedicated to a panoply of Chinese deities, and secret societies which provided the institutional structures within which social, cultural, religious, and recreational activities were performed (Yen, 1986: 317). Through these institutions, Chinese groups had access to a certain range of services which supported immigrant life such as the provision of medical care, job protection, education, entertainment, and facilities which catered to the observance of the rites of passage. The social infrastructure of migration was relatively well developed, and provided the bridgeheads for the chain migration of relatives, friends and clan members. The traditional core area of the Chinese was Chinatown south of the Singapore River in an area originally marked out by Raffles as the Chinese *kampung*,[1] but with rapid growth, the Chinese soon came to dominate the area directly north of the Singapore River, originally designated "European Town" by Raffles. The port area around Tanjong Pagar also constituted another overspill area adjacent to "old" Chinatown as well as a convenient location for port workers.

Until the establishment of the Chinese Protectorate[2] in 1877, the British in general did not intervene in the affairs of the Chinese communities. In conformity with the racialized politics elsewhere in the British Empire, the British rulers considered the Chinese a discrete race and there was little attempt to incorporate the Chinese in any meaningful sense into a broader Malayan framework, whether in terms of the legal framework or the provision of education, health care facilities or housing (Yeoh, 1996a). As Freedman (1950: 98) observed, "the internal affairs of the Chinese community largely passed out of the purview of the British administration. Legally and politically, the Chinese contrived to maintain their own world." In economic terms, the Chinese were also assured of a certain degree of autonomy in conducting their own affairs, thereby constituting an *imperium in imperio*. It is in this context, and under the encouragement of the Chinese government during the rise of modern China, that "'the Chinese overseas' became 'overseas Chinese', having come to think of themselves as an entity with rights and duties *vis-à-vis* their homeland" (Rajah, 1997: 13). Pride engendered by the new Chinese nationalism especially after 1911 further strengthened the consciousness of their links with "homeland" among the Nanyang (south seas)

Chinese. Even among the politically untutored, China remained the locus of their existential world, if not in life than at least in death, as Low Ngiong Ing (1983: 112), an early-twentieth-century Hockchiu immigrant, explained in his autobiographical account:

> An immigrant, if he could afford it, would return to China every few years. In his perambulations he would keep his eyes open for a desirable burial-plot, a knoll commanding a good view, and auspicious according to the laws of geomancy. For we did not mind being men of Nanyang, but that dying, we would hate to be ghosts of Nanyang. If we prospered, we would pile up money in China in order to renovate the ancestral graves and the ancestral homes, to redeem the ancestral fields and add to them . . . so that men might know we were somebody.

Clearly then, for most of the colonial period, immigrant Chinese who sought their livelihoods in the Nanyang continued not only to frame their identities with reference to China as their homeland where return, if not foreseeable in the immediate future, was at least desired as the ultimate rite of passage.

POST-INDEPENDENCE SINGAPORE: CHANGING DYNAMICS AND DISCOURSES

Chinese immigration continued to feature strongly in Singapore's population dynamics right up to the Japanese Occupation, along with a continuous flow of return and secondary migration. Such movements persisted up to the early 1960s, after which they dwindled (Kwok, 1998a: 200). At the same time, as Singapore moved towards the end of British rule in the late 1950s, the lines between immigrant and resident became more clearly drawn. The Singapore Citizenship Ordinance of 1957 was a watershed. Requiring a residential requirement of only eight years, the ordinance admitted the majority of those born in China to Singapore citizenship (Kwok, 1998a: 211).

With independence in 1965 also came new policies and plans as well as a new state rhetoric about nation building that pervaded public discourse. Policies and plans were put in place to tackle major socioeconomic problems (such as unemployment, housing and education) and hence improve living conditions, but they were also mounted so that the government could secure political legitimacy, build ideological consensus and transform the population into a disciplined industrial workforce (Chua, 1991). The state's strategy in forging a new "nation" rested in the forging of a common consciousness and a sense of identity with the nation-state, beyond meeting the immediate and more long-term material needs of the people. Singapore's leaders had to fundamentally reshape the "primacy of places" in people's consciousness and in turn replace it by "an abstractly conceptualized and much less immediate linkage with a generalized area," in this case, a "nation" defined by political and territorial boundaries (Benjamin, 1988: 3). This was particularly crucial since Singapore's population consisted primarily of immigrants hailing from different "homelands."

A corollary of place-bonding in the construction of nationhood is the welding of individuals within the legitimized borders of the independent "nation" into "one people." The state's vision was to integrate the "nation" to create a "multiracial, non-communist, non-aligned, and democratic socialist state" (Chan, 1991: 158). In 1966, a Constitution Commission was appointed to enshrine the multiracial ideal in the Constitution in order to safeguard the rights of racial, linguistic and religious minorities (Chan, 1991: 159). Multiracialism (along with multilingualism, multireligiosity and multiculturalism) has since then been promulgated as a social formula to forge a single identity out of the heterogeneous population riven by racial, religious, language and cultural lines (Betts, 1975; Benjamin, 1976; Siddique, 1989: 365). This state-vaunted formulation designates four "official" races—Chinese, Malays, Indians and "Others"—viewed as separate but equal, and encourages acceptance of the coexistence of different religious practices, customs and traditions of the various communities "without discrimination for any particular community" (Chan and Evers, 1978: 123). The PAP government had consistently regarded racial chauvinism as one of the two main threats to nation building (the other being communism) and strove to ensure a balance between the interests of the different racial groups through its policies relating to education, housing, language (Chiew, 1985; Shee, 1985), and most recently, the formation of self-help groups. While each race is urged to maintain and draw sustenance from a carefully contained sense of ethnic and cultural identity, they are also encouraged to develop a larger identity based on secular, non-cultural, national values. Communalist sentiments based on race, dialect, surname or regional affinity must be broken down and replaced with social relationships which derived their meaning from the overarching "nation-state framework" (Benjamin, 1988: 36). By appeasing and containing ethnic demands, the multiracial ideology "contributes to the nation-building process" (Hill and Lian, 1995: 5).

The process of nation-building thus requires that the state interferes with the consciousness of its new citizens, turning people's attention away from more parochial concerns towards the nation-state. This process of constructing a "nation" and a "people" from their "almost non-existent past" has a short history of no more than 30 years and is thus "relatively shallow and extremely fluid and formative" (Chua and Kuo, 1990: 5). In the immediate post-independence era, the reality and rhetoric of national survival in the face of threats (e.g., communism) and heavy odds (e.g., the lack of natural resources) became the major rallying point to mobilize the population and inculcate national consciousness. At least before the 1980s, the national values selected to form the bedrock of national identity were deliberately pragmatic rather than associated with any one cultural tradition, "universalistic" values relating to modernity, development and economic success (Chan and Evers, 1978: 122, 125). In more recent times, economic success has brought with it "substantial injection of self-definition and national pride," contributing significantly to the development of national culture and identity (Chua and Kuo, 1990: 6). In the climate of success, the rhetoric of "survival" and "necessity," while not totally abandoned, is no longer compelling in mobilizing people to unite in their strivings; instead, with affluence opening up the avenues of choice and individual preferences, new imperatives had to be found which could justify the moulding of a singular national identity (Chua, 1985: 42; Hill and Lian, 1995: 11). The focus of national identity construction from the mid-1980s has in turn broadened to include an emphasis on the collective history, heritage and struggles of "one people," a revival of "Asian values," and the development of a national ideology, "shared values" (*The Straits Times,* 6 January 1991) culled from a selective distillation of "eastern" and "western" mores, and of traditional and progressive elements. "Janus-faced," the state in the process of nation building "select[s] from the past and reconstitute[s] those elements which are identified as possible sources of cultural ballast and therefore of stability while simultaneously orienting citizens towards the achievement of future goals" (Hill and Lian, 1995: 36).

The broad canvas on which we have painted the state's nation-building rhetoric and action hints at policies and actions which sought to achieve nation-building aims through submerging Chinese links and identity. In the next section, we spotlight two such policies.

Submerging and Subverting Chinese Links and Identity

Policies on language and "community" building played crucial roles in forging common ties among Singaporeans of different groups. At the same time, in effecting these policies, ties within the Chinese community and Chinese identity were subdued. These policies were achieved using a combination of hegemonic but sometimes more apparently coercive measures.

In the early 1960s, while Singapore was part of Malaya, Malay was designated the national language of the state of Singapore, Chinese was recognized as the "mother tongue" of the overwhelmingly Chinese population, and English a useful commercial language (PuruShotam, 1998: 58). This was, however, not undisputed, for "proponents of the (Malay) language, mainly from across the Causeway were impatient for the installation of the Malay language as the language of all Malaysians. For them, the identification and play on the meaning of Chinese, even if 'only' as a mother tongue, was considered a barrier to the institution of the National Language" (PuruShotam, 1998: 60). They also wanted the dominance of English to be replaced by Malay.

Once Singapore became independent in 1965, the government made it clear that the policy of multilingualism would hold. It also announced that Malay would remain the national language while Mandarin, Tamil and English would be Singapore's official languages. This reflected national concerns, since the choice of Malay was borne of historical and geographical considerations: Singapore's original population of Malays and location in a predominantly Malay world. As various writers have explained, the most recent being PuruShotam (1998: 63),

> The choice of Malay . . . was linked to concern with profiling Singapore, then a fairly defenceless republic, in terms that would be favourable to its position in the region. Indeed, in one of his warnings about keeping the issue of language low, Lee Kuan Yew referred to the "only one mile of water across the Causeway" that separated Singapore from the Federation of Malaysia. Referring to this again in 1970, the then Minister for Communications, clarified that while it would have been "democratic" to choose Mandarin as the National Language of Singapore, the government's decision to retain Malay was in some important part due to the "unfriendly foreign references now and again to Singapore being a Third China."

As a counterbalance to naming Malay the national language, the accordance of official status to the other three languages at the same time indicated a sensitivity to the fact that the other communities should be acknowledged in some way too. However, given that the majority of Singapore's population (74.9 percent) at that point was Chinese, the decision not to privilege any of the Chinese languages in fact could be interpreted as a policy that discounted the Chinese. This interpretation did not escape some Chinese and attempts were indeed made to reassert their own identity. In 1965, the Chinese educated elites categorically asked the then-Prime Minister for the institutionalization of Mandarin as *the* official language of Singapore (PuruShotam, 1998). The request was denied.

The ideal of multilingualism as espoused in the Constitution is not without contradiction. This is most clearly borne out in the bilingual policy. While multilingualism upholds an ideal that Singaporeans have the freedom to use any language they wish, the bilingual policy is designed to promote specifically the use of English for pragmatic reasons and the "mother tongue" for cultural development. English is encouraged because it is recognized that in order to attract foreign investors and to participate effectively in the international economic system, an English-speaking labor force was needed, facilitating communication, the development of commerce, trade and industry, science and technology (Altbach, 1982). The "mother tongue," taught as a "second language" in school, is believed to anchor cultural roots, and is defined as "language of [one's] racial origin" (PuruShotam, 1998: 57), using a 1956 recommendation by the All Party Committee of Singapore Legislative Assembly on Chinese Education (APR). There, it is specified that

> Mandarin should be the only language to be taught for all Chinese pupils as the compulsory language in English schools, Tamil for all Indian children (or Hindi or whatever language the Indian community chooses) and Malay for all Malaysian races. In the case of the Eurasian, since English is the mother tongue, the choice of the vernacular should be left to the parents. (APR, 1956: 41)

For the Chinese, freedom of language is more apparent than real. In particular, where the Indian community appeared to have had choices open to them in the interpretation of "mother tongue," the Chinese did not have that option. In forcing a common "mother tongue" for all Chinese pupils, an attempt was made to impose a homogeneity and common identity among the Chinese in Singapore which did not exist.

The relegation of Mandarin to second language status was not received without resistance. In April 1966, the Singapore Chinese Chamber of Commerce, the Singapore Chinese Schools Conference, the Singapore Chinese Middle School Teachers' Union, the Singapore Chinese Secondary School Principals Association, and the Singapore Chinese Second Language Teachers' Association organized a month-long "Promote Mother Tongue Education," with the aim of urging more Chinese parents to send their children to Chinese schools. They also hoped that by doing so, Mandarin would be elevated from second language to first language status, since it would then be the main medium of education. In what was an astute move which appeared to respond and yet not capitulate, the state announced a new ruling on the second language soon after the campaign was launched in which the second language became a compulsory primary and secondary school subject with immediate effect. This was in contrast to the earlier policy where the second language subject only existed in the primary school curriculum. The state therefore gave more acknowledgement to the need to have Mandarin taught in schools but did not concede first language status to it.

Even while the state was clear that Mandarin was not to threaten the predominance of English, it nevertheless attempted to use Mandarin as the unifying factor amongst Chinese through reducing dialect use. This attempt, however, took a long while to effect. Twelve years after the introduction of compulsory bilingual education in primary and secondary schools, a Report on the Ministry of Education in 1978 found, *inter alia,* that the policy of bilingualism had not been very successful in the sense that students found it difficult to be proficient in two languages. One of the main hindrances for those with an English-Mandarin combination was the use of Chinese dialects in everyday situations. Indeed, the Report acknowledged that since 85 percent of Singapore's Chinese came from dialect-speaking homes, Mandarin had been wrongly dubbed as the mother tongue of the Chinese! Rather than leading to a reevaluation of the measures that were designed to homogenize the Chinese in the first place, this realization led to intensified efforts to valorize Mandarin. Specifically, findings from the Ministry of Education report led to a forum on promoting Mandarin among the Chinese in Singapore, organized by the Singapore Baolin Recreation Club, two Chinese dailies and the English language daily. Following this, a panel, spearheaded by the Chinese Chamber of Commerce and Industry was set up in August 1979, to promote the use of Mandarin (PuruShotam, 1998: 68–69).

At the launch of the Speak Mandarin campaign on 7 September 1979, the then-Prime Minister Lee Kuan Yew "made repeated pleas . . . to Chinese parents to drop dialects at home and speak Mandarin to help lighten the load of their children (in school)." He also pointed out that learning Mandarin, "apart from being culturally worthwhile would also be economically useful because China, after successful implementation of its "Four Modernizations" program would become a major trading partner—accessible not through Hokkien but Mandarin" (*The Straits Times,* 8 September 1979). Endorsement of Mandarin above Chinese dialects was therefore forthcoming from the highest level. The commitment to this policy is evident in that the Speak Mandarin campaign continues to this day, and now relies on a host of strategies to achieve its aims. The mass media has been mobilized through the years to spread the campaign message and help teach the language as well. Dialect programs over radio, television and Rediffusion (a Singapore media group), except for small segments of news broadcasts on radio and Rediffusion, have since been phased out. Publicity materials such as songs, stickers, advertisements and posters have been produced to encourage Chinese Singaporeans to utilize the language more. Both public and private organizations, and various constituencies have also organized campaign activities, including visits made by Members of Parliament and members of grassroots organizations such as the Citizens' Consultative Committees, Community Centre Management Committees and Residents' Committees to residences, markets, food centers and shops to distribute publicity material and to encourage the Chinese community to speak more Mandarin (*A Decade of Mandarin, 1979–1989:* 23–25). Less hegemonic measures have also been used: Mandarin-speaking officers have replaced ethnic Chinese officers who do not do so at public counters; Chinese officers have also been asked not to use dialects during office hours when dealing with the Chinese public, as far as possible. For those officers who do not know Mandarin but need to use the language in the course of their work, conversational Mandarin courses are offered for them. The Ministry of Education also conducts a Proficiency Examination in Conversational Mandarin for officers who have completed the Conversational Mandarin Course, and one of the incentives given to these officers is that, together with their ability to speak Mandarin and other factors, is a greater chance of being promoted. Since September 1979, the government has made the ability to speak Mandarin one of the criteria for new Chinese applicants for taxi-driving licenses. The government also encourages the use of *hanyu pinyin*[3] names instead of dialect transliterations in English for signages of food stalls, new companies and businesses, the Housing and Development Board's new towns, new street names,[4] private estate and building names, and newborn Chinese babies' names. To oversee the proper usage of Mandarin, a Standard Chinese Language Committee was set up by the Ministry of Education in 1981 to conduct research on the use of the Chinese language in Singapore, to upgrade the quality of usage and to provide standardized Mandarin terms (*A Decade of Mandarin, 1979–1989*: 27–31).

The combined effect of all the different measures is that, in Singapore today, English has grown in importance both in the public and private sphere, while the use of Mandarin has eroded the use of dialect. This is reflected in the shifts in language usage pattern within households between 1980 and 1990 (see table 8.1). Furthermore, between 1959 and 1984, the enrollment in Chinese-medium primary schools (those which used Mandarin as the medium of instruction) dropped from 46 percent to 0.7 percent (*The Straits Times,* 3 May 1987). Similarly, the number of those who qualified to enter Nanyang University (a Chinese-medium university) and chose to do so rather than go to the University of Singapore (an English-medium university) also dropped (Lee, 1980). Indeed, this was one of the reasons cited for the closure of Nanyang University (Lee and Tan, 1996). This was not surprising, as English-educated graduates came into more favor with employers and were paid higher wages than their Chinese-educated counterparts, whose degrees were sometimes not even recognized by employers (Lee and Tan, 1996; PuruShotam, 1998). State policy, which emphasized the construction of a national identity, the building of a "nation" and the development of a sound economy plugged in to a global economy, therefore had the effect of eroding assertions of Chinese identity and transforming the markers of such identity through influencing language use.

Lily Kong and Brenda Yeoh

Table 8.1. Persons Aged 5 Years and Over in Resident Private Households by Percentage of Language Spoken to Parents, Spouse, Siblings and Grandparents, 1980 and 1990

Language	To Parents		To Spouse		To Siblings		To Grandparents	
	1980	1990	1980	1990	1980	1990	1980	1990
English	6.2	12.2	12.7	19.5	14.7	22.0	2.0	4.7
Mandarin	5.7	22.0	9.7	21.8	9.5	26.6	1.1	11.4
Chinese Dialects	66.9	46.9	58.0	40.5	55.6	33.9	79.7	63.3

Sources: Singapore Census of Population 1980 (1981); *Singapore Census of Population 1990* (1993).

Apart from its language policy, the state in Singapore also drew on other strategies in its nation-building endeavor that impinged on the evolution of ethnic identity among the Chinese. We will focus here on attempts at "community" building. Prior to independence, the notion of "community" was often defined in racial terms. Among the Chinese, clan associations played a key role in pulling together the community, or at least, sub-communities, for example, in terms of dialect or surname group. Particularly in the early to mid-twentieth century, clan associations played important social, economic, cultural and even political roles in the lives of Chinese migrants, providing mutual help programs, education, temporary housing (particularly for those who had just arrived), recreational facilities and charity. As Cheng (1990) illustrated, historically, they played an important role in inculcating strong ties among particular communities of Chinese in Singapore.

With independence and importance accorded to the nation-building enterprise, the state began to pay significant attention to community-building activities, defining community in cross-racial terms. State-initiated institutional efforts at community development in Singapore found expression particularly in the activities of residents' committees (RCs) and community centers (CCs). Residents' committees were created as more and more people of different races (mainly Chinese, Malays and Indians) moved into new housing estates,[5] leaving behind the close-knit racial enclaves such as Chinatown for the Chinese and Kampong Glam for the Malays. It was with the intention of encouraging the growth of pan-racial community cohesion and neighborliness that RCs were organized. RCs initiate activities for residents, including social and recreational programs (such as excursions and get-together parties) and educational ones (such as forums and exhibitions). In addition, other forms of service to the community include the organization of senior citizens' programs and tuition classes. The intended aim is to provide residents with opportunities for social interaction.

Like RCs, community centers were created to cater to various social and recreational needs of residents (Wong, 1988). They cater generally to the entire population in defined areas as well as more specifically to women (through the Women's Executive Committees) and youths (through the Youth Executive Committees) in these areas. They are involved in the organization of a range of activities, from recreational (such as Chinese chess) to vocational (dressmaking), cultural (musical instruction) and educational (talks) ones. They are often strategically located to capture hinterlands of population.

CCs and RCs have taken over many of the roles of traditional associations and new associational and neighborhood interaction networks have been encouraged which are no longer oriented along racial lines. The decline in the growth of clan associations is evident in the fact only 39 Chinese associations were established between 1960 and 1970 while the period from 1945 to 1959 witnessed the establishment of 138 such associations. There was also declining membership in many of these associations (Cheng, 1990).

As Cheng (1990: 61) pointed out, clan associations have not been able to compete with the multifarious programs offered by the CCs in particular because of the "shortage of space, manpower and finance." The traditional roles of providing shelter, jobs and education, for example, have also been fulfilled by the state. The state's efforts at community and nation building have thus been achieved through submerging and subverting ethnic Chinese identity.

Recreating and Reclaiming Chinese Links and Identity

The attempts to de-emphasize Chinese links and identity took a turn from the mid to late 1980s as various policies and actions appeared to revalorize such ties. Yet, as we will illustrate, the state continues to emphasize "nation" above "community" defined racially, thus constantly striving to keep a fine balance between reclaiming Chinese cultural identity while keeping at bay the development of any political affiliations with China. In this section, we will illustrate these developments by elaborating on the reignition of Chinese clan association ties, the establishment of racially based self-help groups, the inscription of "Chineseness" in Chinatown to recreate the quintessential "Chinese hearth" and the call to regionalize, building on Chinese networks. We will illustrate in each of these cases how the Chinese community has responded, sometimes heeding the state's exhortations to "rediscover" their roots and ties, at other times, rejecting the state's attempts to impose a constructed "Chineseness," and at yet other times, renegotiating their Chinese identity as previously constructed, given new dynamics and discourses.

One of the key state discourses that has persisted through the last three decades is the idea that Singapore must retain its "Asian values" even as it modernizes and is open to "western" influences. The growth of Singapore as a global city, manifest in, *inter alia,* the increased use of the English language, the exposure to western media, and the growth in travel and tourism, has also meant that Singapore has been exposed to "western" values and ways of doing things. This has caused concern, expressed in a number of remarkably similar ways through the years (see Kong, 2000). Common in public discourse were calls to avoid the perceived erosive effects of the west, and to root cultural values in Asian cultural traditions, while avoiding the privileging of any particular Asian tradition.[6] In 1988, for example, Ho Kah Leong, Senior Parliamentary Secretary, Ministry of Communication and Information, argued that

> In order to resist the erosive effect of western culture, we encourage our people to keep their traditions and cultural roots. [However] care should be taken not to over-emphasize activity that is confined to a certain race only because this could inadvertently lead to racial polarization. (Parliamentary Debates, 14 March 1988, col. 723–724)

Such concerns continue to persist in the 1990s. As George (*The Straits Times,* 31 December 1994) highlighted, the foreign threat that the government seems most worried about is that of "bad Western values." Hence, "[a]t home, politicians told the people to hang on to their traditional Asian ways. Abroad, Senior Minister Lee Kuan Yew and diplomat Kishore Mahbubani continued to counter Western proselytizing blow for blow."

As part of the effort to counter "bad western values," the state saw fit to revitalize the activities of clan associations. The then-Second Deputy Prime Minister (DPM) Ong Teng Cheong first mooted the idea of forming the Singapore Federation of Chinese Clan Associations (SFCCA) in October 1984 at a meeting with Chua Gim Siong, a prime mover of the clan association movement and other community organizations. The Second DPM Ong "confirmed the government's endorsement for clan activities" (Cheng, 1990: 63) and "gave his approval for holding a national seminar of Chinese clan associations aimed at reexamining the associations' role in nation-building" (Cheng, 1990: 63). In the keynote address at the seminar held on 2 December 1984, Mr. Ong outlined five directions of future development for the associations:

- to open their membership to all Singaporeans, irrespective of race and dialect;
- to groom a younger leadership for renewal;
- to intensify cultural and educational activities such as organizing large-scale cultural and recreational activities to promote arts and festivals, publishing books and magazines, and collecting, preserving and exhibiting cultural heritage of associations;

- to set up homes for the aged, creches, and care-centers for different age-groups; and
- to coordinate with other community organizations for community development.

The seminar concluded with the passing of various resolutions that eventually led to the formation of the SFCCA in 1986 (Cheng, 1990: 63–64).

The Second DPM's vision for revitalized Chinese clan associations represented a balance between calling on racial ties while achieving national goals. The state hoped to tap the organizational setup of clan associations and the former spirit of self-help and community assistance that pervaded the early immigrant Chinese communities. However, it hoped to see membership and activities open to non-Chinese as well. This balance was reinforced several years later in 1992 when a new Deputy Prime Minister Lee Hsien Loong outlined his vision for Chinese clan associations. He encouraged activity among Chinese clan associations while emphasizing the commonality of Asian traditions and urging recognition that development of one community was not at the expense of another, to allay fears of divisiveness among communities. He therefore identified the role of clan associations to be:

> . . . to continue imparting values like filial piety, hard work, thrift and honouring one's obligations to the older generation: values which have enabled Asian civilisations to endure for thousands of years. We have to preserve and strengthen these traditional values, especially as our society becomes increasingly affluent and open to outside influences (Lee, 1992: 121).

At the same time, he was keen on the idea that Chinese clan associations "help other community groups with donations and joint projects," a step which will make clear to all that "the progress made by one community is not at the expense of the other communities" (Lee, 1992: 122).

The formation of the SFCCA has been accompanied by a minor revival of sorts of clan association activities in the 1990s. Reports indicate a younger membership and leadership, and renewed efforts at the organization of cultural and educational activities in at least some associations. Yet, while the Chinese community appears to have awoken to state calls to rejuvenate their community ties, the simultaneous state vision that these ties would be developed in tandem with other inter-community links do not appear to have taken root. In 1998, none of the membership registers of the six major clan associations[7] indicated membership of non-Chinese (as envisioned by the then DPM Ong Teng Cheong in 1984). Only one association reported joint organization of one cultural/educational event with a community center in recent years (field notes, November 1998). State attempts to shape the development of inter-community ties via encouragement of links between strengthened racial and national community organizations have therefore not taken the precise shape desired. What appears to have happened instead is a revival of Chinese community ties per se.

In a move similar to the revival of Chinese clan associations, the state also sought to make racial ties work for the "nation" through the establishment of racially based self-help groups. The underlying rationale was again to take advantage of racial affinities to better the conditions of those less well-off and less well-developed within each community and to achieve improvement across all communities eventually. In 1992, through the Singapore Federation of Chinese Clan Associations (SFCCA) and the Singapore Chinese Chamber of Commerce and Industry (SCCCI), the Chinese Development Association Council (CDAC) was set up to help lower-income, under-achieving Chinese households (defined as households in which heads or main wage earners took home S$1,212 or less per month, and who did not have at least GCE O-level qualifications) (*The Straits Times,* 11 November 1992). Although it was set up by nongovernmental organizations, the common wisdom is that "the government's hand is all too visible" (*The Straits Times,* 28 November 1992). The help rendered by CDAC would take various forms, for example, self-help vocational training and tuition programs, and would be funded by contributions from the Chinese community in Singapore. It started with a fund-raising drive spearheaded by three Chinese newspapers (*Lianhe Zaobao, Lianhe Wanbao* and *Xinmin*) and is sustained by auto-deductions of negligible sums from individual Chinese adults' salaries on a monthly basis. Those who do not wish to make the contribution may opt out of the system.

At the inaugural dinner of CDAC in 1992, Prime Minister Goh Chok Tong called explicitly on the racial bonds and spoke about seeking to strengthen and replicate such bonds:

> The Government is aware of the importance of self-help in building an enduring community. The community network built by immigrant forefathers helped them survive through wars, depression and other disasters. We want to strengthen and replicate it. (Goh, 1992: 7)

As with the revival of clan associations, the state's vision has not been completely successful with CDAC. Not all Chinese Singaporeans have subscribed to the notion of self-help. In 1992 when the scheme was initiated, 8.25 percent or 60,000 out of the total 760,000 working adult Chinese had opted out of the system to facilitate contributions from their monthly salaries even though the amount per individual was negligible. It is also likely that those who remained in the scheme did not necessarily do so because they subscribed to the notion of community self-help. For some, the amount was so negligible as to make the process of opting out too troublesome. For others, whether the contribution was channelled to the target population through a racially based community organization or some other organization was immaterial. In turn, for those who opted out, various reasons were cited on the grounds of principle: while some were against the automatic deduction system, which they viewed to be "undemocratic . . . and an infringement of human rights" (Goh, 1992: 13), others were against the "racial" approach of getting a community to help its own kind (*The Straits Times,* 28 November 1992). After all, since independence in 1965, the state had taken over the role of providing basic necessities "rather than to leave each community to help its own kind [as in the colonial era] because this approach accentuates the differences, or fault-lines within multi-racial Singapore" (*The Straits Times,* 28 November 1992). Many also saw CDAC "largely as a Government outfit, and thus not in any dire need of money or other forms of help" (*The Straits Times,* 28 November 1992). It is believed that most of those who opted out were the English-educated because when CDAC set up a hotline in August 1992 to answer public queries on the contribution scheme, nine out of 10 callers of the 3,000 phone calls received were English speaking, with the remaining one speaking in Mandarin or dialect (Goh, 1992: 13). In highlighting this fact, the Prime Minister appeared to suggest that the English-educated Chinese did not feel the sense of community that Chinese-educated Chinese did. Regardless of the veracity of that inference, the fact remains that the state had constructed and called upon a notion of "Chinese community" that did not necessarily exist.

In the same way that a "Chinese community" was being constructed, the state also sought to create a "Chinese landscape." The example of urban renewal and conservation in Chinatown illustrates yet another attempt to address the perceived need to anchor young Singaporeans in particular in their cultural roots. It also illustrates another tension between the state's recreation of emblems while paradoxically heralding the ethnically neutral notion of "nation."

Beginning in the 1960s and 1970s, while Singapore's planning juggernaut rolled relentlessly and transformed myriad landscapes, including Chinatown, into a modernist landscape, there was a recurring apprehension that such a landscape would deprive younger generation Singaporeans of "a daily visual reminder of . . . the degree or form of ruggedness of life" in the past (*The Straits Times,* 6 April 1971), of the importance of the city's "roots," and its architectural and cultural heritage. This concern was addressed when a new conservation ethos that placed the accent on reclaiming heritage and capitalizing on the city's "more traditional assets" (*URA Annual Report,* 1986/1987: 2) emerged in the late 1980s. As part of this conservation effort, the state capitalized on what it deemed to be positive Chinese cultural traits. State agencies such as the Urban Redevelopment Authority (URA) and the Singapore Tourism Board (STB) have identified Chinatown with the pioneering spirit and enterprise of early Chinese immigrants to Singapore and showcased it as a distinctively Chinese cultural area which "brims over with life, capturing the essence of the old Chinese lifestyle in its temples and shophouses and nurturing a handful of traditional trades [such as] herbalists, temple idol carvers, calligraphers and effigy makers . . . in the face of progress" (*Singapore: Official Guide,* 1991: 28–29). Against a backdrop of shophouses and temples, large scale festival activities, fairs, *wayangs,* puppetry and trishaw rides were to be "staged" to provide both locals and tourists with "a different kind of experience" (*Conservation within the Central Area,* 1985: 15). Particularly during Chinese festivals, lion and dragon dances are brought in; national Chinese calligraphy competitions and exhibitions are held; ancient Chinese lantern quizzes are hosted; and Cantonese operas are performed (*The Straits Times,* 19 February 1985). In conserving Chinatown as a testimony to the vibrance of Chinese culture, state strategies focus in the main on refurbishing the traditional architectural facade of Chinatown buildings. Where market forces do not preclude, resurrecting "vanishing trades" which are perceived to epitomize the Chinese past are also encouraged. Conserved Chinatown is conceived as a quintessential Chinese hearth, both for the tourist gaze as well as for locals in search of the vanished past.

The conservation of Chinatown, both in terms of physical facade and activities, reflects attempts to anchor a particular version of Chinese identity in order that Singaporeans may find cultural anchor and rootedness in a world besieged by western influences. Yet, at the same time, in the attempt to reclaim Chineseness, the state is also careful to tread the thin line between recreating ethnic identity and embracing the larger "nation." Indeed, the state seeks to elevate Chinatown to national importance as a civic asset, "a common bond place" for "Singaporeans living in outlying new towns" (*Conservation in the Central Area,* 1985: 15). Conserving Chinatown as a veritable repository of tradition, history and culture can thus be understood as an attempt to render heritage in material form, and hence serve the sociopolitical purpose of binding Singaporeans to place, to the city, and ultimately and vicariously, to the "nation."

The urban planning and conservation in Chinatown reifies a particular version of the visual past and of Chinese culture. However, these ideological designs are neither entirely hegemonic nor totally transparent in the lived Chinatown landscape. Indeed, people living and working in Chinatown have negotiated and resisted the two sets of landscape meanings ascribed by the state: the revitalization and embodiment of a "quintessential Chinese culture" in the conserved Chinatown and the role of the conserved landscape as "a common bond place" for Singaporeans.[8]

For many Singaporean Chinese who live and work in Chinatown, the Chinese cultural life of the place does not simply reside in the architectural form but in the full range of trades and lifestyles from "the traditional makers of paper houses and cars for ancestor prayer offerings, the barber who cuts hair in the backlane, the old coffeeshops where residents gather to chit chat" and so forth (*The Straits Times,* 16 October 1991). Notwithstanding URA's stance that traditional Chinese trades would be given every encouragement, many retailers fear that an open tender system would inevitably squeeze out the small, traditional businesses who would have to make way for more upmarket shops. Small family-run businesses selling food and daily necessities and myriad other enterprises, which cannot afford the post-conservation hike in rentals, have in fact faded out (*The Straits Times,* 29 April 1988). Others which have survived conservation such as small Chinese teahouses and herbal medicine halls have been upgraded into *dim sum* cum herbal tea restaurants (*The Straits Times,* 21 January 1990). While conservation has fostered a state-envisioned "Chineseness" embodied in distinctive architecture, a scattering of unique "dying trades" to represent the Chinese past and a variety of "Chinese" festive activities, it has also led to the demise of much more prosaic elements which go into the making of a Chinese-lived culture. Shopkeepers, families and street vendors lament the rapid attrition of long-standing small businesses which have been part and parcel of the familiar landscape where the retailer-client relationship goes back a long way. This is contrasted to the cautious way in which they view the sudden influx of gentrified shops managed by new people. They are far from persuaded that what the URA promotes as "adaptive reuse" of traditional buildings has revitalized the "traditional Chinese way of life." In coming to terms with the rapid changes of the landscape, old-time residents see themselves as the generation which marks the passing of the old way of life: the future is uncertain and all one can do is, in the words of a longtime resident, to live "a day at a time." The state's rewritten version of the Chinese cultural landscape is hence one which ignores "the inner workings of culture" (Wagner and Mikesell, 1962: 5), choosing instead to identify culture solely with architecture and a few "representative" trades. The Chinese in Chinatown have, however, remained aloof to such a version of the landscape and are not entirely oblivious to the irony that in its attempt to refurbish Chinese architecture and revive Chinese "dying trades," the state's conservation efforts have essentially damaged the day-to-day cultural life of the place.

From the attempts to revalorize local Chinese ties and the efforts to reshape a "Chinese landscape" locally while keeping a view on "larger" national needs, we move now to discuss how the state has recently called upon external Chinese cultural ties for economic ends in its regionalization drive, and what this has meant for those Chinese Singaporeans who have heeded the call to develop a "second wing" for the Singapore economy. In the 1990s, encouraged by the state, various Singapore-based companies have moved their operations to regional locations, a strategy aimed at enhancing their competitiveness and expanding Singapore's economic space beyond its limited geographical boundaries. While particularly active in the 1990s, this regionalization drive originated in 1986 when an Economic Committee, charged with charting economic directions for future growth, suggested measures to create a niche for regional operational headquarters and the export of services (Hui, 1997). Singapore companies responded to these exhortations by investing in the region, especially in China, which experienced the greatest increase in the number of Singapore companies established, from zero in 1981 to 16 in 1985 and then 181 in 1993 (Hui, 1997: 112).

In encouraging the development of a second wing for Singapore's economy, the state has called on Singaporeans to realize the value of their ethnic ties. As Senior Minister Lee Kuan Yew (1993: 42) pointed out:

> We are ethnic Chinese. We share certain characteristics through a common ancestry and culture. We can build up trust and rapport easily between ourselves. . . . it would be a mistake for Singaporean entrepreneurs not to participate in one of the greatest transformations of our age, the industrialisation and modernisation of the countries of East Asia, and not least of China. And we would be foolish not to use the ethnic Chinese network to increase our reach and our grasp of these opportunities.

Yet, he was also quick to point out that, despite the affinities, Singaporeans had to recognize that their "fundamental loyalties [were] to [their] home [Singapore], not ancestral countries," a view repeated in various public discourses by government leaders in various other contexts. At the opening of the Chinese Heritage Centre at one of the local universities, for example, then-Information and the Arts Minister George Yeo reminded ethnic Chinese here and in the region that in celebrating their cultural connections, they must remember that their political loyalty goes to the countries they belong to (*The Straits Times,* 17 June 1995; see also Education Minister Teo Chee Hean's caution against "overzealousness" in *The Straits Times,* 30 May 1993). Other leaders have also categorically proclaimed that Singapore's China policy is founded on the premise of economic opportunities, not ethnic affinity (Wong Kan Seng, Minister of Home Affairs, cited in *The Straits Times,* 17 June 1995). Similarly, he has argued that the Chinese in China engage in business transactions with Chinese in Singapore "with their own interest in mind. Not because we are 76 percent Chinese, not because we can speak Mandarin. But because there is something we can contribute to their development." These qualifications have been persistently made in order to avoid any concerns that greater economic interaction among the Chinese across national boundaries implies political unity. As Scalapino (quoted in Lee, 1993: 38) indicated, this issue needs particularly sensitive handling as any economic advances of the Chinese community could "exacerbate ethnic relations in key Southeast Asian societies" for

> ethnicity is the one permanent factor in politics; it can be rendered quiescent by skilful policies, but it never disappears. The spectre of Chinese economic dominance would be certain to cause it to loom up as a factor of heightened importance.

For this reason, Muslim Affairs Minister Abdullah Tarmugi has gone out of his way to assure non-Chinese Singaporeans that the opportunities in China are for all to exploit, not just the Chinese, and that there was no such thing as giving an edge to the Chinese community over other communities. In response to concerns that the choice of China as part of Singapore's regionalization strategy was to give Chinese Singaporean businessmen an edge over others, he responded:

> I don't think we should look at it as an ethnic issue, but as an economic issue. The gains are there, the potential is there and the opportunities are there, for us, indeed for anybody, to try and grab. (*The Straits Times*, 20 May 1995)

Even while the state seeks to negotiate the line between exploiting Chinese links and awakening/igniting political ties, Kong (1999a, 1999b), in discussing the reassertion of national identity and the renegotiation of ethnic identity among transmigrant Singaporean workers in Beijing, illustrates how the state currently has little cause for concern. Indeed, the transnational location of Singaporean transmigrants in Beijing appears to enhance their sense of national identity, leading to assertions of "Singaporeaness" and rootedness. In order to keep alive their identity and sense of place from afar, they engage in their own processes of consolidating that identity and/or building community—*Singaporean* community—through the activities they organize (for example, National Day celebrations), the language they speak (Singlish), the food they eat ("Singapore food"—see Chua and Rajah, 1997), the company they keep, and the business precepts and strategies they implement (Kong, 1999b). In so doing, they seek to (re)create Singapore in Beijing, engaging in tradition (re)invention and ritual-making, thus validating and asserting their "Singaporeaness."

While these same Singaporeans also engage in the process of rediscovering their ethnic Chinese identity, their activities point to a cultural and economic (re)negotiation rather than a political one. Hence, Singaporean Chinese in Beijing would seek "authentic" Chinese practices to maintain and recover their Chinese identity, including Chinese rituals, traditions and customs common in Singapore but sometimes obsolete or non-applicable in China, such as the Chinese New Year, revalorized through reunion dinners, and mid-autumn festivals, celebrated with the consumption of mooncakes, and the parading of lanterns by children. Singaporean Chinese also engage in "culture building" efforts, for example, striving to improve competence in Chinese arts, culture and history, learning to play a Chinese instrument, developing calligraphic skills, taking up Chinese painting, and learning classical Mandarin (Kong, 1999b). For these Singaporeans, ethnicity is also an "economic resource" that can be called upon to work for them, such as when they use their Chineseness to bargain and to pay local rates at the markets and tourist sites. At another level, in the world of business and capital movements, many also seek to emphasize their affinities with the Chinese in several ways: some seek to accentuate the ability to communicate; others, through engaging in Chinese cultural activities, find a platform for facilitating opportunities and negotiating business deals; yet others highlight family and ancestral ties (Kong, 1999b).[9]

The professed identity of this group of transnational Singaporean Chinese appear to vindicate the state's policies and strategies pertaining to regionalization in achieving economic goals without compromising national/political affiliation. Where ethnic identity is (re)awakened, it is largely cultural-aesthetic rather than cultural-political in nature. This is most markedly expressed by one Singaporean in Beijing (quoted in Kong, 1999b) who professed earlier political inclinations with China that later changed with his experience in China:

> Before I came to China, I always felt that I was a Chinese deep in my bones. . . .
> But only after I came to China, then I realised that I am a Singaporean because
> they don't treat you as a Chinese. They actually treat you as a foreigner.

CONCLUSION

Historically the product of multiple diasporic communities, Singapore exemplifies the place-based dynamics of the intersection between cultural maintenance within specific ethnic communities on the one hand and nation building predicated on a multiracial logic on the other. It also demonstrates a situation where the basic "markers" of being "Chinese"—what legitimately constitutes the language, the communal associations, the forms of self-help and the heritage landscapes of the Chinese, and how "ethnic" networks may be exploited for business gains in a globalizing world—have been very much part of state "management" and "engineering"[10] to ensure Singapore's success.

While the state has continued to propound Singapore's founding logic of four "separate" but "equal" races in a nation of "one people" as Singapore's multiracial formula for success, this has not meant that state policies have remained monolithic or unidirectional over the past three decades. As we have shown, the more immediate post-independence concerns to submerge and subvert ethnic identity to the larger purposes of nation building and national identity construction gave way in the late 1980s and 1990s to much more complex policies and actions, some of which at least have appeared to revalorize and reclaim Chinese links and identity. These moves have generated a host of tensions and contradictions which continue to emerge as Singapore enters the twenty-first century. A sense of these dilemmas is well captured in a recent piece by Singapore sociologist Kwok Kian Woon for *The Encyclopaedia of the Chinese Overseas* (1998b) and excerpted in the Singapore press intriguingly entitled "How to Be Singaporean, Chinese and Modern All at Once" (*The Sunday Times,* 25 October 1998). Kwok (1998b: 125) argues that "Chineseness" has developed into a "discourse of the 1990s" which has been drawn on by individuals and the state to further specific ends. What this has obscured is the fact that cultural identity changes on the ground all the time even as the state chooses to ignore the multiple slippages between "Chinese identity" as a discursive construct and as played out in everyday practices.

Another contributor to the Singapore press, this time to the Forum page which features letters from readers, expressed more specific anxieties about the revalorization of Chinese ethnic identity in a multicultural context. In a letter entitled "Why Abandon the Vision of Ethnic Synthesis?" Mathilda Gabrielpillai (*The Straits Times,* 17 July 1998) writes:

> The nation emerged from the push of multi-culturalism. It was a cultural vision that I took great pride in and identified with while growing up in the 1960s and 1970s. . . . These days, however, we counter this vision by "racialising"[11] everything, from school performances and drug-taking habits to various other social phenomena. . . . The emphasis on the learning of ethnic languages was targeted at providing "cultural ballast" to the nation. But I wonder if a different note is being struck when the need for a local Chinese cultural elite is linked to the regional revival of East Asian culture. I hope that we are still talking about national ethnic heritages here, and not about race—the demon we have so busily and intensely warded off in the past. There are several reasons for us to feel nervous about the "racialising" of culture. For a start, this would break faith with an original and significant cultural contract. It would also introduce vulnerability into the national fabric, exposing the country to extra-national loyalties and placing Singaporeans within the sphere of influence of international racial conflicts. Another fear is the more local threat of cultural dislocation caused by sudden changes in policy. We need also to consider if our cultural experiences, past

and present, can sustain a cultural shift of Singapore from South-east Asia to East Asia, and whether an emphasis is placed on racial origins in a context of English education and globalisation is viable. Otherwise, our cultural policy could give rise to unexpected outcomes.

The concerns of Kwok and Gabrielpillai exemplify some of the underlying dilemmas as Singapore navigates between its history as an immigrant society of multiple diasporas and its vision of becoming a globalized yet unified, modern nation-state. In doing this, it has variously positioned itself both "inside" and "outside" the "Chinese diaspora," giving weight to the view expressed elsewhere (Van der Veer, 1995; Yeoh and Huang, 2000) that "diaspora" describes not so much a settlement pattern but an imagined geography between being "home" and "away."

NOTES

1. A Malay word for village.

2. This had the aim of effective liaison between the authorities and the poorer immigrant sections of the Chinese population.

3. This is a Mandarin system of romanizing Chinese characters used in China.

4. The attempt to apply the *hanyu pinyin* system to street and place names in the 1980s is more fully discussed in Yeoh (1996b).

5. For a history of Singapore's public housing program, see Perry, Kong and Yeoh (1997, chapter 8).

6. It is debatable whether this avoidance was successful. A call to embrace Confucian values in the 1980s (see Wong and Wong, 1989) could be interpreted to be a privileging of Chinese values.

7. These are: Hokkien Huay Kuan, Teochew Poit Ip Huay Kwan, Kwantung Huay Kuan, Nanyang Khek Community Guild, Singapore Hainan Hui Kuan and Fuchou Hui Kuan.

8. The following discussion is drawn from Yeoh and Kong, 1994.

9. However, Kong (1999b) also notes how ethnicity as a resource that is mobilized for gain can sometimes work in reverse. For example, one may not be given the same service as a non-Chinese (particularly Caucasian) foreigner because "Beijingers are basically very proud. They don't want to serve another Chinese, especially southerners" (Singaporean Chinese interviewee). Being a Chinese superior at the workplace may also mean that employees try to take advantage and make demands (of extra employment benefits) which they would not make on a non-Chinese foreigner.

10. Both terms are drawn from the title of two important works on Singapore— Sandhu and Wheatley's (1989) *The Management of Success: The Moulding of Modern Singapore*, and Mahizhnan and Lee's (1998) *Singapore: Re-engineering Singapore*— and imply the significant hand of the state in producing socioeconomic success.

11. The political ideology and effects of "pervasive racialisation" in Singapore has been discussed in greater detail in a number of places, recently in Clammer (1998).

REFERENCES

The All Party Committee of the Singapore Legislative Assembly on Chinese Education, 1956.

Altbach, P. G. 1982. "Higher Education in Singapore: A Permanent Revolution," *Phi Delta Kappa,* Nov. 64(3): 200–201.

Benjamin, Geoffrey. 1976. "The Cultural Logic of Singapore's Multiculturalism," in Riaz Hassan, ed., *Singapore: Society in Transition,* Kuala Lumpur: Oxford University Press, 115–133.

———. 1988. "The Unseen Presence: A Theory of the Nation-State and Its Mystifications," National University of Singapore, Department of Sociology, Working Paper No. 91, 55 pp.

Betts, Russell H. 1975. "Multiracialism, Meritocracy and the Malays in Singapore," unpublished Ph.D. dissertation, Massachusetts Institute of Technology.

Chan, Heng Chee. 1991. "Political Developments, 1965–1979," in Ernest C. T. Chew and Edwin Lee, eds., *A History of Singapore,* Singapore: Oxford University Press, 157–181.

Chan, Heng Chee and Hans-Dieter Evers.1978. "National Identity and Nation Building in Singapore," in Peter S. J. Chen and Hans-Dieter Evers, eds., *Studies in ASEAN Sociology: Urban Society and Social Change,* Singapore: Chopmen Enterprises, 117–129.

Cheng, L. K. 1990. "Reflections on the Changing Roles of Chinese Clan Associations in Singapore," *Asian Culture,* 14: 57–71.

Chiew, Seen-Kong. 1985. "The Socio-cultural Framework of Politics," in Jon S. T. Quah, Chan Heng Chee and Seah Chee Meow, eds., *Government and Politics of Singapore,* Singapore: Oxford University Press, 45–67.

Chua, Beng Huat. 1985. "Pragmatism of the People's Action Party Government in Singapore: A Critical Assessment," *Southeast Asian Journal of Social Science,* 13(2): 29–46.

———. 1991. "Modernism and the Vernacular: Transformation of Public Spaces and Social Life in Singapore," *Journal of Architectural and Planning Research,* 8(3): 203–221.

Chua, Beng Huat and Eddie K. Y. Kuo. 1990. "The Making of a New Nation: Cultural Construction and National Identity in Singapore," National University of Singapore, Department of Sociology Working Paper No. 104, 36 pp.

Chua, Beng Huat and Ananda Rajah. 1997. "Hybridity, Ethnicity and Food in Singapore," Singapore: Department of Sociology, National University of Singapore, 29 pp.

Clammer, John. 1998. *Race and State in Independent Singapore 1965–1990,* Aldershot: Ashgate.

Conservation within the Central Area, 1985. Singapore.

A Decade of Mandarin, 1979–1989. Mandarin Campaign Secretariat, Ministry of Communications and Information, Republic of Singapore.

Demaine, Harvey. 1984. "Furnivall Reconsidered: Plural Societies in South-East Asia in the Post-colonial Era," in Colin Clarke, David Ley and Ceri Peach, eds., *Geography and Ethnic Pluralism,* London: George Allen and Unwin, 25–50.

218	*Lily Kong and Brenda Yeoh*

Freedman, Maurice. 1950. "Colonial Law and Chinese Society," *Journal of the Royal Anthropological Institute of Great Britain and Ireland,* 30: 97–125.
Furnivall, J. S. 1948. *Colonial Policy and Practice: A Comparative Study of Burma and the Netherland Indies,* Cambridge: Cambridge University Press.
Goh, Chok Tong. 1992. "Self-Help in the Chinese Community," *Speeches,* 16(5): 7–16.
Harper, T. N. 1997. "Globalism and the Pursuit of Authenticity: The Making of a Diasporic Public Sphere in Singapore," *Sojourn,* 12(2): 261–292
Hill, Michael and Lian Kwen Fee. 1995. *The Politics of Nation Building and Citizenship in Singapore,* London and New York: Routledge.
Hui, Weng-tat 1997. "Regionalization, Economic Restructuring and Labour Migration in Singapore," *International Migration,* 35(1): 109–128.
Kong, Lily. 1999a. "Globalisation and Singaporean Transmigration: Re-imagining and Negotiating National Identity," *Political Geography,* 18(5): 563–589.
———. 1999b. "Globalisation, Transmigration and the (Re)negotiation of Ethnic Identity," in K. Olds, P. Dicken, P. Kelly, L. Kong and H. Yeung, eds., *Globalization and the Asia-Pacific: Contested Territories,* London: Routledge, 219–237.
———. 2000. "Cultural Policy in Singapore: Negotiating Economic and Sociocultural Agendas," *Geoforum,* 31: 409–429.
Kwok, Kian Woon. 1998a. "Singapore," in Lynn Pan, ed., *The Encyclopedia of the Chinese Overseas,* Singapore: Archipelago Press and Landmark Books, 200–210.
———. 1998b. "Chinese in the Modern World," in Lynn Pan, ed., *The Encyclopedia of the Chinese Overseas,* Singapore: Archipelago Press and Landmark Books, 121–126.
Lee, Edwin and Tan Tai Tan. 1996. *Beyond Degrees: The Making of the National University of Singapore,* Singapore: Singapore University Press.
Lee, Hsien Loong. 1992. "Clans: Remaining Vibrant and Relevant," *Speeches,* 16(5): 120–112.
Lee, Kuan Yew. 1993. "Developing a Global *guanxi,*" *Speeches,* 17(6).
Lee, K. Y. 1980. "Nanyang Needs a Clean Break," *Speeches* 3(11): 4–5.
Low, N. I. 1983. *Recollections: Chinese Jetsam on a Tropical Shore,* Singapore: Eastern Universities Press.
Mahizhnan, Arun and T. Y. Lee 1998. *Singapore: Re-engineering Singapore,* Singapore: Institute of Policy Studies and Oxford University Press.
Parliamentary Debates: Singapore.
Perry, M., L. Kong, and B. Yeoh. 1997. *Singapore: A Developmental City-State,* Chichester: John Wiley.
PuruShotam, Nirmala Srirekam. 1998. *Negotiating Language, Constructing Race: Disciplining Difference in Singapore,* New York: Mouton de Gruyter.
Rajah, A. 1997. "Immigration and Labour: History, Structure and Process in Peninsular Malaya," paper presented at a seminar on "Nation-Building and Citizenship," Centre for Advanced Studies, Faculty of Arts and Social Sciences, National University of Signapore, 25 January.
Roff, William R. 1964. "The Malayo-Muslim World of Singapore at the Close of the Nineteenth Century," *Journal of Asian Studies,* 24: 76–90.
Sandhu, Kernial Singh and Paul Wheatley. 1989. *The Management of Success: The Moulding of Modern Singapore,* Singapore: Institute of Southeast Asian Studies.

Shee, Poon Kim. 1985. "The Evolution of the Political System," in Jon S. T. Quah, Chan Heng Chee and Seah Chee Meow, eds., *Government and Politics of Singapore*, Singapore: Oxford University Press, 3–24.

Siddique, Sharon. 1989. "Singaporean Identity," in Kernial Singh Sandhu and Paul Wheatley, eds., *Management of Success: The Moulding of Modern Singapore*, Singapore: Institute of Southeast Asian Studies, 563–577.

Singapore: Official Guide. 1991. Singapore: Singapore Tourist Promotion Board.

Singapore Census of Population 1980: Languages Spoken at Home. 1981. Release No. 8, Singapore: Dept. of Statistics.

Singapore Census of Population 1990: Literacy, Languages Spoken and Education. 1993. Statistical Release 3, Singapore: SNP Publishers Pte Ltd.

The Straits Times, various issues.

Turnbull, C. M. 1977. *A History of Singapore, 1819–1975*, Kuala Lumpur: Oxford University Press.

URA Annual Report. 1986/1987. Singapore: Urban Redevelopment Authority.

Van der Veer, Peter. 1995. "Introduction: The Diasporic Imagination," in Peter van der Veer, ed., *Nation and Migration: The Politics of Space in the South Asian Diaspora*, Philadelphia: University of Pennsylvania Press, 1–17.

Wagner, Philip L. and Marvin W. Mikesell. 1962. "General Introduction: The Themes of Cultural Geography," in Philip L. Wagner and Marvin W. Mikesell, eds., *Readings in Cultural Geography*, Chicago and London: The University of Chicago Press, 1–24.

Wong, J. and A. Wong 1989. *Confucian Values As a Framework for Singapore's Economic Development*, Taipei: Chung-Hua Institute for Economic Research.

Wong, K. S. 1988. "What Is a Community?" *Speeches*, Singapore: Ministry of Communications and Information, 12(3): 47–49.

Yearbook of Statistics. 1996. Singapore: Department of Statistics.

Yen, Ching Hwang. 1986. *A Social History of the Chinese in Singapore and Malaya, 1800–1911*, Singapore: Oxford University Press.

Yeoh, Brenda S. A. 1996a. *Contesting Space: Power Relations and the Urban Built Environment in Colonial Singapore*, Kuala Lumpur: Oxford University Press.

———. 1996b. "Street-Naming and Nation-Building: Toponymic Inscriptions of Nationhood in Singapore," *Area*, 28(3): 298–307.

Yeoh, B. S. A. and S. Huang 2000. "'Home' and 'Away': Foreign Domestic Workers and Negotiations of Diasporic Identity in Singapore," *Women's Studies International Forum*, 23(4): 413–429.

Yeoh, B. S. A. and L. Kong 1994. "Reading Landscape Meanings: State Constructions and Lived Experiences in Singapore's Chinatown," *Habitat International*, 18(4): 17–35.

9

Ethnic Identity and Business Solidarity: Chinese Capitalism Revisited

You-tien Hsing

What is the making and the working of ethnic identity? How does the making of ethnic identity affect the working of it? How does the increasing recognition of identity diversity and construction shed light on the relationship between culture and economic behavior? More specifically, what does the recognition of diverse Chinese identities inform us about Chinese entrepreneurial practices? This chapter explores these questions in the following sequence: first, a critical review of existing works on Chinese entrepreneurial practices, which assumed a universal Chineseness; second, a modification of anti-essentialist writings with an emphasis on historical condition of identity construction; third, the way shifting identities affect the utility of identity. I argue that the making and the working of ethnic identity are historically embedded. The materials for construction are provided by historical possibilities; and constructed identities at the global and national level are not always consistent with conduct and interpretations at the local level. The utility of identity is also historically conditioned. Identity is not a given economic or political asset. There is a process of conversion from shared identity to economic and political utility. The process and results of the conversion is shaped by historical and territorial particularities. Historical and territorial experiences at the local level set the boundary of imagination. Therefore, the assumed business solidarity among co-ethnics has to be qualified.

DIVERSITY OF CHINESE ENTREPRENEURIAL PRACTICES

The diversity of ethnic Chinese and the construction of Chinese identities have received increasing attention from scholars (cf. e.g., Cheng, 1996;

Smart, 1994; Nonini, 1997; Ong, 1997, 1999; Jesudason, 1997). Chinese entrepreneurial practices vary in different institutional, territorial and historical
contexts. The state-business relationship in different Chinese societies serves
as an example of such diversity. In Southeast Asia where ethnic Chinese are
the minority, Chinese entrepreneurs were treated as subordinate compradors
under the colonial rulers, or pariah entrepreneurs dependent on local patrons
following political independence (Riggs, 1966; Trocki, 1997). Since the
1960s, Chinese entrepreneurs in Southeast Asia have gained more political
influence and are no longer "minority capitalists" (Hewison, 1993). Yet ethnic Chinese with economic forces are still politically vulnerable, and the
state-business relationship in Southeast Asia is still colored by the issue of
ethnic divide, as demonstrated by the 1998 financial crisis in Southeast Asia
and the blame on ethnic Chinese in Indonesia (not to mention the riots associated with such blame).[1] Hamilton suggested that ethnic Chinese merchants
and traders in Southeast Asia have expanded their economic influence overseas *despite* the neglect of the Chinese state and the suspicious and extractive
host states. They developed a collective entrepreneurship through building
exclusive business networks across national boundaries in the region (Hamilton, 1996). In other words, in a society in which the Chinese are the minority
politically and socially, the dividing line between the political and economic
elites is decisive. The Chinese economic interests have to play the double-
edged role of facilitating the regime financially while at the same time keep
their heads low. As a contrast, in Taiwan, where ethnic Chinese are the majority and export manufacturing have been the foundation of rapid industrialization since the 1970s, the state-business relationship has been different.
This relationship is usually analyzed within the context of "state-led development." The developmental state has played a more active role in facilitating domestic industrialists to grow; and the social networks of economic and
political elite are much tighter (Wade, 1990; Gold, 1986).

    The institutional and historical conditions that have shaped the state-busi-
ness relationship in turn conditioned the way Chinese entrepreneurs strategize
and operate. The assumed features of Chinese businesses such as Confucian
paternalism, personalistic trust, informal and secretive financial arrangements
(Redding, 1990, 1995) are not always present in the various forms of businesses operated by Chinese across time, space, and sectors. For example, in
nineteenth-century Southeast Asia the basic unit of Chinese economies was
the *kongsi*. It was a shareholding partnership dominated by people sharing
the same surname or kinship link, sometimes with fictive kinship ties in the
form of sworn brotherhood. The *kongsi* often undertook the responsibility of
government in Chinese communities and had the control of both capital and
laborer. Some *kongsi* had grown so powerful financially and ambitious polit-

ically that they eventually were seen as a threat to the state (Trocki, 1997). This type of business organization is very different from that of the firms in late-twentieth-century Taiwan, which is characterized by highly segmented ownership and a networked production and marketing system. They have little direct involvement in community governance.

The idea sketched here, of diversified Chinese firms and different Chinese entrepreneurial practices, is not consistent with the literature that paints a more universal picture of Chinese businesses. The underlying assumption in essentializing Chinese and Chinese businesses is the existence of definite and static cultural (if not genetic) boundaries, and a consistent association of a people with a particular (usually referred to as "inherited") culture defined by a bundle of attributes. There is also negativity related to this analysis. Confucian paternalism is usually associated with rigid hierarchy that limits innovation; informal financial arrangements lead to insufficient legal protection and therefore instability. The Chinese way is often used interchangeably with the "traditional" way. For the most part it was the next best option when modern legal and financial institutions were not in place. As to the question of transformation, writers of this camp have assumed a linear path of change: it is historically inevitable that when Chinese firms grow, they transform from the traditional Chinese style to the modern, Western style of business organization and management.[2]

Essentialism is not only found in the literature that sees Chinese entrepreneurial practices as traditional and irrational, therefore an inferior other. Chinese triumphalists (and East Asian triumphalists alike) who rejected Western hegemony of business norms and promoted the Chinese way also have not avoided the problem of essentializing Chinese. They too assumed a bundle of cultural attributes that were supposed to be "Chinese" and "Confucian," such as hierarchy, harmony, collectivism, and family loyalty (Kahn, 1979). The difference is that these assumed, fixed cultural attributes are seen as the cause of recent economic success in East Asia, rather than failure.[3] The economic success in East Asia's overseas Chinese economies since the 1970s and the more recent growth in post-Mao China has inspired what Nonini (1997) called "high romance of transnational Chinese capitalism." Nonini argued that Chinese identity is never fixed nor singular. Diaspora Chinese identities in Southeast Asia, for example, "can only be seen contrastively . . . vis-a-vis alternative and opposed identities of citizenship and indigenousness" (p. 206). From this perspective, ethnicity is an imagined community. Ong (1997) further asserted that identity becomes a "regime of power that imagines a nation beyond the state." Ong also dismissed labeling. She called it self-orientalization of Asian scholarship because of the truth claim and cultural essentialism involved in such an exercise (Ong, 1999). In other words, for critical culturalists like Nonini and Ong, Chinese triumphalists' resistance of Western hegemony fell into the same trap of essentializing Chinese and Chinese businesses.

FROM ESSENTIALISM TO FUNCTIONALISM

The recognition of ethnic identity as "becoming" instead of "being" (Hall, 1990) and as politics instead of inheritance (Ong, 1997) defies the absoluteness and timelessness of ethnic identity. One of the most frequently used examples of identity construction is Singapore's Confucianization project under the leadership of the former premier Lee Kuan Yew (Ong, 1997; Blanc, 1997). Another example is the making of the "Greater China" or the "Pacific Rim" (Dirlik, 1993). By focusing on the cultural politics of identity construction, writers seem to assume that such exercises have a clear purpose and utility. The state and the dominant global forces are master planners; and capitalist expansion is the main purpose of such geographical invention. However, what is less clear is the way such global polity is transformed and interpreted at the local level. How is the project of the state connected with individual conduct? What happens to the tension between master plans and historical contingencies? What happens to the holes that seem to exist everywhere in our lives yet suddenly disappear in our analysis of the world? The state's project of constructing national identity is not always successful; nor is the process smooth. The construct is not necessarily most efficient economically, nor is it most effective politically. In Singapore, for example, the state's promotion of Confucianism as a part of the project of building a national identity has met resistance from both Chinese and non-Chinese groups and caused irreversible setbacks (Wong, 1996; Kuo, 1996).

The implicit functionalist assumption can be found in my earlier work on Taiwanese investment in China. By proposing that the blood connection has facilitated the rapid flow of overseas Chinese capital into China, Hsing (1996) assumed a group of people with a shared identity always have consistent and persistent views, clear intentions and coherent goals, i.e., profit maximization. Ethnic ties, constructed or not, were examined through the lenses of economic utility. Etzioni (1988) criticized such functionalist and economist tendency as making simple and exclusive use of economic reasoning in all human conditions. Economism sees ethnic ties as having the exclusive function of reducing transaction costs, reducing competition and facilitating cooperation, and information flows, and maximizing utility of resources. It assumes culture serves the purpose of economy.[4] But in a world in which goals are often multiple, ambiguous and in conflict, the most efficient form does not always predominate. In fact it is not always possible to identify what is more efficient (Etzioni, 1988). Recruiting kins or subcontracting within kin networks may be the result of paying back emotional debts, or out of obligation, but not necessarily a result of cost-benefit analysis. There are also malfunctions and abuse of trust among kins and co-ethnics, as demonstrated by Smart and Smart's (1993) study of Hong Kong investors in southern China.[5] They suggested that the utility of ethnic ties is contingent. Ethnic identity is not necessarily a basis of business success, but can be a resource to be utilized. In other words, not every Chinese is a master of building *guanxi* (interpersonal relationships). It is a learned skill. In addition, the presumed "function" of cultural traits, such as building of *guanxi*, is not always equally functional for all participants. When *guanxi* is supposed to build on the basis of reciprocity and mutual benefit, it is not necessarily equally beneficial; and reciprocity in *guanxi* building is not necessarily symmetrical—it can be asymmetric reciprocity (Buraway and Wright, 1990), and unequal patronism (Oi, 1989).

HISTORICAL CONDITIONS OF IDENTITY CONSTRUCTION

Between the two approaches of problematizing Chineseness—the essentialist one that sees Chineseness as a given with fixed boundaries; and the critical culturalist one that treats Chineseness as an imagined category and invented representation, I propose to approach the question of Chinese entrepreneurial practices by examining specific historical and territorial contexts at the micro level. The meaning of boundary negotiation and the politics of constructing Chineseness have to be investigated through actual practices of a group of people who label themselves, or are labeled as Chinese, and through their interaction with others, in commerce or other areas of activities. Identity, if understood as something induced by shared experiences in history and territory, reinforced by and intersected with ethnicity, kinship, language and religion (Castells, 1998), has a tangible historical and spatial association that is not to be reduced to texts and presentations, nor is it simply a matter of arbitrary invention (Huang, 1998). The most challenging task here is not about choosing between the polar options of decoding texts and enlisting cultural traits. While we dismiss essentialization of Chineseness, we do have to make empirical observation critically of the intersection between texts and interpretations, constructs and conduct, histories and imageries of histories. The making and using of ethnic identities is not separated from social, political, cultural and economic factors in particular historical and territorial conjunctures.[6]

The historical experiences of Chinese entrepreneurs in the last two centuries may be recapitulated in what Hamilton (1996) has proposed as "collective entrepreneurship."[7] Such general prototypes are to be cross-examined with the transformation of institutional and social contexts, as well as the interaction between specific ethnic Chinese groups with other Chinese and non-Chinese groups in such contexts. Chinese identities, like other ethnic identities, do not exist in the abstract and cannot be analyzed properly in isolation from political, economic, and sociocultural elements. They find expression in specific activities (e.g., business organization, property ownership, family relations, and so on) and in the interaction with groups that are defined as "others."

In my research on Taiwanese investment in China since the late 1980s (Hsing, 1996, 1998), I proposed that the blood connection—the cultural and linguistic affinity between Taiwanese investors and their local Chinese workers and partners, has facilitated smooth and speedy capital flows across regional boundaries from Taiwan to China. It has helped Taiwanese manufacturers bypass bureaucratic red tape in China, created a more flexible production environment, and maintained its competitiveness in the world market. I have discussed the cultural tools of building interpersonal relationships (*guanxi*) and disciplining workers on the basis of the blood connection. The cultural tools of building *guanxi* included the understanding of both the spoken and unspoken languages, shared sense of time and space, and the common measurement of the value of material and nonmaterial gifts exchanged in the process of building *guanxi*.

The expression "blood is thicker than water" requires qualification. The flexible arrangement between Taiwanese investors and local Chinese officials was not simply the result of the "blood connection" or the "naturally born" trust between co-ethnics. The utilization of and selection from a "cultural repertoire"[8] on the basis of shared ethnic background was made possible under several historical and institutional conditions at the global and local levels. The late 1980s witnessed Taiwan's economic expansion in the face of surging protectionism in the Organization for Economic Cooperation and Development (OECD) markets. A labor shortage and mounting competition in the world market created great pressure for economic restructuring and pushed Taiwanese export manufacturers to look for new markets and cheaper overseas production sites. At the same time, China accelerated its open door policy by offering generous investment packages to overseas Chinese investors, calling for their patriotic sentiment toward the motherland. The campaign of attracting overseas Chinese capital escalated after the Tiananmen massacre in 1989, when many non-Chinese foreign firms fled China. Taiwanese and Hong Kong medium-scaled manufacturers, who had limited resources and experiences in overseas production,[9] filled the investment vacuum in China. Taiwanese and Hong Kong investors found their local business partners in highly entrepreneurial government officials in Chinese cities and towns. The local Chinese officials have been enjoying their newly gained economic autonomy, as part of the post-Mao reforms in fiscal decentralization, since the 1980s. Their enthusiasm and willingness to take initiative in business ventures were induced by post-Mao fiscal reform and nourished by the long tradition of local autonomy in China.[10] Local officials have been eager to meet the demands of Taiwanese investors with maximum flexibility; they have simplified the process and regulation of investment and made concessions in taxes and fees for Taiwanese investors. Such flexibility, which was crucial to the success of Taiwanese investment, was made possible under the circumstances in which autonomous and entrepreneurial local Chinese officials and small- and medium-sized Taiwanese export manufacturers had matching needs.

Moreover, the "blood connection" between Taiwanese and Chinese is more distinctive in relative terms. Taiwanese investors' advantage in building *guanxi* with local Chinese officials, and the sense of togetherness between the Taiwanese and their Chinese agents was more apparent when compared to American or European investors in China. Non-Chinese investors often complained about their lack of *guanxi* with local officials, which put them in a disadvantageous position in China.[11] Also, the shared identity between Taiwanese and Chinese is often built on negativity. Taiwanese are considered, and consider themselves closer to mainland Chinese for what they are not as much as for what they are—both of them are not English speaking, not part of the advantageous and dominant group in the capitalist world. Their mutual understanding is as much the result of shared historical experiences of being late industrializers as being Chinese. The qualification of the blood connection within the historical and institutional contexts leads to the question of business solidarity between co-ethnics at the local level.

ETHNIC IDENTITY AND BUSINESS SOLIDARITY

Ethnic identity—inherited or constructed, can be an economic asset only when other conditions are met. What are the factors that induce solidarity, that is, trustworthy behavior on the basis of kinship and/or ethnicity? Smart and Smart (1993) suggested "effective management" as a variable. Ethnicity and kinship can induce kin-worker's compliance and consent to work hard only upon effective management. In other words, its utility is an accomplishment, not an automatic outcome of a particular set of cultural resources/ propensities. There is a process of conversion that transforms ethnic and family ties into business assets. The process of conversion involves searching for the balance between sameness and differences, and for the balance between inclusion and exclusion.

Similarities do not always facilitate solidarity. While taking advantage of their familiarity with certain Chinese customs, Taiwanese investors in China also have disadvantages because of their status as half-insiders. Taiwanese investors often complained about the higher expectations placed on them by local Chinese. They were expected to demonstrate patriotism by donating to charity and public works. On the other hand, many mainland Chinese professionals have preferred to work for non-Taiwanese firms in China, because Taiwanese "know too much about Chinese and their way of conducting business is too Chinese."[12] The fact that both groups have been at peripheral and semiperipheral positions has made Taiwanese more reluctant to transfer technologies to China for fear of Chinese competition. Taiwanese manufacturers commented that it is relatively easy for Chinese to expropriate their technologies and market connections through their linguistic and cultural affinity.[13]

Taiwanese investors and their Chinese partners also have visible differences. To begin with, business cultures in Taiwan and China are distinctively different. Networks of production and marketing among Taiwanese export manufacturers are established through time in specific territories (Hsing, 1999). Export-oriented manufacturing in Taiwan has built a regime of timely delivery, cost reduction, quality control, and product variation, in contrast to the production culture of the Chinese industrial system. In addition, the customary practices of Taiwanese businesses, such as sales on credits (delayed payment to suppliers until buyers pay for the delivery), and interlocking share-holding among manufacturers, suppliers and subcontractors, are not shared by their mainland Chinese counterparts. Most of all, these business practices are based on time-honored and territorially bounded interpersonal networks. Established among those who are involved in a specific industrial circle, such networks cannot be replicated easily or expanded quickly to new production sites in China. The trust relationship Taiwanese entrepreneurs have established among themselves has had historical and territorial bases.

In addition, the half-century-long political rivalry between the regimes of Chinese communists and Taiwan's nationalists has resulted in deep suspicion between Taiwanese and mainland Chinese. The income gap between Taiwan and the mainland in the past three decades has made some Taiwanese see the mainlanders as untrustworthy, backward and second-class co-ethnics. The boundary between Taiwanese investors and their local Chinese agents is further reinforced by language. Most Taiwanese investors can trace their ancestry to Southern Fujian Province in southern China. Although they can speak the official language of Taiwan and China, Mandarin, most Taiwanese investors speak southern Fujian dialect as their mother tongue. Southern Fujian dialect has become the basis of primary identity of Taiwanese investors and a a symbol of Taiwanese solidarity in China.[14] As a result, the inclusiveness of the Taiwanese identity-based network can be exclusive to non-Taiwanese on the mainland. This in turn has reduced the possibility of building production linkages between Taiwanese and local enterprises in China. Instead of using local suppliers and contractors, Taiwanese manufacturers would move the entire networks of production to the mainland, similar to the Japanese style of overseas expansion (Hsing, 1999).[15] In short, it is the interplay of the similarities and differences, inclusion and exclusion, that determines the investment strategy of Taiwanese firms and forms of business collaboration between Taiwanese and their mainland partners.

BOUNDARY CROSSING AND SHIFTING IDENTITIES

But the binary structure of "similarity and difference" can be too linear in our understanding of ethnic identity and business solidarity. The dividing line between the Chinese on the mainland and Taiwanese is not always clear, nor is it fixed. The multiple dimensions of identity built upon multiple bases such as language, place of origins, gender and class can contradict one another and blur the dividing line. They also provide the possibility of boundary crossing from one dimension of identity to another under different circumstances. The politics of language on the shop floor in Taiwanese-invested factories provide a good example of such blurring boundaries.

While most Taiwanese bosses and high-ranking managers speak southern Fujian dialect as the mother tongue, most mainland Chinese workers speak other Chinese dialects and Mandarin. Taiwanese managers speak southern Fujianese among themselves when they do not wish to be heard by local workers. Southern Fujian dialect has become the language of the power circle and the symbol of power in Taiwanese-invested firms in southern China (except for southern Fujian). In Guangdong Province, where the majority of Taiwanese investors are concentrated, I met a mainland foreman from southern Fujian, who spoke southern Fujian dialect, the language of power. When talking to me in private, he often complained about the lack of empathy for the mainland employees of his Taiwanese boss. But he also liked to speak Fujianese to his Taiwanese boss as a way to get close to the boss and to distance himself from the rest of the low-ranking local managers. The Taiwanese boss and managers of the factory talked to him in southern Fujian dialect too. The boss explained to me: "when I talked to the foreman in southern Fujian dialect, it pleased him and made him feel that he was a part of the inner circle of the factory."[16] Patronage through the use of language was used to gain the loyalty of the foreman to his Taiwanese boss. Yet the

Fujian foreman was never invited by his Taiwanese boss to the drinking ses-
sions in local karaoke bars, which was a more important indicator of one's
power status in the factory.

The blurring boundaries that mix class, territorial and ethnic identities have
created the space for transferring capitalist ideology of production from Taiwan to the mainland. Chinese low-level managers and clerks were crucial in
the success of Taiwanese investment on the mainland (Hsing, 1998). While
they were aware of the exploitative nature of labor relationship in many Taiwanese factories, they tended to identify themselves with the Taiwanese boss
when they talked about "progress" and "modernization." Most of the Chinese
low-level managers started at the bottom as operators and gradually moved
up to low-level managerial positions. The same Fujian foreman mentioned
above told me that China is making good progress towards modernization
"just like Taiwan." He explained that local workers did not have time for
lunch, just like what he heard from his boss about the hard-working, devoted
workers in Taiwan. During my fieldwork in the Pearl River Delta in Guangdong Province, a local clerk in a Taiwanese firm complained to me about the
long working hours. Most days she could not leave the office until midnight.
Then she commented on how much more efficient the Taiwanese firm was,
compared to local firms. She said, "If this was a mainland firm there would
be at least twice as many people doing the same amount of work we did
here."[17] A mainland manager in another Taiwanese firm, who used to work
for a mainland state-owned enterprise, reasoned that "mainland firms are not
as competitive as Taiwanese firms because of the burden of welfare system in
mainland firms."[18]

I saw a mainland woman foreman lecturing to a group of woman workers,
after receiving the news that a delivery was rejected by the buyer because of
poor quality.[19] She blamed the workers for being "selfish" and "ungrateful"
for the Taiwanese boss who had established the factory to help them escape
the hopeless and jobless countryside and make cash income in the prosperous city. Therefore, workers should not create troubles for the boss and
should share the boss' burden by devoting themselves to the factory. She
emphasized the common fate of workers and the boss. It was not clear how
much those overworked employees appreciated her preaching. But the foreman herself, like other low-level mainland managers in Taiwanese factories,
seemed to believe in the perspectives she espoused. They were aware of the
heavy workload and complained about the discrimination of their Taiwanese
boss against the mainland staff, feeling like secondary citizens in the factories.[20] Yet the capitalist Taiwanese modernity, as they knew it from working
in Taiwanese factories, gave them another identity affiliation. The transfer of
capitalist ideology was made easier through these blurred boundaries and the

intermediaries with multiple identities. In these in-between zones, the flows of capitalist ideologies merged with flows of capital itself. Also, the global construct of identity, either by the Chinese government, that is, preaching China-centered Chinese identities to overseas Chinese, or by the Singaporean state promoting Singapore as the center of "global Chinese networks," did not seem to receive direct compliance from these young mainland middle- or low-level managers in Taiwanese factories. Their fluid and often contradictory identities can be the result of the "multiple logics of action and shift among systems of script and norms" (Friedland and Alford, 1991). When rotating through different roles and identities in their daily operations, they may not be always conscious about it nor are they always purposeful.

CONCLUSION

Ethnicity is a convenient vehicle of identity building. Ethnicity-based identity has the potential of securing businesses solidarity, therefore reducing transaction costs, facilitating information flows, reducing competition, inducing cooperation, and maximizing resource utilization. But materialization of such potential is contingent upon specific historical and institutional conditions. The historical contingencies come from the following sources. First, between the monumental and absolute identity built by the state, and the rotating, often incoherent identities of individual citizens, there are vast discrepancies. Actions of individuals and groups may follow multiple logics and may not be the result of conscious or rational decisions. The successfulness of the identity building project initiated at the macro level has to be assessed at the micro level. Identity may not even be the central concern for many business and nonbusiness people. Second, the utility of ethnic identities, be they constructed or evolved, is determined by particular conditions at the macro and micro levels. Identity does not guarantee solidarity.

What we learn from such historical contingency is that identity is not an isolated or a systematic being. The making and the working of identities are not separated from the historical and territorial processes that involve economic, political, social and cultural factors. The meaning of boundary negotiation and the construct of Chineseness are exhibited through the actual practices of people and their interaction with others. The politics of identity is so highly localized that we are left with the question not about whether there is such a thing as Chineseness, but the question of how Chinese as individuals and collectives exercise their multiple identities in daily operations. The balance between the loosely drawn commonality and the novelty of particular action in specific time and space remains the issue for further analysis. We also have to redefine the problematic of Chineseness: instead of searching for a coherent system based on a coherent conceptual framework, one might have to trace multiple threads of historical possibilities and interpretations at different levels simultaneously and interactively. How to handle such muddy tasks while keeping some form of analytical consistency remains a great challenge. One way of handling it is to focus on more specific activities, such as business operations or through labor regimes. When Chinese capitalism is in question, it may be more fruitful to differentiate (and compare) Chinese businesses in different sectors, such as labor-intensive manufacturing versus high-tech industries, or manufacturing versus real estate and financial services. The specificity of different sectors in financing, organization and personnel will affect the way ethnic identity is converted into business solidarity.

NOTES

1. See, for example, Gilley (1998) and Cohen (1998) in *Far Eastern Economic Review*.

2. For example, Linda Lim (1983), when looking at the transformation and diversity of Chinese businesses, suggests that spatial and temporal variations of Chinese business strategies imply that "Chineseness" is an adaptive strategy rather than an identity. She further contends that, considering that many overseas Chinese firms are evolving into transnational business groups, they need to change from a traditional style. This involves the introduction of Western management into traditional family firms, and the expansion and separation of ownership from management. On this basis, the uniqueness of Chinese entrepreneurial practices must be questioned. Lim proposes a thesis of convergence of ethnic differences in business practices through growth.

3. The characteristics of the Chinese Confucianism, loyalty and hierarchy, in Max Weber's work, for example, are seen as the reason for the lack of capitalism in China at the beginning of the twentieth century. But the same characteristics are seen as the reason for the economic miracle in 1970s in East Asia. Thus the same conduct and characteristics in these two cases led to opposite consequences. To put it plainly, good or bad, capitalism or no capitalism, it is because they are Chinese and they are Confucianists. It does not really avoid the trap of essentialism, while at the same time assigning a causal relationship to coexisting phenomena.

4. The abuse and overuse of the term "capital" in the discussion of social relations and economy, such as social capital, cultural capital, symbolic capital also bears the danger of neglecting the multiple logics of action (i.e., cultural, political, and economic logics). See Alan Smart, 1994.

5. Granovetter (1995) reminded us with the old saying: the one you love can hurt you the most.

6. We also have to remind ourselves a sad fact that although a popular topic in cultural studies, identity is not necessarily on the top of the mind of our "research objects." In fact identity itself is a very Western idea (Trocki, 1997).

7. Chinese collective entrepreneurship is based on networks of family firms. Chinese family firms are not individual firms, but are organized in networks of many family firms. Hamilton suggested that this characteristic makes Chinese family firms different from Western family firms.

8. This is Granovetter's (1995: 143) term. He also used "culture as a tool kit."

9. Some have failed in other overseas production sites like Indonesia, the Philippines, even South Africa.

10. See Hsing, 2000.

11. Many foreign firms from North America or Europe tried to compensate for their "cultural disadvantage" by sending staff of Chinese ethnicity to their operations in China. Some of these staff may be American-born Chinese with limited Chinese language proficiency or sociocultural experiences. The appearance of Chineseness does deal with a wide range of cultural identities.

12. China interview M-36, November 1995. (All interviews are anonymous.)

13. China interview A-2, March 1991.

14. Except for those in southern Fujian Province, which, surprisingly enough, is not the primary site of Taiwanese investment in China.

15. There are regional variations in this regard. In Wenzhou, where there is a long history of private business operation, Taiwanese investors have established a more extensive production network with local industries than they have in other regions in China.

16. China interview A-1, March 1991.

17. China interview G-1, March 1991.

18. China interview F-4, April 1991.

19. In fact, the true reasons for the rejection were not so simple, see Hsing, 1998.

20. See Hsing 1998.

REFERENCES

Blanc, Cristina Szanton. 1997. "The Thoroughly Modern 'Asian': Capital, Culture, and Nation in Thailand and the Philippines," in Aihwa Ong and Donald Nonini, eds., *Ungrounded Empires: The Cultural Politics of Modern Chinese Transnationalism*. New York: Routledge, 261–286.

Buraway, Michael and Erik O. Wright. 1990. "Coercion and Consent in Contested Exchange," *Politics and Society* 18 (2): 251–266.

Castells, Manuel. 1998. *Power of Identity*. Cambridge: Blackwell.

Cheng, Lucie. 1996. "Chinese Americans in the Formation of the Pacific Regional Economy," unpublished manuscript, Department of Sociology, University of California at Los Angeles.

Cohen, Margot. 1998. "Moving Targets," *Far Eastern Economic Review* 161 (8): 51.

DiMaggio, Paul. 1994. "Culture and Economy," in Neil Smelser and Richard Swedberg, eds., *The Handbook of Economic Sociology*. Princeton: Princeton University Press, 27–57.

Dirlik, Arif. 1993. "Introducing the Pacific," in Arif Dirlik, ed., *What Is in a Rim? Critical Perspectives on the Pacific Region Idea*. Boulder, CO: Westview, 3–12.

Etzioni, Amitai. 1988. *The Moral Dimension.* New York: The Free Press.

Friedland, Roger and Robert Alford. 1991. "Bringing Society Back In: Symbols, Practices, and Institutional Contradictions," in Walter Powell and Paul DiMaggio, eds., *The New Institutionalism in Organizational Analysis.* Chicago: Chicago University Press, 232–263.

Gilley, Bruce. 1998. "Ready, Set," *Far Eastern Economic Review* 161(8): 46–50.

Gold, Thomas. 1986. *State and Society in the Taiwan Miracle.* Armonk, NY: M. E. Sharpe.

Goodman, David. 1997. "The Ethnic Chinese in East and Southeast Asia: Local Insecurities and Regional Concerns," paper presented at the conference on the Economics of East Asian Security, International Institute for Strategic Studies (London) and Council for Advanced Policy Studies (Taipei), March 3–5, 1997, Vancouver.

Granovetter, Mark. 1995. "The Economic Sociology of Firms and Entrepreneurs," in Alejandro Portes, ed., *The Economic Sociology of Immigration: Essays on Networks, Ethnicity, and Entrepreneurship.* New York: Russell Sage, 128–165.

Hall, Stuart. 1990. "Cultural Identity and Diaspora," in J. Rutherford, ed., *Identity: Community, Culture, Difference.* London: Lawrence and Wishart, 222–237.

———. 1991. "The Local and the Global: Globalization and Ethnicity," in Anthony King, ed., *Culture, Globalization, and the World System.* Binghamton, NY: Department of Art History, SUNY at Binghamton, 20–39.

Hamilton, Gary. 1996. "Overseas Chinese Capitalism," in Tu Wei-ming, ed., *Confucian Traditions in the East Asian Modernity.* Cambridge, MA: Harvard University Press, 328–342.

———. 2000. "Reciprocity and Control: The Organization of Chinese Family-Owned Conglomerates," in Henry Wai-chung Yeung and Kris Olds, eds., *Globalization of Chinese Business Firms.* New York: St. Martin's, 55–74.

Hewison, Kevin. 1993. "Of Regimes, State and Pluralities: Thai Politics Entered the 1990s," in K. Hewison, R. Robson and G. Rodan, eds., *Southeast Asia in the 1990s: Authoritarianism, Democracy, and Capitalism.* St. Leonards, Australia: Allen and Unwin, 161–189.

Hsing, You-tien. 1996. "Blood, Thicker Than Water: Interpersonal Relations and Taiwanese Investment in Southern China," *Environment and Planning A* 28: 2241–2261.

———. 1998. *Making Capitalism in China: The Taiwan Connection.* New York: Oxford University Press.

———. 1999. "Trading Companies in Taiwan's Fashion Shoe Networks," *Journal of International Economics* 48: 101–120.

———. 2000. "Spaces of Local Autonomy: Entrepreneurial Officials in Post-Mao China," unpublished manuscript.

Huang, Philip. 1998. "Theory and the Study of Modern Chinese History," *Modern China* 24 (2): 183–209.

Jesudason, James. 1997. "Chinese Business and Ethnic Equilibrium in Malaysia," *Development and Change* 28: 119–141.

Kahn, H. 1979. *World Economic Development: 1979 and Beyond.* London: Croom Helm.

Kuo, Eddie C. Y. 1996. "Confucianism As Political Discourse in Singapore: The Case of an Incomplete Revitalization Movement," in Tu Wei-ming, ed., *Confucian Traditions in the East Asian Modernity.* Cambridge, MA: Harvard University Press, 294–309.

Lim, Linda Y. C. 1983. "Chinese Economic Activity in Southeast Asia: An Introductory Review," in Linda Lim and Peter Gosling, eds., *The Chinese in Southeast Asia,* vol. 1. Ann Arbor: University of Michigan, Center for South and Southeast Asian Studies: 1–29.

Nonini, Donald. 1997. "Shifting Identities, Positioned Imaginaries: Transnational Traversals and Reversals by Malaysian Chinese," in Aihwa Ong and Donald Nonini, eds., *Ungrounded Empires: The Cultural Politics of Modern Chinese Transnationalism.* New York: Routledge, 203–227.

Oi, Jean. 1989. *State and Peasant in Contemporary China: The Political Economy of Village Government.* Berkeley: University of California Press.

Ong, Aihwa. 1997. "Chinese Modernities: Narratives of Nation and of Capitalism," in Aihwa Ong and Donald Nonini, eds., *Ungrounded Empires: The Cultural Politics of Modern Chinese Transnationalism.* New York: Routledge, 171–202.

———. 1999. *Flexible Citizenship: The Cultural Logics of Transnationality.* Durham: Duke University Press.

Redding, Gordon. 1990. *The Spirit of Chinese Capitalism.* New York: de Gruyter.

———. 1995. "Overseas Chinese Networks: Understanding the Enigma," *Long Range Planning* 28 (1): 61–69.

Riggs, Fred. 1966. *Thailand: The Modernization of a Bureaucratic Polity.* Honolulu: East-West Center.

Sanders, Jimy and Victor Nee. 1987. "Limits on Ethnic Solidarity in the Enclave Economy," *American Sociological Review* 52: 745–773.

Smart, Alan. 1994. "Gifts, Bribes, and Guanxi: A Reconsideration of Bourdieu's Social Capital," *Cultural Anthropology* 8 (3): 388–408.

Smart, Alan and Josephine Smart. 1993. "Obligation and Control: Employment of Kin in Capitalist Labor Management in China," *Critique of Anthropology* 13 (1): 7–31.

Smart, Josephine. 1994. "Business Immigration to Canada: Deception and Exploitation," in Ronald Skeldon, ed., *Reluctant Exiles?: Migration from Hong Kong and the New Overseas Chinese.* Hong Kong: Hong Kong University Press, 98–119.

Trocki, Carl. 1997. "Boundaries and Transgressions: Chinese Enterprise in Eighteenth- and Nineteenth-Century Southeast Asia," in Aihwa Ong and Donald Nonini, eds., *Ungrounded Empires: The Cultural Politics of Modern Chinese Transnationalism.* New York: Routledge, 61–88.

Wade, Robert. 1990. *Governing the Market: Economic Theory and the Role of the Government in East Asian Industrialization.* Princeton: Princeton University Press.

Wong, John. 1996. "Promoting Confucianism for Socioeconomic Development: The Singapore Experience," in Tu Wei-ming, ed., *Confucian Traditions in the East Asian Modernity.* Cambridge, MA: Harvard University Press, 277–293.

Woodside, Alexander. 1998. "Reconciling the Chinese and Western Theory Worlds in an Era of Western Development Fatigue (A Comment)," *Modern China* 24 (2): 121–134.

10

Notions of Home among Diaspora Chinese in Germany

Maggi W. H. Leung

The organizer of a recent conference "Locality, Identity and Diaspora" (held in Hamburg in February 2000) opened her introductory speech by reporting the results of an internet search with the keyword "Diaspora." She ended up with a list of hundreds of entries just from the German language web pages, ranging from stories about the diaspora of aliens from outer space to reports on the diaspora of the Swabians (*Schwaben,* a German ethnic and dialect group with a presence in the area of modern Stuttgart) from southern Germany. Her humorous reporting aroused not only a round of laugher, but also some serious thoughts about what "diaspora" should mean. The biblical concept of *The Diaspora*—exile of the Jews from their historic homeland and their dispersion among the Gentiles—has been more generally applied to other systems of population dispersion. "Diaspora" now carries an array of definitions. While some argue that the Jewish Diaspora is the "model," "genuine" or "ideal" diaspora (e.g., Safran, 1991), some use the term broadly, overlapping with other vocabularies of migrancy such as immigrant, expatriate, refugee, guest-worker, exile community, overseas community and ethnic community (Tölölian, 1991). More and more scholars use the concept metaphorically to map out other aspects of migrancy created by increased transnational movements of people, commodities, images, service and information in the globalized political economy (Hall, 1987, 1990; Gilroy, 1993; Clifford, 1994, Brah, 1996; Lavie and Swedenburg, 1996; Mitchell, 1997; Ong and Nonini, 1997). In spite of the contentious usage of the concept, it is generally agreed that the idea of diaspora embodies an image of leaving "home," going on a long-term journey and putting "roots" someplace else, establishing "a home away from home." This chapter is an attempt to bring to light different notions of this central element in diaspora: "home."

I use the term "diaspora" both literally to illustrate the distinct experiences of geographical movement among overseas Chinese in Germany, as well as metaphorically to explore the transnationality of these people-on-the-move and their transforming multi-placed identities. Diaspora, in my mind, is a dynamic patchwork, or a fluid collage made up of multiple and diverse journeys, sometimes diverging while other times overlapping, embarked upon by individuals of a dispersed community. By diasporic "journeys," I do not only mean their movements across geographical space, but also the long-term or lifelong processes undergone, interactively, with their social environments in identity (re)construction, (re)interpretation of their positions in the host society and ongoing negotiation in defining the meanings of "home." In this chapter, based on my observations of life-experiences of diaspora Chinese in Germany, I seek to uncover the diverse, fluid and dynamic nature of "home" among them.[1]

Methodologically, in order to better understand the nature of migration processes, a number of population geographers and migration scholars have recently called for a move away from grand narrative toward a more careful analysis of the situatedness and positionality of migrants achieved by ethnographic research methods (White and Jackson, 1995; Lawson, 2000; McHugh, 2000; Silvey and Lawson, 1999). My study involves collecting narratives of diaspora Chinese to explore the relationship between place(s) (in this case, the places called "home") and identities among them, as well as their sense of belonging and alienation as transnational beings. During the year May 1999–April 2000, I conducted personal interviews with over forty individuals, mainly ethnic Chinese women and men of diverse national, class, linguistic and age/generational backgrounds. My informants ranged from business migrants from Taiwan to refugees from war-torn Vietnam; from first- to third-generation migrants; from bankers, businesspeople, restaurant and hotel owners, government officials, religious workers, to housewives, retired seamen, and university students. They ranged in age from their mid-twenties to early eighties. Some of them were born in Germany, some have been there for just a few years, while almost all of them have been in Germany for more than eight years. Interviews were conducted in Mandarin Chinese, Cantonese Chinese, German and English (or a mixture of them) as the informants preferred. Most of the interviews took about one to two hours, some were products of a few meetings with informants. During the interviews, I especially engaged subjects that seemed to be important to my interview partners, attempted to guide the conversation to points which I wished to investigate including: migration motivations, reasons for their place of resettlement, meanings they attached to "home," nature and roles of ethnic networks at different geographical scales and adaptation strategies.

MAPPING GEOGRAPHIES OF MIGRANCY WITH "DIASPORA"

In *Nations Unbound,* Basch, Schiller, and Blanc-Szanton (1994) contribute a more precise and realistic transnational analytical framework to the field of migration studies, pointing out the insufficiency of terms such as "emigrant" and "immigrant" as categories to understand experiences of people moving across geographical boundaries in the age of intensified globalization. Not that transnationalism is a new phenomenon, it has however become more and more obvious in the late twentieth century that migrants develop and maintain networks and activities that span their "home" and the host society. Diasporic communities are prime examples of such transnationality. Diaspora, by definition, involves a "stretching out" of social relations between people across space (Massey and Jess, 1995), across geographical and cultural boundaries, as people in diaspora maintain connections through physical visits, letters and parcels, telecommunication and transnational mass media. Identities and narratives of a diaspora group are therefore rooted in multiple places, formed and transformed both within and beyond national boundaries. With this subtext of multiple belongings to multiple places, the concept of diaspora is helpful in debunking notions that associate "home" identity and culture strictly with fixed and bounded territories such as nation-states (Hall, 1987, 1990; Gilroy, 1993; Bhabha, 1994; Clifford, 1994; Brah, 1996; Lavie and Swedenburg, 1996; Silvey and Lawson, 1999). The idea of diaspora opens up space for rethinking the relations between place and identity, which is required in unraveling people's connections and identifications with places in an era when migrancy has become a normal state of affairs.

In her book *Cartographies of Diaspora,* Avtar Brah (1996) develops the concept of "diaspora space" which challenges absolutist notions of fixed origins and permanent homeland. Her idea underlines the "entanglement of genealogies of dispersion with those of staying put" (181) and emphasizes "the *configurations of power which differentiate diasporas internally as well as situate them in relation to one another*" (183). Diaspora space is a conceptual space inhabited by those constructed as "natives" and those as "migrants." It relocates the discourse of migration from the "exotic," "displaced migrants," and "the Others" to an understanding which takes into consideration those who move and those stay. Furthermore, her stress on the configurations of power *within* diasporas warns us from the common traps in applying ideas such as "diaspora" or "migrant community": the erroneous suggestion of a homogeneous and unified group that shares a set of characteristics and values, the idea that all members of a diasporic community have common goals (such as a perpetual desire to return to the original homeland, or to contribute to the prosperity of this historical, geographic origin as characterized by Safran, 1991),[2] or sweeping descriptions of the homebound emotions among overseas Chinese (narrated by Pan, 1990, for example).

If we remind ourselves that, in talking about the Chinese diaspora, we are referring to tens of millions of individuals scattered on every continent of the globe,
then we realize how illogical it is to generalize about them in such crude ways.

Thus, when we discuss diasporas as distinct historical experiences, we
ought to pay significant attention to the particularities of the many journeys
that join, intersect, overlap to form the collage. We learn that a diaspora is
hard to define, diasporic cultures are dynamic and fluid, and that not all members of a diaspora yearn to return to their homeland all the time, or that the so
thought-of "community" is also characterized by diversity and power hierar-
chies. It might be unsettling to some as the identities of an imagined diasporic
community no longer (if they ever did) conform to the traditional, neatly
trimmed, and often timeless Orientalist images. But we proceed to understand
how diasporas are differentiated and contested in space, and how a diasporic
group comprises communities of different identities and interests. Social
boundaries among these communities are not fixed or given, rather they fluc-
tuate in the continuous play of history, culture, and power both *within* and
without the diaspora. It is in this contested space that narratives and identities
of a diaspora are produced and negotiated, while some are foregrounded, dismissed, or forgotten at a particular time/space (Hall, 1987, 1990; Lowe, 1991;
Brah, 1996; Nagar and Leitner, 1998). Instead of sculpturing fruitlessly a
static image of how a diaspora should look, thinking about it as unclosed and
fluid allows us to understand and appreciate its complexity and dynamism.

HOME IS ALWAYS HOME?

The notion of home is particularly intriguing for those who are often *en route,*
crossing borders, embedded in webs of always transforming social relations
that stretch across geographical and cultural boundaries, who are identified
with multiple places. For some in migrancy, "home" is where they originally
come from, a place of nostalgia; for others, "home" is the place for which
they have left, a new way of life; some make home in their migrancy, carry
their "mobile home" with them like snails; while some have multiple homes.

Home is an important place. It is probably the very first place with which
we identify ourselves—a place we take for granted. But home is not always
just home. It is in fact a problematic concept, especially when we examine it
under a geographical light. "Home" signifies places of different geographical
scales. Home can be a country, a city, a village, a neighborhood, a house, or
apartment where one usually feels anchored, safe, and belonging. In the Chinese language, the multiple-scale characteristics of "home" is signified in the
vocabulary. *Jia* is home, country is *guojia,* one's home village is *jiaxiang,* and

one's original home is *laojia*, which is a more general term that can be applied for a whole array of "homes" of different geographic scales. Depending on one's social background and the circumstances in which one has to identify "home," the location of home changes along this geographic scale from household to the world scale (in such environmental slogans like "The Earth is our Home!"). During my interviews, I explore the concepts of home among my informants by posting questions "Where is home?" or *"Jia zai na li?"* (in Chinese) or *"Wo ist Heim?"* (in German). Responses of my informants reflect the multiplicity and fluidity of the place called "home." I shall return to this topic with more concrete examples in a later part of the chapter.

While recognizing the multiplicity in the meanings of "home," in the sense of geographic scales as mentioned above, it is also essential to underline that "home" at each of the multiple geographic scales, whether at the national or household level, is not bounded or fixed. Informed by Massey's (1994) concept of place, I understand "home" as any other place to be constituted out of a particular set of social relations (at different geographical scales) intersecting at a particular location. Home, as a social product, alters in response to changing social interrelations at multiple geographical scales.

In the last decade, many geographers have inquired into the interrelations between place and diasporic experience, to examine how processes at multiple scales intersect to shape migrants' life paths (e.g., Anderson, 1991; Western, 1992; Keith and Pile, 1993; Li and Findlay, 1996; Mountz and Wright, 1996; Stack, 1996; Nagar, 1997; Nagar and Leitner, 1998). Studies on the question of "home" identity or sense of belonging in migrancy have been conducted along several trajectories. The diverse trajectories of this body of literature also reflect multiple understandings of "home." Anderson's (1991) work on Chinatown in Vancouver highlights the social and political constructedness of "race" and place, and powerfully underscores how Chinatown, the often unquestioned "home" of overseas Chinese, is socially and politically produced and contested. In an essay on identity politics among South Asian communities in Dar es Salaam, Richa Nagar and Helga Leitner (1998) assess how processes of multiple scales intersect and shape the negotiation of geographic and social space among different diasporic South Asian groups in their neighborhood, a "home" which might appear to outsiders as a closed and homogenous space. Carol Stack's (1996) work on the return migration of African-Americans to their homelands in the rural Carolinas uncovers meanings of home and family among migrants. Her account of the motivations of migrants' movements challenges the traditional developmentalist and economistic assumptions in migration research (see also Silvey and Lawson, 1999). Focusing on the connection between place, identities and sense of belonging, John Western (1992) examines the concepts of "home" among Barbadian Londoners.

In this chapter, I examine the dynamic and multiple notions of "home" at the individual level to uncover the feelings among diasporic Chinese for the importance of home as place. Though personal, the feelings of migrants should not be seen as trivial as their senses of belonging are not only an individual's feelings and meanings, but are also importantly a product of the social environments in which they are embedded. For those in diaspora, whether one feels "at home" or is able to claim a place to be his or her home depends on journeys undertaken, both experienced and planned, and how one is embedded in and works through the social relations experienced in multiple places. These factors affect the meanings she attaches to her social environment, which in turn informs her actions. Since one in diaspora is often *en route* and the social relations in which an individual is embedded are also constantly transformed, so are people's ideas of "home" and senses of belonging. The examples presented in this chapter will underscore the multiple and fluid nature of "home" in diaspora. Before explaining my findings about "home," a brief description of the diaspora Chinese in Germany is in order.

DIASPORA CHINESE IN GERMANY: AN OVERVIEW

Contrary to the migration narratives of Chinese to Southeast Asia and North America, Europe has no core history of Chinese migration. Chinese in Europe are scattered and diverse in their origins. Significant Chinese settlement in Germany began in the 1870s. These early settlers were mostly men, ranging from peddlers, laborers, seamen at one end of the social ladder, to diplomats and students at the other. Before the First World War, there were only a few hundred Chinese settlers. Between the two World Wars, there were a few thousand Chinese in Germany, which were concentrated in Hamburg and Berlin. The Second World War disrupted the Chinese populations in Germany, and most of them left. The current geography of Chinese settlement can be traced back to the end of the 1950s when larger numbers came from Hong Kong and Taiwan, most of whom went into the catering and restaurant business. In the 1960s and 1970s, considerable numbers of ethnic Chinese from Indonesia, Vietnam, Laos and Cambodia arrived in Germany largely due to the anti-Chinese sentiment in their homelands. Since the late 1970s, there has been a sharp increase in the number of students and business people coming from the People's Republic of China (PRC) and Taiwan. Nationals from these countries officially comprised about 48,300 people (42,925 from the PRC and 5,331 from Taiwan) at the end of 1999 (Statistisches Bundesamt, 2000), who make up only a portion of the diasporic Chinese community. The Chairman of the Federation of Chinese Organizations in Europe (interview: October 31, 1999) estimates that there are currently 150,000 ethnic Chinese residing in Germany, but this is often considered to be an overestimation among my informants. The number is derived mainly by extrapolating from the 13,000 to 14,000 Chinese restaurants in Germany, together with the number of Chinese firms, and students. Figure 10.1 shows the distribution of 3,286 of the restaurants whose locations I obtained from *China-Branchenbuch,* the first ever published Chinese business directory in Germany. The picture is by no means complete, but it gives some indication of the perceived geography of the Chinese diaspora or the "imagined Chinese community" in Germany. Population concentrations are located in big urban areas, namely Berlin, Hamburg, Frankfurt am Main, the Düsseldorf-Cologne-Bonn region, and Munich.

Figure 10.1.   Distribution of 3,286 Chinese Restaurants in Germany (Source: *China-Branchenbuch* [*Chinese Directory*]. 1998. Dülmen: Chinesisches Handelsblatt.)

Shipping

A few factors are particularly important in tracing the specific development of Chinese settlement in Germany. A large portion of the early settlers in Germany were involved in the shipping industry, working for European shipping lines. Together with other major European ports, namely London, Liverpool, Amsterdam, Rotterdam and Antwerp, Hamburg was home to a Chinese population that dates back to the nineteenth century. In order to compete with the Japanese and American shipping lines, the Hamburg-Amerika Linie, Nord-Deutsche Lloyd, and Rickmers Linie began to employ Chinese, who were paid 40 to 50 percent less than their European counterparts, as firemen, oilers, or coal carriers on cargo ships in 1890s. More fortunate ones were employed as laundrymen or cooks on passenger ships. In 1898, in response to the German seamen who feared losing their jobs, the state drafted a bill aiming to partly ban the use of non-German or "colored" staff (*farbige Mannschaften*) aboard German ships. On 30th October 1898, employment of these "colored" crew on the main shipping route to Australia was banned. They were still allowed to work on main lines to China and Japan, but only to take the work that was considered to be detrimental to the health of "white" workers, such as working in the boiler- or engine-room. The number of Chinese seamen employed fluctuated with political-economic conditions. During the World Wars, for instance, the demand for foreign seamen and laborers at ports rose steeply to substitute for local laborers who were directed to the battlefields. When the Chinese seamen were laid off or decided not to sail anymore, many settled down and entered the catering business in cities such as Hamburg, Bremen and Berlin (Rübner, 1997; Gütinger, 1998).

Colonial Influence

Unlike the situations in England, France, or the Netherlands, direct colonial impact on the immigration of foreigners to Germany is minimal. In March 1898, German military occupied Qingdao in Shangdong Province, which was then ceded to the Japanese after the First World War. This colonial connection plays no significant role in the immigration of Chinese into Germany. Rather, the British colonial history in Hong Kong resulted in the resettlement of many Hong Kong Chinese in Germany. The vast majority of these Hong Kong Chinese came from the New Territories and were eligible for the right of abode in Britain. Since most of them entered the same business, in the restaurant and food services trade, the market in Britain was quickly saturated and many made their next journey to Germany.

Intra-European Movements

Germany, though not an immigration country, has attracted a number of Chinese who re-migrated from Britain and the Netherlands. Italy, Portugal and Spain have served as more lax points of entry of many migrants into Europe due to their less stringent immigration policies. Before 1992, nationals from the PRC did not need a visa to enter Hungary, which was also another jumping off point for many Chinese to enter western Europe. Romania, the Czech Republic, and Poland have also served similar functions for migrants who eventually settle in Germany (International Organization for Migration, 1995; Giese, 1999).

DIASPORA CHINESE: COMMUNITIES OF DIVERSITY

Chinese restaurants, snack bars, and Asian groceries are what many Germans associate with Chinese people. This was most telling when the Statistisches Bundesamt (Federal Statistical Office) suggested to me that I consult the *Deutscher Hotel- und Gaststättenverband e.V.* (Hotel and Restaurant Association) when I inquired about data regarding the Chinese minority. Indeed the Chinese themselves also share this perception. Estimating the size of the "Chinese community" and its geography from the number and location of Chinese restaurants is a common practice among scholars and community organizations. Though much less often, some Germans also associate the Chinese with criminal activities and drug trafficking. During a casual dinner with two German families, which included conversation about my research project, the first question someone asked me was "Do they also tell you about their criminal activities?" In another example, Thomas Weyrauch (1995), contrary to what his book's title suggests, *Escapee's Destination: Germany: Migrants from the People's Republic of China; Background, Determination and Motives,* devotes only a small portion of his writing to Chinese experiences in Germany. In that short coverage, however, he includes a detailed description of the Chinese triad and various police arrests of these gangsters.

These perceived dominant occupations and economic activities of the Chinese often stereotype "the Chinese" in predefined and limited social space, and obscure the diversity within the Chinese communities. In the memoir *Chenfu laiyinhe* (*Life along the Rhine*), by contrast, Hu Tou recounts perspectives of difference from within the Chinese community:

> In *Chouloude Zhongguoren* (*The Ugly Chinese*) Bo Yang asserted that the Chinese are best at forming cliques. The Chinese here [the German university at

which the author studies] are the same. To form a clique a line is needed. South-
erner, Northerner, from Shanghai, from Beijing, on scholarship, self-financed,
with Chinese partners, with German partners. . . These lines are drawn and re-
drawn . . . , the relationships are confusing. (Hu 1995: 123, my translation)

Hu points out vividly that complex social boundaries along axes of place, language and socioeconomic status play important roles of inclusion and exclusion *within* the "mainland Chinese student community." It is therefore erroneous to suppose that the "Chinese community" in Germany is homogenous
and shares a defined set of interests. In the inquiry into the migration experiences of Chinese in diaspora, one of the fascinating trajectories of diversity
among them is how they "place" themselves, specifically the various meanings they attach to the important place called "home."

NOTIONS OF "HOME" AMONG CONTEMPORARY DIASPORA CHINESE

We belong to the planet now, Mama. Does it make sense to you that if we're no
longer attached to one piece of land, we belong to the planet? Wherever we happen to be standing, why, that spot belongs to us as much as any other spot.
(Kingston, 1975: 107)

So says the protagonist of *The Woman Warrior* to her mother who has found
out that "[they] are not going back to China for sure now," as "[they] have no
more China to go home to" (Kingston, 1975: 106). The relatives have taken
over their land in the village with her father's permission. After her daughter's "comforting," Mama said "I don't want to go back anyway," " I have
gotten used to eating" (107).

This episode illustrates some aspects of the complexity of "home," especially for those in diaspora. While the daughter points out the multi-place
quality of home and her global belonging, her mother struggles with her hap-
hazard desire to return to her *laojia* which is identified with a piece of land in
the village. In the following, I shall bring to light some of the diverse sentiments of my informants about "home." In particular, my examples will uncover their living experiences with regard to the location(s) of home and their
making themselves at home in Germany. These pieces of the diasporic collage show that, contrary to traditional wisdom, home is not simply a family
inheritance, that is, determined by where or to whom one was born. Rather,
for those in diaspora, the meaning of "home" undergos change with time and
relocation, and is shaped by the constantly transforming social environments
in which they find themselves.

Multi-placed Home

When I asked "Where is home?" to a Chinese man in his 40s from the PRC, who has lived in Germany for 12 years (interview: November 3, 1999), he answered that he achieved some relief when he stopped searching and yearning for "home":

> My life is the present, the journey I am on. I live the everyday, not thinking so much where I will eventually be. I don't ask myself anymore where my home will be. Then I feel relieved. I can shed the burden.

His sentiment confirms Paul Gilroy's (1993) idea that being in diaspora is simultaneously about *roots* and *routes*. Not yearning for the *laojia* does not mean feeling homeless; being rootless about home can also be experienced within migrancy. My informant reassured me, he "feels at home" in Hamburg, as he said "our roots are now in the soil here [in Hamburg]." Reflecting the case of many, as a sojourner for whom *laojia* is not always in sight or in touch, he resorts to creating "homes" *en route*. The "created home" can take a variety of forms, which lie on different geographic scales depending on the specific circumstances in which one defines, or has to create, a "home." My informant above considers Hamburg "home at the present" where he and his family's roots are inserted, supporting Susan Pattie's (1994: 186) observation, about the Armenian diaspora in the United States, that "home" for many is both mobile and nomadic, more synonymous with family than a particular place. A woman in her early 30s who immigrated to Germany at the age of 12 echoed this idea of home:

> I think our home, [short pause], we say *genru youxiang* [there is a home when roots are inserted], for me, my root is not in China, not in Germany, but in my family. (interview: February 15, 2000)

Migration has increased in scope in the age of accelerated and intensified globalization. It has been estimated that at least 100 million people in the world today have left their homes to seek or improve their safety and/or livelihood (Phizacklea, 1998: 22). Many of these people who have left home, as Kingston's quote at the beginning of this section propounds, do not feel that they belong to a particular piece of geographical territory, but rather to an array of different places where they have set foot. Regarding this phenomenon, Brah (1996: 194) asserts, "the double, triple, or multi-placedness of 'home' in the imagery of people in the diaspora does not mean that such groups do not feel anchored in the place of settlement." This multi-placedness of home has been made more attainable in this new age of rapid communication and transportation. Nowadays one can (at least, most of my informants can afford to) switch on the television anytime of the day, be at home and make a virtual journey to another "home," view programs via satellite from the PRC, Taiwan, and Hong Kong, ranging from news to MTV and soap operas. In addition, telecommunications and air travel have become increasingly affordable, enabling those in diaspora to maintain more frequent face-to-face contact as well as establish new kin and friendship ties with those in the original "home," or those who have established another home someplace else in the diaspora.

Enjoying his mobility, a Taiwanese businessman in his 40s who had worked in South America for five years before coming to Germany, and has lived in Hamburg for over ten years, remarked with a celebratory note when he talked about his multiple-roots:

> Taiwan has become a psychological home. . . . I feel comfortable living any-where. It was great when I worked in South America, and then I returned to Taiwan, it was of course good. Or in Hong Kong I also have many good business partners, friends. And here [Hamburg], I am also used to living here. . . . The world has become so small. It is a global village. (interview: November 26, 1999)

While this kind of resilient, transnational identity is commonplace among mostly young male professional diaspora Chinese who live a jet-set way of life, it is also worth noting, however, that this hyper-mobility also has its cost. A government official from Singapore in his late 30s, who has been posted overseas for the last seven years, doubted if he "qualified" to be my inform-ant as he expressed his frustration with his "nomadic" lifestyle:

> I can introduce you to people I think more appropriate. But not me. You want to interview people who live here, right? I don't really live here. Yesterday I just came back from Russia and then I am off again the day after tomorrow. Some-times I come home [in Frankfurt] just having enough time to say hello to my apartment and bye again. Like a dog! Really! [Laugh.] My family gave me a *tieshu* ["iron tree"] as a present. You know? This plant is supposed to survive anything like iron, right? And it died on me! It did. Even an iron tree died on me! I am never home. Just running around like a dog! (interview: March 27, 2000)

The frustration of my informant cautions us from the danger of over-glorifying the mobility and flexibility among Chinese elites who are often assumed not to need a home. Their nostalgic yearning for a home base, a geographic anchor-age, does not necessarily cease even though these young professionals have the financial means to shuttle between the many places where they could make "home."

In addition to problematizing the notion of hyper-mobility among the elite diasporic Chinese, it is also crucial to underscore the "power geometry" (Massey, 1993) of this flexibility and mobility. As the elites stretch their socio-economic "playing field" across oceans and continents, many "lower-skilled" migrant laborers do not enjoy the privileges of such frequent border crossings, including facing more restrictive border controls. In addition to the class differential, the gender dimension of this elite diasporic space should also be examined. A few studies conducted recently on so-called corporate wives have brought to light the gendered nature of highly skilled labor migration (e.g., Weyland, 1997; Li and Findlay, 1999; Yeoh and Willis, 1999). In order for the geographically mobile male elites to be able to spread their wings and cruise carefree across oceans and continents, many corporate wives (also reflected in most cases of my corporate informants) may stay in the home country or migrate with their husbands, having to forego their career and/or other aspirations to take over the reproductive needs of these elite diaspora households. These women are also more likely to restrict their life space to the household(s). In his study of the Hong Kong "astronaut families," who strategically disperse different members of the family in different continents (often the husband or father works in Hong Kong while the rest of the family lives in the United States, Canada, Australia or New Zealand), Chan Kwok Bun (1997) points to the gendered nature of a "typical" transnational household:

> The dispersed family, fashioning itself in a duality, or rather (in the future, if not now) a plurality of places, provides him with a structure, form, and context to articulate his multiplicity of selves and identities, in motion, "in the cracks" between psychologies, ethnicities, cultures, and civilizations, touching all. (Chan, 1997: 204, emphasis mine)

Chan's quote illustrates the highly gendered nature of the "typical" transnational household. In most of these families, the prerequisites for the relatively carefree mobility of the males is women's geographically bounded home-making duties, which the men use as a basis of enjoying their journeys, knowing that there is a secure "home base" preserved by their wives.

To sum up, I have in this section looked into the notion of multi-placed home, which is commonly recognized among contemporary diasporic Chinese. "Home," for most of them, no longer takes a fixed form situated only in bounded geographical territory. This finding has provided a powerful critique of previous narratives of rootedness of the "natives" and uprootedness of "those who come"; it is however extremely important to keep in mind the limits of this "new freedom of modern diaspora Chinese," such as the salient class and gender differences as discussed above. In the next section, I shall bring the discussion to a different geographical scale and consider the space available for ethnic Chinese migrants in claiming the country Germany as "home." In this respect, "home" represents a negotiated terrain not merely for those who have moved, but also with those who have not. "Home" embodies then intersections of power relationships between the so-constructed "natives" and "strangers."

Claiming a Place Home

Ong's (1996: 738) re-theorization of "cultural citizenship"[3] reminds us that immigrant or minority groups cannot always "escape the cultural inscription of state power and other forms of regulation that define the different modalities of belonging." Her concern can be detected in the German context only if we think about the meanings embodied by terms used for different groups of people in the country. Migrant and minority groups, no matter how long they have lived in Germany, are generally called *Ausländer* or *Fremde*—both referring to foreigners (while the latter means literally "strangers," it also applies to Germans from other parts of the country, such as tourists or short-term visitors). "Indigenous Germans" use the term *Einheimische,* literally meaning "those who are at home here" to describe themselves. So migrants and minorities, as foreigners or strangers, may *"feel* at home" but not *"be* at home."

The issue of immigration continues to be one of the most hotly debated social and political topics in Germany. *Ausländer,* especially those from the less industrialized regions of the world, are often scapegoats for socioeconomic problems, such as persistent unemployment and economic recession, and are targets of right-wing political parties and populist groups. "Germany is not an immigration country" is one of the most commonly heard statements in the immigration/minority discourse. This claim clashes, however, with the reality that over 7.3 million foreigners live in Germany, amounting to almost nine percent of the total population at year end 1999 (Statistisches Bundesamt, 2000).[4] Until the recent reform that was put into force on January 1, 2000,[5] the German citizenship and nationality law had been based on the principal of *jus sanguinis* (citizenship by descent), thus excluding or making it very difficult for those who are not of ethnic German descent to stake claim politically in the German territory as "home." One of my informants in her 30s, a naturalized German, who has lived in Germany for almost 20 years, said about the recent citizenship reform:

> I think [radical changes] are not what you can expect. You know Germany, or Europe in general is too small. It is not a traditional immigration country. If you need this idea to change in the general societal level, you might need a few generations' time. (interview: February 15, 2000)

Before the recent reform of the citizenship law, it had been possible to apply for naturalization. But admission to citizenship through naturalization had been rare: only those who are considered to be particularly "valuable" to the German state would be granted this "exceptional privilege" (Jones, 1996: 121). All the second-generation Chinese migrants I have interviewed are formally German citizens. Political inclusion does not, however, necessarily waive social exclusion from the German nationhood, which is conventionally based on skin color (i.e., being "white") and religion (i.e., being Christian). One second-generation woman in her 20s, whose parents migrated from Hong Kong to Germany in the 1950s, considers herself "Hong Kong Chinese" even though she was born and raised in Hamburg. She explained to me her sense of being out of place as we were waiting for her friends in a pub:

> Many people say that I am very "German." But if you call yourself a German, they say, "No." You can't be a German looking like me, right? At school I did not have many "German" friends. You will see who my friends are when they come. They are all, but one, atypical Germans [i.e., not those whose parents are both "indigenous Germans" born and raised in Germany]. They [the "Germans"] do not understand us. I don't feel that we are alike. It is strange, I don't know why (interview: September 25, 1999).

Her friend, also in her 20s, whose parents came from Jakarta, Indonesia, in the 1960s interjected:

> Or like, they praise, "You speak German really well!" Hello! That is all I spoke until I started learning Chinese in the university! [They both laughed.]

Another young woman in her 30s, who came to Germany as a teenager, also pointed to the importance of physical identities, which often determine where one belongs. She related to me her strategy of "going global" to escape from her transterritorial sense of belonging, the state of in-betweenness:

> Many people ask me this kind of question [of "Who are you?"]. I say I am a *shijieren* [world citizen]. Because I feel that I am not totally a Chinese, except I look Chinese and I speak Chinese. But there are a lot of living habits, I am more "Germanized." But then if I say, I am German, that is also not quite right. I have a German passport, but from my appearance, I cannot be a German. So I have this feeling, I prefer not to have a nationality, then I feel the most comfortable. (interview: February 15, 2000)

The above examples resonate Brah's (1996) argument that "diaspora space" is inhabited not only by those who have moved and their descendants, but also by those who have "stayed put," the "indigenous." Where one feels belonging depends much on the perceptions of the others. One of my informants in her 30s whose partner is a "German-looking" German recalled angrily:

> He works in China and last time when he came back to Hamburg, we went out with his friends. And they all thought, "Aha, he has brought her back from China." I had never felt so "Chinese" before. I have lived here all my life! I was

shocked. I expected that kind of prejudice from my parents' generation. But you
still hear that from our generation. (interview: October 19, 1999)

At the beginning of our conversation, she told me that because her mother
was German and she was raised as a German child in Hamburg, the city was
no doubt her home where she felt belonging. Even though she is not much attached to China, where her father came from and where her mother grew up,
she cannot escape from being categorized as an identity-carrier of that nation-
state, a "home" that "Others" ascribe to her. By the same token, the possession of political citizenship does not necessarily guard one from being gazed
at as the "Other." The few narratives above illustrate how the body is a site of
cultural symbols, a social product to be understood in the context of the historically rooted symbolic system, in which the "Chinese" and the "German"
are defined. This last case shows also clearly that the body is not only racialized, but also gendered, in the sense that my informant was not only viewed
as "Chinese" but also as a "woman," the passive "Other" to be brought back
from the "Orient." In this way being a member of a diaspora can entail carrying identities, memories, and narratives, which include not only those lived
and relived, produced and reproduced, told and retold by those *within* the diaspora, but also those who "stayed put" *without* it.

Due to its anti-Semitic history and the too frequent occurrence of racist at-
tacks, xenophobic sentiment and violence in Germany are important topics in
public discourse. The most recent annual survey conducted by the *Bundesamt
für Verfassungsschutz* (Federal Office for the Protection of the Constitution) reports that in 1999 the number of members of far-right political parties and
groups reached 51,400, which was 2,200 members lower than in 1998. The
number of violent far-right extremists has, however, risen 10 percent from the
previous year, reaching 9,000 people. The number of Internet homepages which
propagate far-right ideas has also increased from 200 in 1998 to 330 in 1999.
These reflections of racial prejudice do not seem to disturb most of my informants. Some of them consider Hamburg and Frankfurt as safe compared to
Bavaria, or the former East Germany where the majority of anti-foreigner violence has taken place. A few of my informants hypothesized that the small number and scattered distribution of the Chinese, who work hard but do not compete with the Germans for work (as many of them are entrepreneurial), do not
make political demands, and do not stand out ("unlike the Turks who wear their
hats and headscarves around," said one), renders them "invisible," and thus
safer from vulgar racism. Nonetheless, when one looks around and observes the
recent increased momentum of anti-migrant and anti-foreign sentiment in Germany, as well as in other European countries, namely Austria, France and even
in Scandinavia, one should perhaps not be too complacent. In his article in one
of the Chinese community newspapers, Peng (2000) reflects on repeated inten-

tional damage to Jewish graves in eastern Germany and stresses that diaspora Chinese in Germany, and in Europe in general should guard themselves from possible development of this anti-Semitic attitude.

CONCLUSION

In this chapter, I have sought to bring together some of the multiple meanings of "home" for those in diaspora and to examine their daily negotiations of this important place. Based on published accounts and personal interviews, I have provided an overview of Chinese migration to Germany and a more in-depth inquiry into the various issues pertaining to the notion of "home" among diaspora Chinese. Specifically, I have referred to Massey's conceptualization of place to uncover my informants' ideas of home. As my examples have hopefully illustrated, "home," especially for diasporic subjects, is not a place taken for granted, bounded and fixed in a certain geographical territory. Rather, "homes" are more often placed at different geographical scales and multiple locations. "Homes" can thus be appropriately understood as social constructions, intersections of social relationships at different spatial scales. "Home," and a sense of belonging, is identified with a particular place at a particular time, informed by one's social identities (including gender, class and ethnic background), experiences along many diasporic journeys, past and future, as well as the broader socioeconomic and political environments in which one is situated. As those in diaspora sojourn physically and/or mentally between their new homes and *laojia*, diasporic individuals incorporate and blend experiences of multiple places and various homes to help make sense of their physical and social environments. These multi-placed experiences partially inform migrants' identities—who they are, where they belong, as well as how "Others" view who they are and where they belong—which in turn shape their adaptation strategies and further mobility patterns. Diasporic identities are always transforming and being transformed, always (re)producing and being (re)produced. By appreciating the heterogeneity and diversity of diasporic experiences, we take a leap beyond the backward-looking conceptualization of diaspora as "the old, the imperialising, the hegemonising, form of 'ethnicity'" against which Hall (1990: 235), has written, citing the traumatic expulsion of the Palestinians by the "home-coming at all cost" of the Jewish diaspora.

By collecting rich stories from individuals in diasporas, I have sought grounded data on the diverse and changing meanings they attach to the notion "home," as well as their experiences of the complex processes of inclusion and marginalization in Germany. These narratives allow me to feel the texture and color of some pieces of the collage of the Chinese diaspora. Listening to migrants' stories has enabled me uncover some of the multiple ways of "being Chinese" and "feeling Chinese" in the contemporary Chinese diaspora.

NOTES

This chapter presents findings from my ongoing dissertation research project funded by the German Academic Exchange Service. I am grateful to my informants who had trust in me, and were generous to share their valuable time, experiences, sentiments and ideas with me. Many thanks to Richa Nagar and the editors of this volume for their helpful comments on earlier drafts of this paper.

1. Unless otherwise noted, the term "Chinese" refers to ethnic Chinese, regardless of their national background, throughout the chapter.

2. Safran (1991: 83–84) asserts that expatriate communities should carry several of the following six key features in order to be qualified to be a diaspora: (i) a history of dispersion (ii) memories of homeland, (iii) alienation or a feeling of being insulated from the host society, (iv) a desire to return to their homeland, (v) a collective commitment in maintaining or restoring their homeland and contribute to its safety and prosperity, and lastly (vi) they maintain personal or vicarious relationships with their homeland and a sense of collective cultural consciousness. Following his classification, Safran identifies the following contemporary diasporas, all of which do not, however, conform to the "ideal type" of the Jewish Diaspora. They are diasporas of the Armenian, Maghrebi, Turkish, Palestinian, Cuban, Greek, Chinese at present, Polish of the past.

3. The concept of "cultural citizenship" was first introduced by Rosaldo (1994: 57). He defines it as "the right to be different (in terms of race, ethnicity, or native language) with respect to the norms of the dominant national community, without compromising one's right to belong, in the sense of participating in the nation-state's democratic processes. . . . From the point of view of subordinate communities, cultural citizenship offers the possibility of legitimizing demands made in the struggle to enfranchise themselves."

4. At the end of 1998, the largest group of foreigners living in Germany came from Turkey (28.8 percent of total foreign population). Over 80 percent of the foreigners came from other European countries. The second largest contingent came from Asia, who made up about 10 percent of the total foreign population. In 1998, the growth rate of Thai nationals was the highest (6.7 percent) while the PRC nationals comprised the second-fastest growing group (5.5 percent).

5. After the introduction of the reform on 1 January 2000, children who are born to foreign nationals will receive German citizenship when one of the children's parents has resided legally in Germany for at least eight years and holds entitlement to residence or has had an unlimited residence permit for at least three years. These children acquire German citizenship at birth and also their parents' citizenship under the principle of descent (when applicable to the laws of the country of their parents' origin). The children have to decide within five years after turning eighteen (i.e., by the age of twenty-three) whether they want to retain their German citizenship or their

other citizenship. In addition, the reform has also shortened the mandatory waiting period for naturalization from fifteen years to eight years of legal residence in Germany, provided that the applicant (i) professes loyalty to the German constitution, (ii) possesses a resident permit or the right of unlimited residence, (iii) is able to support himself without the help of welfare benefits or unemployment assistance, (iv) has renounced or lost his/her previous citizenship, (v) does not have a criminal record, and (vi) has an adequate command of the German language.

REFERENCES

Anderson, Kay. 1991. *Vancouver's Chinatown: Racial Discourse in Canada, 1875–1980,* Montreal, Buffalo: McGill-Queen's University Press.

Basch, Linda, Nina Glick Schiller, and Cristina Blanc-Szanton. 1994. *Nations Unbound: Transnational Projects, Postcolonial Predicaments, and Deterritorized Nation-States,* Langhorne, PA: Gordon and Breach.

Bhabha, Homi. 1994. *The Location of Culture,* London: Verso.

Bowles, Edith. 1992. *The Chinese of Hamburg, Germany: Migration and Community,* M.A. Thesis, University of Hawaii.

Brah, Avtar. 1996. *Cartographies of Diaspora: Contesting Identities,* London: Routledge.

Chan Kwok Bun. 1997. "A Family Affair, Migration, Dispersal, and the Emergent Identity of the Chinese Cosmopolitan," *Diaspora,* 6(2): 195–213.

China-Branchenbuch (Chinese Directory). 1998. Dülmen: Chinesisches Handelsblatt.

Clifford, James. 1994. "Diasporas," *Cultural Anthropology,* 9(3): 302–338.

Cohen, Robin. 1997. *Global Diasporas: An Introduction,* London: UCL Press.

Eberstein, Bernd. 1988. *Hamburg—China. Geschichte einer Partnerschaft (Hamburg—China. The History of a Partnership),* Hamburg: Christian Verlag

Giese, Karsten. 1999. "Patterns of Migration from Zhejiang to Germany," in Frank Pieke and Hein Malle, eds., *Internal and International Migration: Chinese Perspectives,* Surrey, UK: Curzon Press, 199–214.

Gilroy, Paul. 1993. *The Black Atlantic: Modernity and Double Consciousness,* London: Verso Press.

Gütinger, Erich. 1998. "A Sketch of the Chinese Community in Germany: Past and Present," in Gregor Benton and Frank Pieke, eds., *The Chinese in Europe,* London: Macmillan Press, 197–208.

Hall, Stuart. 1987. "Minimal Selves," *ICA Document on Identity,* 6: 44–46.

———. 1990. "Cultural Identity and Diaspora," in Jonathan Rutherford, ed., *Identity, Community, Culture and Difference,* London: Lawrence and Wishart, 222–237.

Hu, Tou. 1995. *Chenfu laiyinhe (Life along the Rhine),* Beijing: Jiefangjun Wenhua Chubanshe.

International Organization for Migration. 1995. *Chinese Migrants in Central and Eastern Europe: The Cases of the Czech Republic, Hungary and Romania,* Brussels: International Organization for Migration.

Jackson, Peter and Jan Penrose, eds. 1994. *Construction of Race, Place and Nation,* Minneapolis: University of Minnesota Press.

Jones, Philip. 1996. "Immigrants, Germans and National Identity in the New Germany: Some Policy Issues," *International Journal of Population Geography*, 2(2): 119–131.

Keith, Michael and Steve Pile. 1993. "Introduction Part 1: The Politics of Place," in Michael Keith and Steve Pile, eds., *Place and the Politics of Identity*, New York: Routledge, 1–21.

Kingston, Maxine Hong. 1975. *The Woman Warrior: Memoirs of a Girlhood among Ghosts*, New York: Vintage International.

Knödel, Susanne. 1995. "Die chinesische Minderheit (The Chinese Minority)," in Cornelia Schmalz-Jacobsen and Georg Hansen, eds., *Ethnische Minderheiten in der Bundesrepublik Deutschlan— Ein Lexikon (Ethnic Minorities in the Federal Republic of Germany— An Encyclopedia)*, München: Beok Verlag, 119–134.

Lavie, Smadar and Ted Swedenburg. 1996. *Displacement, Diaspora, and Geographies of Identity*, Durham, NC: Duke University Press.

Lawson, Victoria. 2000. "Arguments with Geographies of Movement: The Theoretical Potential of Migrants' Stories," *Progress in Human Geography*, 24(2): 173–189.

Li, F. L. N. and Allan Findlay. 1996. "Placing Identity: Interviews with Hong Kong Chinese Immigrants in Britain and Canada," *International Journal of Population Geography*, 2(4): 361–377.

———. 1999. "To Follow the Chicken or Not? The Role of Women in the Migration of Hong Kong Professional Couples," in Paul Boyle and Keith Halfacree, eds., *Migration and Gender in the Developed World*, London: Routledge, 172–185.

Lowe, Lisa. 1991. "Heterogeneity, Hybridity, Multiplicity: Marking Asian American Differences," *Diaspora*, 1(1): 24–44.

Massey, Doreen. 1993. "Power-Geometry and a Progressive Sense of Place," in Jon Bird, Barry Curtis, Tim Putman, George Robertson and Lisa Tickner, eds., *Mapping the Future: Local Cultures, Global Change*, New York: Routledge, 59–69.

———. 1994. *Space, Place and Gender*, Minneapolis: University of Minnesota Press.

Massey, Doreen and Pat Jess, eds. 1995. *A Place in the World? Places, Culture and Globalization*, London: Oxford University Press/The Open University.

McHugh, Kevin. 2000. "Inside, Outside, Upside Down, Backward, Forward, Round and Round: A Case for Ethnographic Studies in Migration," *Progress in Human Geography*, 24(1): 71–89.

Mitchell, Katharyne. 1997. "Different Diasporas and the Hype of Hybridity," *Environment and Planning D: Society and Space*, 15(5): 533–553.

Mountz, Alison and Richard Wright. 1996. "Daily Life in the Transnational Community of San Augustin, Oaxaca and Poughkeepsie, New York," *Diaspora*, 5(3): 403–428.

Nagar, Richa. 1997. "The Making of Hindu Communal Organizations, Places, and Identities in Postcolonial Dar es Salaam," *Environmental and Planning D: Society and Space*, 15(6): 707–730.

Nagar, Richa and Helga Leitner. 1998. "Contesting Social Relations in Communal Places: Identity Politics among Asian Communities in Dar es Salaam," in Ruth Fincher and Jane Jacobs, eds., *Cities of Difference*, New York: Guilford Press, 226–251.

Ong, Aihwa. 1996. "Cultural Citizenship As Subject-Making: Immigrants Negotiate Racial and Cultural Boundaries in the United States," *Cultural Anthropology,* 37(5): 737–762.

Ong, Aihwa and Donald Nonini. 1997. "Towards a Cultural Politics of Diaspora and Transnationalism," in Aihwa Ong and Donald Nonini, eds., *Ungrounded Empire: The Cultural Politics of Modern Chinese Transnationalism,* London: Routledge, 323–332.

Pan, Lynn. 1990. *Sons of the Yellow Emperor: A History of the Chinese Diaspora,* London: Mandarin.

Pattie, Susan. 1994. "At Home in Diaspora: Armenians in America," *Diaspora,* 3(2): 185–198.

Peck, Jeffrey, Mitchell Ash and Christiance Lemke. 1997. "Natives, Strangers, and Foreigners: Constituting Germans by Constructing Others," in Konrad Jarausch, ed., *After Unity: Reconfiguring German Identities,* Providence: Berghahn Books, 61–102.

Peng, Xiaoming. 2000. "Deguo youtairen he Deguo huaqiao (Jews and Overseas Chinese in Germany)," *Chinesische Allgemeine Zeitung,* February 2000, 5.

Phizacklea, Annie. 1998. "Migration and Globalization: A Feminist Perspective," in Khalid Koser and Helma Lutz, eds., *The New Migration in Europe: Social Constructions and Social Realities,* Basingstoke: Macmillan, 21–37.

Rosaldo, Renato. 1994. "Cultural Citizenship in San Jose, California," *POLAR: Political and Legal Anthropology Review,* 17(2): 57–63.

Rübner, Hartmut. 1997. "Lebens-, Arbeits- und gewerkschaftliche Organisationsbedingungen chinesischer Seeleute in der deutschen Handelsflotte: Der maritime Aspekt der Ausländerbeschäftigung vom Kaiserreich bis in den NS-Staat (Conditions of Life, Work and Labor Organization of Chinese Seamen on German Trade Fleets: The Maritime Aspect of the Foreigner Employment from Empire to the Nazi State)," *Internationale wissenschaftliche Korrespondenz zur Geschichte der deutschen Arbeiterbewegung,* 33: 1–41.

Safran, William. 1991. "Diasporas in Modern Societies: Myth of Homeland and Return," *Diaspora,* 1(1): 83–99.

Said, Edward. 1979. *Orientalism,* New York: Vintage.

Silvey, Rachel and Victoria Lawson. 1999. "Placing the Migrant," *Annals of the Association of American Geographers,* 89(1): 121–132.

Stack, Carol. 1996. *Call to Home: African Americans Reclaim the Rural South,* New York: Basic Books.

Statistisches Bundesamt. 2000. *Statistisches Jahrbuch für die Bundesrepublik Deutschland* (*Statistical Yearbook for the Federal Republic of Germany*), Wiesbaden: Statistisches Bundesamt.

Tölölian, Khachig. 1991. "The Nation State and Its Others: In Lieu of a Preface," *Diaspora,* 1(1): 3–7.

Vertovec, Steven and Robin Cohen. 1999. "Introduction," in Steven Vertovec and Robin Cohen, eds., *Migration, Diasporas and Transnationalism,* Cheltenham: Edward Elgar, xiii–xxviii.

Western, John. 1992. *A Passage to England: Barbadian Londoners Speak of Home,* Minneapolis: University of Minnesota Press.

Weyland, Petra. 1997. "Gendered Lives in Global Space," in Ayçe Öncü and Petra Weyland, eds., *Space, Culture and Power: New Identities in Globalizing Cities,* Highlands: Zed Books, 82–97.

Weyrauch, Thomas. 1995. *Fluchtziel Deutschland: Migranten aus der Volksrepublik China: Hintergründe, Determinanten und Motive (Escapee's Destination: Germany: Migrants from the People's Republic of China; Background, Determination and Motives)*, Dortmund: Projekt Verlag.

White, Paul and Peter Jackson. 1995. "(Re)theorising Population Geography," *International Journal of Population Geography,* 1(2): 111–123.

Yeoh, Brenda and Katie Willis. 1999. "'Heart' and 'Wing,' Nation and Diaspora: Gendered Discourses in Singapore's Regionalisation Process," *Gender, Place and Culture,* 6(4): 355–372.

IV

MIGRATION AND SETTLEMENTS
IN NORTH AMERICA

11

Chinese Americans: Immigration, Settlement, and Social Geography

C. Cindy Fan

It has been estimated that as of 1990 there were 37 million Chinese living outside the People's Republic of China (PRC) and Taiwan (Poston et al., 1994). The vast majority, 32.3 million, lived in Asia. Of the Chinese in non-Asia countries, more than one-third were in the U.S., making it home to the largest Chinese community outside of Asia. Yet systematic studies of Chinese Americans, despite their increasing size and stature in the U.S. as well as internationally, are relatively scant. A recent book on "overseas Chinese" (Sinn, 1998), for example, has chapters on Chinese in France, the Netherlands, Canada, Japan, Australia, Britain, Malaysia, and South Africa, but no separate analyses of Chinese in the U.S. This chapter aims at documenting the salient processes that have shaped the experiences of Chinese Americans, focusing on their history of immigration, growth and composition, spatial distribution and migration, socioeconomic statuses, and identities and ties. I employ an integrative approach that emphasizes the geography of and interactions among the above aspects, highlights the complexities and heterogeneity of the experiences of Chinese Americans, and focuses on the connections between their experiences and the larger structural, political, and economic contexts in the U.S. and internationally.

In this chapter, the term "Chinese Americans" is used to describe the population who reside in the U.S. and who consider Chinese as their race, ancestry and/or heritage, and is used interchangeably with the term "Chinese in the U.S." It includes Chinese immigrants and their descendants living in the U.S., regardless of where they were born and whether they are citizens. Here, Chinese Americans is preferred to the term "overseas Chinese," in order to emphasize the shared yet heterogeneous experiences of the Chinese in the U.S., as well as the specific contexts in the U.S. that have been so central to their experiences.[1] Since "China" has been commonly used to refer to the PRC, this chapter uses these two terms interchangeably. Similarly, "Taiwan" is used to refer to the Republic of China (ROC).

As much as possible, in this chapter I shall use the most up-to-date information available, including data from the 2000 Census of the U.S. At the time of writing, however, only summary files from that census are available. Therefore, data from past censuses will also be used to provide a more complete picture of Chinese in the U.S. Several points need to be clarified in regards to U.S. census data. First, for the sake of convenience, I use the terms "Asians" and "Asian Americans" to include Pacific Islanders. Second, I shall aggregate Taiwanese with non-Taiwanese Chinese, though they are treated as two separate categories in the census. Third, wherever possible I shall separate out the race categories from the Hispanic/non-Hispanic ethnicity category, so that White refers to non-Hispanic White, Black refers to non-Hispanic Black, etc. Nevertheless, data so far available from the 2000 Census do not permit distinguishing detailed Asian races from the ethnicity category, so that most of the data for Chinese Americans from that census overlap with Hispanics. However, that overlap is expected to be very small, as less than 2% of Asian Americans reported Hispanic ethnicity. Fourth, for the first time in U.S. history, the 2000 Census permitted the selection of more than one race. Two or more races accounted for 2.4% of U.S. population and 15.5% of all those who selected Chinese as one of their races. There is insufficient information on what other races were selected by those who reported more than one race. Therefore, in this chapter, unless otherwise specified, I shall focus specifically on the population that selected one race only. This approach underestimates the population and hence interpretation of the 2000 Census data should be done with special caution.

HISTORY OF CHINESE IMMIGRATION

The majority of Chinese Americans are foreign born. Specifically, the foreign born accounted for respectively 76.6% and 70.7% of Chinese in the U.S. in 1980 and 1990. Among the foreign-born Chinese in 1990, the majority were recent immigrants who entered the country since 1980 (table 11.1). Though the number of native-born Chinese has increased over time, immigration continues to be a determining factor of the growth of Chinese Americans. To understand the experiences of Chinese Americans, one must first understand the history of Chinese immigration, which has been a direct function of changes in the American economy, U.S. immigration legislation, geopolitics in East Asia and U.S.-China relations.

Table 11.1. Growth and Composition of Major Ethnic Groups and Asians in the United States, 1980–2000

	1980 Population		1990 Population		1990 Composition (%) Native Born	Foreign Born Entered Before 1980	Entered Since 1980	2000* Population		Annual Average Growth Rate 1980–1990	1990–2000
	Number (thousands)	Percent	Number (thousands)	Percent				Number (thousands)	Percent		
Total U.S. population**	226,546		248,710		90.8	5.3	3.9	281,422		0.9	1.2
Non-Hispanic White	180,603	79.7	188,128	75.6	96.1	3.0	0.9	194,553	69.1	0.4	0.3
Non-Hispanic Black	26,092	11.5	29,216	11.7	95.3	2.3	2.5	33,948	12.1	1.1	1.5
Hispanic	14,604	6.4	22,354	9.0	57.3	22.0	20.7	35,306	12.5	4.3	4.7
Non-Hispanic Asian	3,551	1.6	6,968	2.8	32.5	28.8	38.7	10,477	3.7	7.0	4.2
Asian***	3,551		6,968		32.5	28.8	38.7	10,642		7.0	4.3
Chinese	812	22.9	1,645	23.6	29.3	30.6	40.1	2,433	22.9	7.3	4.0
Filipino	782	22.0	1,407	20.2	30.0	35.5	34.5	1,850	17.4	6.0	2.8
Japanese	716	20.2	848	12.2	64.5	17.1	18.4	797	7.5	1.7	-0.6
Asian Indian	387	10.9	815	11.7	22.7	31.7	45.6	1,679	15.8	7.7	7.5
Korean	357	10.1	799	11.5	17.5	35.0	47.6	1,077	10.1	8.4	3.0
Vietnamese	245	6.9	615	8.8	17.9	31.9	50.2	1,123	10.6	9.6	6.2
Cambodian, Hmong, Laotian	69	1.9	387	5.6	23.2	13.9	62.9	510	4.8	18.8	2.8

Sources: Lee (1998); U.S. Department of Commerce (1983; 1992; 1993; 2002).

*Data for non-Hispanic White, non-Hispanic Black, non-Hispanic Asian and all detailed Asian categories include only those who reported one race. Data for detailed Asian categories overlap with the Hispanic ethnicity category.

**Percentages do not add to 100 because American Indians and Alaska Natives are not included, and for 2000 also because the non-Hispanic population of two or more races are not included.

***Data include other Asian ethnic groups and Pacific Islanders not shown in this table.

The first Chinese immigrants to the U.S. came to work as miners during the California gold rush in the 1850s. Between 1850 and 1860 the number of Chinese in the U.S. increased from less than 1,000 to approximately 35,000 (Brown and Pannell, 1985). They were followed by a second wave between the 1860s and 1880s as workers for the transcontinental railroads, as well as farmers and laborers. The demand for labor in the U.S. precipitated the contracting and transportation of "coolies" from China. As a result, the peak of Chinese immigration to the U.S. in the nineteenth century was reached in 1871–1880, when more than 120,000 Chinese were admitted (figure 11.1).

Most of the early Chinese immigrants were from rural villages in the Pearl River Delta and spoke the Cantonese dialect (Pan, 1998: 261). The vast majority were men. As sojourners, they worked hard and led a thrifty lifestyle, hoping to accumulate as much fortune as they could before returning to their homelands. But many eventually stayed. Yet to the American public the Chinese were brought to the U.S. only to meet the demand for labor. Their increasing number was greeted with prejudice and discrimination, which grew even more severe during economic recessions in the 1870s and 1880s. Anti-

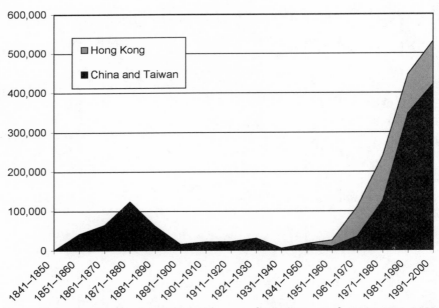

Figure 11.1.   Immigration from China, Taiwan, and Hong Kong to the U.S., 1841–2000 (Source: U.S. Immigration and Naturalization Service [1997; 2002].)
Note: Immigration by country of last residence. Data for China and Taiwan were not reported separately since 1957 and were therefore aggregated. Data for Hong Kong were not reported separately until 1952.

Chinese sentiment culminated into the first nationality-based immigration law in the U.S., namely, the 1882 Chinese Exclusion Act, which suspended immigration of Chinese laborers and barred those already in the U.S. from becoming citizens. Until after the Second World War, an assimilationist philosophy dominated U.S. immigration legislation, which aimed at excluding individuals deemed "unassimilable" into the American society. The 1924 Immigration Act established a national origins quota system, and effectively banned all immigrants from Asia, except for a small number of diplomats and students. After the 1880s, therefore, the number of Chinese immigrants dropped drastically (see figure 11.1), and the size of the Chinese population in the U.S. decreased and hovered around 60,000 to 90,000 until after the Second World War (Brown and Pannell, 1985).

After the founding of the PRC in 1949, an increasing number of Chinese immigrants were admitted, including refugees and students from Taiwan and Hong Kong. But it was not until the 1960s civil rights movement that legal discrimination against Asian immigration was eliminated. The 1965 Immigration and Nationality Act Amendments, which abolished the national origins quota system and eliminated national origin, race, or ancestry as bases for immigration to the U.S., was a watershed legislation. It established a preference system for granting immigrant visas based on family unification and special occupational skills criteria, and effectively opened the gate for new waves of immigrants from Asia and Latin America. Improvement in U.S.-China relations since Nixon's 1972 visit to China further motivated many Chinese, including students, to go to the U.S. Meanwhile, concerns over the PRC's increasing power, and the U.S.'s recognition of its legitimacy, prompted many Taiwanese to emigrate. The number of immigrants from China, Taiwan and Hong Kong increased from 109,771 in 1961–1970 to 237,793 in 1971–1980, 444,962 in 1981–1990, and 528,893 in 1991–2000 (see figure 11.1). As a result, the number of Chinese in the U.S. increased by 1.8 times from about 237,000 in 1960 to 435,000 in 1970, another 1.8 times to 812,000 in 1980, and more than doubled to 1.65 million in 1990 (Brown and Pannell, 1985; see table 11.1). By the year 2000, the number of (one race) Chinese Americans reached 2.43 million.

Two other immigration laws have had direct, though smaller, effects on Chinese immigration. The first was the Immigration Act of 1990, which increased the total number of immigrants to the U.S., and granted permanent residency to immigrants on investment bases. Then, the 1992 Chinese Student Protection Act, in response to the 1989 Tiananmen incident, provided permanent resident status to China nationals who were in the U.S. between June 4, 1989, and July 11, 1990.

In addition to changes in immigration laws, two relatively new channels have affected Chinese immigration to the U.S. The first is adoption of Chinese orphans by U.S. residents. Since the 1990s, the American media has widely publicized the notion that China's one-child policy had left many girl babies unwanted and accelerated female infanticide. With the aid of adoption agencies, China has since the mid-1990s replaced Korea and the former Soviet Union as the largest source of immigrant-orphans adopted by U.S. citizens. Second, smuggling of laborers from China has been rampant since the early 1990s, resulting in several large waves of illegal immigration to the U.S. Many illegal immigrants were brought from villages in Fujian, to work as laborers in sweatshops, restaurants, and farms in New York, New Jersey, and other parts of the U.S. (Pan, 1998: 268). They are heavily controlled by "snakeheads"— persons in charge of the smuggling operations—to whom they may owe several years of wages as fees for smuggling. Unlike most Chinese immigrants who are relatively free to pursue social mobility, these illegal immigrants' social, economic, and political isolations have rendered them among the most entrapped in the U.S. society and economy.

China, Taiwan and Hong Kong are the leading places of birth of Chinese immigrants to the U.S. In 2000, a total of 60,111 immigrants born in these three places were admitted, accounting for 7.1% of all immigrants to the U.S. that year (see table 11.2). Three-quarters of Chinese immigrants were born in China, which has become the second-largest country of birth of immigrants, after Mexico, to the U.S. Not surprisingly, China, Taiwan and Hong Kong were also the leading places of birth for foreign-born Chinese Americans, according to the 1990 Census. The importance of Taiwan and Hong Kong as sources of Chinese immigrants has increased since the 1960s. For example, according to the 1990 Census, the proportion of Chinese Americans identifying with Taiwanese ancestry had increased from 4.0% among pre-1965 immigrants to 15.9% among 1980–1990 immigrants. This trend is attributable to both economic and geopolitical factors. As two of the "four little dragons" in East Asia, they have emerged as thriving Newly Industrializing Economies (NIEs). Increasing wealth has not only made it possible for emigration to take place, but has also enabled more parents to send their children to the U.S. for education. This has led to a popular perception that recent immigrants from Taiwan and Hong Kong are mostly from affluent backgrounds. Second, persistent concerns over China as a potential threat to the well-being of residents in Taiwan and Hong Kong have motivated some to emigrate. Worries over Communist influence and the return of Hong Kong to China in 1997 triggered waves of emigration from Hong Kong to Western countries, especially to Canada, Australia and the U.S., as early as the 1960s (see figure 11.1). Therefore, despite its relatively small size, Hong Kong was the birth place of almost 10% of Chinese immigrants who entered during the 1980s, according to the 1990 Census. Other prominent places of birth of foreign born Chinese Americans are primarily Southeast Asian countries, especially Vietnam.

Table 11.2. Characteristics of Immigrants to the United States Born in China, Taiwan, and Hong Kong, 2000

	China	Taiwan	Hong Kong
Total Admission	45,652	9,040	5,419
Sex ratio	67.0	75.6	—
Class of Admission (%)			
Family unification			
Family-sponsored	27.6	45.7	64.3
Immediate relatives of U.S. citizens	41.0	23.3	16.6
Employment-based	30.2	30.6	15.6
Refugee and asylee	1.1	0.0	0.7
Orphans Adopted	4,943	24	14
% female	97.2	58.3	35.7
Selected States of Intended Residence (%)			
California	29.0	49.7	—
New York	19.6	6.6	—
Texas	5.0	6.6	—
New Jersey	4.1	6.3	—
Selected Urban Areas of Intended Residence[a] (%)			
California			
Los Angeles	8.7	19.8	—
San Francisco	7.1	3.1	—
Oakland	4.2	6.0	—
San Jose	3.1	8.4	—
Orange County	1.1	5.3	—
New York			
New York	16.9	4.7	—
Texas			
Houston	2.0	2.5	—
New Jersey			
Suburban New Jersey	3.0	5.0	—
Other			
Boston	3.2	1.3	—
Washington, D.C.	3.0	3.8	—
Occupation[b] (%)			
Professional, technical	37.6	50.0	30.1
Executive, administrative, managerial	13.2	22.4	30.6
Sales	2.5	8.8	7.2
Administrative support	6.9	11.9	13.6
Service	0.8	0.5	2.0
Precision production, craft, repair	12.1	0.9	5.6
Operator, fabricator, laborer	20.6	0.5	0.1
Farming, forestry, fishing	6.2	4.9	10.7

Source: U.S. INS (2002).

[a] Individual Metropolitan Statistical Areas (MSAs), except Suburban New Jersey which consists of five different MSAs in New Jersey (Middlesex-Somerset-Hunterdon; Newark; Bergen-Passaic; Monmouth-Ocean; and Jersey City).

[b] Excludes homemakers, students, unemployed or retired persons, and others not reporting or with an unknown occupation.

As expected, the proportion of Chinese who speak at least one non-English language at home was the lowest among the native born (41.7%) and the highest among post-1980 immigrants (95.5%), according to the 1990 Census. The vast majority of the foreign-born Chinese speak Chinese at home, which in the census definition includes Cantonese, Yueh, and Min dialects that are widely spoken in the southern Chinese provinces of Guangdong, Guangxi and Fujian, as well as Hong Kong. Formosan, which includes southern Min and is commonly spoken in Fujian and Taiwan, and Mandarin, the popular dialect among most mainland Chinese and Taiwanese, represent respectively the distant second and third non-English languages spoken by foreign-born Chinese at home. Since the census definitions of the three languages are neither exact nor mutually exclusive, it may be that many Chinese Americans selected the "Chinese" category regardless of the specific dialects they spoke. Nevertheless, the proportion of foreign born selecting Formosan and Mandarin increased with recency of arrival, which hints at increasing proportions of immigrants from northern China and Taiwan over time.

GROWTH AND COMPOSITION

Chinese are the largest Asian group in the U.S., accounting for 22.9% of all Asian Americans in 2000 (see table 11.1). Though Asian Americans constitute a relatively small proportion of the U.S. population (3.7%), they were the fastest growing ethnic group in the 1980s and were outpaced only by Hispanics in the 1990s. The average annual growth rate of Chinese was near average for all Asians. Its decline from 7.3% in the 1980s to 4.0% in the 1990s reflect the low fertility rates among Chinese Americans. In 1990, the total fertility rate for Chinese Americans was 1.4 children per woman, significantly lower than the fertility level of the U.S. population as a whole (2.1) and that of all Asian Americans (2.0) (Lee, 1998).

Except Japanese and Pacific Islanders, the majority of Asian Americans are foreign born. The dominance of the foreign born who entered since 1980 is especially marked for Vietnamese, Cambodians, Hmongs and Laotians (see table 11.1). According to the 1990 Census, among the 1.65 million Chinese in the U.S., 29.3% were native born, 7.0% entered before 1965, 23.7% entered between 1965 and 1979, and 40.1% entered since 1980. These groups differ in many ways, including age and sex structures. Though as a whole the mean age of Chinese Americans (33.1) was close to that of the U.S. population (34.8), the native born were significantly younger (20.8), those who entered before 1965 were the oldest (57.1), and those who entered during 1965–1979 and 1980–1990 were somewhat older (41.4 and 33.2 respectively). The modal age groups were consistent with the above differences, and the foreign born corresponded to the young adult ages (approximately 25–34) during the time of immigration, reflecting the age-selectivity of that process.

In 1990, foreign-born Chinese who entered before 1965 had the highest sex ratio (111.5), indicating that men were more highly represented among early immigrants. A sex ratio favoring men among the native born (104.9) is indicative of their young age structure, which is usually associated with higher sex ratios. But the sex ratios of post-1965 immigrants favored women, a direct result of immigration based on family unification, which involved large numbers of female family members. In 2000, the sex ratio of immigrants born in China and Taiwan was respectively 67.0 and 75.6 (see table 11.2). A large proportion of "immediate relatives of U.S. citizens" immigrants (41.0%) also explained the extremely low sex ratio among immigrants born in China. While "immediate relatives" included spouses, children, and parents, the spouses were more likely wives than husbands, and the children consisted of a large number of adopted orphans, predominantly girls. In 2000, 4,943 adopted orphans from China, 97.2% girls, were admitted, accounting for 27.3% of all adopted orphans admitted to the U.S. that year.

SPATIAL DISTRIBUTION AND MIGRATION

Since the 1850s the largest Chinese communities in the U.S. have settled in the West, especially California. According to the 2000 Census, the proportion of Chinese in the West, Northeast, South and Midwest was respectively 48.8%, 28.4%, 14.1%, and 8.7%. California and New York had the largest Chinese populations, with 40.3% and 17.5% respectively (see table 11.3). None of the other states accounted for more than 5% of Chinese in the U.S. Note that the apparent decline of the number of Chinese in Hawaii from 1990 to 2000, and consequently the state's drop in rank from third to eighth, are artifacts of the large proportions of two-or-more-races population in that state. Specifically, 21.4% of Hawaii's population reported more than one race, compared to 2.4% for the U.S.; and 66.9% of Hawaii's Chinese population (of any number of races) reported more than one race, compared to 15.5% for the nation. Detailed examination of the 1990 Census data shows that the regional distribution of Chinese did not vary significantly between the native born and foreign born, nor among the foreign born that entered in different periods of time. In 2000, California was the largest state of residence for all major ethnic groups, except Blacks, in the U.S. The relative concentration of Chinese in that state, however, was higher than any other major ethnic group, and was surpassed only by Filipinos (49.7%), Cambodians (40.9%), and Indonesians (44.7%).

Table 11.3.   States with the Highest Numbers of Chinese Americans, 1990 and 2000

| | 1990 | | | 2000 | | | Migration 1985–1990 | | | | | |
| | | | | | | | From Abroad | | | Interstate Migration | | |
	Number of Chinese	Rank	Percent of Total	Number of Chinese (one race)	Rank	Percent of Total	Number	Rank	Rate[a] (%)	Net	Rank	Rate[a] (%)
California	706,090	1	43.3	980,642	1	40.3	119,990	1	17.0	18,666	1	2.6
New York	282,132	2	17.3	424,774	2	17.5	54,191	2	19.2	-11,069	51	-3.9
Hawaii	66,007	3	4.1	56,600	8	2.3	4,755	11	7.2	-1,547	48	-2.3
Texas	62,166	4	3.8	105,829	3	4.4	12,889	3	20.7	-4,485	50	-7.2
New Jersey	57,670	5	3.5	100,355	4	4.1	8,696	6	15.1	6,721	2	11.7
Massachusetts	53,621	6	3.3	84,392	5	3.5	11,112	4	20.7	399	10	0.7
Illinois	48,243	7	3.0	76,725	6	3.2	9,681	5	20.1	-2,102	49	-4.4
Washington	33,963	8	2.1	59,914	7	2.5	6,690	7	19.7	1,018	5	3.0
Maryland	29,732	9	1.8	49,400	10	2.0	5,832	9	19.6	1,973	3	6.6
Pennsylvania	29,636	10	1.8	50,650	9	2.1	6,640	8	22.4	-5	16	0.0

Sources: Calculated from U.S. Department of Commerce (1993; 2002).
[a]Percent of 1990 population.

Like most other Asian groups in the U.S., Chinese Americans are highly urbanized. In 2000, 97.7% of them resided in urban areas. Figure 11.2 shows the metropolitan areas that had at least 5,000 Chinese in 2000. New York City, Los Angeles, and San Francisco, the three traditional and most popular ports of entry for Chinese immigrants, are the main reasons for the large concentrations of Chinese in the states of New York and California, and for their persistent bi-coastal settlement pattern. Though the number of Chinese in San Francisco, the oldest major Chinese settlement in the U.S., has been surpassed by that in New York and Los Angeles, the former continued to have the highest percentage of Chinese—11.9%—compared with respectively 4.0% and 3.5% in New York and Los Angeles. Adjacent to these three traditional centers are newer and less densely populated metropolitan areas that have attracted significant numbers of Chinese immigrants and internal migrants, including San Jose, suburban New Jersey, and Orange County. Their growth suggests that Chinese are attracted to newer settlements, but proximity to traditional large Chinese communities and an urban setting continue to be important locational determinants. The only exception is Seattle, which is not among or near traditional ports of entry but has become one of the larger Chinese settlements in the nation. Seattle's West Coast location and concentration of high-technology employment (e.g., Microsoft and Boeing) are two main attributes that appeal to Chinese Americans.

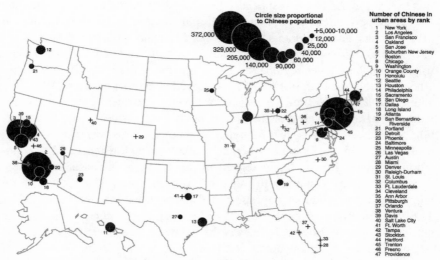

Figure 11.2.   Distribution of Chinese in the United States by Metropolitan Areas, 2000 (Source: Calculated form the U.S. Department of Commerce [2002].)
Note: **Only Metropolitan Statistical Areas (MSAs) with more than 5,000 Chinese are shown. Data for Suburban New Jersey represent the sum of five MSAs (see Table 11.2.).**

Chinese communities in other ports of entry, such as Chicago, Houston, and Honolulu, remain large but have not grown as much as those in California and New York. Large metropolitan areas such as Boston, Washington, D.C., and Dallas continue to have sizable Chinese settlements. On the other hand, Chinese communities are considerably smaller in much of the Midwest, South and the Great Plains areas, with typically not more than a few thousand in major urban areas.

Immigration is an important factor of the geographical distribution of Chinese in the U.S. Table 11.3 shows that with the exception of Hawaii, the 10 states with the largest number of Chinese in 1990 and 2000 were also among the 10 states with the largest number of Chinese migrants from abroad between 1985 and 1990. Migration from abroad accounted for between 15.1% and 22.4% of Chinese in these states in 1990. Not only were California and New York the leading states of Chinese Americans, they were also leading states of Chinese migrants from abroad. The impact of immigration is even more profound when one examines the proportions of the foreign born who entered since 1980 (not included in table 11.3), who accounted for on average 38.0% of Chinese in these 10 states in 1990.

In 2000, California and New York continued to be the most popular states, and Los Angeles, New York City, and San Francisco the most popular metropolitan areas, for new immigrants from China and Taiwan (see table 11.2). Compared with immigrants from China, those from Taiwan had a stronger preference for California (especially Los Angeles) than New York, and they were also more interested in newer metropolitan areas adjacent to traditional urban centers, such as Orange County, San Jose, and suburban New Jersey.

In addition to immigration, internal migration of Chinese further contributed to their uneven regional distribution. Among the 1.33 million Chinese who resided in the U.S. in 1985, 45.1% moved to another house by 1990, and about 21.5% (129,000) of the movers migrated to another state. These ratios were comparable to those of the U.S. population as a whole, but the proportion of interstate movers that migrated to another census region was significantly higher among Chinese Americans (59.4%) than the general U.S. population (51.8%). This is likely related to the former's bi-coastal settlement pattern and their propensity to move to Western states. The West was the biggest gainer of internal migration of Chinese Americans, with a total of 14,605 net in-migration between 1985 and 1990. All other census regions were net losers, and the biggest loser was the Midwest whose net migration was −7,560. The westward movement of Chinese was more prominent than that of the U.S. population as a whole. While the westward movement of the U.S. population has continued since the 1970s, it was the South that was the biggest net gainer between 1985 and 1990. The net flow to the West accounted for 13.4% of all interregional net flows among the U.S. population, but as high as

42.8% of the interregional net flows among Chinese Americans, further underscoring the dominance of the West as the latter's most popular destination.

Within the West, California was the most popular destination of Chinese internal migrants, registering 18,666 net in-migration between 1985 and 1990 (see table 11.3). Though interstate migration was a less important factor of population growth than migration from abroad, the former highlights important spatial dynamics within the U.S. The 10 states with the largest Chinese population were also among the states with the largest (most positive) net migration (California, New Jersey, Maryland, Washington) or those with the smallest (most negative) net migration (New York, Texas, Illinois, Hawaii). This indicates that internal redistribution of Chinese Americans occurred across the largest Chinese settlements. Three patterns seemed to have emerged. The first is the aforementioned movement from the Northeast, Midwest and South to the West. Another is the movement from older settlements, namely New York, Texas, Illinois, and Hawaii, to newer settlements along the eastern or western coast, namely New Jersey, Maryland, and Washington. A third pattern relates to the migration from older metropolitan areas to newer but adjacent metropolitan areas. The positive net migration in New Jersey, in conjunction with the net loss in New York, is the most prominent example of this trend.

Within metropolitan areas, Chinese settlements have also experienced changes. The oldest Chinese settlements are typically near central cities and in large metropolitan areas centering around Chinatowns. Chinatowns serve multiple functions, including first depots for new Chinese immigrants seeking information and employment, locations for firms oriented to a Chinese clientele, and commercial and cultural centers for Chinese communities across the city. But the newer waves of immigration since 1965 have accelerated the growth of new Chinese settlements in "ethnoburbs," a term coined by Li (1998; 1999) in her study of the San Gabriel Valley in Los Angeles. Li argues that the Chinese ethnic suburbs are brought about by new immigrants' desire for suburban living and have taken on a new "global economy outpost" function, by serving the residential and services needs of new immigrants whose economic and social networks are more international in scope than older immigrants. From a different perspective, Zhou's (1998) work shows that Chinese producer service firms that do not aim at an ethnic market, such as computer firms, are not necessarily located in Chinatowns or Chinese ethnic suburbs.

Figures 11.3, 11.4 and 11.5 respectively show the percentages of Chinese by census tract in Los Angeles for 1980, 1990 and 2000. They highlight first of all the tremendous growth of Chinese in Los Angeles County, from 93,747 in 1980 to 244,907 in 1990 and 329,352 (one race) in 2000. Second, Chinese settlements have expanded from Chinatown to more suburban locations. In 1980, Monterey Park and adjacent neighborhoods already emerged as important Chinese settlements, but the relative concentration there was still much smaller than that of

Chinatown. Specifically, in 1980, the proportion of Chinese in the three census tracts that constitute Chinatown (197100, 197700, 207100) ranged from 41.9% to 63.9%, but the proportion of Chinese in two of the most central tracts in Monterey Park (482101, 4822) was only 19.0% and 12.6% respectively. By 1990 and especially 2000, however, Monterey Park and adjacent neighborhoods have replaced Chinatown as the largest Chinese settlement in Los Angeles. This was signified by the splitting of census tracts (due to rapid population growth) in Monterey Park and the rising proportions of Chinese in these tracts. For example, the proportion of Chinese in census tract 482101 increased to 42.4% in 1990 and 48.9% in 2000, and the proportions in 482201 and 482202 (formerly parts of 4822) increased respectively to 42.4% and 44.1% in 1990 and 49.6% and 49.2% in 2000. These proportions are still lower than those of 207100, the most central Chinatown tract—72.4% in 1990 and 68.8% in 2000. Declining proportions of Chinese in Chinatown and adjacent tracts, however, further signify the suburbanization trend. In particular, the increasing spatial extent of Chinese settlements extending northward and eastward from Monterey Park—generally referred to as San Gabriel Valley—represents a relatively new and more popular suburban type of settlement with lower population density and less defined spatial boundaries. Meanwhile, the shares of Chinese-Vietnamese, and of poorer and less educated individuals, in Chinatown have increased (Allen and Turner, 1997: 121). Monterey Park (and its adjacent communities), on the other hand, has been transformed into a city accommodating large numbers of recent immigrants from Taiwan, so much so that it has been nicknamed "Little Taipei."

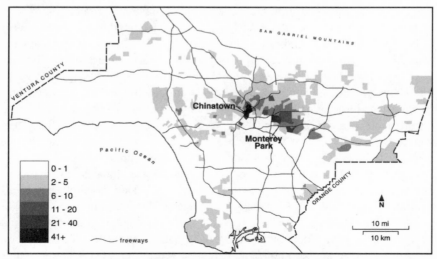

Figure 11.3. **Proportion of Chinese in Southern Los Angeles County by Census Tract, 1980 (Source: U.S. Department of Commerce [1982].)**

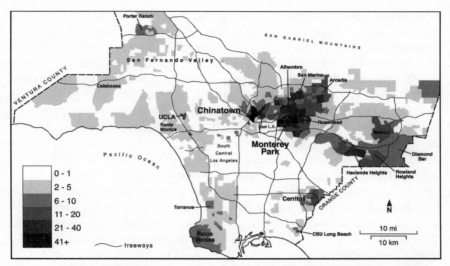

Figure 11.4. **Proportion of Chinese in Southern Los Angeles County by Census Tract, 1990 (Source: U.S. Department of Commerce [1991].)**

The spatial evolution of suburban Chinese communities in Los Angeles is by design and not by accident. The arrival of large numbers of new immigrants since 1980 fueled the demand for housing beyond the supply in Chinatown and Monterey Park. The higher population density, older housing stock, and central-city setting of Chinatown were considered less desirable by the new

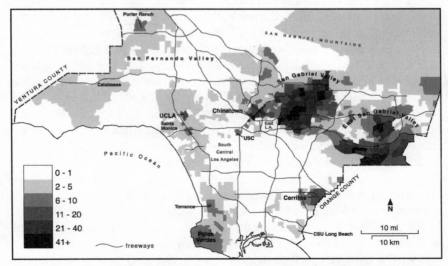

Figure 11.5. **Proportion of Chinese in Southern Los Angeles County by Census Tract, 2000 (Source: U.S. Department of Commerce [2002].)**

immigrants (Li, 1998). From Monterey Park, Chinese communities expanded into adjacent suburban cities such as Alhambra and Rosemead. Then, further to the north the well-known school district and affluent hilly neighborhoods of and near San Marino, still within reasonable reach to commercial and cultural establishments in Monterey Park, became attractive to them. Developers also began to focus on cities further east, namely, Walnut, Hacienda Heights, Rowland Heights and Diamond Bar in East San Gabriel Valley, where population density was relatively low and new tracts were available for building large and new residential and shopping complexes and amenities specifically serving new Chinese immigrants. Hacienda Heights, in particular, is well known as the site of Hsi Lai Temple—the biggest Buddhist temple in the Western Hemisphere. These cities have become the newest suburban Chinese settlements in Los Angeles that are no longer dependent on the commercial and cultural amenities in Chinatown or Monterey Park and adjacent communities. Figure 11.5 shows that by 2000 East Gabriel Valley has become a full-fledged ethnic suburb for the Chinese, perhaps even rivaling Monterey Park. Not only has the proportion of Chinese in Walnut, Rowland Heights and Hacienda Heights increased, but as a result of population growth many tracts in these communities had to be split and new tracts created. For example, the proportion of Chinese in tract 408701 in Rowland Heights was 12.3% in 1990, and by 2000 the tract was further subdivided and the proportion in one of the split tracts—408703—had increased to 55.2%. Such rapid growth reflects the attractiveness of new suburban housing development and suggests that the eastward suburbanization of Chinese in Los Angeles continues unabated.

The expansion of Chinese communities to the east and to the north, but not to the south and west, of Monterey Park, is attributable to ethnic geography and residential preferences. New Chinese settlements have generally been away from inner-city areas with high population density and high proportions of Blacks and Hispanics. Research has found that preferences and avoidance, in addition to socioeconomic factors such as income differences, are important determinants of residential segregation (Allen, 1997; Clark, 1992; Darden, 1985–86). East Los Angeles and South Central, for example, are neighborhoods with high proportions of Hispanics and Blacks, and where the number of Chinese in many tracts is zero or close to zero.

Other pockets in Los Angeles where the proportions of Chinese are more marked fall under four categories. The first consists of neighborhoods along the coast that are largely White with more expensive and older housing stock, such as Santa Monica and Torrance. The second category includes Porter Ranch and West San Fernando Valley that are also mostly White but where newer housing is available. Palos Verdes, Cerritos and Calabases are examples of the third category of neighborhoods, characterized by well-known school districts. Finally, census tracts with colleges that enroll large numbers of Chinese students, such as University of California-Los Angeles (UCLA), University of Southern California (USC), and California State University (CSU)-Long Beach, constitute the fourth category.

The settlement pattern described above suggests a high level of residential segregation among Chinese in Los Angeles. To ascertain this observation, the similarity index (S) and the modified exposure index (E')[2] are applied to census tract-level data for 1980, 1990, and 2000. The similarity indices, which range from 0 which indicates complete segregation to 1 which denotes no segregation, depict that the level of segregation of Chinese was most severe with Blacks, followed by Hispanics and Whites, and least severe with other Asians (see table 11.4). From 1980 to 2000, the similarity indices declined for all ethnic groups, indicating increases in residential segregation of Chinese. Positive values for the modified exposure indices denote that exposure to members of an ethnic group is higher than the citywide level, and negative values signify exposure levels less than the citywide level. Modified exposure indices between Chinese and other Asians were positive, but were near zero for Whites, negative for Blacks, and near zero or negative for Hispanics, again indicating that Chinese in Los Angeles were most segregated from Blacks, somewhat segregated from Whites and Hispanics, and least segregated from other Asians. These statistics further confirm that between 1980 and 2000 the level of residential segregation of Chinese increased, as signified by declining exposure indices with Blacks, Hispanics, and other Asians. This trend reflects the persistence of old ethnic enclaves and suggests that Chinese ethnic suburbs in San Gabriel Valley and East San Gabriel Valley

Table 11.4. Similarity and Modified Exposure Indices: Chinese and Other Ethnic Groups in Los Angeles County, 1980-2000

	1980	1990	2000
Similarity index (S)			
White	0.47	0.40	0.33
Black	0.19	0.20	0.18
Hispanic	0.42	0.35	0.28
Other Asian	0.60	0.52	0.47
Modified exposure index (E')			
White	−0.13	−0.11	−0.12
Black	−0.57	−0.67	−0.70
Hispanic	0.05	−0.15	−0.34
Other Asian	1.13	0.63	0.82

Sources: Calculated from U.S. Department of Commerce (1982; 1991; 2002).

have become new spatial entities of concentrated Chinese settlements. The predominance of recent immigrants among the Chinese population in Los Angeles, and their desire for settlements near other Chinese, are among the major reasons for their continued residential segregation, despite massive suburbanization that occurred in the past two decades.

SOCIOECONOMIC STATUS

Asian Americans as a whole have been portrayed as a model minority, but this notion downplays the diversity within the group and the continued resistance Asians face in their efforts to reach the top of the socioeconomic ladder (Cheng and Yang, 1996). While Chinese are among the most highly achieved Asian Americans, they are also a considerably heterogeneous group. The following examines in detail their attainments in education, occupation, and income.

Education

An important indicator of one's socioeconomic well being and human capital is educational attainment. According to the 1990 Census, 44.7% of Asian Americans aged 25 and over had at least college education, compared with respectively 28.4%, 16.7%, and 14.0% for the White, Black, and Hispanic groups. But the proportions varied considerably among specific Asian ethnic groups, ranging from 8.0% for Hmongs to 64.0% for Asian Indians. The proportion for Chinese Americans (47.7%) was only exceeded by that of Asian Indians and Filipinos. Among Asian Indians the foreign born had higher levels of educational attainment than the native born, but among Chinese it was the native born that had the highest education—61.5% of the native born aged 25 and over had college education or above, compared with 45.3% of their foreign-born counterparts (see table 11.5). Though on the whole the educational attainment of immigrants who entered since 1965 was higher than that of immigrants who entered before 1965, the differences were relatively small. They shared a bimodal pattern of educational attainment, that is, the majority had high-school education or above but significant proportions received only education at eighth grade or below.

Unlike the foreign born, the native-born Chinese did not have a bimodal structure. Instead, very high proportions of them had college education or above, which can be explained by two prevailing views. The first explanation is cultural, focusing on the value ethnic Chinese all over the world have placed on education. In this view, the high priority given to education is rooted in Confucianism, and is transferred from immigrants to their children

Table 11.5.   Educational and Occupational Attainment, Income, and Poverty of
Chinese Americans, 1990

	Native born	Entered before 1965	Entered 1965-1979	Entered 1980-1990
Educational attainment (%) (aged 25+)				
8th grade or below	3.2	24.1	17.0	18.7
9th–12th grade	4.6	9.7	10.3	11.0
High school	30.7	22.1	26.2	25.7
College	43.1	21.9	26.7	26.5
Graduate school	18.5	22.1	19.8	18.1
Occupational attainment (%) (aged 25–64)				
Managerial, professional	48.1	47.1	37.4	29.0
Technical, sales, administrative support	34.3	25.0	30.3	28.7
Service	5.9	12.9	16.4	21.4
Precision production, craft, repair	5.8	5.0	5.4	6.2
Operators, fabricators, laborers	4.9	9.3	10.0	14.0
Mean personal income (US$) (aged 15+), 1989	21,856	29,071	22,750	11,077
Percent below poverty line (%) (aged 15+), 1989	7.8	6.1	8.4	22.4

Source: Calculated from U.S. Department of Commerce (1993).

and transplanted to Chinese settlements in the U.S. through immigration. The
second explanation is structural, which suggests that high educational attainment among native-born Chinese is a strategy to compensate for discrimination in the labor market. In this view, Chinese share the experience of other
Asian Americans and other ethnic minorities who continue to be subject to
discrimination because of their race and ethnicity. High level of educational
attainment has become a means to overcome race-based obstacles in achieving social mobility (Cheng and Yang, 1996).

Occupation

In general, high levels of educational attainment are translated into high levels of occupational attainment. According to the 1990 Census, 36.4% of Chinese Americans aged 25–64 were in managerial/professional occupations,
compared with 29.8% of Whites, 17.7% of Blacks, and 14.6% of Hispanics.
But the proportions for Japanese Americans (39.1%) and Asian Indians
(45.0%) were even higher. Compared to Chinese Americans, the proportion
of Japanese Americans aged 25 and over with college education or above was
slightly lower (44.4%), but their high proportion of native born (64.5%) has

enabled higher levels of occupational attainment. Many Chinese immigrants, on the other hand, are disadvantaged because of inadequate English ability and lack of knowledge of the labor market. The high level of occupational attainment among Asian Indians is largely due to the very high level of educational attainment among the foreign born—64.3% of them had college education or above.

Table 11.5 shows in more detail the occupational attainment of Chinese Americans. The native born had the highest levels of occupational attainment, as evidenced by their very high proportions in managerial/professional occupations and very low proportions in service occupations and as operators, fabricators, and laborers. This is a direct function of their high level of educational attainment, as well as their more advantaged positions as native born in the labor market. Among the foreign born, the earlier the date of entry, the higher the proportions in managerial/professional occupations, and the lower the proportions in less prestigious occupations such as operators, fabricators, and laborers. Since educational attainment did not differ significantly among the foreign born, the occupational differences are attributable to other reasons. First, occupational attainment is a function of age. Second, the foreign born who entered before 1965 had more time and opportunities to move into managerial and more prestigious positions. Their longer duration of stay has helped them gain greater acceptance in a White-dominated society. Recent immigrants, on the other hand, must first overcome difficulties in entering the mainstream white-collar labor market, including relevant U.S. credentials and English ability. These difficulties have rendered them more highly represented than earlier immigrants in less prestigious occupations such as operators, fabricators, and laborers. Another alternative is to engage in service occupations, such as restaurant and motel sectors, where U.S. credentials and English ability are relatively less important.

A more detailed breakdown of the occupational categories shows the niches of Chinese in the U.S. labor market (see table 11.6). I define the niche index as the ratio between the proportion of Chinese Americans engaged in a specific occupation to the proportion of the U.S. population engaged in that occupation. For example, the niche index of cooks is 3.3 since respectively 6.1% of Chinese Americans and 1.9% of the U.S. population were cooks. An occupational niche is defined as an occupation whose niche index is at least 3, that is, the proportion of Chinese Americans engaged in the occupation is at least three times the proportion of the U.S. population in that occupation. Table 11.6 lists for 1990 the top 10 occupations for Chinese Americans aged 16 and over, as well as other occupations with more than 4,000 Chinese Americans employed and with niche indices bigger than 3. The occupational niches support an earlier observation of a bimodal occupational structure—on the one hand, Chinese Americans are highly represented in professional, mostly technical, occupations such as engineers, physicians, computer scientists, and postsecondary teachers; on the other hand, they are also highly represented in restaurant services and menial work such as textile machine operators and dressmakers. A closer scrutiny of the 1990 Census shows that occupational niches in restaurant services and of menial nature were highly represented by recent immigrants.

A bimodal occupational structure also characterizes recent immigrants from China and Taiwan to the U.S. (see table 11.2). In addition to family unification, employment-based admission is indeed an important channel for the

Table 11.6. Occupational Niches of Chinese Americans Aged 16 and above, 1990

	Number	Rank	%	Niche index
Cooks	61,047	1	6.1	3.3
Managers and administrators, not elsewhere classified	39,804	2	3.9	1.0
Textile sewing machine operators	39,173	3	3.9	5.6
Waiters and waitresses	32,697	4	3.2	2.4
Cashiers	30,507	5	3.0	1.1
Accountants and auditors	29,605	6	2.9	2.5
Supervisors and proprietors, sales occupation	27,207	7	2.7	1.0
Managers, food serving and lodging establishments	25,247	8	2.5	3.2
Computer programmers	23,994	9	2.4	4.9
Postsecondary teachers, subject not specified	23,966	10	2.4	5.0
Technicians, not elsewhere classified	17,000	11	1.7	4.2
Computer systems analysts and scientists	15,498	16	1.5	4.6
Electrical and electronic engineers	14,279	17	1.4	4.1
Physicians	12,979	18	1.3	3.0
Engineers, not elsewhere classified	9,943	22	1.0	3.8
Civil engineers	6,796	29	0.7	3.6
Pharmacists	5,216	45	0.5	3.8
Chemists, except biochemists	4,848	49	0.5	4.6
Dressmakers	4,189	53	0.4	4.6
Aerospace engineers	4,106	56	0.4	3.8

Source: Calculated from U.S. Department of Commerce (1993).
Note: This table shows the top 10 occupations for Chinese Americans, as well as the occupations with more than 4,000 Chinese and whose niche indices are at least three.

immigration of Chinese, accounting for respectively 30.2% and 30.6% of those from China and Taiwan in 2000. As expected, Chinese immigrants are highly represented in professional and technical occupations, which in 2000 accounted for respectively 37.6% and 50.0% of immigrants born in China and Taiwan. They, together with those in executive, administrative, and managerial occupations, suggest that Chinese immigrants as a whole are a highly selected group. On the other hand, significant proportions of them worked in less prestigious occupations, such as operators, fabricators, and laborers. This bimodal distribution reflects the two-track immigration processes, whereby employment-based admission brought in high-skilled immigrants and family unification brought in immigrants with a range of occupational skills.

Income and Poverty

It is widely known that Asians have the highest median household incomes among all major ethnic groups in the U.S. But this generalization hides two important observations. The first is that Asian households are larger in size and have more workers (Cheng and Yang, 1996). Personal income is therefore a better measure. According to the 1990 Census, the mean personal income of Asians aged 15 and over in 1989 was $17,488, which was higher than that of Blacks ($12,026) and Hispanics ($11,782) but lower than that of Whites ($19,368). Second, Asians are a very heterogeneous group. The mean personal incomes of Japanese ($22,352) and Asian Indians ($22,393) were significantly higher than that of other groups. On the other hand, the mean personal incomes of Laotians ($9,149), Cambodians ($9,095) and Hmongs ($6,130) were extremely low, and their levels of poverty were many times higher than the U.S. average. In 1989, the mean personal income of Chinese Americans was $17,984, which was slightly higher than the average for Asian Americans as a whole but lower than that of Whites.

What is more interesting is the differences between native-born and foreign-born Chinese, and among immigrants of different dates of entry. Table 11.5 shows that Chinese immigrants who entered before 1965 had the highest mean personal income and lowest level of poverty, which was partly due to their older ages. Among the foreign born, there was clearly a positive correlation between income and duration of stay, and a negative correlation between level of poverty and duration of stay. While age may partially explain these correlations, differences in their levels of occupational attainment, described earlier, are perhaps a more determining factor. Income differences were the highest among the 1980–1990 immigrants, whose coefficient of variation was 1.56, compared with 1.20 for the native born, 1.18 for immigrants who entered before 1965, and 1.24 for 1965–1970 immigrants. A significant proportion (22.4%) of the 1980–1990 immigrants were below the poverty line. These statistics highlight the internal stratification of recent Chinese immigrants, and question the widely held perception that they are predominantly affluent individuals.

IDENTITIES AND TIES

The experiences of Chinese Americans, including the evolution of their identities and ties with their homelands, are intricately related to the changing contexts of race relations in the U.S. For example, the prejudice and discrimination experienced by early Chinese immigrants have made social and nativity-based organizations such as *huiguan* an indispensable part of their lives. These organizations, most highly represented in San Francisco and New York since the nineteenth century, provided early sojourners shelter, protection, resources, and means for maintaining ties not only with China but also with specific social groups based on lineage and/or native place.

Since the 1960s, both the larger structural contexts and the composition of immigrants have changed, which have in turn transformed the means by which identity is formed and social ties are maintained. First of all, the civil rights movement refocused Americans' attention on race relations, and on the structural discrimination and historical legacies that had impeded upward mobility of minorities. Two of the outcomes of that movement were Affirmative Action programs, which aimed at widening the opportunities for minorities to attain higher education and to work in occupations where they were underrepresented, and the elimination of exclusionary immigration legislation. The movement also precipitated a reexamination of the dominant American social order based on the assimilationist paradigm, and motivated research that employed a pluralist perspective. The latter emphasizes multiculturalism, including immigrants' roots and connections with the home countries, rather than the extent to which they are assimilable (Cheng and Katz, 1998).

The term "Asian Americans" (and "Chinese Americans," etc.), which foregrounds identity as Americans, also has its origins in the 1960s civil rights movement. It offered a drastic alternative to prevailing notions of Asians as foreigners and outsiders. "Chinese Americans" has become a distinct identity that emphasizes the processes of racialization and race formation, rather than a hybrid halfway between Chinese and Americans. It describes more appropriately the experience of descendants of Chinese immigrants who left their homelands a long time ago, for whom the concepts of "diaspora" and "homeland" may have lost their meanings (Leong, 1989). Increases in intermarriage with other Asians and non-Asians, especially among the native born and younger Chinese Americans, have further strengthened the identities rooted in nationality rather than ancestry.

A common membership to Asian Americans highlights the similar historical experiences shared by many Asian groups in the U.S., such as exclusionary immigration laws and labor market segregation. It also compels politicians to recognize the importance of looking at race relations beyond the Black-White dichotomy. Joining forces with other Asians has enabled larger blocs of constituencies and empowered Asian Americans as a whole. Scholarly and institutional foci on ethnic studies, and artistic and literary expressions of ethnic themes, have also been key processes in the formation of an Asian American identity. Classes and programs in Asian American Studies began in the late 1960s in selected universities, including University of California–Berkeley, University of California–Los Angeles, and San Francisco State University. Many more U.S. colleges, including private universities such as Stanford and Cornell, have since developed Asian American Studies programs. Chinese American experiences is a central component of these programs, which have greatly facilitated the documentation and systematic analyses of the experiences of Asian Americans, including individual and collective identities, struggles, aspirations, and voices. In addition, Chinese Americans are increasingly exploring themes of ethnic identity, including intergenerational conflicts, in creative ways. Amy Tan's "Joy Luck Club," Ang Lee's "The Wedding Banquet," and Wayne Wang's "Dim Sum," are among the most well-known examples.

Chinese Americans have increasingly excelled in traditional as well as nontraditional fields. Among early immigrants, the most well-known individuals are mostly in scientific fields, including Nobel laureate C. N. Yang. Many Chinese Americans continue to show great achievements in sciences and related fields, including David Ho in AIDS research, but more recently they have also gained national and international recognition in sports (e.g., Michael Chang, Michele Kwan), architecture (e.g., Maya Lin, I. M. Pei), journalism (e.g., Connie Chung), and education (e.g., Chang-Lin Tien). In politics, Gary Locke was elected governor of the state of Washington in 1996 and is the first Chinese American to head a governor's office. In 2001, Elaine Chao was confirmed as Secretary of Labor and became the first Chinese American to be appointed as a cabinet member. With Norman Mineta, the Secretary of Transportation also confirmed under the George W. Bush administration, they represent two historic Asian American appointments in the cabinet.

Despite achievements by the above individuals, in general Chinese Americans have only a small presence in top-level management and in federal politics. The difficulties Chinese Americans have experienced in U.S. politics may be attributable to two factors. The first factor is a lack of political cohesion that is critical for establishing an influential constituency. In response, a group of prominent Chinese Americans are developing strategies to enable greater representation of Chinese in politics, including an organization called "The 80-20 Initiative" founded in order to cultivate Asian American political clout and to make Asian American voters a crucial factor in the year 2000 presidential election. Second, Chinese Americans are subject to two types of racial domination (Wang, 1995). The first is domestic, and has to do with the long-standing exclusion and repression U.S. minorities experienced and are still experiencing. The second type of domination is extraterritorial, and refers to the implications of international relations for Chinese Americans. The ups and downs of U.S.-China relations since the late 1970s, in particular, have complicated the experiences of Chinese Americans. Many have become investors, or liaisons for American investors, in China since it opened its doors to the world. But the 1989 Tiananmen incident, charges of human rights violations, controversies over U.S. presidential campaign funds, accusations of Chinese American scientists stealing U.S. nuclear technology, and the reportedly accidental bombing of the Chinese embassy in Belgrade, have culminated into very tense relations between the two nations. In the U.S. media, China has been portrayed as an enemy rather than a friend ("Special Report: Friend or Foe?" 1996; "The Next Cold War?" 1999). Regardless of how "American" Chinese Americans have become, these external developments continue to constrain their opportunities in politics, technology, management and other fields.

Many examples illustrate the enduring perception and labeling of Chinese Americans as foreigners. Wen Ho Lee, a first generation immigrant originally from Taiwan and a Chinese American scientist, was falsely accused of stealing American nuclear technology for China in 1999, dismissed from his job arbitrarily by the University of California and the Department of Energy, and subjected to nine months of solitary confinement with neither a trial nor a conviction. In September 2000, he was found guilty of only one minor charge of "mishandling classified data," but for over a year and a half "politicians and media incited mass hysteria and engaged in a national witch-hunt, rendering Asian American synonymous with treason and espionage" (Wang, 2002). In February 2002, figure skating veteran Michelle Kwan, a second generation Chinese American, lost the Winter Olympics gold medal to Sarah Hughes, a White American. The MSNBC network and Seattle Times respectively headlined "American Beats out Michelle Kwan" and "American Outshines Kwan," despite the fact that Kwan was born and raised in the U.S. In April 2002, Abercrombie & Fitch (A&F), an upscale retailer, put out a new line of T-shirts with derogatory portrayals of Asians. One of the designs shows Asians in laundry services, referring to a popular livelihood of Chinese immigrants in the nineteenth century, again illustrating the stereotyping, racialization, and social construction of Asian Americans and Chinese Americans as permanent foreigners.

Emergence of a Chinese American identity has occurred side-by-side with renewed efforts to maintain strong and multiple ties across the Pacific. New immigrants are much more resourceful than their predecessors in using modern telecommunication technologies for this purpose. Videos and newspapers flown in from overseas, and locally published Chinese newspapers and locally based television stations, have also kept immigrants abreast of current news in Asia. Second, the U.S. has become an important market for investors from Asia. The enormous commercial development in suburban communities such as Monterey Park is not only a product of the demand by immigrants, but is also evidence of the tremendous infusion of Asian capital to the U.S. Referred to by Omi (1993) as "private cultures," the expansion and multiplication of goods and services for Chinese Americans further question the assimilationist assumption that Anglo-conformity is inevitable. In addition, Asian products are increasingly globalized and designed for the international market. The Asian entertainment industry, for example, has evolved from the Bruce Lee–genre focusing on ethnic and nationalistic themes, to more recent works targeting mass American and Hollywood-style consumption, such as the films by Jackie Chan, John Woo, Gong Li, Michele Yeoh, Jet Li and Chow Yun-Fat.

Third, many new immigrants have direct business ties with their homelands. Frequent travels between the U.S. and Asia are not only common among business people, but they also characterize immigrants who maintain their primary jobs in the homelands. Nicknamed "astronauts," these frequent flyers are mostly male heads of households, who are unwilling to give up satisfactory employment in their homelands and resort instead to commuting across the Pacific between jobs and family. For households where both parents stay most of the time in Asia, the children who live and are educated in the U.S. are referred to as "parachute kids," a source of social problems including juvenile delinquency and youth gangs.

CONCLUSION

The above examination of the history, geography, socioeconomic status and identities of Chinese Americans has highlighted the key roles immigration has played in the experiences of the Chinese in the U.S. Not only is immigration important because the foreign born account for the vast majority of Chinese Americans, but it also is among the determining factors of their spatial distribution and migration, levels and heterogeneity of attainments in education, occupation, and income, and processes of identity formation. The changing structural, political, economic, and social contexts in and outside the U.S. have further complicated their experiences, as a diaspc nity and as a racial minority.

Post-1965 immigration has been the reason for the tremendous   ..r ol Chinese Americans, resulting in a more than tenfold increase from approximately 237,000 in 1960 to 2.43 million in 2000. Their settlement and migration patterns are heavily shaped by immigration. Specifically, major ports of entry, especially those in California, are the most popular sites of large Chinese communities and destinations of Chinese internal migrants. Movements to newer metropolitan areas and ethnoburbs are again a function of immigration, more specifically of new waves of immigrants who prefer suburban locations with large numbers of Chinese, and who are no longer dependent on Chinatown-based resources and networks. Accordingly, a bi-coastal settlement pattern and high levels of residential segregation will continue to characterize the geography of Chinese Americans.

The heterogeneity of Chinese Americans is closely related to immigration history. In general, the native born have achieved higher and more uniform levels of educational, occupational, and economic attainments. The achievements of recent immigrants, however, are highly bimodal. They are characterized by an elite group with high levels of educational and occupational attainment that partially reflect employment-based immigration legislation, and a less advantaged group with greater constraints in social mobility. One of the indications is lower income among recent immigrants, a net result of the bimodal socioeconomic structure and an evidence countering the prevailing view that recent Chinese immigrants are predominantly affluent.

Rather than converging in one identity, representations of Chinese Americans are increasingly complicated by immigration history, racial relations in the U.S., and international politics. Heterogeneous sources of immigrants, from China, Taiwan, Hong Kong, and other Southeast Asia countries, have engendered placed-based communities, differing settlement patterns, and multiple ties to the homelands. Earlier immigrants and the native born are more motivated than recent immigrants in establishing a Chinese American identity. On the other hand, as immigrants and as a racial minority, Chinese Americans are constrained by stubborn impediments that prevent them from rising to the top, as evidenced by their occupational niches and low representation in top-level management and federal politics. Prominent among these impediments is the lingering perception and continued construction by the mainstream society of Chinese Americans (and Asian Americans) as foreigners. Changes in U.S.-China relations have further complicated their experiences. Despite more than a century of settlement in the U.S. and the heterogeneity among Chinese Americans, they continue to be confronted, as a group, with burning questions of diaspora, immigration, and racialization.

NOTES

An early version of this chapter was presented at the Annual Meeting of the Association of American Geographers, Pittsburgh, Pennsylvania, April 4–8, 2000.

I would like to thank Chase Langford for cartographic assistance and Wenfei Wang for research assistance. Research for this chapter was partially supported by the Asian American Studies Center at UCLA.

1. See Poston and Yu (1990) for a brief discussion of the debate concerning the use of the terms "Chinese Americans" and "overseas Chinese."

2. The computation of the dissimilarity index (D) is based on the difference between the proportion of one ethnic group and the proportion of another ethnic group in subunits such as census tracts. For example,

$$D = \frac{1}{2} \sum_{i=1} \left| \frac{w_i}{W} - \frac{b_i}{B} \right|$$

where w_i = number of Whites in census tract i;
   b_i = number of Blacks in census tract i;
   W = number of Whites in the city;
   B = number of Blacks in the city.

D measures to what extent population of an ethnic group is evenly distributed with respect to another ethnic group and is conceptually related to the Lorenz Curve (Duncan and Duncan, 1955). Its theoretical range is from 0 (no segregation) to 1 (complete segregation). In this chapter, I modify D by subtracting it from 1:

$$S = 1 - D$$

S is a "similarity index," and ranges from 0 for complete segregation to 1 for complete desegregation. This modification is done in order to associate higher values with more potential interactions, and lower values with fewer potential interactions, with members of another ethnic group.

The exposure index is another popular measure of residential segregation. Assuming a two-group situation:

$$E_{WB} = 1 - P = 1 - \frac{\sum_i w_i b'_i}{WB'}$$

where w_i = number of Whites in census tract i;
   b'_i = proportion of Blacks in census tract i;
   W = number of Whites in the city;
   B' = proportion of Blacks in the city.

E_{WB} measures the degree of exposure of Whites to Blacks at the census-tract level, relative to the city-wide level of exposure of Whites to Blacks. It refers to segregation in a sociological sense and is built upon the probability of contact of one ethnic group with another within a spatial context (White, 1986). Its theoretical range is from 0 to 1: 0 indicates complete balance or no segregation, when Whites would encounter Blacks at a rate equal to the city-wide level; 1 indicates complete isolation or segregation, when Whites would tend toward contact only with other Whites. However, in a multiethnic setting the theoretical minimum may be less than 0. In order to more adequately measure the exposure between ethnic groups in a multiethnic setting, I modify the exposure index by subtracting E from 1:

$$E' = 1 - E$$

$E' = 0$ depicts a situation where the census-tract exposure level is equal to the city-wide level of exposure; and $E' = -1$ indicates complete segregation. But E' does not have a theoretical maximum because the exposure level between two ethnic groups in a multiethnic city can be many times greater than the citywide exposure level. Like the similarity index, the modified exposure index also associates higher values of the index with more potential interactions, and lower values with less potential interactions, with members of another ethnic group.

REFERENCES

Allen, James P. 1997. "Asians in Los Angeles: Comparative Residential Distributions." Paper presented at the 2nd Sino-American Symposium on Human Geography, June 23–25, 1997, Xian Foreign Language University, Xian, China.

Allen, James P., and Turner, Eugene. 1997. *The Ethnic Quilt: Population Diversity in Southern California,* Northridge, CA: Center for Geographical Studies, California State University.

Brown, Catherine L., and Pannell, Clifton W. 1985. "The Chinese in America." In *Ethnicity in Contemporary America: A Geographical Appraisal,* ed. Jesse O. McKee, 195–216. Dubuque, IA: Kendall/Hunt.

Cheng, Lucie, and Katz, Marian. 1998. "Migration and the Diaspora Communities." In *Culture and Society in the Asia-Pacific,* ed. Richard Maidment and Colin Mackerras, 65–87. London: Routledge.

Cheng, Lucie, and Yang, Philip Q. 1996. "Asians: The 'Model Minority' Deconstructed." In *Ethnic Los Angeles,* ed. Roger Waldinger and Mehdi Bozorgmehr, 305–44. New York: Russell Sage Foundation.

Clark, William A. V. 1992. "Residential Preferences and Residential Choices in a Multiethnic Context." *Demography* 29: 451–66.

Darden, Joe T. 1985–86. "Asians in Metropolitan Areas of Michigan: A Retest of the Social and Spatial Distance Hypothesis." *Amerasia* 12(2): 67–77.

Duncan, O. D., and Duncan, B. 1955. "A Methodological Analysis of Segregation Indexes." *American Sociological Review* 20: 210–7.

Lee, Sharon M. 1998. "Asian Americans: Diverse and Growing." *Population Bulletin* 53(2).

Leong, Russell C. 1989. "Asians in the Americas: Interpreting the Diaspora Experience." *Amerasia Journal* 15(2): vii–xvii.

Li, Wei. 1998. "Los Angeles's Chinese Ethnobourb: From Ethnic Service Center to Global Economy Outpost." *Urban Geography* 19(6): 502–17.

———. 1999. "Building Ethnoburbia: The Emergence and Manifestation of the Chinese Ethnoburb in Los Angeles' San Gabriel Valley." *Journal of Asian American Studies* 2(1): 1–28.

"The Next Cold War?" 1999. *Time* 153(22): June 7, 30–44.

Omi, Michael. 1993. "Out of the Melting Pot and into the Fire: Race Relations Policy." In *The State of Asian Pacific America, A Public Policy Report: Policy Issues to the Year 2020,* ed. LEAP Asian Pacific American Public Policy Institute and UCLA Asian American Studies Center, 199–214. Los Angeles: LEAP Asian Pacific American Public Policy Institute and UCLA Asian American Studies Center.

Pan, Ling (ed.). 1998. *The Encyclopedia of the Chinese Overseas.* Hong Kong: Joint Publishing (H.K.) Co.

Poston, Dudley L., Jr., and Yu, Mei-Yu. 1990. "The Distribution of the Overseas Chinese in the Contemporary World." *International Migration Review* 24(3): 480–508.

Poston, Dudley L., Jr., Mao, Michael Xinxiang, and Yu, Mei-Yu. 1994. "The Global Distribution of the Overseas Chinese around 1990." *Population and Development Review* 20(3): 631–45.

Sinn, Elizabeth. 1998. *The Last Half Century of Chinese Overseas.* Hong Kong: Hong Kong University Press.

"Special Report: Friend or Foe?" 1996. *Newsweek,* April 1, 28–53.

U.S. Department of Commerce, Bureau of the Census. 1982. *Census of Population and Housing, 1980 (United States): Summary Tape File 2A (Computer file).* Washington, D.C.: U.S. Department of Commerce, Bureau of the Census.

———. 1983. *1980 Census of Population: General Social and Economic Characteristics (Vol. 1, Part 1: United States Summary).* Washington, D.C.: U.S. Department of Commerce, Bureau of the Census.

———. 1991. *Census of Population and Housing, 1990 (United States): Summary Tape File 1A (Computer file).* Washington, D.C.: U.S. Department of Commerce, Bureau of the Census.

———. 1992. *1990 Census of Population: General Population Characteristics.* Washington, D.C.: U.S. Department of Commerce, Bureau of the Census.

———. 1993. *Census of Population and Housing, 1990 (United States: Public Use Microdata Sample: 1-Percent Sample Computer File), 2nd release.* Washington, D.C.: U.S. Department of Commerce, Bureau of the Census.

———. 2002. http://factfinder.census.gov.

U.S. Immigration and Naturalization Service (INS). 1997. *Statistical Yearbook of the Immigration and Naturalization Service, 1996.* Washington, D.C.: U.S. Government Printing Office.

———. 2002. http://www.ins.usdoj.gov.

Wang, L. Ling-Chi. 1995. "The Structure of Dual Domination: Toward a Paradigm for the Study of the Chinese Diaspora in the United States." *Amerasia Journal* 21(1 and 2): 149–69.

———. 2002. "Statement of Prof. L. Ling-chi Wang in Response Today's NY Times Story." March 26, 2002. http://www.wenholee.org.

White, M. J. 1986. "Segregation and Diversity Measures in Population Distribution." *Population Index* 52(2): 198–221.

Zhou, Yu. 1998. "Beyond Ethnic Enclaves: Location Strategies of Chinese Producer Service Firms in Los Angeles." *Economic Geography* 74: 228–51.

12

Community As Catalyst: The Chinese in Honolulu

Sen-dou Chang

Among islands of the Pacific, the Hawaiian group was the earliest destination for Chinese migrants. The location of the Hawaiian chain at the crossroads of the Pacific drew British and American sailing ships to layover for provisions and provide a break for crew and passengers. Early sailing ships sometimes employed Chinese crews, who were the first Chinese to visit the islands and a number of them stayed on. Historians of Hawaii consider 1789 the year of the first Chinese arrivals, who came aboard the schooner *Eleanora*. Under the command of American Captain Simon Metcalf, the *Eleanora* reached Maui from Macao with a crew of ten Americans and forty-five Chinese (Char, 1975: 37). As a consequence of this historic event, in 1989 the Chinese community in Hawaii celebrated the 200th anniversary of the arrival of the Chinese in Hawaii.

In the remaining years of the eighteenth century and the first half of the nineteenth century, substantial trade developed between China and Hawaii, based largely on sandalwood, which was the major export commodity to China. Although the number of Chinese staying in Hawaii was not large at the time, sandalwood commanded such high values in China that by the year 1852, when the first contract Chinese laborers came to the sugar cane plantations in Hawaii, sandalwood in Hawaii was almost exhausted. The historical significance of Hawaii to the Chinese has been preserved in the Chinese name for Hawaii, *Tan-xiangshan* (Sandalwood Mountains), a name that continues to be used today.

In the middle of the nineteenth century, the tropical climate and rich volcanic soil of Hawaii were recognized as an ideal location for the development of sugar plantations by new migrants from New England. However, during the early nineteenth century, the Hawaiian population experienced a drastic decline due to the spread of leprosy. The number of native Hawaiians fell from 130,313 in 1831–1832 to 73,138 in 1853 (Nordyke, 1989:

52). Importation of laborers from Asia appeared necessary to operate the flourishing sugar cane fields. Colonists recognized the hardworking nature and diligence of Chinese farm laborers, and commissioned British Captain John Cass to obtain a supply of Chinese laborers for employment on the sugar plantations. The first group of 200 contract laborers from China arrived in Hawaii on January 3, 1852 (Schmitt, 1977: 11; Chang, 1968). A second trip later in 1852 increased the Chinese influx to 293 in that year. The contract was for five years at three dollars per month, in addition to the passage fees, food, clothing, and dormitory. There were also 20 Chinese boys engaged by Honolulu residents as house servants for five years at two dollars a month. This was a factor in explaining why Chinese were dispersed throughout Honolulu earlier than in many other cities in the United States. The early Chinese also made greater contributions to Hawaii after their five-year contracts expired in the late 1850s and 1860s. Many of them started rice cultivation, developed irrigation systems, introduced a variety of crops, vegetables, and fruits from China, and set up sugar refining facilities based on traditional technologies used in their home villages in Zhongshan. Considering that Zhongshan is located at 22 degrees, 30 minutes N, approximately one degree north of Honolulu, the similarity of latitudinal location between the place of origin and place of destination was a factor in the Chinese community's contribution to Hawaii's agricultural development. The intermarriage between Chinese men and Hawaiian women was also an important factor that led the Chinese to be accepted easily by local communities in early Hawaii. However, by the second half of the 1880s Hawaii instituted regulations designed to slow Chinese immigration, and Chinese arrivals were further diminished in 1890 when Hawaii was annexed by the U.S. and came under the 1882 U.S. Chinese Exclusion Law.

In the past 150 years, Chinese in Honolulu have made important contributions to Hawaiian society, certainly more than their population numbers would indicate. They achieved higher socioeconomic status than all other ethnic groups in Hawaii. They also integrated socially and economically with the local community more than other Chinese communities on the mainland. In many respects, the Chinese in Honolulu are ahead of other Asian communities in the United States in achieving socioeconomic status, and perhaps indicate a direction Asian minorities are heading in the twenty-first century. This chapter offers some points of comparison between the socioeconomic and residential characteristics of the Chinese in Honolulu and Chinatowns in other cities of the United States, and provides explanations as to why and how these characteristics were formed throughout the 150 years of history of Chinese immigration in Hawaii.

EARLY URBANIZATION AND THE CHINESE

The development of Chinatown in Hawaii has been closely connected with early stages of urbanization in Honolulu, and the Chinese community in Honolulu has been a multiethnic settlement from the outset. Practically all Chinatowns in the United States developed in proximity to the Central Business District (CBD) of large cities, but they emerged after the CBDs of the cities were well established. Chinatown in Honolulu, by contrast, started with the onset of the city's urbanization in the middle of the nineteenth century. In fact, the aggregation of Chinese men (after the expiration of their contracts) in the vicinity of Honolulu's harbor was the beginning of the formation of Honolulu itself. As a result, the major streets of Nuuanu and Maunakea in Chinatown today were a part of the CBD in downtown Honolulu in the second half of the nineteenth century. Few Chinatowns in the United States were located so close to the financial district as Honolulu's Chinatown. Bishop Street, the main street of Honolulu's CBD, is only three blocks away from Chinatown. To many office workers in the high rises of that street and King Street, Chinatown is a daily lunch place, and functions in relation to the CBD in ways few other Chinatowns in the United States are able to enjoy (Kenneth, 1996).

Concentration of the Chinese in Honolulu's Chinatown began in the 1850s. Between 1860 and 1900, almost all of the Chinese business establishments were located in Chinatown (Glick, 1942). However, Chinatown was never a ghetto in the true sense. As early as 1866, only half of the 370 Chinese in Honolulu lived in Chinatown (Glick, 1980). For many decades, in the late nineteenth century, Honolulu's Chinatown was known among Caucasians as the "Native Quarter" since more Hawaiians lived there than Chinese (Glick, 1980). In 1885 and 1886, the Hawaiian government ended Chinese contract labor immigration, and the Chinese population more or less stabilized (Nordyke, 1989). The great man-made fire of 1890, started in an attempt to eliminate the bubonic plague by burning out rats, caused an exodus of many Chinese from Chinatown. By 1920 a little over a half of the population in Chinatown was Chinese, and by 1930 only 47 percent of Chinatown's population was Chinese (Horman, 1956). The population of the Chinese in Chinatown peaked in the 1920s, and since then it has experienced gradual decline (Rapkin, 1971).

Between 1970 and 1990, the number of Chinese in Chinatown and the population of the Chinese in Hawaii transformed. The number of Chinese in Chinatown declined rapidly, in both absolute numbers and in proportion to the total Chinese population in Honolulu. This decline was due in part to the dying out of many single male laborers who arrived in Hawaii in the late nineteenth and early twentieth centuries. Recent immigrants from China are largely relatives of Hawaii Chinese and sponsored by affluent Chinese residents. The new immigrants from Taiwan are relatively few in number, but are usually successful businessmen or professional people who are scattered all over the high-rent residential areas of Honolulu, such as Waialae Iki and Hawaii Kai. The Chinatown of Honolulu has increasingly become dominated by new immigrants from the Philippines and Korea, including smaller but still sizable numbers from Japan and Vietnam (figure 12.1). In 1990, the Chinese constituted a little over 21 percent of the total residents in the whole area of Honolulu's Chinatown; this is small by comparison to Chinatowns in the U.S. mainland, where Chinese have tended to constitute the majority of the population. Many Chinese still operate their businesses in Chinatown, but they usually live outside Chinatown, such as in the Kukui housing area to the north.

The small number of Chinese living in Honolulu's Chinatown is largely due to the geographic dispersion of the Chinese in Honolulu and the rise of Chinatown as a multiethnic community. Since the 1920s, Honolulu's Chinatown has ceased to function as a place for residential transition for the newly arrived immigrants. Even in the first few decades of immigration to Hawaii, between the 1850s and 1880s, the number of Chinese was comparatively small. Then, in 1885 and 1886 Hawaiian government regulations practically ended Chinese contract labor immigration. Subsequently, the number of Chinese arrivals could not exceed the number of departures, and Chinese were

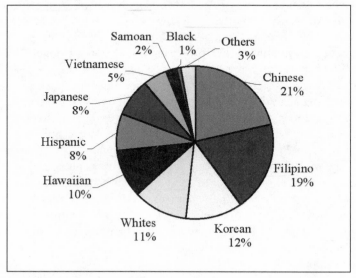

Figure 12.1.   Ethnic Composition in Honolulu's Chinatown, 1990
(Source: *1990 Census of Population and Housing, Census Tracts and Block Numbering Areas,* Honolulu MSA, p. 103.)

permitted to enter Hawaii under conditional work permits that required departure in five years. Even though the system had restrictions, the work permit system meant that virtually all Chinese immigrants coming to Hawaii were legally admitted. Consequently, the Chinese had no need to physically hide, like many did in New York's Chinatown.

ECONOMIC SUCCESS

The Chinese in Honolulu may have achieved economic success sooner than other Asian immigrants in the United States. After the expiration of their five-year labor contracts, there were no compulsory regulations in the Kingdom of Hawaii forcing the Chinese laborers to return to China. In fact, due to the drastic decline of the native Hawaiian population and rapid urbanization as a result of the emergence of the plantation economy in the nineteenth century, the Chinese had significant opportunities to engage in a variety of agricultural activities, including rice farming, as well as service jobs in the rapidly growing urban economy. The fortunes of Chinese in Honolulu resembled those of the Chinese in Southeast Asia, where the Chinese quickly occupied a variety of employment niches, more than their late-nineteenth-century counterparts in California. In the early decades of the twentieth century, with a more balanced sex ratio, many Chinese built their own houses in various parts of the city, in which no particular ethnic group dominated. The Chinese as a whole were treated more cordially in Honolulu than their counterparts in California or New York. In the late 1880s and 1890s, when the Chinese Exclusion Law was in effect and Japanese immigrants poured in, the proximity of Chinatown to the harbor made it an arrival point for this new ethnic group. This is one important reason why Chinatown in Honolulu became a multiethnic community at a very early time. In the meantime, the Chinese in Honolulu had gained practical control of all business in laundry, tailoring, restaurants, and retailing. When these services were gradually taken over by the Japanese in the early twentieth century, the Chinese had already established dominant positions in white-collar occupations, such as federal government services, state government jobs, real estate, insurance, banking, and education. The high achievement of the Chinese in education in Honolulu is reflected most clearly in per capita income among ethnic groups. By the 1930s, the Chinese per capita savings deposits in Hawaii totaled more than twice as much as Filipino or Japanese. According to 1990s statistics, except for a very small population of Asian Indians who were mostly scientists and engineers, the Chinese were ahead of all other ethnic groups in household income ($53,560), although just slightly ahead of the Japanese group ($52,766) (Bureau of the Census, 1993) (table 12.1). The well-being of the Chinese in Honolulu is also reflected in life expectancy. According to the State of Hawaii Department of Health, the Chinese in Hawaii can expect to live longer than all other ethnic groups. Female Chinese babies born in 1996 were expected to live for 86 years (Hawaii Department of Health, 1998).

Why the Chinese in Honolulu have such a distinctive demographic profile is hard to explain but the social and economic well-being of the community is an important condition. The rapid transition from manual laborers to professional workers in a few decades can be attributed to the high value placed on education, generation after generation. The 1950 U.S. Census reported that almost 9 percent of Honolulu Chinese over 25 years old had graduated from college, as compared with 2.4 percent for the Hawaiians, 3 percent for the Japanese, and 0.3 percent for the Filipinos (Brunsman, 1952: 76). The high ratio of the Chinese in Honolulu receiving higher education has been maintained in recent years. Among Chinese, Japanese, and Koreans receiving a higher education in 1990, the Chinese were still ahead of other ethnic groups in this category, although the Japanese were making gains (Bureau of Census, 1993).

As most contract workers from China in the early years were illiterate, education for their children was not really their top priority. A priest who performed missionary work in Guangzhou established the first class of Chinese language in 1883. The class was located in the YMCA building on Beretania Street and attracted about 20 students. The class was closed two years later due to lack of funds. The Chinese language education initiated by the Chinese community occurred only in the twentieth century. The first Chinese school in Honolulu, Ming-Lum School, was founded in February 1911, and stressed traditional Confucian ethics. In the same year, the Nationalist Party founded another school, the Chung Shan School. Both were located in Chinatown with the purpose of giving Chinese language training to students after regular school hours in the late afternoons. All classes were conducted in Cantonese. With donations and contributions from various associations and enterprises, their enrollments increased remarkably in the 1920s and 1930s, with peak enrollment reaching more than 1,000 in the late 1930s. After the Pearl Harbor

Table 12.1. Per Capita Savings Deposits in Hawaii by Ethnic Group, 1910–1930 (US$)

Group	1910	1915	1920	1925	1930
Chinese	13.35	27.37	59.32	153.01	150.76
Portuguese	40.85	76.72	95.37	108.46	116.11
Hawaiian	6.02	15.94	20.74	42.96	81.53
Filipino					69.38
Japanese	2.40	3.36	17.91	23.72	64.83

Source: Lind (1938: 266).

incident in December 1941, all foreign language schools were closed. It was not until October 1947 that Chinese language schools were permitted to re-open after a prolonged judicial process initiated by the Overseas Chinese Education Alliances of Honolulu.

Enrollment in these two language schools has been sustained by new immigrants in recent years. But how to promote the enrollment in third and fourth generation young people has become a great challenge to the Chinese community in Honolulu. One bright spot of Chinese language education in Hawaii is that several public schools have installed Chinese language curricula, with progressive levels. Two private schools, Iolani and Punahou, have Chinese curricula from the seventh through twelfth grades. Almost every community college in the city has a two-year Chinese language curriculum. The University of Hawaii at Manoa is known for its Asian language programs, including Mandarin Chinese and Cantonese. The majority of students in these classes, not surprisingly, are of Chinese ancestry.

The Chinese families in the United States have tended to send their children to the most reputable high schools in their communities. Honolulu's Chinese families have also followed this trend (Young, 1972). Iolani School, a private K–12 school, is considered one of the two best schools in Honolulu, and in the past ten years it has been ranked one of the top 20 secondary schools in the country in terms of achievements in SAT and ACT scores. Dr. Sun Yat-sen was enrolled in this school for three years in the early 1880s, and the education he received had a profound influence in the formulation of his ideas in his book, *Three Principles of the People* (Lum and Lum, 1999), which for some 60 years served as the basic blueprint for the Republic of China's national development. In the past ten years, virtually every graduate of Iolani has gone on to college, many to Ivy League schools. Among the 232 graduates of the Class of 1999, 51 were of Chinese ancestry, forming 22 percent of the total (Iolani School, 1999). In general, Chinese students formed nearly a quarter of the population of the school, even as the Chinese population of Honolulu amounts to only about seven percent of the city total (7.6 percent in 1990) (Planning Department, 1994).

Compared with the size of other ethnic groups in Honolulu, such as Koreans and Filipinos, the growth of the Chinese population in Honolulu has been relatively slow in recent decades. One of the important factors accounting for the slow growth of the Chinese has been out-migration of college graduates to the mainland. Significant numbers of college-age students in the Chinese community attend universities on the mainland, and after graduation, they often find high-paying jobs and do not return to live in Hawaii. Such brain drain, together with highly educated young adults of other Asian groups in Hawaii, has contributed significantly to the relatively slow population growth of Hawaii's Chinese in the past few decades.

EXOGENOUS MARRIAGE

Multiethnic marriages have been a common phenomenon in Hawaii in the past 150 years, and there is a long tradition of exogenous marriage for both genders in Honolulu's Chinese community. This represents a unique case for the Chinese migrants to the United States in the last 150 years of Chinese migration history. Whereas in recent decades it has been quite common for the Chinese, especially for the highly educated, to marry non-Chinese, exogamous marriages in the early years of migration were rare, even when the sex ratios of the migrants were highly unbalanced and single Chinese males often had to remain bachelors for life. The Chinese in Hawaii, however, have married other ethnic groups almost since they first arrived in the 1850s. The early contract laborers were all males from Zhongshan. The only persons the Chinese had social contact with were the Hawaiians both in Chinatown areas and on plantations, and it was common for the Chinese laborers to marry Hawaiian women at that time.

There were also other socioeconomic factors in Hawaii that induced more Chinese to marry non-Chinese than many Chinese communities on the mainland. First, according to the regulations of the Kingdom of Hawaii, a contract laborer was able to obtain the privilege to stay in Hawaii legally if he married a Hawaiian woman after the expiration of his contract. Second, the traditional Hawaiian society treated all ethnic groups equally without any feelings of being racially superior or inferior. In fact, to replenish the dwindling population, the government in Hawaii encouraged intermarriage between native Hawaiian women and "respectable foreigners," which included Chinese. Third, the Chinese were considered ideal husbands by the Hawaiian women, because they were considered diligent, thrifty and energetic with a keen business sense and a desire for upward mobility. They and the children of such marriages also often benefited from the resultant higher family status (Wittermans-Pino, 1964: 122). An early-twentieth-century survey conducted among 140 female students at Kamehameha School, a high school exclusively for Hawaiians or part-Hawaiian students, revealed that the Chinese male ranked second only to whites as preferred dates among all ethnic groups in Hawaii (Beaglehole, 1939).

During the period 1840–1870, there were about 400 legal marriages of Chinese men to Hawaiian women. In the period of 1871–1899, there were 400–500 such intermarriages in Hawaii, mostly in Honolulu. In addition to the legal marriages, there were several hundred cases in which a Chinese man and a Hawaiian woman maintained a common-law marriage (Adams, 1937: 146). Based on various estimates, prior to 1900 there were as many as 1,500 Chinese men who had entered into marital relations with native Hawaiians. During the period 1900–1916, another 550 Chinese men took Hawaiian wives. The interracial marriage of Chinese slightly declined since the 1920s as the sex ratio among the marriage-age Chinese gradually became normalized (figure 12.2).

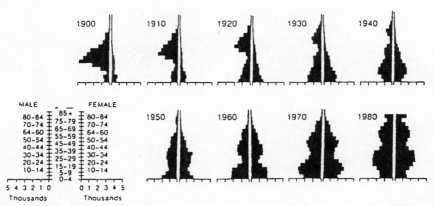

Figure 12.2. Age and Sex Structure of the Chinese Population in Hawaii, 1900–1980 (Source: Nordyke, Eleavor. 1989. *The Peopling of Hawaii* [Honolulu: University of Hawaii Press]: 58.)

The marriage of the Chinese in Hawaii continues to be dominated by the multiethnic pattern, and in terms of the proportion of multiethnic marriages to the total population, Chinese have continued to lead other ethnic groups in Hawaii. In 1996, among 508 Chinese men getting married in Hawaii, only 244, or 48 percent, married Chinese women, the rest marrying non-Chinese (see table 12.2a). Among the 427 marriages involving Chinese brides, only 36.8 percent of the grooms were Chinese (see table 12.2b). Compared to Chinese men, Chinese women tended to marry Caucasians more frequently, followed by Japanese and Hawaiians. Multiethnic marriage contributes to the idea of Hawaii as a "melting-pot" of various ethnic groups, and the Chinese in Hawaii have contributed substantially to this perception.

Table 12.2a. Marriage of 508 Chinese Grooms in 1996

Ethnicity of Bride	Number	Percentage
Chinese	244	48.0
Japanese	97	19.1
White	68	13.4
Filipino	36	7.1
Hawaiian	27	5.3
Korean	20	3.9
Vietnamese	6	1.2
Samoan	2	0.4
Black	2	0.4
Others	6	1.2

Table 12.2b.   Marriage of 427 Chinese Brides in 1996

Ethnicity of Groom	Number	Percentage
Chinese	165	36.8
White	100	23.4
Japanese	85	19.9
Hawaiian	35	8.2
Filipino	17	4.0
Black	20	2.3
Vietnamese	8	1.9
Korean	3	0.7
Others	3	0.7

Source: Hawaii Department of Health, 1998.

INTRA-URBAN DISPERSION OF THE CHINESE

Intra-urban dispersion of the Chinese community occurred earlier than in most Chinese communities in other large cities in the United States. Most Chinatowns in the United States have been ghettoes of the Chinese for a large part of their history, such as those in San Francisco, Seattle, and New York. Honolulu's Chinatown served as a ghetto for the Chinese probably only in the first fifty years of its history in the second half of the nineteenth century. Even in those years, Honolulu's Chinatown was not really a ghetto as only a little more than half its population were Chinese. Chinatown did function as a social and communication center for plantation laborers in the early years of Chinese immigration, because Chinatown was the headquarters for many clan associations, native-place organizations, and information centers for news from hometowns in China. After the expiration of the five-year contracts, the laborers were free to choose their own professions. With Hawaiian women as their spouses, many Chinese were able to purchase land or urban real estate in a few short years and moved their residences in newly developed subdivisions all over the city. To a great extent, Chinese residential movement coincided with the expansion of urban land use in Honolulu in the latter part of the nineteenth century. The Legislature in Hawaii passed an act to abolish the disabilities of aliens to acquire and convey land as early as 1850, two years prior to the arrival of large numbers of Chinese laborers (Chinen, 1974; Linnekin, 1983). The institutional provision of land ownership in the Kingdom of Hawaii has been an important reason why the Chinese have the highest percentage of land ownership among all ethnic groups today and why the Chinese have dispersed from Chinatown at an early date (map 12.2).

Two disastrous fires in Chinatown in 1886 and 1900 also had an important effect on the dispersion of Chinese residences away from Chinatown in those years. The 1886 fire was started with the burning of lottery chits by Chinese gamblers during a raid by the city's police force. Nearly 60 acres of the city were burned, 523 buildings destroyed, and 7,000 left homeless, mainly Chinese. The January 1900 fire was started purposefully by the Honolulu Board of Health to burn out the source of the bubonic plague on Nuuanu Street between Beretania and North King. The blaze lasted for 17 days and destroyed 38 acres and the homes of 4,000 people, mainly Chinese. By late 1900 only 40 percent of the Chinese in Honolulu lived in Chinatown. Ever since, the Chinese population in Chinatown has experienced a gradual decline (Scott, 1968).

The diversified occupations of the Chinese laborers after the expiration of the five-year contracts in the sugar plantations were also instrumental in their residential dispersion. Among Chinese laborers who came to Hawaii in the early 1850s, there were a number of young men in domestic jobs in well-to-do families that were located in high-value residential areas outside of Chinatown. In the 1870s, the Chinese started to develop the rice, coffee and pineapple plantations, in addition to fishing, and bakery industries. By the turn of the century, Chinese in white-collar professions, such as banking, medicine, law, government service, and education, located their offices in various localities within the city. The areas first penetrated by the Chinese were the districts of Bingham (near what is now the University of Hawaii), Makiki, Nuuanu, and Kaimuki.

At first, the Chinese clustered together according to their native places in China from which they came and in which a common dialect was spoken. For example, the Hakka were concentrated along Pauoa Street in Nuuanu Valley, while the Punti (*bendiren* in Mandarin, meaning the locals) people who spoke Cantonese were mainly in the Liliha area. The years after the bombing of Pearl Harbor in 1941 also facilitated further dispersion of the Chinese, as many whites sold their homes and moved to the mainland. The Chinese gained a number of valuable properties at reasonable prices during that time in the Makiki and Manoa areas, and both have large concentrations of Chinese today.

As urbanization proceeded at a faster rate and English gradually became a common language among the Chinese in the postwar years, the Chinese further dispersed, and the linguistic association of residential choice gradually weakened. A total of nearly 50,000 Chinese scattered in every residential area of the city, and almost every census tract had some Chinese, according to the 1990 U.S. Census.

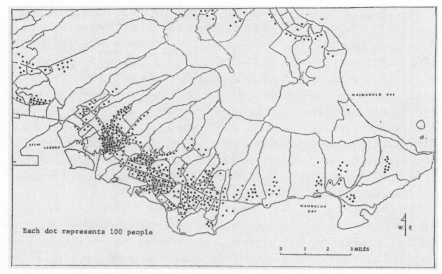

Map 12.1.   Distribution of Chinese in Honolulu, 1990 (Source: 1990 US Census)

At a micro-scale, Chinese residence patterns display the following characteristics. First, Honolulu's Chinatown has a population so diversified that the
Chinese constituted only 21 percent of the total population in 1990 (see map
12.1). It would not be a big surprise if the Filipinos became the largest ethnic
group in Honolulu's Chinatown. Second, there are four census tracts in the
city where the Chinese population constitutes more than 25 percent of the total population. Two of these are near Chinatown, and the other two are high
quality residential areas in Honolulu, one in the Makiki Heights near the central part of the city and the other in the Waialae Iki Ridge whose elevated
property commands spectacular views. The Makiki Heights residences reflect
Chinese preference to live near the city center and the Waialae Iki Ridge area
is a concentration of immigrants from both Hong Kong and Taiwan since the
1970s. Third, although the Chinese have been dispersed from Chinatown in
Honolulu since the 1880s, their residential mobility has been low once they
have settled. Unlike the average American household that moves at least five
times in a lifetime, the Chinese household in Honolulu appears to move much
less frequently. Based on a survey conducted on residents named Ching that
appeared in the telephone books of Honolulu in 1960, 1970, 1980, and 1990,
only about 35 percent of them changed their residential addresses (Chang,
n.d.). Many changed first names but maintained the same address, reflecting
the fact that the younger generation continued to stay at the same residence.
Therefore, the contemporary Chinese residence often reflects the historical

Chinese distribution of the early, or middle part of the twentieth century. During that time, relatives often shared a common neighborhood and residents with the identical surname lived next to each other.

STRONG INTRA-DIASPORIC LINKAGES WITH ZHONGSHAN

The Chinese have not only made important contributions to the socioeconomic development in Honolulu in the past 150 years; they have also donated human and monetary resources for the well-being of their hometowns in Zhongshan County. According to the estimates made by the Chinese Chamber of Commerce in Honolulu, approximately 70 percent of the Chinese in Honolulu were from towns and villages in Zhongshan County in the Pearl River Delta. Honolulu may well be the place with the largest concentration of people from Zhongshan outside the county itself. In the past when contract laborers came to Hawaii, they left their families at home. As they settled down and succeeded in a variety of occupations in the last decades of the nineteenth century, they sent a large portion of their savings back to their families through fellow provincials visiting their home villages. Practically every village in Zhongshan had at least one person operating a store in Honolulu's Chinatown. These stores often became banks and post offices for delivering money and letters to their homes in Zhongshan. While the amount of remittances to Zhongshan must have been quite substantial each year, there was no reliable data indicating the exact amount. In recent decades, most Chinese in Honolulu have been in the third or fourth generation and their relatives at home have gradually died off. However, their enthusiasm for financial assistance to their home villages has not diminished, as remittances from the Chinese community in Honolulu are still pouring into Zhongshan to construct schools and hospitals or municipal infrastructure such as roads and parks. Continuous contributions to the improvement of Zhongshang's living conditions by the Chinese community has been instrumental in winning recognition for Zhongshan Mayor Huang Zijiang, who was awarded the Habitat Scroll of Honor by the United Nations Habitat Center for "his outstanding role in the sustainable development and management of human settlement" in Zhongshan (UNCHS, 1997).

For the purpose of promoting Chinese culture and enhancing social linkages with Zhongshan and China, the Chinese Chamber of Commerce sponsors the selection of the Narcissus Queen and four princesses every December. The Narcissus Queen attends many social events held in the Chinese community, and she is the leader of an annual tour to China in the summer. The tour, lasting more than twenty days, is probably the most eventful undertaking of the

Chinese community in Honolulu and is normally joined by approximately one hundred people. The tour usually makes a stop in Zhongshan toward the end so that many people in the tour are able to visit their relatives and friends in their home villages.

Besides the official tour to China annually sponsored by the Honolulu Chinese Chamber of Commerce, there are various shorter tours to Zhongshan organized by family or township associations, which involve different members of the community. The spring tours in early April often coincide with the Qingming festival, a Chinese memorial day when ancestors' graves are cleaned and their spirits are worshipped with candles, incense, and sacrificial foods and delicacies. The autumn tours often overlap with October 1, China's national day when official receptions for overseas Chinese are held by local officials of the city and towns of Zhongshan. During the period of homecoming, houses and buildings are often renovated or remodeled.

For those who have no relatives in Zhongshan, contributions or donations in the form of cash or checks are made to local schools, hospitals, or the local government. Most visible and frequent are donations given to the schools that their ancestors attended many years ago. A most common scene in schools in both Zhongshan City and rural towns is a sign hanging by the door of a classroom indicating the name of the donor for its construction. This is an important reason why the illiteracy rate in Zhongshan has been the lowest among all cities and counties in Guangdong Province. Ties between Honolulu and Zhongshan are distinctive and have endured through events and activities that combine traditional holidays and native-place ties with contemporary programs and festivals.

CONCLUSION

The majority of the Chinese in Honolulu now are the third or fourth generation immigrants, and nearly half are descendents of multiethnic marriages. As they are residentially dispersed among all ethnic groups in Honolulu, they are characterized by a multicultural identity, although their degree of acculturation in Hawaiian and "American" society is quite varied. Bilingual speakers have drastically declined in the second and third generations, but Chinese cultural identity has been demonstrated in various social contexts and events, such as the celebration of the Chinese New Year, the custom of Chinese cooking, and watching Chinese programs on television. The upkeep of cultural customs in the Chinese community has been revitalized in the past twenty years as the new immigrants from Taiwan, Hong Kong, and Vietnam have enhanced the traditional celebrations of various festivals based on the lunar calendar. Exhibitions of calligraphy and painting, the public showing of Chinese movies and popular lectures related to current events are periodically sponsored by community organizations such as the Chinese Alliance and Sino-American Friendship Associations. The auspicious dragon dance, which often kicks off the beginnings of community events in Honolulu, appears as popular in Honolulu as in other communities of the Chinese diaspora.

The social and entertainment-related contexts of popular Chinese culture in Honolulu also point to how political interests of contemporary Chinese appear to be quite minimal. While Dr. Sun Yat-sen's portrait is often seen in various same-surname and native-place associations, as he received his high school education in Honolulu during 1879–1883, his image does not indicate avid support for any contemporary Chinese regime. Dr. Sun's ties with Honolulu are simply very strong: in addition to being educated in Honolulu, he returned five times up to 1910, soliciting financial and moral support for his revolution in China. It is widely considered that the generous assistance and support of the Chinese community in Honolulu was instrumental in his successful overthrow of the Manchu Dynasty and the founding of the Nationalist Party (Lum and Lum, 1999). The apathetic nature of the Chinese community in Honolulu toward politics can be clearly seen by the presence of delegations from both Taiwan and mainland China during the inauguration of the new president of the Chinese Chamber of Commerce. The inauguration ceremony usually ends with a large banquet with the presence of the Consul General of the People's Republic in Los Angeles and the Director of the Taipei Economic and Cultural Office in Honolulu. The entertainment after the banquet usually stresses the cultural aspect of traditional China without political overtones.

Support of representatives of both the People's Republic of China and Taiwan underscores the prosperousness and achievements of the Chinese community in Honolulu. The evolution of this distinctive Chinese community in Hawaii has arguably depended upon opportunities and conditions that were not common in other Chinese immigrant destinations. For more than 110 years prior to the statehood of Hawaii in 1959, the Kingdom of Hawaii provided a less restrictive and more congenial socioeconomic environment for Chinese immigrants than other places in the U.S. Over time, the Chinese took advantage of relatively hospitable local conditions and achieved socioeconomic status that not only surpassed that of other Chinese communities on the East and West Coasts of the U.S. mainland, but also other Asian immigrant communities in Hawaii. The Chinese in Honolulu have demonstrated that a transnational community can achieve social distinction equal to or surpassing host communities and other immigrant groups. Despite its relatively small population size in Hawaii and Honolulu, the Chinese community, at various historical junctures, has catalyzed social and economic change, from building up new industries to establishing patterns of exogenous marriage. While the long-term future of the Chinese community in Honolulu is uncertain, given the possibility of continued population decline, its historic place in the Chinese diaspora is assured.

REFERENCES

Adams, Romanzo. 1937. *Interracial Marriages in Hawaii,* New York: McMillan Company.

Beaglehole, Ernest. 1939. *Some Modern Hawaiians,* Honolulu: University of Hawaii Research Publications, No. 9, 124–41.

Brunsman, Howard G. 1952. *Detailed Characteristics: Hawaii,* Washington, D.C.: U.S. Bureau of the Census.

Bureau of the Census, U.S. Department of Commerce. 1993. *1990 Census of the Population: Social and Economic: Hawaii,* Washington, D.C.: Government Printing Office.

———. 1991. *Survey of Minority Owned Business Enterprises: Asian Americans, American Indians and Other Minorities,* Washington, D.C.: Government Printing Office.

Chang, Sen-dou. 1968. "Distribution and Occupations of Overseas Chinese," *Geographical Review* 58(1): 89–107.

———. n.d. Longitudinal Telephone Book Survey of Honolulu Residences by Surname Ching, 1960–90.

Char, Tin-Yuke. 1975. *The Sandalwood Mountains,* Honolulu: University Press of Hawaii.

Chen, Ta. 1940. *Emigration Communities in South China: A Study of Overseas Migration and Its Influence on Standard of Living and Social Change,* New York: Institute of Pacific Relations.

Chinen, Jon J., ed. 1974. *The Great Mahele, Hawaii's Land Division of 1848,* Honolulu: University Press of Hawaii.

Dye, Bob. 1997. *Merchant Prince of the Sandalwood Mountains,* Honolulu: University of Hawaii Press.

Glick, Clarence. 1942. "The Relation between Position and Status in the Assimilation of Chinese in Hawaii," *American Journal of Sociology* 157(5): 667–79.

———. 1980. *Sojourners and Settlers,* Honolulu: University Press of Hawaii.

Godley, Michael R. 1991. *The Mandarin-Capitalists from Nanyang: Overseas Chinese Enterprise in the Modernization of China, 1893–1911,* Cambridge: Cambridge University Press.

Hawaii Department of Health. 1998. *Vital Statistics 1996,* Honolulu: State Office of Health Status Monitoring.

Horman, Bernhard. 1956. "Certain Ecological Patterns of Honolulu," *Social Process in Hawaii* 20(1): 23–29.

Iolani School. 1999. *1998–99 Student-Parent Directory,* Honolulu: Iolani School.

Kenneth, Ames L. 1996. *On Bishop Street,* Honolulu: First Hawaiian Bank.

Linnekin, Joycelyn. 1983. "The Hui Lands of Keanae: Hawaiian Land Tenure and the Great Mahele," *Journal of Polynesian Society* 92(2): 169–88.

Lum, Yansheng and Lum, Raymond M. K. 1999. *Sun Yat-Sen in Hawaii: Activities and Supporters,* Honolulu: University of Hawaii Press.

Nordyke, Eleanor. 1989. *The Peopling of Hawaii,* Honolulu: University of Hawaii Press.

Nordyke, Eleanor and Lee, Richard K. C. 1989. "The Chinese in Hawaii: A Historical and Demographic Perspective," *Hawaiian Journal of History* 23(2): 196–216.

People's Daily, Overseas Edition. April 20, 1990.

Planning Department. 1994. *Statistics Profiles of Oahu Neighborhood Areas (1980–90),* Honolulu: City and County of Honolulu.

Rapkin, Chester. 1971. "The Current Status of Two of America's Chinatowns: New York's—Purpose Renewed, Honolulu's—Purpose Dispelled," Paper presented at *Chinatown Urban Renewal Workshop,* sponsored by National Association of Housing and Development Officials and The Honolulu Redevelopment Agency. Honolulu, September 28.

Schmitt, Robert C. 1977. *Historical Statistics of Hawaii,* Honolulu: University Press of Hawaii.

Scott, Edward B. 1968. *The Saga of the Sandwich Islands,* Lake Tahoe, NV: Sierra-Tahoe Publishing, 193.

Spickard, Paul R. 1989. *Mixed Blood: Intermarriage and Ethnic Identity in Twentieth Century America,* Madison: University of Wisconsin Press.

Taylor, Frank J. 1947. "Labor Moves in on Hawaii," *Saturday Evening Post,* June 26.

UNCHS (UN Centre for Human Settlements [Habitat]). 1997. Press Release. September 22.

Wittermans-Pino, Elizabeth. 1964. *Inter-ethnic Relations in a Plural Society,* Groningen: J. B. Walters.

Young, Nancy. 1972. "Changes in Values and Strategies among Chinese in Hawaii," *Sociology and Social Research* 56(2): 228–41.

13

From Downtown Slums to Suburban Malls: Chinese Migration and Settlement in Canada

David Chuenyan Lai

The history of Chinese migration to Canada epitomizes the dramatic transformation of the nature of the Chinese diaspora as a set of geographic processes. Aside from the increase in number and the change in occupational structure outlined in the introductory chapter of this volume, the Chinese in Canada have also experienced major spatial expansion from the old and small Chinatowns in British Columbia, where earlier migrants tended to stay, to other provinces. The Immigration Act of 1967, based on nondiscrimination and universality, is a significant demarcation in the study of Canadian immigration policies. For the first time in the history of Canada, ethnic origins of immigrants were not a criterion for admission to the country. As a result, after 1967 the racial distribution of immigrants drastically changed and the numbers of Chinese immigrants substantially increased. From a historical perspective, the Chinese diaspora in Canada can be divided into three major periods: pre-immigration, 1788–1857; pre-universal immigration, 1858–1966; and post-universal immigration, 1967–present. This chapter focuses on the origins and destinations of Chinese migrants to Canada, the impacts of Canadian immigration policies on the growth and distribution of the Chinese population, the spatial expansion of the Chinese since the late eighteenth century, and the changing characteristics of Chinatowns in Canada.[1]

PRE-IMMIGRATION PERIOD, 1788–1857

The earliest written evidence of Chinese appearance on the western coast of Canada is found in Captain John Meares' (1790) memoirs of his voyages from China to the northwest coast of America in 1788 and 1789. Captain

Meares was a British fur trader and a retired Naval officer. In January 1788, he recruited fifty Chinese sailors, smiths, and carpenters at Macao and Guangzhou (Canton), and shipped them to Nootka Sound on Vancouver Island where they helped him build a small fortress, a dockyard and a schooner. In the following year Captain Meares recruited another seventy Chinese laborers at Guangzhou, and shipped them to Nootka Sound. He recorded his favorable impressions with the Chinese workers' obedience, diligence and willingness to work hard, and predicted that they would be indispensable laborers in the opening up of the virgin land of British Columbia.

The duration of stay of the Chinese laborers in Nootka Sound was very brief. In the summer of 1789 the Spaniards under the command of Captain Martinez arrived and took possession of Nootka Sound, seized Meares' vessels, and imprisoned his Chinese crew. What happened to the 120 Chinese laborers afterward is still a mystery. It was reported that some of them might have been shipped to San Blas in Mexico, some might have escaped from their Spanish captors, and some might have been killed later by the native Indians (Howay, 1930). These early Chinese arrivals were contract laborers and not immigrants. For sixty-nine years after the so-called Nootka Sound Controversy between the British and Spanish, there was no written evidence of further Chinese arrivals in British Columbia.

PRE-UNIVERSAL IMMIGRATION, 1858–1966

The first wave of Chinese immigration was associated with the gold rushes in British Columbia during the late 1850s and 1860s, and the second wave with the construction of the Canadian Pacific Railway in British Columbia from 1880 to 1885. After 1885, the Canadian government adopted monetary measures to restrict Chinese immigrants from entering Canada. As these measures failed to curb immigration, the government decided in 1923 to close its door to Chinese immigrants. The policy of exclusion lasted for twenty-three years during which Chinese residents in Canada could not bring their families from China to join them.

The First Influx

Chinese migration to Canada began when gold was discovered in the lower Fraser River in British Columbia during the summer of 1858. A few hundred Chinese joined in the gold rush by boat from San Francisco or by overland routes from the Washington territory. Soon many Chinese gold-seekers came directly by ship from Hong Kong. This marked the first wave of Chinese migration.

The colonial government of British Columbia could only estimate population figures because of the miners' great mobility during this period (United

Kingdom, 1867: 140). The annual average Chinese population between 1867 and 1870 was estimated at about 1,900 persons, of whom over 1,000 Chinese miners were found in the gold-mining areas in the Lower Fraser Region and the Cariboo Region (United Kingdom, 1968: 142; 1869: 150; and 1870: 135–136). In 1871 British Columbia entered the Confederation and became the sixth province of Canada.[2] By that time the gold rushes were over and most of the Chinese miners had left the gold-bearing creeks on the mainland and settled down in the capital city of Victoria, the coal-mining town of Nanaimo, and the salmon-canning city of New Westminster. In 1879, according to the data compiled from the polling district officers' reports submitted to T. B. Humphries for October 1879 to February 1880, the Chinese population in British Columbia was estimated at about 4,000, of whom 2,300 lived in Chinatown in Victoria, 435 in Nanaimo, and 300 in New Westminster. The Chinese population in the gold-mining areas had been greatly reduced: for example, only 149 still remained in Barkerville, 41 in Yale, and 33 in Kamloops.

The Chinese population of Canada was reported for the first time when British Columbia was included in the national census of 1881: the Chinese population of British Columbia was 4,350, with 22 in Ontario, 7 in Quebec, and 4 in Manitoba (Canada, 1882–85). The predominance of the Chinese population in the Canadian far west explains why the initial protests against Chinese immigration by white workers were limited to British Columbia.

The Second Influx

The second wave of Chinese migration was in response to the demand for laborers to build the Canadian Pacific Railway. Andrew Onderdonk, a railway contractor, recruited thousands of Chinese laborers from the United States and China to build his section from Port Moody to Eagle Pass in British Columbia (Lai, 1998: 3–4). By 1882, the total labor force on the railway had reached about 9,000 men, of whom 6,500 were Chinese and 2,000 were white. Hundreds of the Chinese laborers died from winter cold, malnutrition, sickness, and accidents. They were constantly replaced by new arrivals from China. By 1884, the total Chinese population in British Columbia amounted to 10,492, of whom 3,510 Chinese railway workers lived in makeshift tents along the route of the railway line. The largest Chinese communities were in Victoria, with a Chinese population of 1,767, in New Westminster, where the Chinese population numbered 1,680 and in Nanaimo, with 969 Chinese residents (Canada, 1885a: 363–365) (map 13.1). In addition, about 700 Chinese still remained in the gold-mining Cariboo area, where Forks Quesnelle and Stanley had the largest concentration of Chinese miners. Pockets of Chinese gold miners and farmers were also distributed throughout the lower and upper Fraser River valley. In the far north, along the Skeena River, about 300 Chinese worked in fish canneries.

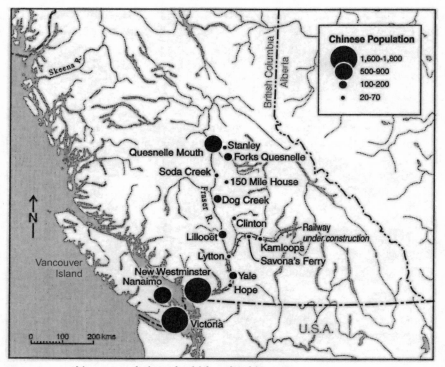

Map 13.1.   Chinese Population of British Columbia, 1884

The Chinese population in 1884 was predominantly male, with fewer than two hundred persons listed as married women, young girls, and prostitutes. Nearly all married women and young girls lived in the Chinatowns of Victoria, New Westminster, or Nanaimo where a small merchant class had become established. Other Chinese communities in small mining or farming towns were comprised of single male laborers, and did not have any Chinese female members, except for a few prostitutes. In those days, all the Chinatowns or Chinese quarters consisted of wooden shacks or small frame-houses and were located usually on the fringe of a town center and separated from the white community.

Between 1881 and 1884, a total of 15,701 Chinese from China, San Francisco, and Puget Sound landed at Victoria (Canada, 1885a: 398). This influx of Chinese laborers coincided with a period of slow economic activity and increased unemployment, and resulted in a tumultuous outcry against Chinese immigration in British Columbia. To appease the widespread anti-Chinese sentiment in British Columbia, the federal government decided in 1885 to tighten Chinese immigration.

Head Taxes

The federal government passed a Chinese Immigration Act in 1885, the year the Canadian Pacific Railway was completed to Port Moody, which imposed a head tax of $50 on every person of Chinese origin entering Canada (Canada, 1885b). The intention of this Act was to impose a financial burden on the Chinese laborers and discourage them from coming to Canada. However, the head tax failed to curb Chinese immigration and the number of arrivals increased steadily from 211 in 1886 to 4,385 in 1899. Accordingly, the federal government passed a Chinese Immigration Act in 1900 that increased the head tax to $100. In 1903, another act was passed that raised the head tax to $500 (Canada, 1900 and 1903). In spite of these increases, many youths in China still considered it advantageous to leave their villages, where they were unemployed or earning only about $2 a month, for Canada where they could earn over ten times as much. Furthermore, after the American Congress passed the Chinese Exclusion Act of 1882, and subsequent immigration acts that prohibited Chinese laborers from entering the United States, many Chinese immigrants paid the heavy head tax as a trade-off for possible opportunities to enter the United States from Canada (Huang, 1954: 82–83). Consequently, the number of Chinese emigrants to Canada continued to increase throughout the 1910s.

The Canadian Pacific Railway was terminated at Port Moody in 1885 but extended to Vancouver in 1887. Vancouver was incorporated in 1886 on the former site of Granville Village, and transformed rapidly from a frontier town to a major entrepôt on the Pacific coast. As the Pacific terminus of the transcontinental railway, Vancouver soon replaced Victoria as the Asian gateway to Canada (Nicol, 1970: 56). Scores of adventurous Chinese immigrants also migrated eastward along the railway line to the new towns of Calgary, Moose Jaw, and Regina in the hope that racial antagonism on the prairies might be less severe and job opportunities better than in British Columbia. By the late 1890s a steady stream of Chinese immigrants settled in Winnipeg, Toronto and Montreal and another stream moved into Canada from the United States. By 1911 the Chinese population in Canada stood at 27,774, of whom 71 percent were in British Columbia, 10 percent in Ontario, 6.4 percent in Alberta, and 5.7 percent in Quebec (table 13.1).

In 1911, the four major Chinatowns in British Columbia were located in Vancouver, Victoria, New Westminster and Nanaimo (map 13.2). The living conditions were extremely poor. In Vancouver's Chinatown, for example, most of its 3,480 residents were male laborers who were crowded in small wooden shacks or wooden tenement buildings on both sides of Dupont Street (now called Pender Street). Located close to a tidal flat, the

Table 13.1. People of Chinese Ethnic Origin in Canada, 1911 and 1941

Province/Territory	Number of Persons		Increase in Population	Percent Increase
	1911	1941		
British Columbia	19,568	18,619	−949	−4.8
Ontario	2,766	6,143	3,377	122.1
Alberta	1,787	3,122	1,335	−4.7
Quebec	1,578	2,378	800	50.7
Saskatchewan	957	2,545	1,588	165.9
Manitoba	885	1,248	363	41.0
Nova Scotia	134	372	238	177.6
New Brunswick	93	152	59	63.4
Prince Edward Is.	6	45	39	650.0
Yukon	0	0	0	0
NW Territories	0	3	3	300.0
Total	27,774	34,627	6,853	24.7

Sources: Census of Canada, 1911 and 1941.

place was odorous and viewed by whites as "an incubation of leprosy, smallpox, cholera, and other diseases" (*Daily World,* 23 March 1893 and 7 April 1899). Victoria's Chinatown, centred on Fisgard and Cormorant Streets on the northern bank of the Johnson Street ravine, had 3,458 Chinese residents who lived in densely packed wooden-frame or brick buildings on narrow alleys or around tiny enclosed courtyards, littered with the detritus accumulated from living off marginal resources. Both Vancouver and Victoria city governments condemned the overcrowding and unhygienic living conditions in the Chinatowns and viewed them as separate slums for the Chinese only, not as part of the urban fabric of the cities. Nanaimo's Chinatown, with about 600 Chinese residents, was located on the southern boundary of the coal-mining town consisting of an array of wooden structures on both sides of the unpaved Pine Street, which ran between two deep gullies (*Nanaimo Free Press,* 22 June 1908). There were no utilities because the northern side of Pine Street was within the city of Nanaimo and the southern side belonged to the provincial district of Harewood. Consequently, neither the city nor the provincial government felt responsible for the schools, water supply, or street maintenance in the Chinatown. Hence, Pine Street was paved and had electricity only up to the point where it reached Chinatown.

By 1911 small Chinatowns had also emerged outside the province of British Columbia. For example, the largest Chinatown in the province of Alberta was in Calgary, which, with 485 Chinese residents, was located on the southern bank of the Bow River near the Centre Street Bridge, an area con-

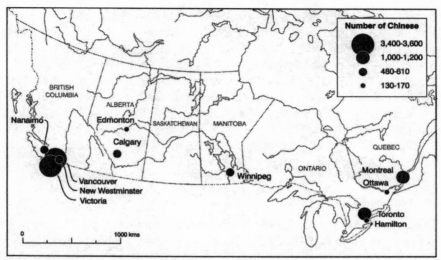

Map 13.2. Chinese Population of Canada, 1911

sidered by the white community as a "cheap dumping ground." In the province of Ontario, the greatest concentration of Chinese was in Toronto where 1,036 Chinese residents were concentrated on Queen Street East and on York Street, where two embryonic Chinatowns emerged (Toronto, 1910). Other Chinese immigrants, following the Canadian Pacific Railway, had travelled beyond Ontario and settled in the province of Quebec, although an undetermined number had also come by train from the United States (Aiken, 1984: 52). In 1911 Montreal had 1,197 Chinese residents, or 95 percent of the province's total Chinese population, and nearly all of them lived in Chinatown on Laguachetiere Street West in Dufferin District, which was a rundown residential area with warehouses, machine shops and some light industries (Robert, 1928: 14).

Home Origins

It is generally known that most Chinese immigrants in Canada originated from the Zhujiang (Pearl River) Delta in Guangdong Province, but demographic data about the county origins of these emigrants have never been officially collected and published. I used two types of archival materials from Victoria's Chinese Consolidated Benevolent Association (CCBA) as documentary evidence of the home county origins of Canada's Chinese immigrants, which provide a perspective on diversity within the larger Chinese community and demonstrate a basis for immigrant community formation. The first archival source is the set of 5,064 CCBA donation receipt stubs, dated 1884 and 1885, and the second source is the 6,155 CCBA's hospital donation receipt stubs, dated from 1892–1915 (Lai, 1975, 1977). In both cases, the full name and home county of the donor was recorded on the donation stubs. An analysis of the 11,211 donation receipt stubs reveals that during the late nineteenth and early twentieth centuries, nearly 69 percent of the Chinese in Canada had come from Siyi (the Four Counties), of which natives of Toishan (Taishan) County alone accounted for one-third. Natives from Sanyi (the Three Counties), Panyu, Nanhai, and Shunde, represented 14 percent and those from other counties 17 percent of the total Chinese population in Canada (table 13.2).

Interwar Years

Great changes characterized the growth and distribution of the Chinese population and communities in Canada between the two World Wars. After World War I, the economy of Canada was disrupted and workers were dislocated: there were factory layoffs, jobless war veterans, and other prob-

Table 13.2.   Home County Origin of People of Chinese Ethnicity in Canada at the Turn of the Twentieth Century

County	Number of Persons	% of Total
Siyi		
Taishan	3,245	28.94
Kaiping	1,916	17.09
Xinhui	1,744	15.56
Enping	772	6.89
Sanyi		
Panyu	1,361	12.14
Nanhai	121	1.08
Shunde	116	1.03
Other counties		
Zhongshan	522	4.66
Heshan	435	3.88
Zengcheng	306	2.73
Baoan	104	0.93
Dongguan	97	0.87
Yangjiang	66	0.59
Huaxian	66	0.59
Others	340	3.03
Total	11,211	100.00

Sources: Donation receipts of the Chinese Consolidated Benevolent Association (1884–1885); Chinese Hospital (1892–1915).

lems during the general economic slump (Wickberg, 1982: 137). The Chinese were again made the scapegoats and blamed for having taken jobs from white laborers. As the number of Chinese arrivals soared from 769 in 1918 to 4,333 in the following year, it became evident that the heavy head tax had failed to stop the Chinese influx. Hence, the outcry for exclusion grew louder and louder (Woodsworth, 1941: 287; Canada, 1904–17; Canada, 1918–34). Eventually, in 1923, the federal government passed the Chinese Exclusion Act which prohibited the entry of any person of Chinese origin or descent except for Chinese consular officials, children born in Canada, merchants, and students (Canada, 1923). Even these exempted classes were harassed to the point of being excluded because the Act did not define the meanings of "merchants" and "students." The Act effectively prevented Chinese residents from bringing their wives and children from China. After the last group of Chinese immigrants who had already paid the $500 head tax arrived in 1924, Chinese immigration to Canada virtually came to a halt.

Chinese bachelors in Canada found it difficult to get married because there were few Chinese women, and intermarriage was virtually impossible. Most married Chinese men left their wives behind in China. In order to reunite with their families, they had to, and did, return to China. As a result, the Chinese population in Canada declined and many small Chinatowns were depopulated and eventually abandoned. For example, the Chinese population in Canada decreased from 46,519 in 1931 to 34,627 in 1941, a decrease of 26 percent (table 13.3). Even the Canadian-born Chinese who enthusiastically participated in the social activities of Canadian society were still denied Canadian citizenship and barred from practising law, medicine and other professions during the interwar years. Although more widely dispersed than in previous decades, the 1941 Canadian census showed that nearly half of the Chinese were concentrated in six major Chinatowns: Vancouver with 7,174; Victoria, 3,307; Toronto, 2,326; Montreal, 1,703; Calgary, 799, and Winnipeg, 719 (map 13.3). These Chinatowns were virtually self-contained, complete with stores, schools, hospitals, temples and *tong* (association) buildings. The residents were primarily single male laborers and small business owners. The types of business were remarkably consistent from one Chinatown to another: restaurants, grocery stores, laundries and the like. *Tong* buildings, store signs, merchandise, and other aspects of the townscape were visibly Chinese. With hidden alleys and underground tunnels, these areas symbolized for outsiders secrecy and danger. Despite similar characteristics, they varied in historical development, size and areal extent, population, and socioeconomic conditions. These variations tended to increase as one moved eastward, reflecting the general movement of Chinese immigrants from British Columbia to eastern Canada (Lai, 1988: 68–70).

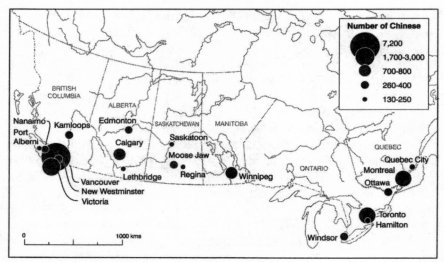

Map 13.3.   Chinese Population of Canada, 1941

Selective Entry

During World War II, about 600 Chinese youths in Canada served in the Canadian forces, and after the war these Chinese veterans demanded equal treatment. Other Chinese residents and many Caucasians in Canada also lobbied parliament to end the exclusion. Eventually in 1947 the Canadian government

Table 13.3.   Growth of People of Chinese Ethnic Origin in Canada, 1881–1996

Census Year	Number of Persons	Increase Over Previous Census	% Increase	% of Canada's Population
1881	4,383	—	—	0.10
1991	9,129	4,746	108.3	0.19
1901	17,312	8,183	89.6	0.32
1911	27,831	10,519	60.8	0.39
1921	39,587	11,813	42.5	0.45
1931	46,519	6,932	17.5	0.45
1941	34,627	−11,892	−25.6	0.30
1951	32,528	−2,099	−6.1	0.23
1961	58,197	25,669	78.9	0.32
1971	118,815	60,618	104.2	0.55
1981	289,245	170,430	143.4	1.20
1991	652,630	363,385	125.6	2.32
1996	921,585[a]	268,955	41.2	3.23

Source: Census of Canada, 1881–1996
[a]This figure does not include 7,770 respondents who stated their origin as "Taiwanese" and 780 respondents who stated their origin as "Tibetan."

repealed its 1923 Chinese Immigration Act and permitted Chinese to be naturalized as Canadians and to sponsor their wives and children to come to Canada (Canada, 1947b). Nevertheless, although exclusion was abolished, government policy continued to restrict Asian immigration in order to maintain "the fundamental composition of the Canadian population" (Canada, 1947a). In other words, the immigration policy was based on the principle of preserving Caucasian predominance. The more fundamental turning point in Canadian immigration policy was the adoption of the Bill of Rights in 1960, a federal statute that barred discrimination on the grounds of national origin, race, colour, religion, or sex. Subsequently, in 1962, the Canadian government introduced a significant change in its immigration policy by which the country of origin was no longer a major criterion for admission to Canada (Canada, 1962).

The Chinese population in Canada increased after the abolition of the Chinese Exclusion Act but the number of Chinatown residents decreased through the 1950s and 1960s due to death and departure. Deaths among the aging population were not counterbalanced by births because there were few adult Chinese women in these settlements. Furthermore, when many elderly people retired, they returned to their home villages in China where the cost of living was much lower. In 1959 the federal government permitted Canadians living outside Canada to continue receiving their old age pensions, which further encouraged elderly Chinese to return to Hong Kong or China. Consequently, many of the smaller Chinatowns in New Westminster, Hamilton, Cumberland, Moose Jaw and other cities simply vanished. As a result of decentralization, declining numbers of Chinese residents also characterized the large metropolitan cities. In Winnipeg's Chinatown in 1951, 86 percent of its 700 residents were old bachelors (Da Rosa, 1971: 1–3). Twenty years later, the population had further decreased to 540 persons, which represented only 20 percent of the Chinese population in Metropolitan Winnipeg. Montreal's Chinatown once had a residential population over a thousand, but by the early 1970s most of the Chinese had moved out to better neighbourhoods such as St. Laurent, LaSalle, Brossard, and Outremont (*Chinatown News,* 3 February 1982: 33). After the 1950s, many young Canadian-born Chinese who were better educated and economically better-off than their parents, moved out of Chinatown and established their families in more upscale neighbourhoods, partly because they could afford a higher standard of living and partly because discrimination against them had greatly reduced. The third-generation Chinese and many postwar Chinese immigrants did not regard Chinatown as home because they had not been brought up there, and they more widely participated in the activities of the larger society. Unlike the generations of sojourners before them who were closely tied to the traditional associations in Chinatowns, based on place of origin, common dialect, and clan relations, the new generation had little to do with these organizations.

The changing social structure of the Chinatowns accompanied a decline in their commercial functions. New Chinese businesses were set up outside Chinatowns, drawing away many former customers. Many small stores and cafes in Chinatowns had to close after their original proprietors retired or died because their educated children did not want to work long hours, as their parents had done, and refused to run the family business. Ottawa's Chinatown on Albert Street is a case in point: it disappeared as the last few stores ceased to operate (Lee, 1983).

Slum clearance or urban renewal projects also played an important role in the decline and destruction of Chinatowns throughout the 1960s and early 1970s. Physical deterioration of the buildings made them vulnerable to land speculation or to demolition in the course of downtown revitalization programs. In Kamloops, for example, many of the old buildings in Chinatown were levelled during the construction of the new Overlander Bridge in 1961, and the entire Chinatown was demolished in 1979 for the expansion of Victoria Street (June, 1987).

POST-UNIVERSAL IMMIGRATION, 1967–PRESENT

The Immigration Act passed in 1967 introduced for the first time a policy for admitting immigrants that was not based on country of origin or racial category (Canada, 1968: 227). Instead of nationality and race, a "100-points system" was introduced whereby points were allotted for education and training (20 points), occupational skill (10 points), knowledge of English and French (10 points), and other merits. For example, an "independent immigrant," irrespective of his or her ethnic origin, would be admitted to Canada as long as he/she had at least 70 out of 100 points. In addition, the new immigration policy contained provisions that facilitated family reunion (Canada, 1984).

The 1967 Immigration Act resulted in dramatic changes in Chinese communities across Canada. Chinese immigrants came from many lands and cultures: Hong Kong, Taiwan, China, Southeast Asia, Britain, the United States, to name a few, but unlike their predecessors, many post-1967 Chinese immigrants entered Canada under the "independent category," and listed their intended occupations as professionals such as medical doctors, nurses, engineers, architects, and teachers, and other skilled occupations such as clerical workers and machine technicians. Many chose to stay in Toronto, Vancouver, and other large cities for job opportunities, but lived in the suburbs and went to Chinatown only on weekends or holidays for Chinese food and groceries.

Immigrants from China

After 1967, the Canadian government ceased to identify ethnic origin in immigration statistics, listing instead the country of the immigrant's last permanent residence. In statistics, for example, from 1967 to 1970, a total of 28,440 immigrants came from "China," which included Hong Kong, Taiwan, and the People's Republic of China (Canada, 1967–70). Most of these immigrants were definitely Chinese, but they also included English, Indians, Sikhs, and other ethnic groups. Furthermore, statistics on landed immigrants from Vietnam, Malaysia and other Southeast Asian countries included an undetermined number of persons of Chinese ethnic origin. Therefore, the exact number of Chinese immigrants coming to Canada after 1967 is not known. After Canada recognized the People's Republic of China in 1970, the numbers of landed immigrants from Hong Kong, Taiwan, and China were recorded individually in immigration statistics. For example, from 1971 to 1977, 66,900 landed immigrants came from Hong Kong, 7,582 came from Taiwan, and 3,045 were from China (Canada, 1972–77). Most of them were definitely persons of Chinese ethnic origins. This influx of Chinese from Hong Kong was caused by three main factors: (1) the 1967 riots in Hong Kong and the subsequent fear of Communist takeover of the British Colony; (2) the new "point-system" and "family reunion" immigration policy of Canada; and (3) educational and economic opportunities in Canada. Under a new immigration regulation introduced in 1973, students holding student visas who had entered Canada before November 1972 were permitted to apply for permanent residence status while staying in Canada (Canada, 1973). Thus about 500 Hong Kong students holding student visas applied and obtained permanent residence status. As a result, Hong Kong immigrants soared from 5,009 in 1971 to a record high of 14,662 in 1973 (Canada, 1973).

A "Swinging Door" Policy

In the 1950s, European immigrants accounted for nearly 90 percent of total immigrants to Canada, while Asian immigrants made up only 2 percent. But by the late 1960s and early 1970s, the proportion of European immigrants had dropped to 50 percent while Asian immigrants had risen to nearly 17 percent of the total (Canada, 1975). The number of immigrants from Latin American and African countries also increased. The significant increase in non-White immigrants led to simmering discontent among some groups in the white community. In response to their concerns, and after many consultations with communities across Canada, the federal government passed a new Immigration

Act in 1976, effective in 1978, in which the "points system" was revised and placed greater emphasis on occupational experience and job creation (Canada, 1976–77). These changes introduced a new immigration category called "business immigrants" by which the federal government issued visas to prospective immigrants whose business proposals met the economic needs of the province in which they would reside.

Another major change was the implementation of an annual immigration level by which, every October, the Minister of Employment and Immigration would specify the number of immigrants admissible for the following year after consultation with the provincial governments in regard to regional demographic conditions and labor market considerations. Thus, in 1978, the Minister set the first immigration level at 100,000 for 1979 (Canada, 1988: 40). The door of immigration was swung open in the following two years as the level was increased to 120,000 for 1980 and 130,000–140,000 for 1981. Most of the Chinese immigrants entering at this time settled in Ontario, which by 1981 overtook British Columbia as the leading province in the size of Chinese population (figure 13.1).

From late 1981 to 1984, Canada experienced a deep economic recession, which resulted in increased unemployment. Accordingly, the government partially closed the door of immigration by reducing the annual immigration level from 130,000–135,000 in 1982 to 85,000–90,000 in 1985. The reduction did not affect immigrants from Hong Kong, mainly because they were professional people, investors, or entrepreneurs. During the Sino-British negotiations on the future of Hong Kong between 1982 and 1984, thousands of Hong Kong residents emigrated to Canada, the United States, and Australia because of the uncertainty over Hong Kong's future. Even after the Sino-British joint Declaration agreement was signed in December 1984, most of the well-to-do Chinese still planned to leave because they worried that the policy of "one country, two systems" might not be honoured if China were once again controlled by radical leftists. In 1985, for example, about 10,000 Hong Kong residents emigrated to Canada.

A Report on the Review of Future Directions for Immigration Levels, which was tabled in the House of Commons in 1985, revealed that the birth rate in Canada had dipped to about 1.66 children for every woman of child-bearing age, and that unless more immigrants were accepted, the economy of Canada would be negatively affected by population decline. There was broad consensus in government as well as in the private sector that immigration had been too low in the previous years, and that business immigrants should be encouraged as a means of complementing Canada's strategies of attracting foreign investment and alleviating problems of unemployment (Canada, 1988: 28). Accordingly the federal government

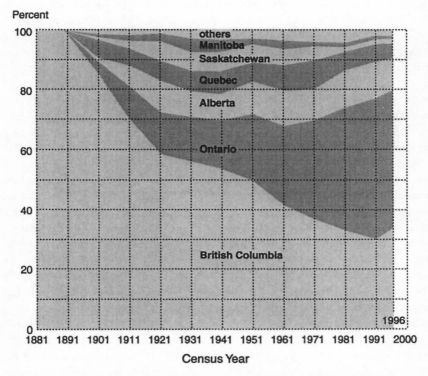

Figure 13.1.   Chinese Population by Province, Percent of Total, 1881–1996

opened the door of immigration again by raising the immigration level from 105,000–115,000 for 1986 to 150,000–160,000 for 1989 and 250,000 for 1992–1996.

Immigrant Investor Program, 1986–2000

In 1986 the Investment Canada Act was introduced. Central to the Act was the Immigrant Investor Program, which sought to promote economic growth in Canada by attracting new investment capital and experienced businessmen (Canada, 1988: 2). The investor class comprised three types of business migrants: investors, entrepreneurs, and self-employed persons. The act specified that (1) a migrant investor must maintain a residence in Canada and make a three-year investment of not less than Can$250,000, which would create jobs; (2) a migrant entrepreneur must have bona fide financial and managerial ability, and buy or start a business where he or she would have an active managerial role, and create jobs for Canadians; and (3) a self-employed migrant must maintain employment and contribute to the economy or enrich Canada's cultural-artistic life. A prospective business immigrant would be given a two-year conditional visa based on his or her business experience, wealth, and potential to establish a business in accordance with the economic goals of a province. This program encouraged many Chinese entrepreneurs and investors from Hong Kong and Taiwan to migrate to Canada with large amounts of capital. Chinese business immigrants from Hong Kong and Taiwan accounted for 32 percent and 5 percent respectively of 7,518 business immigrants to Canada in 1986; by 1990, the percentages had increased to 37 percent and 13 percent respectively of a total 18,445 business immigrants (Canada, 1986–90). Most of these immigrants invested in Ontario and British Columbia. In order to encourage wider geographic distribution of investment, in 1990 the federal government amended the Immigrant Investor Program in order to encourage investor immigrants to set up businesses in less popular destinations: the minimum amount of investment in the provinces of Ontario, British Columbia, and Quebec was increased from $250,000 to $350,000 while the amount in other provinces and territories remained at $250,000 (Canada, 1990). The amendment also changed the length of time that investment funds were locked in from three to five years.

Through the late 1990s, and in response to complaints from some provinces, the federal government consulted the provincial governments about revisions to the Immigrant Investor Program. For example, immigrants could invest and obtain immigrant status easily in Quebec because Quebec operated its own investor program under the terms of the 1991 Canada-Quebec Accord.[3] Exercising their freedom under the Charter of Rights to live in the province of their choice, many investor immigrants who landed in Quebec subsequently moved to Ontario, British Columbia, and other provinces, which had to bear the cost of their settlement expenses (*Ming Pao Daily,* 21 March 1997). Since 1986 British Columbia had received only 10 percent of the $3.2 billion in federal support for the immigrant-investor program although it had more than half of the immigrants and bore the heavy cost of settlement services (such as adult language training) (*Vancouver Sun,* 15 April 1997). Between 1971 and 1991, Ontario, Alberta, Prince Edward Island, and British Columbia registered the highest percentage increases in population, reflecting immigrant settlement (table 13.4). Both Ontario and British Columbia experienced the highest increase between 1991 and 1996 because more than half of all the investor immigrants arriving in Canada during this period indicated their intention to settle in these two provinces (table 13.5) (Hiebert, 1999).

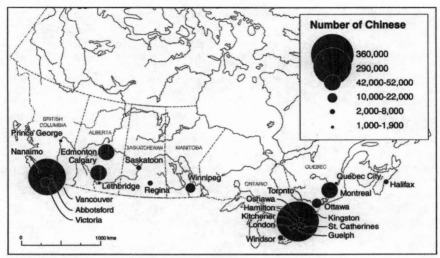

Map 13.4.   Chinese Population of Canada, 1996

Most of the Chinese immigrants were bound for large metropolitan cities. By 1996, about 70 percent of the Chinese population in Canada were concentrated in Metro Toronto and Metro Vancouver, and 15 percent in the metropolitan cities of Montreal, Calgary and Edmonton (map 13.4).

In 1999, the federal government implemented a new Immigrant Investor Program which increased the minimum investment to $400,000 for all investors,

Table 13.4.   People of Chinese Ethnic Origin in Canada, 1971 and 1991

Province/Territory	Number of Persons		Increase in Population	% of Increase
	1971	*1991*		
Ontario	39,325	304,755	268,430	675.0
British Columbia	44,315	196,725	152,410	344.0
Alberta	12,905	80,210	67,305	521.0
Quebec	11,905	41,620	29,715	249.6
Manitoba	3,430	13,730	10,300	300.3
Saskatchewan	4,605	9,335	4,730	102.7
Nova Scotia	935	2,885	1,950	208.6
New Brunswick	575	1,550	975	169.6
Newfoundland	610	1,125	515	84.4
N.W. Territories	115	380	265	230.4
Yukon Territory	85	195	110	129.4
Prince Edward Island	25	120	95	380.0
Total	118,815	652,630	533,815	449.3

Source: Census of Canada, 1971 and 1991

Table 13.5. People of Chinese Ethnic Origin in Canada, 1991 and 1996

Province/Territory	1991		1996	
	No. of Persons	% of Total	No. of Persons	% of Total
Ontario	304,755	46.70	422,770	45.87
British Columbia	196,725	30.14	312,330	33.89
Alberta	80,210	12.29	98,135	10.65
Quebec	41,620	6.38	55,870	6.06
Manitoba	13,730	2.10	14,485	1.57
Saskatchewan	9,335	1.43	9,970	1.08
Nova Scotia	2,885	0.44	3,675	0.40
New Brunswick	1,550	0.24	1,830	0.20
Newfoundland	1,125	0.17	1,415	0.15
North West Territories	380	0.06	455	0.05
Yukon Territory	195	0.03	410	0.04
Prince Edward Island	120	0.01	235	0.03
Total	652,630	100.00	921,585	100.00

Source: Census of Canada, 1991 and 1996

regardless of the province of capital investment (Canada, 1999). The federal government acts as an agent to the select investors on behalf of the provinces and the territories, which determine where to invest the money. Consistent with the spirit of the Canada-Quebec Accord, Quebec agreed to harmonize its regulations with the new program but has retained its prerogative to select investors. Investors chosen by Quebec must be destined for Quebec whereas investors selected under the federal program can be destined for any other province of their choice.

Renovation of Old Chinatowns and the Emergence of New Chinatowns

New immigrants and new investments have led to the rehabilitation of pre–World War II Chinatowns and the development of new Chinatowns and new Chinese shopping centres in the suburbs of metropolitan cities. The only two surviving old Chinatowns in British Columbia have been revitalized and transformed into tourist attractions. Victoria's Chinatown had lost its former luster but much of its nineteenth-century built environment remained intact (Lai, 1991: 12–13). This was the first Canadian Chinatown to carry out a comprehensive rehabilitation program, which occurred from 1979 to 1986 and included the restoration and painting of building facades, beautification of streets, construction of a gateway, and establishment of an elder care facility and a subsidized housing project. The other surviving old Chinatown is in Vancouver, which has been booming since the 1980s, mainly because of new investment by Hong Kong entrepreneurs and investors. As commercial spaces on East Pender and Keefer streets were fully occupied, new immigrant investors began to set up businesses on Main, East Hastings and other streets near Chinatown (Lai, 1988: 133). New indoor malls such as Chinatown Centre and Sun Wah Centre were constructed, which contributed to revitalizing the district.

The province of Alberta is one of the favored destinations of recent Chinese immigrants to Canada. In Edmonton, the old Chinatown on 97th Street was demolished and replaced by a New Chinatown on 102nd Avenue (also known as Harbin Road) where an Elders' Mansion, a Multicultural Centre, and a Chinese arch were erected (Lai, 1988: 139–140). Chinese Vietnamese investors and entrepreneurs played an important role in the birth of another New Chinatown in Edmonton, which centers mainly between the 97th and 98th Streets (Lai, 1995: 258). The historic decline in Alberta's Chinese population left Calgary's old Chinatown district subject to redevelopment, and the original Chinatown buildings were virtually replaced by high-rise residential and commercial apartments, making Calgary a "Replaced Chinatown." It is different from Victoria, Vancouver or Montreal, which still retain many buildings built during the early twentieth century. They are rehabilitated old Chinatowns, which have been much reduced in size because of postwar development by Chinese as well as non-Chinese developers during the 1960s and 1970s. In Montreal, for example, many old buildings in Chinatown were razed and replaced by Complexe Desjardins, Complexe Guy Favreau and other massive complexes of high-rise offices and apartment buildings, which were regarded by city officials as catalysts for urban revitalization (Lai, 1988: 150). And in Toronto, nearly two-thirds of the old Chinatown on Elizabeth and Chestnut streets was obliterated in the 1960s to provide space for Nathan Phillips Square and the new City Hall (Lai, 1988: 146). Businesses and residents moved out and reestablished further west along Dundas Street West between University and Spadina Avenue where Chinatown West, a new Chinatown, emerged. During the 1970s an increasing number of low-income Chinese and Vietnamese immigrants took up residence in Riverdale, about three miles east of Chinatown West, where properties were several thousand dollars cheaper than Chinatown West, and rents were much lower (Lai, 1988: 168). Hence, in Toronto a new Chinatown East was born at the intersection of Broadview Avenue and Gerrard Street East.

Suburban Asian-Themed Plazas and Malls

The social geography and economic landscape of large metropolitan cities have been distinctively reshaped by the post-1967 Chinese immigrants. An increasing number of recent immigrants have preferred to live in suburban municipalities rather than in the inner city, which has changed the function and form of commercial developments in the suburbs. In 1991, for example, only about 23 percent of the 231,795 Chinese of Metro Toronto lived in the inner city whereas 51 percent lived in the inner suburban municipalities (Scarborough, 28 percent; North York, 17 percent; and East York, Etobicoke and York, 6 percent) and 26 percent in outer suburban municipalities such as Markham, Mississauga and Richmond Hill (map 13.5). During the late 1970s Chinese merchants set up Chinese restaurants, grocery stores, bookstores and other small shops in three small plazas at the intersection of Glen Watford Drive and Bramley Street to meet the need of the growing suburban Chinese population in Scarborough (Lai, 1988: 170–171). By the early 1980s several Chinese investors started to construct enclosed malls such as the Dragon Centre, and open plazas such as the Mandarin Shopping Centre and Pearl Plaza on Sheppard Street (map 13.6). This cluster of Chinese shopping centers had once been called Scarborough's Chinatown. They are known to the public as Chinese plazas or malls because of their unique characteristics such as store signs written in Chinese characters, a predominance of Chinese patrons and Chinese store owners, and the merchandise and services that are oriented nearly exclusively to Chinese customers (Lai, 2000: 110). Many of the Asian-themed malls are strata-titled—in which the shop units are sold individually under condominium-style arrangements—and have been sold quickly at a profit to merchants or investors. Many non-Asian developers are enticed by this quick return of investment and participate in the construction of Asian-themed malls catering to Chinese buyers from Hong Kong and Taiwan. By December 1999, a total of 58 Asian-theme malls had been built in five suburban municipalities of Metro Toronto. Similarly, by 1996, half of Vancouver's Chinese residents lived in the suburbs (table 13.6). In Richmond alone, there were 49 Asian-themed malls in the municipality's central business district in 1999 (Lai, 2000: 112).

CONCLUSION

Poverty, unemployment, hunger, civil war, and the bankruptcy of rural economy originally compelled Chinese villagers to leave their homeland for Canada with hopes for greater economic opportunities. The early Chinese diaspora from the 1850s to 1950s was mainly a result of China's economic weakness and the demand for labor in Canada. Initially the Chinese were welcomed for their cheap labor, but soon after the labor shortage was reduced the Canadian government introduced head taxes to restrict their entry. As the monetary measures failed to curb the number of Chinese immigrants, the pol-

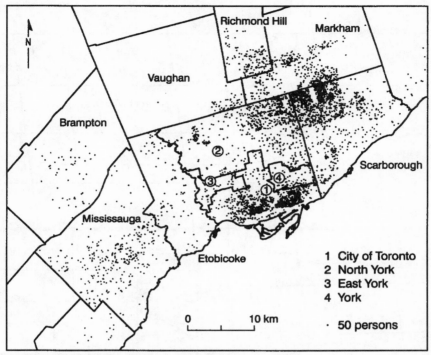

Map 13.5.   Distribution of Chinese in Metro Toronto, 1991

icy of exclusion was carried out and effectively prevented Chinese from entering Canada for over two decades. The Chinese who remained in Canada
confined themselves and their economic activities to one or more city blocks
in the city core or on the fringe of downtown commercial areas where the living conditions were poor and which became known over time as Chinatowns
to the locals and their residents alike. Throughout the 1960s and 1970s a large
number of deteriorating Chinatowns were demolished or relocated in the
course of slum clearance or urban renewal programs.

The year 1967 was the centennial year of the birth of the Dominion of Canada,
but the year was more significant to nonwhite immigrants because it marked the
beginning of Canada's color-blind immigration policy. The new immigration
regulations, based on nondiscrimination and universality, gave people from all
parts of the world an equal opportunity to qualify for admission. For the first
time in Canadian history, prospective Chinese immigrants were treated the same
as immigrants of other nationalities and were selected for admission according
to education, training, skills, and other criteria linked to Canada's economic and

Map 13.6.   Distribution of Asian-Themed Malls, December 1999

■ Asian-themed Malls

1 Midtown Plaza	16 Scarborough Village Mall	31 Finch - Leslie Square	46 Birchwood Plaza
2 Cathay Plaza	17 Silverland Centre	32 Ho - View Plaza	47 Bamburgh Gardens
3 Dragon Centre	18 Scarboro Industrial Centre	33 Golden Plaza	48 Metro Square
4 Glen Watford Drive	19 First Commercial Place	34 Chalmers Gate	49 New Century Plaza
5 Dynasty Centre	20 Milliken Square	35 Golden View Centre	50 Milliken Mews
6 Mandarin Shopping Centre	21 Milliken Business Park	36 Doncrest Plaza	51 Peachtree Centre
7 Pearl Plaza	22 Midland Court	37 Jubilee Square	52 New Kennedy Square
8 Brimley Commons	23 Midland North Business Centre	38 Time Square	53 Regency Place
9 Prince Mall	24 Evergold Centre	39 Shoppes of the Parkway	54 Milliken Wells Shopping Centre
10 Centerview Square	25 Midland Village	40 Commerce Gate	55 Woodside Square
11 Victory Shopping Centre	26 Market Village	41 Glen Cameron Place	56 Scherwood Centre
12 Agincourt Commercial Centre	27 Pacific Mall	42 Central Park on Yonge	57 Swing'n Bowl
13 Agincourt Mall	28 New World Plaza	43 Lexus - Bayview Square	58 First Markham Place
14 Chartwell Shopping Centre	29 Prosperity Centre	44 Richlane	
15 Finch - Midland Centre	30 Victoria Business Centre	45 Huntingwood Square	

human resources requirements. Unlike the early Chinese immigrants who were forced away from their homelands, many Chinese students, professionals, entrepreneurs, or retired people voluntarily left their homeland for Canada for educational and investment opportunities, political security and other reasons. A considerable number of them were entrepreneurs of moderate or great wealth who settled down in large metropolitan cities, such as Toronto and Vancouver, where

Table 13.6. Distribution of Chinese in Metropolitan Vancouver, 1996

Municipality	Number of Persons	% of Total
Vancouver City	143,115	49.56
Richmond City	50,215	17.38
Burnaby City	40,165	13.91
Coquitlam City	15,530	5.38
Surrey City	14,195	4.92
North Vancouver DM	4,285	1.48
Port Coquitlam City	3,960	1.37
Delta DM	3,935	1.36
West Vancouver DM	3,685	1.28
New Westminster City	1,785	0.62
Port Moody City	1,535	0.53
North Vancouver City	1,525	0.53
University Endowment Area	1,285	0.44
Maple Ridge DM	1,135	0.39
Langley DM	1,090	0.38
Others	1,355	0.47
Total	288,795	100.00

Source: Census of Canada, 1996

they invested heavily in Canadian business and industry. Their capital and entrepreneurial skills have helped create employment in Canada. They play an important role in the revitalization of old Chinatowns and the development of new Chinatowns and Asian-themed malls in suburban municipalities of metropolitan cities, contributing directly to the economic growth of Canada and multiculturalism that the government has been promoting in recent decades.

NOTES

The author is grateful to the Vancouver Centre of Excellence for Research on Immigration and Integration in the Metropolis for funding this research, and to Dr. Daniel Hiebert for providing 1996 Census of Canada data.

1. In this chapter, the term "Chinese" refers to people of Chinese ethnic origin residing in Canada regardless of their citizenship and residence status.

2. The Confederation in 1867 was the formation of the Dominion of Canada by uniting Ontario, Quebec, New Brunswick and Nova Scotia. Later other British colonies such as British Columbia, etc. entered the confederation and became a province of the Dominion of Canada.

3. The federal government of Canada recognizes that Quebec has a distinct society and signed the Canada-Quebec Accord, which became effective on 1 April 1991. Under the Accord, Quebec has its own investor regulations and selection criteria for independent immigrants. Canada would not admit any investors, independent immigrants or refugees into Quebec who do not meet Quebec's selection criteria.

REFERENCES

Aiken, Rebecca B. 1984. "Montreal Chinese Property Ownership and Occupation Change, 1881–1981," unpublished Ph.D. thesis, McGill University.

Canada. 1882–85. Department of Agriculture. *Census of Canada, 1880–81,* Printed in Ottawa: Maclean, Roger and Co.

———. 1885a. Royal Commission on Chinese Immigration. *Report and Evidence.*

———. 1885b. *Statutes of Canada. An Act of Respecting and Regulating Chinese Immigration into Canada, 1885. 48–49 Victoria, Chapter 71, 207–12.*

———. 1900. *Statutes of Canada. An Act Respecting and Restricting Chinese Immigration, 1900. Ottawa: 63–64 Victoria, Chapter 32, 215–21.*

———. 1903. *Statutes of Canada. An Act of Respecting and Restricting Chinese Immigration, 1903. Ottawa: 3 Edward VII, Chapter 38, 105–11.*

———. 1904–17. Department of Interior, Superintendent of Immigration, *Annual Reports, 1904–17.*

———. 1918–34. Dominion Department of Immigration and Colonization, *Annual Reports, 1918–34.* Ottawa: Printed by order of the Commission.

———. 1923. *Statute of Canada. An Act Respecting Chinese Immigration, 1923. Ottawa: 13–14 George V, Chapter 38, 301–15.*

———. 1947a. *Debates of House of Commons,* Ottawa: Vol. III, May 1947, 2644–46.

———. 1947b. *Statutes of Canada. An Act to Amend the Immigration Act and to Repeal the Chinese Immigration Act, 1947. Ottawa: 11 George VI, Chapter 19, 107–9.*

———. 1962. Order in Council, P. C. 1962–86m Immigration Act, 18 January, 37–62.

———. 1967–70. Department of Employment and Immigration. *Immigration Statistics, 1967–70.*

———. 1968. *Canada Year Book.* Dominion Bureau of Statistics.

———. 1972–77. Department of Manpower and Immigration. *Immigration Statistics, 1972–77.*

———. 1973. *Statutes of Canada. An Act Respecting Immigration to Canada, 21–2 Elizabeth II, Chapter 27.*

———. 1975. Department of Manpower and Immigration. *Green Paper on Immigration and Population.* Ottawa, 35–39.

———. 1976–77. *Statutes of Canada. An Act Respecting Immigration to Canada, 265–26 Elizabeth II, Chapter 52.*

———. 1984. *Canada's Immigrants, 1984.* Statistics Canada. Pages unfolioed.

———. 1986–90. Department of Employment and Immigration. *Immigration Statistics.*

———. 1988. *Immigration Levels Planning: The First Decade,* Employment and Immigration Canada, March.

———. 1990. Department of Manpower and Immigration. News release, 90–23, 20 August.

———. 1999. Citizenship and Immigration Canada. News release 99-16, 24 March 1999, 1.

Chinatown News, Vancouver.

Da Roza, Gustavo. 1971. *Winnipeg Chinatown: A Proposal,* Winnipeg: Winnipeg Chinese Development Corporation.

Daily World, Vancouver.

Hiebert, Daniel. 1999. "Immigration and the Changing Social Geography of Greater Vancouver," *BC Studies,* 121: 35–82.

Howay, F. W. 1930. "A Yankee Trader on the Northwest Coast, 1791–1795," *Washington Historical Quarterly,* 21: 83–94.

Huang, Tsen-ming. 1954. *The Legal Status of Chinese Abroad,* Taipei: Chinese Cultural Service.

June, Jaime. 1987. Owner of Paradise Café, private interview, Kamloops, July.

Lai, David Chuenyan. 1975. "Home County and Clan Origins of the Chinese in the 1880s," *BC Studies,* 27: 3–29.

———. 1977. "An Analysis of Data on Home Journeys by Chinese Immigrants in Canada, 1892–1915," *Professional Geographer,* 29(4): 359–365.

———. 1988. *Chinatowns: Towns within Cities in Canada,* Vancouver: University of British Columbia Press.

———. 1991. *The Forbidden City within Victoria: Myth, Symbol and Streetscape of Canada's Earliest Chinatown,* Victoria: Orca Rook Publishers.

———. 1995. "Three Chinatowns," in Bob Hesketh and Frances Swyripa, eds., *Edmonton: The Life of a City,* Edmonton: Newest Publishers Ltd., 256–266.

———. 1998. *Canadian Steel, Chinese Grit: No Chinese Labor, No Railway,* A Chinese Grit Heritage Documentary, Vancouver: National Executive Council of Canadian Steel.

———. 2000. "The Impact of New Immigration Policies on the Development of New Chinatowns and New Chinese Shopping Plazas in Canada," *Asian Profile,* 28(2): 99–116.

Lee, Wei-man. 1983. Manager of Cathay House Café, private interview, Ottawa, July.

Meares, John. 1790. "Voyages Made in the Years 1788, and 1789, from China to the North West Coast of America" and "Authentic Copy of the Memorial to the Right William Wyndham Grenvill, dated 30 April 1790, and Present to the House of Commons on 13 May, 1790," unpublished manuscripts held by British Columbia Archives, Victoria, British Columbia, Canada.

Ming Pao Daily, Vancouver.

Nanaimo Free Press, Nanaimo.

Nicol, E. 1970. *Vancouver,* Toronto: Doubleday.

Robert, Percy A. 1928. "Duffering District: An Area in Transition," unpublished Master's thesis, McGill University.

Toronto. 1910. *Toronto City Directory.*

United Kingdom. 1867–70. *Blue Books of Statistics, Colony of British Columbia,* London: Colonial Office.

Vancouver Sun, Vancouver.

Wickberg, Edgar, ed. 1982. *From China to Canada,* Toronto: McClelland and Stewart.

Woodsworth, Charles J. 1941. *Canada and the Orient,* Toronto: Macmillan.

V

TRANSMIGRANTS IN OCEANIA

14

Chinese Immigrants and Transnationals in New Zealand: A Fortress Opened

Manying Ip

FROM WHITE NEW ZEALAND TO OPEN DOOR

The patterns of migration and settlement of the New Zealand Chinese bear striking similarities to those in Australia and North America. The immigration policies of Australia, Canada, and the United States were, and still are, arguably the most decisive factor in determining the formative processes as well as the nature of the Chinese communities that settled in these countries. Since the 1990s, New Zealanders have called their country "an immigrant nation." The term has an egalitarian ring, signifying the fact that the forebears of New Zealand's different citizens had migrated and settled in the country at different stages in its history.

While this description is technically true, it is inaccurate in spirit and even misleading in implication. Historically speaking, immigrants to New Zealand were never treated equally. The founders of the country had never intended it to be a haven for diverse migrants from the Old World. Unlike the Mayflower pioneers of the American colonies, who upheld an idealistic vision that all the persecuted, huddled masses could find refuge in the new continent, the New Zealand dream was much more exclusive and restricted. Early New Zealand settlers wanted to build up a replica of Britain in the South Pacific. New Zealand was to be settled by migrants from Britain, not migrants from other countries. While the Dutch were considered "closest in blood and assimilable" (McKinnon, 1996), such tolerance was extended only with great reluctance to the southern Europeans, including the Greeks, Italians, and Yugoslavs. In this context, the Chinese, who started coming to New Zealand soon after it became British colony, remained "undesirable aliens" and became the focus of many official attempts of exclusion (Ip, 1995).

339

As a country that had always worried about insufficient population, New Zealand nevertheless persistently introduced restrictive immigration legislation against the Chinese until recent times. Furthermore, this country, which has always maintained ideas about taking pride in egalitarianism and fair play, never hesitated to introduce highly discriminatory laws against the Chinese, including those born in New Zealand (Murphy, 1997). Historically, New Zealand only opened its doors twice to the Chinese: once in the Second World War, and once in the 1990s. In the first instance, it was reluctant and cautious, forced by political circumstances (Fong, 1959). In the latter case, it was unintentional and totally coincidental, because the Business Immigration Policy and the Point System favor immigrants with business acumen, capital, and skills, and many of these people happen to be ethnic Chinese.

Policies Affecting Migration: Anti-Chinese Legislation

The first sizeable group of Chinese arrived in New Zealand in 1866, at the invitation of the Dunedin Chamber of Commerce. They came as itinerant laborers to re-work the Otago gold fields abandoned by the European miners. From 1881 to 1920, the New Zealand government passed numerous laws restricting Chinese immigration (O'Connor, 1968). Anti-Chinese prejudice was extremely widespread, and politicians often found it expedient to go with the tide. In reality, the Chinese were hardly a threat. They numbered only 5,004 nationwide when the first anti-Chinese act was passed (Ip, 1990; Murphy, 1997). This act imposed a poll tax of ten pounds and limited the number of Chinese who could be landed to one for every ten tons of each ship's cargo. In 1896, the poll tax was raised from ten to one hundred pounds. In 1907, an additional "reading test" was introduced to screen Chinese immigrants. They were required to read "to the satisfaction of custom officials at the port of entry" one hundred English words picked at random (Ip, 1990).

Simultaneous with immigration restrictions, legislation was introduced against the Chinese residents in New Zealand. In 1908, naturalisation was denied to all Chinese. The denial of citizenship meant the loss of the right to vote, which was not regained until 1952. Historically, the Chinese were the only ethnic group to suffer the poll tax as well as the denial of citizenship. Restrictions were also introduced on their movement. All Chinese wanting to leave New Zealand and then return had to apply for reentry permits, which bore their thumbprints. Even New Zealand-born babies were not exempted. The Chinese were also the only ethnic group excluded from the social welfare benefits enjoyed by all other New Zealanders: old age pension, sickness benefit and unemployment benefits. The severity and effectiveness of such legislation can be seen in the steady decline of the country's Chinese population (Ng, 1993). In 1916, it stood at just around 2,000.

On the immigration front, the most effective legislation was the 1920 Immigration Restriction Act, which required every aspiring immigrant other than people of British and Irish descent to apply for a special entry permit. No selection criteria were proclaimed and no reasons for rejection were given. Decisions rested with the Minister of Customs and immigration matters were no longer debated in the Parliament. The "Great White Walls" were securely erected around fortress New Zealand (Price, 1974).

World War II and the Arrival of Chinese Families

Paradoxically, a significant watershed in New Zealand Chinese history took place not because of legislative relaxation, but because of wartime exigency. In 1939, when the invading Japanese army overran south China, devastating the home villages of the few thousand Chinese residents in New Zealand, the government allowed the men's families to come in temporarily as refugees. Each person had to pay two hundred pounds as bond and sign a pledge that they would return to China as soon as the war ended. They also promised to take away all the children, including any babies who might be born in the interim.

By the time the war ended in late 1945, New Zealand became more aware than ever about the disadvantages of the country's small population and eagerly accepted English and Polish orphans and welcomed European refugees. Preparations were made to repatriate the Chinese women and children but the Dunedin Presbytery made a vigorous campaign to enable the Chinese families to stay (Ip, 1990). The 1947 event was crucial to the development of the Chinese community, marking its transformation from an itinerant bachelor group into a settled community of families (Ip, 1998a). Although the total population was still below the 5,000 mark of 1881, the gender balance was somewhat healthier, with 3,414 men and 1,526 women. Finally, there was a chance for the ethnic Chinese in New Zealand to develop into a community.

However, this was a "one-of" magnanimous gesture of the government, an accepted *fait accompli*. It did not involve any review of existing policy or genuine change of heart. The old 1920 Permit System remained intact, and "confidentiality" remained the watchword of the selection mechanism. Immigrants continued to come from the narrowly selected traditional source countries of Britain and Western Europe. Unbeknown to many of the most discerning critics of the "White Australian Policy," New Zealand practiced an equally stringent and discriminatory policy towards the Chinese and other Asian peoples for a much longer time (Brawley, 1995).

The Chinese population gradually rose from 6,731 in the 1956 census to 10,283 in 1966. The New Zealand Chinese community had become strongly localized by then, with about 60 percent local born. As a small ethnic minority in a closed society, which was strongly monocultural and deprived of any new arrivals, the Chinese looked ready to be totally assimilated (Fong, 1959; Greif, 1974). During those years the Chinese earned the epithet "Model Minority" because they were unobtrusive, law-abiding, and eager to integrate. As recently as 1986, they made up only 0.6 percent of the total population. It was a self-contained, largely middle-class, well-educated and low-profile group numbering only 19,000 people. Proportionally small and politically silent, the Chinese had yet to reach the critical threshold of being a force in the ethnic mosaic of New Zealand.

The 1987 Immigration Policy Change

As always, the single most important determining factor of Chinese migration to New Zealand is the government's immigration policy. The 1987 Act should be seen in the context of the extensive deregulation program introduced by the Fourth Labor Government which came to power in 1984. The government boldly embarked upon the radical path of economic restructuring to stimulate local economy and attract international investment. An innovative immigration policy was part of this larger program of social reform, necessary to offset the effect of a decade of continuous negative migration, with a net loss averaging 18,000 a year (Lidgard et al., 1998).

To offset this brain drain and to increase New Zealand's competitive edge, the 1987 Act boldly declared that "the selection of new immigrants would be based on criteria of personal merit without discrimination on grounds of race, national or ethnic origin," thus opening the country to "non-traditional" immigrants (Trlin and Spoonley, 1997). The Chinese, mostly re-migrants from other parts of the Chinese diaspora, saw New Zealand as a democratic society with an open economy and which welcomed skilled migrants. Many saw it as a land that is less economically competitive than some other countries but which offers superior lifestyle and good opportunities. Most of them migrated to New Zealand largely unaware of the closed and unexamined chapter of its racist past.

DEMOGRAPHIC CHANGE AND EMPLOYMENT PROFILE

The arrival of middle-class Chinese from various Asian countries had dramatic impacts on New Zealand's demography, especially because the base number of the Chinese population was so small. Census returns in 1991 show that the number of Chinese rose by more than 100 percent, to about 40,000, or 1.1 percent of the country's total population of 3.2 million. By 1996, the Chinese population doubled yet again, to 81,309 persons (about 2.2 percent of the country's total population of 3.6 million) (figure 14.1). This total includes over 16,000 persons (about 20 percent) who are part-Chinese, e.g., European-Chinese, Maori-Chinese, or Samoan-Chinese.

A significant feature of the New Zealand Chinese community is its "rawness," with overseas-born immigrants who had arrived in within ten years (59 percent) far outnumbering both the locally born (about 28 percent) and the overseas born who had been resident for more than a decade (about 12 percent) (figure 14.2). Immigrants from Taiwan, the People's Republic of China and Hong Kong made up most of the new arrivals from 1986 to 1996 (figure 14.3). Thanks to the immigration policy's bias towards "quality" immigrants, most of these new arrivals came from urban centers and are highly educated professionals with transferable skills and business experiences (Vasil and Yoon, 1996). Instead of being economic refugees in search of a higher standard of living, the new Chinese migrants are mostly "reluctant exiles" (Skeldon, 1994) who left their countries of origin with ambivalent feelings. Quite often, these migrants left homelands that have enjoyed a significantly higher GNP than New Zealand.

Migrants from Hong Kong mostly came in search of a political haven when China's 1997 takeover loomed large and ominous. Taiwanese migrants shared similar, but less immediate, political worries. Many came in search of a better education for their children and a more relaxed lifestyle for themselves. However, the majority of them also realized that they were giving up

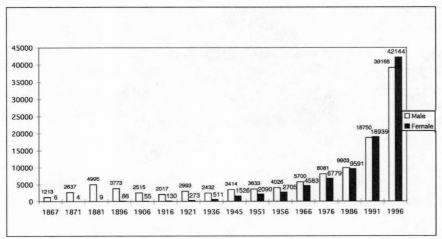

Figure 14.1. Chinese Population in New Zealand by Sex, 1867–1996 (Source: New Zealand Census, 1871–1996)

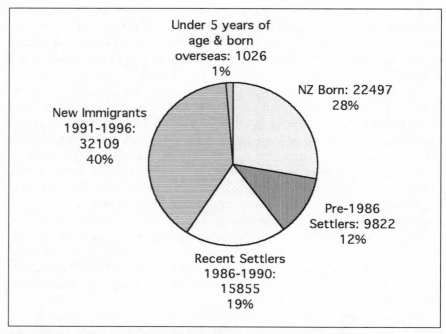

Figure 14.2.   Chinese Population in New Zealand by Periods of Migration (Source: New Zealand Census,1996)

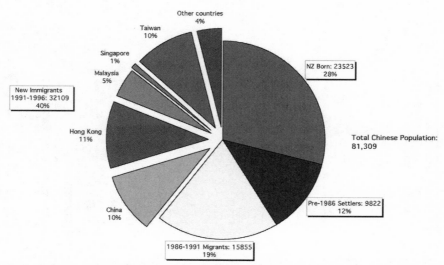

Figure 14.3.   New Chinese Immigrants in New Zealand by Previous Country of Residence (Source: New Zealand Census,1996)

a higher standard of living and higher income in leaving the vibrant and rapidly expanding economies of Asia (Friesen and Ip, 1997).

The 1996 age and gender profile shows that the Chinese are significantly younger than the national average. Most of the New Zealand Chinese are below 50 and belong to the working age group. This is to be expected of a community with a preponderance of new immigrants recruited by an immigration policy especially favoring the young and skilled. However, a closer examination of the gender mix reveals some worrying signs of gender imbalance, with the female population prominently outstripping the male population in the age cohorts of 20–29, 30–39 and 40–49 (figure 14.4). The shortfall of the number of Chinese men seems to be an indication of the "astronaut" phenomenon when men return to their country of origin to continue their business, supporting their families in New Zealand by overseas funds because there is no work for them locally.

The employment status profile of 1996 further supports this theory. Although only 8 percent of the new Chinese immigrants reported that they were officially "unemployed and actively seeking work," over 60 percent of them were "not in the labor force." Only 15 percent of the new immigrants were "full-time and salary earners" and 6 percent of them were full-time self-employed (figure 14.5). In August 1998, the new Minister of Immigration admitted that an immigration policy blunder had left "hundreds of highly skilled settlers facing the prospect of never working in their chosen profession in New Zealand."

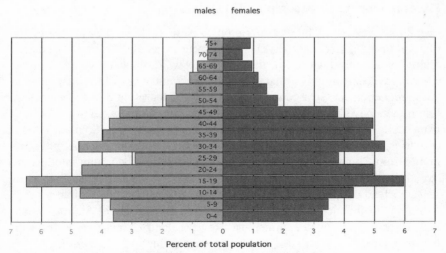

Figure 14.4.   Chinese Population in New Zealand by Age and Sex, 1996 (Source: New Zealand Census,1996)

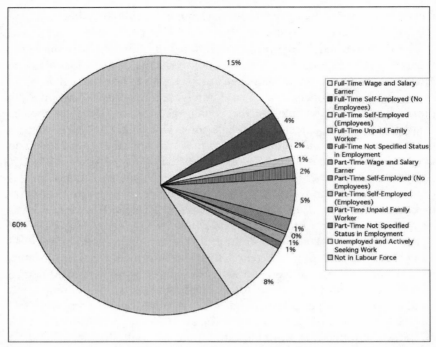

Figure 14.5.   Chinese Population in New Zealand Resident Less than Ten Years by Employment Status (Source: New Zealand Census, 1996)

Places of Origin and Geographical Distribution

In the two waves of Chinese migration to New Zealand, the sources of immigrant origin differ markedly. Up to as recently as the 1987 policy change, the overwhelming majority of the Chinese New Zealanders were Cantonese speakers whose forefathers had come to the country as gold miners or market-gardeners from Guangdong. From 1987 to the present day, the sources of immigrants have been much more diverse. Recent Chinese immigrants came from Hong Kong, Taiwan, Malaysia, Singapore, and other Southeast Asian countries, as well as from the People's Republic of China. Significantly, migrants from China in the last decade are more likely to be young intellectuals from large Chinese cities like Beijing, Shanghai, and Guangzhou (Trlin et al., 1998) instead of from the old "home villages" of rural South China.

Similar to their counterparts who migrated to the United States, Canada and Australia, the nineteenth-century New Zealand Chinese came from the overpopulated, impoverished and war-torn province of Guangdong. While most of the overseas Chinese in general came from the Four Counties (Siyi) of Yunping (Enping), Hoiping (Kaiping), Sunwui (Xinhui) and Toishan (Tai-shan) in Guangdong, situated on the southern coast, many of the early gold miners to New Zealand came from Upper Poonyu (Panyu) county (Ng, 1993), which was poorer and less developed. All these early migrants spoke the dialects of the Pearl River Delta: variants of the Cantonese dialect, which are often mutually unintelligible, thus further accentuating isolation. However, the Chinese population in New Zealand remained so very small that they never experienced violent conflicts similar to the "Tong wars" which tore the American Chinese communities apart.

Spatial Distribution

Since the great majority of the early Chinese came as gold miners, they were heavily concentrated in the goldfields in the South Island, mainly in Otago, Southland, and on the West Coast. The Roundhill goldfields of Riverton, near Invarcargill (the country's southernmost city), was nicknamed "Little Canton" in the 1880s because over 2,000 Chinese miners worked there. It was, incidentally, the world's southernmost Chinese settlement of the time.

Owing to the anti-Chinese legislation, the Chinese population dwindled markedly, with elderly miners dying off in destitution and younger ones driven off by both the depletion of the gold and the virulent racist social climate. The Chinese drifted northwards, moving into the growing cities. Similar to their North American and Australian counterparts, the New Zealand Chinese sold their labor in menial jobs that were too tedious and unpleasant for the mainstream population to pick up. Many became laundrymen. They also quickly established themselves in the niche of growing vegetables (called market-gardening in New Zealand), which was too labor intensive to appeal to the British settlers who preferred dairy farming and animal husbandry.

The early decades of the twentieth century saw the Chinese moving into various cities like Dunedin and Christchurch in the South Island, and Wellington and Auckland in the North Island. The outbreak of the Second World War and New Zealand's becoming an ally of the United States gave an unprecedented opportunity to the Chinese: their vegetables were designated "essential supplies" for the Allies. This both raised their status and gave them a ready market with a guaranteed good income (Ip, 1990).

Chinese Enclaves

By this time, Chinese refugee women and children and babies born in New Zealand were officially given permanent residency, in 1947. This marked the beginning of a real Chinese settlers' community in the country (Ip, 1998a).

Although the population was still too small for "Chinatowns" to emerge, certain streets within the biggest cities began to take on clear Chinese flavors. Among these were Walker Street of Dunedin, Haining Street of Wellington, and Grey's Avenue of Auckland. The headquarters of various clan associations were usually located there. One or more Chinese supply shops run by merchant-community leaders (such as Sew-Hoy of Dunedin, Joe L. Choy of Wellington, and Wah-Lee and the Doo of Auckland) were also there. These shops were multifunctional. Besides supplying essential Chinese produce, dried foods and medicines, they and their owners also served as informal bankers, immigration consultants, job agencies, post offices, boardinghouses for new arrivals, and guarantors for fellow-villagers (Ip, 1990). Very often, private gambling houses as well as Chinese eateries were also located nearby. The same area would also have a Chinese church (Presbyterian churches in both Dunedin and Auckland, and a Baptist church in Wellington). The churches also ran Chinese Sunday schools, which became quite busy as more families arrived in the late 1940s.

These early Chinese communities were spatially compact and socially homogeneous enough to constitute Chinese enclaves in the above-mentioned localities in the early 1950s. They were both places of work and residence, as well as the center of social gathering and entertainment. By then, the Chinese were responsible for producing over 65 percent of the green vegetables of New Zealand and the Chinese Vegetable Growers' Federation had a national membership of several thousand (Sedgwick, 1985). The segregation from mainstream society protected them from the most unpleasant aspects of racism and encouraged solidarity in their niche occupation.

Post-1987 Settlement Configuration

The 1987 policy change had a profound effect on Chinese settlement configuration. Since the new policy favors the highly educated middle-class and business people, most of the new Chinese immigrants are young professionals and are suburban dwellers. They tend to congregate in key suburbs of the big urban centers of the country. According to Statistics New Zealand, in the early 1990s, 97 percent of the total Chinese population lived in urban areas (*New Zealand Now,* 1995). Countrywide, over 90 percent of the Chinese live in the North Island, concentrated heavily in the big cities of Auckland, Christchurch, and Wellington. Fewer than 3 percent of the Chinese lived in rural areas in 1996.

Within the big cities, a definite preference for certain suburbs is quite apparent. For example, in Auckland the Chinese are remarkably concentrated in more affluent suburbs like North Shore, Epsom, Remuera and Howick-

Pakuranga. While the prestigious suburbs close to the city center have always been sought after by upper-middle-class residents irrespective of ethnic origin, the rapid development of Howick-Pakuranga (dubbed the "Far Eastern Suburbs" since the early 1990s) was influenced by the preference of the urban Chinese for brand-new, low-maintenance and brick-and-tile homes. Each of the above-mentioned suburbs is within the school zones of certain well-known state schools. The clustering of the Chinese furthermore reflects the high premium they set on their children's education (Boyer, 1995). Different from the old Chinatown days, these new Chinese enclaves within the suburbs of the big cities are now mainly places of residence, rather than places of work, although one can find the usual Chinese restaurants, supermarkets selling Chinese produce and similar businesses catering to the needs of the local population.

Different places of origin of the Chinese have had little influence on the configuration of settlement. There is little evidence that dialect group or place of origin considerations affect the clustering of the new Chinese immigrants. Very often, the Chinese from Hong Kong, Taiwan, and the local born live next door to each other. The fault lines seems to occur along socioeconomic rankings rather than countries of origin. For example, there are comparatively more immigrants from China and Vietnam living in West Auckland and South Auckland suburbs. But that pattern is most probably due to the generally lower prices of the property there than any preference for living in the same suburb with former compatriots (Friesen and Ip, 1997).

SOCIAL ORGANIZATIONS AND ECONOMIC CHARACTERISTICS

Two golden periods of Chinese association formation have existed in New Zealand history. One lasted from the 1930s to the 1950s, and the other began after 1987. These two periods have coincided with the influx of newcomers who have retained emotional linkages with their homelands, and the presence of a significant percentage of young children whom parents felt needed to be taught Chinese language and Chinese culture. In recent years, professional organizations have formed to bring together groups otherwise divided by their places of origin and associated dialects, although the membership of many Chinese organizations still tends to follow places of origin of their respective presidents and executive committees (Martell, 1998).

Such social organizations have given a considerable amount of social cohesiveness to the Chinese who are non-English speaking and less integrated into the mainstream New Zealand society. In the New Chinese New Zealanders survey (Ip and Friesen, 1997), researchers found that the Taiwanese (who are generally less fluent in English) depend more heavily on their associations and communities for social interaction and information than either the Hong Kong people or the Singaporeans. The Chinese from English-speaking backgrounds, by contrast, tend to be more active in mainstream community groups, such as church groups, school boards, and parent-teacher associations. The Hwa Hsia Society, representing 4,000 Taiwanese households in Auckland, remains numerically the largest Chinese organization in New Zealand, and gives the Taiwanese a remarkable degree of social cohesiveness.

None of the associations, including the Hong Kong Business Association, the New Zealand China Business Association, and the more recent New Zealand Taiwan Business Council, engages in any direct investment in China or the wider Asian region. They are more loose social and information networks of like-minded people whose purpose is to facilitate information sharing among members and aid low-level lobbying rather than cooperation in direct investment (Martell, 1998). The known group investments are based on small groups of personal friends and extended family members rather than along association lines.

Political Affiliations and Involvement in New Zealand Politics

The political affiliation of the Chinese associations has always been pro-China—"China" as represented by whichever government is in power. Before the communists came to power in 1949, Chinese New Zealanders were staunchly pro-Guomindang which, until recently, followed Dr. Sun Yat-sen's view of the overseas Chinese as the "mothers of the [Republican] Revolution," a source of honor for many Chinese abroad. When New Zealand switched political recognition from Taiwan to Beijing in 1972, there was much frustration and feeling of betrayal among the old Chinese New Zealanders. By the 1990s, however, Chinese associations tended to support different home governments. On the whole, political affiliations of the Chinese associations in New Zealand have played only a minor role in these organizations. Most of them are now more interested in promoting their own philanthropic profile and cultural programs.

Since New Zealand has a full-fledged democratic tradition, it is possible for all minority groups to try to seek their fair share of political limelight. The option to participate in the democratic process means that many Chinese immigrants can enjoy more political opportunities than they did in their homelands. Homeland politics, therefore, take a back seat to interest in New Zealand society and local politics. In the election campaigns preceding the 1996 General Election, the Chinese communities were buzzing with unprecedented electioneering activities. For the first time there existed a sizeable population of about 80,000 Chinese, and the introduction of the MMP (mixed-members-proportional) system seemed to give new openings for minority groups (Zhang and Ip, 1996). A racist revival earlier in the year, whipped up by populist politicians scapegoating immigrants, also helped to forge the political consciousness of the Chinese. Two new ethnic political parties were formed, and both major parties, National and Labour, put Chinese candidates on their "party list" in order to draw Chinese voters. In the end, Pansy Wong entered Parliament and became the country's first ever Chinese MP as a list candidate of the National Party. Her election raised the level of political consciousness of the Chinese to a new height.

INTRA-DIASPORIC LINKAGES AND ADAPTIVE STRATEGIES

One of the most noticeable features among the new Chinese settlers in New Zealand is their "frequent flyer" behavior of shuttling across the Pacific for family visits and business deals. Socially, the transnational movements of the new migrants have generated negative comments about their perceived "lack of commitment to New Zealand" (in the words of the populist anti-immigration politician, Winston Peters). In reality, the unsavory image of the "astronaut parent" and the "parachute kid" (see Ma, chapter 1) provides a clue to understanding the intra-diasporic linkages that new immigrants are trying to forge as part of their survival strategies. Analysis of data on long-term external migration of new migrants in the last ten years reveals that the Chinese seldom depart New Zealand permanently or for more than twelve months (Ip, 1997). Chinese from the major source countries of Asian migrants—China, Hong Kong and Taiwan—had comparatively low long-term departure rates. In comparison, citizens of Britain have been the most fluid and transient group, both numerically and percentage-wise. Half of the British migrants in the last decade eventually went home, far out-numbering any group from Asia.

On the other hand, the new Asian immigrants are undoubtedly among the most mobile when short-term movements are examined. Both Taiwan and Hong Kong have short-term departures that are 300 percent higher than their respective long-term arrival numbers during the same period. Highly significant is the fact that citizens of Korea have an even higher rate of short-term departure, and the "frequent flyer" characteristics are also shared by the new arrivals from South Africa. It should be pointed out that most of these new migrants targeted by the post-1986 policies are young, highly educated and highly trained professionals, technocrats and business entrepreneurs. Their transferable skills and internationally recognized credentials which made them qualified to enter New Zealand also make them highly desirable workers to many other countries. The educated middle class has always been the most socially mobile group, irrespective of ethnicity. Based on New Zealand's limited conditions of international exposure, it is widely accepted that young Kiwis newly equipped with university degrees should "do their OE," i.e., acquire overseas experience for several years before returning to settle. The frequent circulatory movements of the new Chinese immigrants are common characteristics shared among this social group from across ethnic and national boundaries. Therefore, the departures of the new Chinese migrants might well share similar features with the popular phenomenon of educated young New Zealanders going overseas. Both groups are motivated by the desire to seek international work experience and wider opportunities.

Multi-locality Strategy

In spite of the New Zealand government's original intention of recruiting Asian talent to jumpstart the economy, the general picture among Chinese new business migrants is grim and anecdotes about frustrated Asian business migrants abound (Chapple, 1992; Jones, 1991). The smallness of the New Zealand population (3.6 million in the latest census of 1996), the high cost of freight in importing and exporting, and the inflexibility of the government bureaucracy have combined to ensure that new Chinese entrepreneurs would feel hampered in efforts to start new ventures. On a practical level, lack of English language fluency and the unfamiliarity with local council bylaws have stumped many entrepreneurial initiatives. The lack of published standard guidelines on general business regulations and tariffs has convinced many new immigrants that the government is only paying lip service to their promise of helping Asian business people forge trade linkages (Friesen and Ip, 1997).

Faced with the threat of prolonged unemployment and repeated failures in starting their own businesses, many new Chinese migrants feel that they have no option but to become "returnees." Shuttling across the Pacific became a survival strategy. The income earner goes back to the country of origin to pick up their former business or engage in ventures in a familiar economic climate, and supports his/her family left in New Zealand with overseas funds (Lidgard, 1996; Boyer, 1995). In many ways this strategy is similar to the old practice of the nineteenth century, when New Zealand was dubbed "New Gold Hill" and the Chinese men migrated as bachelor itinerant gold miners, supporting their families in South China with regular remittances. At the turn of the century, entire villages in the Pearl River Delta were kept prosperous by remittances from the goldfields of Australia, North America, and New

Zealand. At the turn of a new millennium, we witness the reverse phenomenon of Chinese migrants working in Asia, where the economy is expanding faster and where jobs are more plentiful, supporting their families in Canada, Australia and New Zealand.

Going hand in hand with the shuttling between the homeland and the new country of adoption is the building up of multi-locality networks among members of the extended family. Comparatively few new immigrants have their extended families coming to New Zealand with them (Friesen and Ip, 1997). Instead, many new Chinese immigrants have siblings and parents located either in their countries of origin or in various Pacific Rim countries like Australia and Canada rather than in New Zealand. This phenomenon is highly significant and has far-reaching implications for the future of diasporic networks.

CHINESE IDENTITY IN A BICULTURAL NATION

The identity of the Chinese community is necessarily defined by the dominant majority of New Zealand. While many of the immigrant-receiving countries like the United States, Canada, and Australia are officially multicultural, New Zealand is bicultural. The 1840 Treaty of Waitangi gave the sovereignty of the country to the British Crown and also established the partnership between Maori and Pakeha (the word for non-Maori, and at that time denoting the British). For the Chinese as well as other non-British immigrants, the trouble is that they cannot be sure that "Pakeha" includes them as well (Ip, 1998b). To complicate matters further, New Zealand has no written constitution, and the cryptic document of 1840, signed by some 140 Maori chieftains, is widely regarded as the "embryonic constitution" and "the founding document of the nation" (Melbourne, 1995). Since the very presence of the Chinese was considered a historical mistake that threatened the racial and cultural purity of New Zealand, British culture was deemed unquestionably superior right up to the 1970s, and "Chineseness" was often defined in negative ways.

Another obstacle that hampered formation of Chinese community identity is perceived as the geographical remoteness of New Zealand. The idea of the distant island nation combined with restrictive government immigration policies meant that Chinese New Zealanders were cut off from Chinese communities and migrant populations which might help them to be more self-aware: restrictive immigration meant that the community had no new blood for decades. Devoid of any better frame of reference, the Chinese learned to see themselves through European eyes and measure themselves by European standards. Chinese values soon became associated with everything second-rate, backward, and unsophisticated (Ip, 1996). The policy of assimilation pursued by a government absolutely convinced of the superiority of British culture ensured that the Chinese, like the Maori, lost much of the pride in their culture as well as their language competence. For example, recently available archival materials reveal that the 1946 Fraser government covertly sabotaged the Chinese associations' efforts to bring in Chinese teachers for language classes for children. The government felt that these teachers (and Chinese schools in general) would teach Chinese values and thus undermine the children's process of assimilation into British culture (Sedgewick, 1985).

No Assimilation Possible

While their "Chineseness" was almost totally lost, the Chinese New Zealanders can never be fully assimilated by mainstream New Zealand society. The issue is a racial/biological one: the very racial homogeneity of New Zealand has served to mark the Chinese apart. Since New Zealand has such a preponderance of descendants from Britain, the Asian Mongoloid physical features of the Chinese serve to ensure that the Chinese are always regarded as "foreign" and "different."

Chinese New Zealanders have a more marginalized position than their counterparts in the United States and Canada, partly because their country is far more monocultural and has proportionally far fewer immigrants who belong to "other ethnic groups." A case in point is the census questionnaire. All residents of New Zealand can choose to tick their own ethnic group. There are boxes for groups including: New Zealand European/Pakeha, Maori, Chinese, Indian, as well as smaller groups like Poles, Dutch, German, etc. In all the European groups, it is common practice for all the younger people (especially the local-born ones) to identify themselves as "New Zealand European/Pakeha," leaving only their older (usually immigrant) parents or grandparents claiming to be "Poles," "Irish" or "Dutch." With the Chinese, even the fifth generation Chinese New Zealanders will tick themselves as "Chinese" since there is no alternative box marked "Chinese New Zealanders." In this case, their Chineseness is reinforced by government official categorization. The census survey 2001 used the same ethnic categories.

The 1990s: New Immigrants and Cultural Revival

The arrival of new Chinese immigrants in the 1990s witnessed much more concerted effort to enhance the "Chineseness" of the community. In the media arena, new Chinese immigrants especially have found a forum for representation in local Chinese radio stations and newspapers (usually weeklies), established in major cities. The largest radio station is in Auckland, broadcasting 24 hours a day. By 1999, two Chinese daily newspapers were operating steadily: both the *Sing Tao Daily* and the *Independence Daily* are Auckland-centered and distributed throughout the country. Both the local newspapers and the radio stations appear to be well subscribed, especially by new immigrants who do not usually use the English language media. Most of the weeklies are free, supported by advertisers who cater specially to the Chinese niche market. At present, there are at least six free Chinese weeklies in Auckland, and one each in Wellington and Christchurch. Their existence suggests that there must be a sizable number of new arrivals in these cities who are dependent on the Chinese media, thus making them viable ventures.

The Chinese Christian churches, Buddhist temples, and Taoist temples also play their part in enriching spiritual life and enhancing Chinese identity. In addition to religious guidance, each of these religious organizations, together with the numerous place-of-origin Chinese associations, offers Chinese language classes for young people. While most of the classes teach Mandarin, quite a number also teach Cantonese, serving mainly the local Chinese as well as the migrants from Hong Kong. The variety of these religious and educational groups is a fascinating window on the diversity within the New Zealand Chinese community today. Each is a haven, both spiritual and emotional, for the new migrants who are not securely networked into mainstream New Zealand. Each will play its part in enhancing Chinese identity and a sense of pride in Chinese culture.

Relationship with the Indigenous Maori

A great potential hurdle that the Chinese have to overcome is regaining acceptance by the indigenous Maori people, who make up 14 percent of the total population and are becoming increasingly involved in national politics. Historically, the Chinese and the Maori were once close, when both were downtrodden and marginalized. Chinese market-gardeners used to employ Maori helpers and intermarriages were quite common. However, in the 1980s, with the influx of the "new Asians" under the Business Immigration Policy and the Points System, Maori attitudes took a U-turn.

According to some Maori activists, the Treaty of Waitangi was a contract allowing migrants from the United Kingdom only (Walker, 1995). Therefore, the immigration of any other people without extensive consultation with the Maori was a direct affront. The government's 1987 immigration policy of welcoming "quality migrants" was attacked as "a covert strategy to suppress the counter-hegemonic struggle of the Maori by swamping the country with outsiders who are not obliged to them by the Treaty" (Walker, 1995).

This is an example of the widely held view that the arrival of the middle-class Chinese and other Asian immigrants would subvert the Maori struggle for greater power and equality. Some observers made worried comments about the apparent incompatibility of the middle-class Chinese and the rural Maori and argued that immigrants should be tested on their understanding of the Treaty of Waitangi and Maori values before they are granted residence visas.

CONCLUSION

The first Chinese arrived in New Zealand not long after the British settlers, but were relegated to the lowest rung of society. Under the highly restrictive anti-Chinese legislation, their group remained a pitiful, stunted, and "broken-stem" bachelor community for many decades until the Second World War, when their families were allowed to join them. When a new breed of middle-class immigrants came with the relaxation of immigration policy in 1987, the influx brought about strong anti-Asian backlash from both the Europeans and the Maori. Many of these new Chinese immigrants are more transnationals than settlers. They are reluctant to relinquish their homeland businesses, professional networks and client base. Frequent commuting is their normal behavior, to keep up intra-diasporic linkages. They are determined to keep their options open, especially when their new homeland is not totally welcoming.

From 1996 to 1998, the annual arrival figures of the Chinese from various home bases slumped sharply, partly due to the depressed New Zealand economy. A less stringent immigration policy has been put in place since early 1999 and may encourage more immigrants to come in, although the policy is unlikely to result in any numbers close to the previous robust scale. The racist revival, the lack of economic opportunities, as well as the bleak employment situation combine to make New Zealand unappealing as a destination for settlement.

The slowness of the government in establishing multiculturalism as a social policy should remain one of the greatest worries of Chinese New Zealanders. Like the proverbial guest arriving in the middle of a domestic argument, the immigrant communities are caught in between. The long-term future of the Chinese is closely linked with the potential of solutions to the race issues of New Zealand. Where the country's non-European, non-Maori citizens should fit in an officially bicultural policy is a highly problematic issue (Ip, 1998b). At the dawn of the twenty-first century, ethnic diversity is a fact which New Zealand has yet to address.

The future of the Chinese New Zealanders is also closely tied with the ongoing reshaping of the country's national identity. New Zealand has been extremely slow in accepting the reality of its geopolitical position as an Asian-Pacific (instead of a European) country. Whether the Chinese can play a more central role in the country's political and social scene largely depends on whether New Zealand truly embraces diversity and regards non-British and non-Maori nationals as equal New Zealanders.

REFERENCES

Boyer, Tania. 1995. "Home Sweet Home?: An Analysis of Taiwanese Immigration since 1986, and the Present Status of the Taiwanese Community in Auckland," in *An Ethno-Geography of Taiwanese, Japanese and Filipino Immigrants in Auckland.* Auckland, New Zealand: University of Auckland.

Brawley, Sean. 1995. *The White Peril: Foreign Relations and Asian Immigration to Australasia and North America 1919–1978.* Sydney, Australia: University of New South Wales Press.

Chapple, Max. 1992. "The Wok Ethic," *The Metro,* Auckland, October 1992: 91–98.

Fong, Bickleen Ng. 1959. T*he Chinese in New Zealand.* Hong Kong: Hong Kong University Press.

Friesen, Ward and Manying Ip. 1997. "New Chinese New Zealanders: Profile of a Transnational Community in Auckland." *Aotearoa New Zealand APMRN (Asia-Pacific Migration Research Network) Journal,* Massey University, October, 1997: 3–19.

Greif, Stuart W. 1974. *The Overseas Chinese in New Zealand.* Singapore: Asia Pacific Press.

Ip, Manying. 1990. *Home Away from Home, Lifestories of Chinese Women in New Zealand.* Auckland, New Zealand: New Women's Press.

_____. 1995. "Chinese New Zealanders: Old Settlers and New Immigrants," in Stuart W. Greif, ed., *Immigration and National Identity in New Zealand,* Palmerston North, New Zealand: Dunmore Press, 161–203.

_____. 1996. *Dragons on the Long White Cloud: The Making of Chinese New Zealanders.* Auckland, New Zealand: Tandem Press.

_____. 1997. "The Successful Settlement of Migrants and Relevant Factors for Setting Immigration Targets," in *Population Conference Proceedings, People, Communities, Growth.* Wellington, New Zealand: Population Conference, New Zealand Immigration Service.

_____. 1998a. "Racism, Gender and the Politics of Migration," in Rosemary DuPlessis and Lynne Alice, eds., *Feminist Thought in Aotearoa New Zealand: Connections and Differences.* Auckland, New Zealand: Oxford University Press, 43–51.

_____. 1998b. "The Legal and Political Status of Chinese New Zealanders: Implications of the Treaty of Waitangi," in Wang Ling-chi and Wang Gungwu, eds., *The Chinese Diaspora: Selected Essays, Volume II.* Singapore: Times Academic Press, 217–230.

Jones, Lloyd. 1991. "Too Tough to Make Money in New Zealand, Say Business Migrants." *New Zealand Herald* (September 26), 1991.

Lidgard, Jacqueline M. 1996. *East Asian Migration to Aoteoroa/New Zealand: Perspectives of Some New Arrivals*. Hamilton, New Zealand: Waikato University.

Lidgard, Jacqueline, Richard Bedford and Joanne Goodwin. 1998. *International Migration from Northeast Asia and Population Change in New Zealand, 1986 to 1996*. Hamilton, New Zealand: Waikato University.

Martell, Owen. 1998. *Chinese Association in New Zealand 1860s to Present*. Unpublished Master's thesis, Department of Chinese, Asian Languages and Literatures, University of Auckland.

McKinnon, Malcolm. 1996. *Immigrants and Citizens: New Zealanders and Asian Immigration in Historical Context*. Wellington, New Zealand: Victoria University.

Melbourne, Hineani. 1995. *Maori Sovereignty, the Maori Perspective*. Auckland, New Zealand: Penguin.

Murphy, Nigel. 1997. *A Guide to Laws and Policies Relating to the Chinese in New Zealand 1871–1996*. Wellington, New Zealand: New Zealand Chinese Association Inc.

New Zealand Herald [Auckland]. 1991. "Lloyd Jones 'Too tough to make money in NZ says business migrants,'" September 26, 1991, A5.

New Zealand Now: Asian New Zealanders. 1995. Statistics New Zealand, ed. Wellington, New Zealand.

Ng, James. 1993. *Windows on a Chinese Past,* Volume 1. Dunedin, New Zealand: Otago Heritage Books.

O'Connor, P. S. 1968. "Keeping New Zealand White, 1908–1920," *The New Zealand Journal of History* 2 (1): 41–65.

Price, Charles A. 1974. *The Great White Walls Are Built*. Canberra, Australia: Australian National University Press.

Sedgwick, Charles P. 1985. "Persistence, Change and Innovation: the Social Organisation of the New Zealand Chinese 1866–1976," *Journal of Comparative Family Studies* 16 (2): 205–229.

Skeldon, Ronald, ed. 1994. *Reluctant Exiles? Migration from Hong Kong and the New Overseas Chinese*. Hong Kong: Hong Kong University Press.

Thomson, Barbara. 1993. *Ethnic Groups in New Zealand—A Statistical Profile*. Wellington, New Zealand: Department of Internal Affairs.

Trlin, Andrew and Paul Spoonley. 1997. *New Zealand and International Migration*. Palmerston North, New Zealand: Massey University Press.

Trlin, Andrew, Anne Henderson and Regina Pernice. 1998. "Asian Immigration, Public Attitudes and Immigration Policy: Patterns and Responses in New Zealand," in Eleanor Laquian, Apro-diciao Laquian and Terry McGee, eds., *The Silent Debate: Asian Immigration and Racism in Canada*. Vancouver, B.C.: University of British Columbia Press, 214–226.

Vasil, Raj and Hong-Key Yoon. 1996. *Asian New Zealanders*. Wellington, New Zealand: Institute of Policy Studies.

Walker, Ranginui. 1995. "Immigration Policy and the Political Economy of New Zealand," in Stuart William Greif, ed., *Immigration and National Identity in New Zealand*. Palmerston North, New Zealand: Dunmore Press.

Zhang, Yongjin and Manying Ip. 1996. *The Chinese Community and New Zealand Politics*. Auckland, New Zealand: Auckland University Press.

15

New Middle-Class Chinese Settlers in Australia and the Spatial Transformation of Settlement in Sydney

Chung-Tong Wu

Since the 1980s Asian migrants have become the majority of all permanent settlers coming to Australia. Large numbers of Chinese from various Asian states have made Australia a new and dynamic center of Chinese transmigration and an important place in the Chinese diaspora. The settlement of Asian migrants in Australia reflects the success of Australia's Multicultural Policy, which the government initiated in 1979 and formally instituted with the establishment of the Office of Multicultural Affairs in 1987 and the National Agenda for a Multicultural Australia in 1989. Consistently updated through the 1990s, these policies foster respect for cultural diversity and racial tolerance in Australia, and have encouraged Asian migration. The multicultural platform also represents a dramatic shift in the government's position by comparison to the "White Australia Policy," which prevailed from the late nineteenth century to 1973. The Multicultural Policy accepts and promotes the rights of all Australians to express and share their cultural heritage, by contrast to pro-white immigrant and assimilationist expectations of the previous era. Despite noisy backlash in the 1990s, especially by the anti-immigration "One Nation" Party, which has advocated a hostile attitude toward Asian migrants and a policy of "zero net immigration," migrants from Asia have incrementally increased and have become the largest immigrant group in Australia.[1]

This chapter briefly examines the changes in origins of Australian immigrants, and explores the settlement experience from the perspective of the migrants based on a survey of recent Asian migrants to Australia. Many studies of Asian migrants in Australia have focused on the composition of migrant groups and their settlement experiences (Coughlan, 1992; Adelman et al., 1994). While this study confirms previous findings, it extends previous research by explicitly investigating the migrants' perceptions of Australian society before and after arrival, and how perceptions may influence the individual's settlement experience in Australia. The analysis focuses on Chinese migrants, from China, Hong Kong, and Taiwan, and concludes with an analysis of the spatial dynamics of Asian and Chinese settlement in Sydney.[2] The study sample was drawn from recent Asian migrants resident in five state capital cities in Australia, and, where appropriate, interviews were conducted in the migrant's native language. Before discussing the survey and its findings, the next section provides a brief sketch of the changes in the source of migrant settlers to Australia and the significant economic changes that have transformed Australia during the same period.

CHANGES IN SOURCE COUNTRIES OF MIGRANTS TO AUSTRALIA

Beginning in the late 1970s, a sea change occurred in the source countries of migrants to Australia (see table 15.1). While no single Asian country has become the largest source of migrants, the combined contribution of Asian source countries has risen dramatically since the 1970s. Of the top ten source countries of immigration since then, more than half have been Asian nations. Equally remarkable is that the background of migrants has shifted to individuals with professional training, tertiary education, and/or extensive business and managerial experience (Inglis and Wu, 1992). As a consequence, during the final quarter of the century Australia became the recipient of large numbers of well-educated and professionally trained Asian migrants.

During the same two decades, the economy of Australia experienced fundamental economic restructuring, transforming from a resource and manufacturing-based economy to one that is more reliant on services sector industries, and especially international banking and finance. At the same time, the government initiated a series of economic reforms aimed at making Australia's economy more internationally competitive. The Australian government floated the Australian currency, lifted restrictions on foreign banks, and promoted privatization of state-owned assets. These moves have brought about fundamental changes in the economy and the employment prospects of different economic sectors. Between 1970 and 1990, a quarter of a million jobs in manufacturing disappeared. Australian cities transformed, and sought foreign direct investment in international service sector industries. Employment in finance, insurance, real estate, tourism and other professional services boomed in many of Australia's state capital cities, with Sydney becoming the premier commercial center of Australia. The results of this round of restructuring have yielded the "new Australian economy" (Edwards, 1999). Significant changes in the Australian economy have also meant that the employment opportunities and skills required to drive the economy are different, leading the government

Table 15.1. Settler Arrivals to Australia: Top Ten Source Countries of Birth

1968–1969			1978–1989		
Country of Birth	No.	%	Country of Birth	No.	%
UK & Ireland	80,205	45.7	United Kingdom	13,256	19.7
Italy	13,175	7.5	Vietnam	10,776	16.1
Yugoslavia	12,047	7.1	New Zealand	10,776	16.0
Greece	11,489	6.5	South Africa	2,509	3.7
New Zealand	6,243	3.6	Malaysia	1,683	2.5
India	3,494	2.0	Italy	1,282	1.9
Germany	3,490	2.0	Yugoslavia	1,269	1.9
Czechoslovakia	3,448	2.0	Philippines	1,256	1.9
USA	3,126	1.8	Hong Kong	1,180	1.8
Netherlands	2,870	1.6	Lebanon	1,134	1.7
Subtotal	139,947	79.7	Subtotal	45,173	67.2
Others	35,710	20.3	Others	22,019	32.8
Total	175,657	100.00	Total	67,192	100.00

1988–1989			1998–1999		
Country of Birth	No.	%	Country of Birth	No.	%
United Kingdom	23,933	16.5	New Zealand	18,677	22.2
New Zealand	23,539	16.2	United Kingdom	8,785	10.4
Philippines	9,204	6.3	China	6,133	7.3
Vietnam	7,971	5.5	South Africa	5,024	6.0
Malaysia	7,681	5.3	Philippines	3,318	3.9
Hong Kong	7,307	5.0	Yugoslavia	2,912	3.5
Ireland	4,045	2.8	India	2,557	3.0
China	3,819	2.6	Indonesia	2,491	3.0
India	3,109	2.1	Vietnam	2,137	2.5
South Africa	3,024	2.1	Hong Kong (SAR)	1,918	2.3
Subtotal	93,632	64.4	Subtotal	53,952	64.1
Other	51,684	35.6	Other	30,191	35.9
Total	145,316	100.00	Total	84,143	100.00

Source: Department of Immigration and Multicultural Affairs, Australia (1999) *Immigration Update* (June Quarter 1999), Canberra, p. 16. Taiwan is not identified as a separate entity in the available statistics.

to emphasize migration policies that prefer skilled workers and business professionals. These changes have resulted in attracting large numbers of educated Asian migrants with diverse business and professional backgrounds.

PROFILE OF THE RESPONDENTS

The analysis in this chapter is based on a subset of 452 interviews out of a total of 1,217 respondents drawn from five state capitals in Australia: Adelaide,

Brisbane, Melbourne, Perth, and Sydney. The distribution of the sample reflects the distribution of the relevant Asian groups in Australia and the relative size of these groups in each of the five cities. The study included recent migrants from China, Hong Kong, Japan, Philippines, Taiwan, and Vietnam. While this chapter focuses on those who came from China, Hong Kong and Taiwan, it makes comparisons with the other Asian groups included in the study where appropriate. Four of these countries were among the top ten source countries of birth in 1988–1989 and in 1998–1999 (see table 15.1).

For the purposes of this study, recent migrants were defined as those having migrated to Australia no more than five years prior to the date of the interviews. Ninety-one percent of the respondents have never moved from the city where they first settled. Of the 92 respondents who had moved since their arrival in Australia, half had moved from small towns in various states to the capital cities. The others moved between states and usually to the capital city of another state. Due to the difficulties in finding comparable numbers of suitable female and male respondents, the completed interviews included more females than males. Respondents ranged in age from 18 to 65, with 57 percent of the respondents in the 25–34 and 35–44 age groups, the age groups most likely to migrate.[3] Given that the great majority of the respondents were in the age groups most likely to be in the workforce and likely to be raising a family, it was not surprising that 63 percent of the respondents were married, and only 3 percent were divorced. Of those who reported they were married, only 14 percent were married in Australia. Among migrants from Taiwan, all were married prior to migration. Those from the Philippines (34 percent) and Vietnam (22 percent) were the most likely to be married in Australia.

One of the enduring stereotypes in Australia about Asian migrants is that they have large families. But the respondents to this study did not fit this image. Nearly 44 percent of the respondents had no children, and of those who had children, the majority had one or two. Only 11 percent of the respondents reported they had four or more children. Among these respondents, most were from Vietnam and the Philippines, both with very large Catholic communities.

Since Australia has well-defined criteria for immigration, the visa categories under which the individual migrated to Australia will have some influence on their expectations and settlement experience (see table 15.2). For example, those who entered Australia under the "family reunion" category clearly had family members in Australia and presumably would have an easier time adjusting than those who came as refugees or other categories. This is not to say any individual migrant may or may not have friends or relatives in Australia prior to migration, but the "family reunion" visa is granted only to those who have relatives in the country. While the largest percentage of the respondents arrived in Australia under the family reunion visa status, it is important to note that this was the most important category for those who came from China.

Table 15.2.   Visa Status among Chinese Migrants (as percent of total)

Country of Origin	Independent Migrant	Business Migrant	Refugee	Family Reunion	Student	Temporary Business	Other
China	9.48	3.79	3.32	32.70	45.97	0.47	4.27
Hong Kong	52.50	14.38	0	20.63	8.13	0	4.37
Taiwan	5.06	73.42	1.27	10.13	7.59	0	2.53
Total (entire study)	19.79	8.99	9.98	33.60	13.19	2.14	9.32
Total (Sydney only)	22.4	9.1	7.6	33.8	16.2	3.8	7.1

Note: Excludes missing values and "Other" category.

The second largest group of migrants by visa category was "independent migrants," whose entry is based on individual education and skills. This category was significant for many migrants coming from Hong Kong, Japan, and the Philippines, reflecting the educational background of the respondents. By way of contrast, among those who first came to Australia as "students," the largest groups were those from China and Japan. Those from China probably came before the Tiananmen incident in 1989, and those from Japan probably came to study English. The predominance of Taiwanese under the category of "business migrants" stands in stark contrast to the lack of the same from the Philippines and Vietnam. Sydney, being the premier commercial center of Australia, has attracted a slightly higher than average percentage of business migrants and "independents." The state of New South Wales, where Sydney is located, attracted 41.8 percent of all settler arrivals and 43.65 percent of all "skilled" arrivals in 1998–1999, in numbers similar to previous years destination (Department of Immigration and Multicultural Affairs, 1999).[4] At the same time it has attracted a smaller percentage of refugees.

Information on the highest level of education attainment among the respondents supports the data on migrant preference for settlement in Sydney (see table 15.3). Among highly educated migrants, Sydney has attracted a disproportionately higher percentage of those who have completed tertiary education and significantly fewer of those who have only trade qualifications or only diplomas or certificates. This is consistent with the situation of larger numbers of migrants who have entered as "independents" settling in Sydney, meaning they have special skills and qualifications highly sought after in Australia's leading city. Among the most highly educated migrants, even by comparison to migrants from Hong Kong and Taiwan, more migrants from China reported having completed tertiary education, at slightly over half of the total respondents (see table 15.3). Australia has its own system of recognition of foreign qualifications, and the migrants do not necessarily have automatic recognition of their educational and work experience, leading to problems which can impede finding suitable employment. This issue is explored later in the chapter.

Two other characteristics distinguish the settlement locations of recent migrants: prior visits to Australia, and housing arrangements in Australia (as determined at the time of interview). Previous visits to Australia provide some indication of prior knowledge of Australia and influence choice of city of settlement. Sixty percent of those who originated from Hong Kong, Japan and Taiwan had visited Australia prior to migration, the majority as tourists. Still, just over three-quarters of the total respondents had not visited Australia prior to their migration. This is not surprising because large numbers of migrants from Vietnam and China were either restricted from travelling abroad or did not have the means to travel abroad. The influence of economic background is also reflected in housing arrangements. Almost a quarter of those respondents originating from Japan owned their homes outright. Some three-quarters of those from Taiwan and Hong Kong owned their homes outright or were in the process of buying. Migrants from China, Vietnam, and the Philippines, by contrast, generally had higher than average rates of renting, reflecting the socioeconomic status of these countries by comparison to the Asian industrialized and newly industrialized economies.

To summarize, there is significant diversity among the respondents. On the whole, the respondents have been in Australia for five years or less, most of them in the age groups 25–44; close to 45 percent have tertiary education; only a quarter of them had visited Australia prior to migration; and most of them are renting. Given the known diversity among the Asian migrants, their settlement experience may show similar diversity. Those who have settled in Sydney have important differences from the overall group. Sydney has attracted more of the business migrants and "independents," more of them have

Table 15.3. Highest Level of Education among Chinese Migrants (percentage distribution by place of origin)

	Primary	Secondary	Tertiary	Dip/Cert	Trade Q	No Formal Ed/Other	Total
China	1.43	19.52	51.90	15.24	7.62	4.29	100.00
Hong Kong	3.11	18.63	47.83	22.36	5.59	2.48	100.00
Taiwan	1.27	32.91	41.77	13.92	5.06	5.06	100.00
Total (entire study)	5.12	27.17	44.59	15.36	5.04	2.73	100.00
Total (Sydney only)	5.1	25.6	52.4	11.1	4.2	1.6	100.00

Source: Interview data.

tertiary education, and many more are renters. This latter aspect is not surprising given that Sydney is the most expensive city in Australia, with its average housing price some 30 to 40 percent higher than the next most expensive city in the country.

MOTIVATIONS FOR MIGRATION AND THE CHOICE OF AUSTRALIA

To better understand the respondents' motivations for moving to Australia, they were asked to identify the three most important reasons that prompted their migration. By far the most important reason given was "family and personal ties," identified by 24.6 percent of the respondents. Education was a close second (22.1 percent), in a distant third was "political reasons" (16.5 percent), and "employment" was the fourth place response (10.4 percent). These reasons reflect the background of the migrants and the visa categories under which they entered Australia. The significance of "political reasons" needs to be understood in light of the places of origins. First, there were Chinese students who were allowed to stay as a consequence of the Tiananmen incident. Second, many of the migrants from Hong Kong were concerned about the return of Hong Kong to China in 1997 (Skeldon, 1994). Third, migrants from Taiwan perceived political instability in cross-strait relations between Taiwan and China due to the occasional "saber rattling" by the PRC. What is striking about the responses is that economic factors, such as "new opportunities" and "employment," were not the most important reasons prompting individuals to leave their home country. These responses are consistent with the characterization of recent migrants to Australia as "new migrants," in that their motivations are not chiefly based on finding employment like the older generation of Asian migrants who came to Australia (Inglis and Wu, 1990). If migration is conceived as the result of a number of interrelated push and pull factors, then the migrants' motivations to leave their home country should be more closely related to the reasons for choosing Australia as the destination.

Responses to reasons for choosing Australia as the destination were consistent with the reasons for leaving their home country, with 36.8 percent of the respondents choosing "family and personal ties" as the chief reason for coming to Australia. The next most important reason indicated by respondents was "favorable physical attributes" (14.1 percent), followed by "government grant of visa" (9.1 percent). Significantly, "future prospect and opportunities for children" was identified by only 6.3 percent of the respondents as the most important reason for choosing Australia. What is striking is that migrants consistently identified Australia's environment and favorable physical attributes—its geography—as important conditions for a favorable migration decision. On the whole, migrants have viewed Australia as an environmentally attractive place, with good future prospects, high quality of living, social equality, and friendly people.[5] Given the legacy of "White Australia" and the recency of its Multicultural Policy, this is a remarkable set of impressions (Walker, 1999). The question then is whether these impressions are confirmed after migration.

SETTLEMENT EXPERIENCE

Based on their stated expectations, nearly 54 percent of migrants surveyed replied that their experiences in Australia had met or fulfilled their expectations since migration. Twenty-eight percent were uncertain and 21 percent reported that their expectations were not fulfilled. On the whole, the expectations fulfilled were highly consistent. Migrants found a better standard or quality of life, much better physical environment, personal fulfillment, political stability and friendly people. These conditions are consistent with their impressions of Australia prior to migration. Worthy of note is the fact that, again, economic advantages or good employment prospects were not mentioned.

Given that at the time of the interviews the respondents had been in the country for a maximum of five years, with 33 percent in the country for two years or less and 14 percent for one year or less, it is not surprising that 28 percent of the respondents were uncertain as to whether their expectations had been fulfilled. For these respondents, the chief reason identified had to do with the fact that they had not yet had time to assess their potential for fulfillment; some were themselves uncertain about their expectations. Language barriers and doubts about the long-term economic prosperity of Australia were the two other factors migrants identified as factors explaining the lack of certainty about fulfilling their expectations.

The 21 percent of respondents who indicated that their expectations were not fulfilled begs questions about the migrants' chief disappointments. As it turns out, in spite of the fact that the economy and employment opportunities were not identified as important influences bearing on the decision to migrate, or the choice of Australia as the destination, they featured importantly among the disappointments, with nearly 40 percent of the respondents concerned with negative economic impacts in the national economy. "Boring life" was an issue of disappointment particularly prominent among the younger age groups (18.9 percent). English proficiency also emerged as an issue for the settlers (4.1 percent), not just as an issue for settlement, as explained in a later section, but also an issue limiting the basis for interaction in Australian society.

Before delving more closely into the responses about disappointments and settlement difficulties, these responses need to be put into context. Twenty-nine percent of the respondents indicated they found settlement "generally more difficult" or "much more difficult" than they thought. Fifteen percent found no difficulties at all and another 19 percent found their settlement generally not difficult. Thirty-three percent found no more difficulties than expected. Consequently, it is important to bear in mind that the issues raised later about settlement difficulties or problems encountered is in the context of close to three-quarters of the respondents who did not find any difficulties or no more than expected settling in Australia.

Most migrants have to search for suitable employment and to do so many had to have their qualifications recognized. The cumbersome nature of this process and its intricacies are some of the chief problems confronting migrants. In response to a question about recognition of qualifications, 16 percent of those from Hong Kong and 20 percent of those from China reported difficulties. Since many of the Chinese who responded were students in Australia, the low percentage, compared to other Asian groups, is not surprising but this is still a significant proportion of the respondents. Hong Kong was part of the British Commonwealth, so many of those with qualifications should have less difficulty seeking recognition. Most migrants came from large cities with lifestyles very different from those in the suburbs of the typical Australian city. This may be the chief reason why a small group of migrants find life in Australia "boring," which probably magnified domestic problems emanating from having to settle in a new society.

Many of the issues identified by the migrants as disappointments are also cited as settlement difficulties (see table 15.4). Proficiency in English and obtaining employment are closely related, as well as possibly personal and family adjustments. Access to public transportation and the difficulties in coming to terms with a more automobile-oriented society are related to the different types of cities in which the migrants have settled.

Although only about 10 percent of the Chinese respondents cited racial discrimination as a primary settlement issue, over 42 percent cited discrimination as the second or third response among settlement difficulties (see table 15.4). A clearer picture emerged when they were asked a direct question. An average of 38 percent of the respondents indicated that they had experienced racial discrimination after settling in Australia. They identified four major types of discrimination: verbal abuse, inequitable treatment in employment and workplace, feeling of being discriminated against, and condescending attitude by service providers. Analysis of these responses by city of residence and by places of origin did not yield statistically significant differences. Nevertheless, for a better understanding of how different groups experienced racial discrimination, it is instructive to note that groups of different origins reported different encounters with

Table 15.4. Settlement Difficulties among Chinese Migrants

First Responses (N = 385)	Second Responses (N = 211)	Third Responses (N = 150)
Language problems (43.9%)	Racial discrimination (20.4%)	Racial discrimination (22.6%)
Obtaining suitable employment (19.8%)	Language problems (18.7%)	Language problems (13.2%)
Racial discrimination (10.1%)	Obtaining suitable employment (14.7%)	Obtaining suitable employment (11.3%)
Personal and family adjustment (8.7%)	Personal and family adjustment (14.2%)	
Insufficient public transportation (4.5%)	Insufficient public transportation (12.3%)	

Source: Interview data.

racial discrimination and with different types of discrimination (see table 15.5). This exploration into what constitutes the experience of racial discrimination and how these experiences differed among the various groups of recent migrants is an attempt to clarify how migrants experience racial discrimination, rather than an examination of its existence (see also Castles, 1992; Pe-Pua et al., 1998).

Table 15.5. Types of Racial Discrimination Encountered by Place of Origin

Country of Origin	% Encountered Discrimination	Types Encountered
Taiwan	43.0	Verbal abuse (40.7%) Feeling of discrimination (18.5%) Unfriendly neighbors (18.5%) Condescending attitudes of service providers (11%)
China	34.6	Inequitable treatment in workplace (40.3%) Verbal abuse (22.6%) Feeling of discrimination (17.7%)
Hong Kong	31.5	Verbal abuse (31.4%) Feeling of discrimination (21.6%) Condescending attitudes of service providers (19.6%)

Source: Interview data.

Among the ethnic Chinese migrants interviewed, those from Taiwan reported the highest levels of encounter with racial discrimination. This situation may be related to language problems, since compared to the other Chinese groups, they had a low (11.4 percent) level of English language proficiency. The other groups assessed their own ability to speak English a great deal better: those from Hong Kong found themselves the most proficient (41.9 percent) compared to immigrants from China (27 percent), who were still twice as likely to find themselves proficient in English than those from Taiwan. Migrants from China reported experiencing the highest level of discrimination in the workplace. These encounters may emanate from two different sources. Those from China reported high educational attainment, over 50 percent with tertiary education. Twenty-seven percent of the Chinese respondents reported they speak English very well or well. It is therefore possible that part of the feeling that one is treated inequitably in the workplace is due to the lack of suitable employment and that one should be treated better because of one's education background and/or the ability to communicate.

Respondents' perceptions about Australia support a more generous view of their overall experience. The importance of examining the responses in the wider context is borne out by the responses to questions about migrants' perceptions of Australia. Tables 15.6 and 15.7 summarize the key responses to questions about Australian society and ways of life, Australians' attitudes towards Asians, perception of opportunities for Asian migrants, and the Australian business climate. Confirming some of their perceptions of Australia prior to migration, the respondents consider Australia to be a fair and open society, a land of opportunities, and a safe country. Depending where the respondent originated from, there are some differences in their perception whether the standard of living in Australia is high. For example, those from Hong Kong tended not to regard the standard of living in Australia as being high. In terms of social welfare provisions, while the migrants generally regard these to be too generous, they do agree they are very good indeed. Migrants considered university access to be much better than their places of origin, they overwhelmingly endorsed multiculturalism, and a majority accept that it is necessary to have good English to get ahead in Australia. The majority of migrants regarded Australians as tolerant of cultural differences and on the whole; yet 40 percent strongly agreed with or agreed with the statement, "Australians are basically racist," over a quarter agreed with the perspective that "Australians are hostile to Asian immigrants," and a third agreed with the view that "Relatively, Asians are treated badly when renting." Clearly, Asian migrants perceive some race-based discrimination, but more research is required to ascertain increasing or decreasing trends of such concerns.

Table 15.6. Migrant Perceptions of Australia

	Strongly Agree/ Agree	Strongly Disagree/ Disagree	Uncertain
Australia is a fair and open society	81.4	11.3	7.3
Australia is a safe country to live in	83.2	10.4	6.2
Australia has a high standard of living	35.3	50.6	15.1
Australian way of life is too easygoing	60.5	24.4	15.1
Australians are hostile to Asian immigrants	27.9	44.1	25.9
Australians are tolerant about cultural differences	61.9	19.0	19.1
Australians are basically racist	40.9	36.1	23.0
Relatively, Asians are treated badly when renting	33.9	27.5	38.6
Multiculturalism is good for Australia	87.8	3.8	8.4
University access is better in Australia than back home	63.6	23.0	13.3
Welfare provisions are too generous in Australia	69.9	19.1	11.0

Source: Interview data.

The work ethic of the migrant experience emerged in migrants' perceptions that the Australian way of life is too easygoing, that Australians value leisure more than work, and that they tend to spend more than they save. Migrants see themselves as taking on jobs that many Australians do not want, and two-thirds of the respondents also agreed that some Asian employers pay unfair wages. While most of the Asian respondents disagreed that it is difficult for Asian migrants to get ahead in Australia, Chinese migrants tended to have a

Table 15.7. Migrant Perception of Business Climate in Australia

	Strongly Agree / Agree	Strongly Disagree/ Disagree	Uncertain
Labor costs are too high in Australia	53.6	31.5	14.8
Unions are too powerful in Australia	62.7	10.4	26.9
Taxes are too high in Australia	59.6	10.2	15.1
Businesses in Australia are over-regulated	65.0	12.2	22.8
Government policies are anti-development	32.4	29.9	37.7
Too much environmental protection in Australia	38.6	37.9	23.5

Source: Interview data.

relatively harsh judgment about the business climate in Australia (see table 15.7). The angst expressed by those from Taiwan who came to Australian chiefly under the business migration scheme was particularly deep. Most of the migrants felt that it was difficult for them to get ahead in Australia, especially for those who do not know English well and that many Asian immigrants work on jobs that Australians do not want. As a group, the Taiwanese tend to consider that business regulations are too complex while taxes and labor costs are too high. They also regard government policies to be too anti-development, reflected in their opinion that there is too much emphasis on environmental protection.

IMPLICATIONS FOR SYDNEY

The data presented above paint an overall picture of Asian migrants and their settlement in Australia. In the discussion so far, data on Sydney have been interspersed with the data on the Chinese migrant groups and the data from the overall study to illustrate the implications for one Australian metropolitan area. Putting these into sharper relief, this section focuses on the spatial implications for Sydney using data on the Chinese migrants as well as the other Asian migrant groups. The state of New South Wales, which includes Sydney, is the preferred destination of more than 40 percent of all settlers migrating to Australia. By the mid-1990s, Sydney was already dubbed by one journalist as the "southern suburb of Asia" (Macken, 1996).

Sydney is a metropolitan area of some 4 million residents dispersed over a large area serviced by several commuter railway lines.[6] Befitting its status as the global city of Australia, Sydney is Australia's favorite tourist destination as well as the leading commercial center. Sydney is the location of 155 foreign banks (headquarters of 39) and the location of 62 percent of regional headquarters of multinational corporations (Department of Urban Affairs and Planning, 1998). The economy of Sydney is now firmly tied to the growth of the banking, finance, real estate, professional services and other services sector industries. Sydney is also the most expensive city in Australia. Its median price of established housing is some 30 percent higher than the second most expensive city, Melbourne. Compared to most other major cities in the world, Sydney has a low population density, with the majority of the population residing in single detached dwellings. High-rise residential developments have chiefly emerged during the 1990s: in 1987–1988, only 27 percent of new homes were multi-unit dwellings; by 1997–1998, this figure increased to 54 percent.

The case of Sydney illustrates how Chinese and other Asian settlement has impacted a large metropolitan area in Australia and highlights the new migrant residential concentrations and commercial areas. Elsewhere, I have argued that diaspora Chinese capital has made significant impacts on urban development in a number of Asian Pacific cities (Wu, 2000). Although diaspora Chinese capital does not necessarily follow migration flows, it is well known that a number of Asia Pacific cities have received large numbers of Chinese migrants whose capital has significantly fueled urban development. These developments range from the so-called "monster houses" in Vancouver (Mitchell, 1997; Hutton, 1998), Asian malls in a number of other North American cities (Miller and Steinberger, 1998), and "ethnoburbs" in Los Angeles (Li, 1998), to what might be characterized as "cosmopolitanization" in Brisbane, Australia (Ip, Anstee and Wu, 1998)

The concentration of recent Asian migrants in Sydney has a number of implications. First, international migrants have helped maintain a modest population growth in Sydney, balancing out those moving from Sydney to the other parts of suburban coastal Australia. Second, Asian migrants have also dispersed into a large number of suburbs in the metropolitan area. According to the 1996 Census, 11 out of the 46 local government areas have more than 10 percent of their population born in Asia.[7] Third, during the 1980s and 1990s, there emerged several suburban shopping areas dominated either by Asian-owned businesses or businesses catering to Asian residents. In addition, a number of mainstream commercial areas experienced an injection of many more businesses owned and managed by Asians but not necessarily catering only to Asian customers. Fourth, Sydney, like most metropolitan areas of the world, has a Chinatown located on the fringe of the central business district (CBD). In the 1970s and early 1980s, Chinatown expanded to cater to the needs of the growing Asian population, but the emergence of other centers meant that its dominance as the center of commerce and services catering to the ethnic Chinese and other Asian population is vastly diminished.

Sydney has a higher percentage of independent and business migrants as well as students in comparison to Australia overall, as New South Wales is the preferred destination of international students studying in tertiary institutions in Australia. Sydney is also the destination of a much higher proportion of those who have tertiary education. At least two spatial implications of these conditions have emerged: new residential concentrations of recent Asian migrants based more on socioeconomic background than ethnic group identity and new concentrations of commercial areas, some catering to specific groups of co-ethnic Asian migrants. Among recent settlers from Hong Kong and Taiwan to Sydney, most of whom tend to be highly skilled or have the financial resources to be admitted as business migrants, significant numbers have sought housing in the more established suburbs or in suburbs with larger and stylish housing. Cherrybrook, a northern suburb of many new and large houses, has tended to attract a large number of settlers from Taiwan. Many Hong Kong families also settled in the northern suburbs around Chatswood, Killara, and other areas along the northern commuter railway line.[8] During the 1990s, along with the development of Chatswood as a major regional center, a significant number of businesses emerged catering to the needs of both Asian migrants and the mainstream population, especially restaurants, grocery stores, and personal and professional service providers. Settlers from China, many of them students studying in Australia who did not have the same means as many of the other Asian migrants, congregated in suburbs along the western rail line where affordable rental accommodations are available, in the suburbs of Ashfield, Auburn, and Canterbury. A large number of businesses owned and managed by migrants from China emerged in Ashfield, many of whom are from Shanghai.[9]

Australia has been receiving refugees from Vietnam since the 1970s, a fact reflected in the high percentage of those originating from Vietnam among the settlers to Australia (see table 15.1). Many of the Vietnamese refugees were first housed in government hostels. In Sydney, these were located in the western area of the metropolis, near the suburb of Cabramatta. In time, the local government area of Fairfield, of which Cabramatta is a part, has come to house close to 46 percent of the Vietnam-born population of the Sydney metropolitan area. Over the decades of the 1980s and 1990s, a major commercial center of fresh food outlets, restaurants, provision stores, fabric shops and many other types of commercial establishments emerged in Cambratta catering initially to the Vietnamese, but over time, also to the wider community. Settlers of Vietnamese origin also began to move away from the Cabramatta area, into suburbs closer to the city center where they have established new centers of residence and commerce (Knox, 2000).

These Asian suburbanization trends are a few examples of the new commercial enclaves that have emerged in the Sydney metropolitan area.[10] They share three important interrelated characteristics. First, all of them are next to or within walking distance of a commuter rail station. Commercial centers around railway stations are features of all major metropolitan areas in Australia. While there are smaller centers and individual establishments on highway strips, almost all of the ethnic business enclaves in Sydney have emerged around railway stations. Accessibility is clearly an advantage because such locations bring with them exposure to a much larger potential customer base. Second, the new ethnic commercial enclaves in Sydney are grafted on to existing commercial areas; none of them are entirely new developments as are the Asian malls in some North American cities. Asian businesses have carefully integrated investments into existing commercial districts that cater to both the Asian and larger general populations (Ip, Anstee and Wu, 1998). Third, partly because these developments are located in existing business districts, the areas are characterized by a mix of other businesses catering to or run by other ethnic groups. This distinguishing feature of Sydney's ethnic business concentrations, where Asian business enclaves are situated in a mix of businesses catering to other ethnic groups such as Greeks, Lebanese, Koreans and more, is quite different from North American cities. This amalgam reflects the Multicultural Policy in Australia which promotes an open society where people from different parts of the world work and live in harmony. Indeed by comparison to the conflicts that marked some neighborhoods in Vancouver in the 1980s (Ma, this volume; Hutton, 1998), Sydney has absorbed its recent Asian migrants with few incidents. The Asian influx into Australia was not as compressed in time and space as in Vancouver, Canada, and Asian investment in Australia has in many cases paid off over the longer term in the revival of local commercial districts and neighborhood vitality.

CONCLUSION

This study confirmed that the great majority of recent Chinese migrants to Australia had few difficulties settling in Australia. While there are disappointments for many, particularly in terms of limited employment opportunities, most found their expectations fulfilled. Even though the migrants have come from different countries and hold different types of visas, it is remarkable that the choice of Australia for most migrants is chiefly due to family and personal ties and the desire to seek a better physical and social environment for settlement. While new economic opportunities and employment are not entirely unimportant, these were not the chief reasons that prompted the majority of these individuals to migrate, nor were these the chief reasons for their choice to settle in Australia.

Many of the recent Chinese migrants can best be characterized as "new migrants" of Asia's new middle class. They are on the whole very well educated, have professional qualifications, have chosen to migrate for reasons other than economic concerns, and very often consider family ties and a better physical environment as important factors determining their choice of destination. Australia does not necessarily represent to these individuals vast new economic opportunities; on the contrary, few expected such opportunities in Australia. The great majority of the recent Chinese and other Asian migrants found their expectations fulfilled for a better standard and quality of life, better environment, and political stability. At the same time, they are realistic about social problems in Australia. While only a small percentage cited racial discrimination as an impediment to their settlement experience, close to half of those interviewed encountered racial discrimination in the context of their everyday lives. Still the great majority of the recent migrants responded that they perceive Australia as an open society and Australians as tolerant people.[11]

Considerable differences in migrant group histories contribute to a diversity of settlement experiences, which in turn lead to a multiplicity of spatial manifestations in a complex metropolitan area such as Sydney. Migrants from societies that are more experienced with non-Asian influences, such as those from Hong Kong, who have more professional skills, entrepreneurial experience and financial resources, are able to bypass the need for ethnic enclaves either in residential choice or business location. They are able to insert themselves into mainstream business areas without heavily relying on co-ethnic customers. Still, others, for a variety of reasons, such as not being able to access mainstream jobs because their qualifications are not recognized and they lack large financial resources, may be more attracted to ethnic enclaves as "ports of entry" to the new society. This latter group probably includes those from mainland China, many of them being "stranded" in Australia after the Tiananmen incident. The most visible transformations in the ethnic landscape are the new centers of Asian businesses that have emerged across the metropolitan areas of Australia. That many of the new Asian migrants are not confined to traditional enclaves and have eased into existing business centers reinforces the migrants' own positive views about the open nature of Australian society.

Overall, this study points to the conclusion that Australia's Multicultural Policy has had positive effects on the experience of Asian migrants and their perceptions of settlement in Australia. The recent backlash against Asian migration, embedded in the right-wing "One Nation" platform, has also likely had effects in both raising awareness about discrimination against migrants, and at worst, promoting it. But like the originating context of the "White Australia Policy" that characterized much of Australia's twentieth-century outlook on migration, the recent backlash reflects realities and problems of economic restructuring and social change some members of the "host society" fear and blame on migrants. Significantly more obvious now is the degree to which recent Chinese migrants are, through their investments and professional occupations, contributing to the vigor and growth of the Australian economy.

NOTES

1. See the Australian government's multicultural policy page at http://www.immi.gov.au/multicultural/index.html; and Hage (1998) for an analysis of media representations of the "One Nation" controversy.

2. The survey was supported by a Toyota Foundation grant jointly awarded to David Ip, Ikuo Kawakami and Christine Inglis. The assistance of Mwaniki Wa-Gichia

with data analysis is gratefully acknowledged. The study included migrants from China, Hong Kong, Japan, the Philippines, Taiwan and Vietnam.

3. Although there is a category of those in the age group 15–24, this was done to conform to census age categories. None of the respondents were below 18 years of age.

4. Since the great majority of the migrants stay in the capital city, it can be assumed Sydney is the preferred location.

5. Tim Beal and Farid Sos, in their recent book, observed that Taiwanese migrants to New Zealand and Australia migrated for "life style" reasons, confirming the answers given by the respondents to this study (Beal and Sos, 1999).

6. The Sydney metropolitan area is generally considered to be some 60 km east-west and 50 km north-south, encompassing 46 local government areas and a 1996 population of 3.56 million. The Greater Sydney metropolitan area takes in an area 200 km north-south and 100 km east-west.

7. The range of Asian-born in the local government area ranged from 0.58 percent to 21.88 percent.

8. In Sydney, the CBD is used as the reference point for locations. Northern suburbs refer to those suburbs north of the harbor from the CBD served by one of the main commuter rail lines and containing some of the more desirable residential areas. Western suburbs are found along the main western commuter rail line.

9. Many of the new businesses were probably established by those who could not have their qualifications recognized but confirmation of this possibility awaits further studies.

10. There are a number of other emerging Asian enclaves, notably several centers catering to ethnic Koreans.

11. Further research is required to assess the degree to which responses may reflect inhibition about critical or negative replies.

REFERENCES

Adelman, Howard, Allan Borowski, Meyer Burstein and Lois Foster, eds. 1994. *Immigration and Refugee Policy: Australia and Canada Compared,* Vols. 1 and 2. Melbourne: Melbourne University Press.

Beal, Tim and Farib Sos. 1999. *Astronauts from Taiwan: Taiwanese Immigration to Australia and New Zealand.* Wellington: APRI/Steele Roverts.

Castles, Stephen. 1992. "The 'New' Migration and Australian Immigration Policy," in Christine Inglis, S. Gunasekaran, Gerard Sullivan and Chung-Tong Wu, eds., *Asians in Australia: The Dynamics of Migration and Settlement.* Singapore: Institute of Southeast Asian Studies, 45–72.

Coughlan, James E. 1992. "Patterns of Settlement in Australia of Indochinese Refugees," in C. Inglis et al., *Asians in Australia: The Dynamics of Migration and Settlement.* Singapore: Institute of Southeast Asian Studies: 73–116.

Department of Immigration and Multicultural Affairs, Australia. 1999. *Immigration Update—June Quarter 1999.* Canberra, Department of Immigration and Multicultural Affairs.

————. 1999a. *Settler Arrivals 1998–99.* Canberra: Department of Immigration and Multicultural Affairs.

Department of Urban Affairs and Planning, N.S.W., Australia. 1998. *Shaping Our Cities.* Sydney, Department of Urban Affairs and Planning, 29.

Edwards, John. 1999. *The New Australian Economy.* Sydney: HSBC Securities.

Hage, Ghassan. 1998. *White Nation: Fantasies of White Supremacy in a Multicultural Society.* Sydney: Pluto Press.

Hutton, Thomas A. 1998. "International Immigration As a Dynamic of Metropolitan Transformation: The Case of Vancouver," in Eleanor Laquian, Aprodicio Laquian and Terry McGee, eds., *The Silent Debate: Asian Immigration and Racism in Canada.* Vancouver: Institute for Asian Research, University of British Columbia, 285–314.

Inglis, Christine and Chung-Tong Wu. 1990. "The 'New' Migration of Asian Skills and Capital in the Asia Pacific Region: Its Implications for New Directions in Theory and Research," in R. Reed, *Patterns of Migration in Southeast Asia.* Berkeley: Center for South and Southeast Asian Studies. Occasional Paper No. 16: 282–302.

————. 1992. "The 'New' Migration of Asian Skills and Capital to Australia," in C. Inglis, et al., *Asians in Australia.* Sydney: Allen and Unwin, 193–230.

Ip, David, Mark Anstee and Chung-Tong Wu. 1998. "Cosmopolitanizing Australian Suburbia: Asian Migrants in Sunnybank," *Journal of Population Studies,* 19: 53–79.

Knox, Malcolm. 2000."Sweet and Sour," *Sydney Morning Herald* (Sydney), Mar. 8, 13.

Li, Wei. 1998. "Los Angeles' Chinese Ethnoburb: From Ethnic Service Center to Global Economy Outpost," *Urban Geography,* 19(6): 502–517.

Macken, Deirdre. 1996. "Sydney: Asia's Southern Suburb," *Sydney Morning Herald* (Sydney), Sept. 6, S1–S4.

Miller, M. and M. H. Steinberger. 1998. "America's New Voice," *Far Eastern Economic Review,* 161: 29–32.

Mitchell, Katharyne. 1997. "Transnational Subjects: Constituting the Cultural Citizen in the Era of Pacific Rim Capital," in Aihwa Ong and Donald Nonini, eds., *Ungrounded Empires: The Cultural Politics of Modern Chinese Transnationalism.* New York: Routledge, 228–256.

Pe-Pua, Rogelia, Colleen Mitchell, Stephen Castles, and Robyn Iredale. 1998. "Astronaut Families and Parachute Children: Hong Kong Immigrants in Australia," in Elizabeth Sinn, ed., *The Last Half Century of Chinese Overseas.* Hong Kong: Hong Kong University Press, 279–298.

Skeldon, Ronald, ed. 1994. *Reluctant Exiles? Migration from Hong Kong and the New Overseas Chinese.* New York: M. E. Sharpe.

Walker, David. 1999. *Anxious Nation: Australia and the Rise of Asia 1850–1939.* Brisbane: University of Queensland Press.

Wu, Chung-Tong. 2000. "Diaspora Chinese Capital and Urban Development in Asia Pacific," in Gary Bridge and Sophie Watson, eds., *Blackwell Companion to the City.* London: Blackwell, 365–390.

16

Conclusion: Regions of Diaspora

Carolyn Cartier

The geography of the Chinese diaspora is one of the great demographic subjects of the modern era. Emigrants from China have formed significant overseas communities worldwide. The scholarly field of Chinese diaspora studies has been a productive interdisciplinary arena, enlivened by renewed migration from China in the late twentieth century. The chapters in this volume examine especially geographical conditions of the diaspora to assess spatial complexities of diaspora and the importance of the concept of place in the formation of diasporic communities and Chinese overseas identities. In all the ways that geographical subjects have become popular in recent scholarship in the social sciences and humanities, our interest has been to foreground the geographical realities (rather than metaphorical geographies) of diasporic processes, and from different methodological and theoretical perspectives among geographical approaches. As an ongoing process of migration, relocation, negotiation of place, and community formation, our interest is the Chinese diaspora as a set of dynamic geographical subjects.

Still, as several chapters in this volume discuss, defining the Chinese diaspora has been an unwieldy task: diverse interpretations characterize both the word diaspora itself and the subjects it implicates. This brief conclusion revisits the definitional problem in geographical terms by asking about the territorial assumptions and implications of the Chinese diaspora. What does the idea of the Chinese diaspora imply about the origins of the migrants? What does "Chinese" mean in Chinese diaspora? The goal of posing these questions is to destabilize the sense of an equation between "Chinese" and "China" in the context of diaspora and reorient territorial implications of diaspora away from the nation-state container of interest to the realities of places and regions of migrant origins and destinations.

REGIONAL ORIGINS AND REGIONAL SETTLEMENTS

Time and again the chapters in this volume point to the origins of the Chinese diaspora on the southeast coast of China, in Guangdong and Fujian Provinces, and, to a somewhat lesser degree, in Zhejiang Province as well. The historic diaspora has not been equally represented by migrants from diverse regions of China—though small numbers of people from northern and western provinces have emigrated—but has been regionally specific to the southern coastal provinces. The southeast coast is China's maritime region, the center of historic international economy, port cities, long-distance trade, and overseas migration. When European mercantilists first ventured into the South China Sea in the sixteenth century, mariners of the south coast had been regularly sailing to Taiwan, Japan, and Southeast Asia for hundreds of years, if not millennia. Understanding the south China coast as a maritime trading region distinguishes the region from the larger landed empire of China, where the experience of traveling overseas was relatively unknown and ideas about it, as Lin points out in his chapter, in the context of Confucian society, were disdained.

The counterpart to the origins of diaspora in the south China coast is the overwhelming concentration of Chinese diasporic settlement in coastal urban centers of the Southeast Asian region. As Ma's chapter documents, among the worldwide population of ethnic Chinese overseas, over three-quarters are in Southeast Asia. The concentration of the Chinese overseas population in Southeast Asia has had significant social and economic impacts in the region itself, where settlement has also concentrated regionally in the major port cities and mercantile centers. These geographies of Southeast Asian settlement have both historic and contemporary dimensions. As Rigg recalls, throughout the first half of the nineteenth century the population of Bangkok was over half Chinese. In Vietnam, the largest Chinese settlement concentrated in the main port and trade center of the country, Saigon, in the district of Cholon, which has been one of the largest Chinese settlements in the diasporic world. During the French colonial period, estimates of the numbers of Chinese residents of the Saigon-Cholon area were upwards of half the total population. Like Bangkok, the Chinese population dominated Saigon by shear numbers until after the turn of the century. In Malaysia too Chinese migrant populations came to be the preponderant group in mercantile towns. The British colonial Straits Settlements, Malacca, Penang, and Singapore, were centers of migrant residence whose economies depended on the activities of Chinese merchants and traders. In the built environments of these cities today, Straits Chinese architecture represents the historic prominence of these communities. Migrant groups from Zhejiang have also left regional imprints.

Zhejiang migrants, especially from the Wenzhou area, have especially settled in Europe, and this migration flow continues in the contemporary period.

Even as the weight of historic diasporic settlement was predominantly urban, important communities of Chinese overseas also settled rural areas. In his chapter exploring meanings of the diaspora, Skeldon reminds us of the importance of Chinese labor in nineteenth-century primary resource economies. Chinese workers opened up tin mines in Malaysia and worked goldfields in Australia, California, and South Africa. Their labor contributions to colonial plantation economies undergirded the expansion of cash crop production in the evolving world economy. In the middle of the nineteenth century the south China coast was the leading region from which colonial administrators worldwide sought contract workers for labor-strapped economies. As a result, shiploads of Chinese workers left Fujian and Guangdong for places like Java, Belize, Cuba, Martinique, Peru, Demerara, and Hawaii, in addition to the more conventional destinations in the Straits Settlements. Where indentured labor was concerned, ship captains often told the men they were bound for the Straits Settlements—the most desirable destination—when in fact they were heading for the Pacific Islands or the Caribbean. In his chapter on Honolulu, Chang discusses the centrality of Chinese workers to the success of sugar plantations in the islands. Sugar was already an important cash crop on the south China coast, and workers from the region proved indispensable in reproducing the regime of sugar production on Oahu. Skeldon points out too the role of Teochiu migrants from northern coastal Guangdong in introducing sugar cultivation to Thailand. Chinese migrants also proved central to the transformation of colonial Malaya and they were the primary force in planting rubber on the peninsula. Where the need for workers in mining declined, communities of Chinese agriculturalists were maintained through the twentieth century, though their numbers have decreased with industrialization and urbanization. While substantially smaller in numbers, migrant workers from the northern Chinese provinces of Shandong, Hebei, and Henan also worked in the South Africa gold mines in the first decade of the twentieth century, but the vast majority of these workers returned and these flows did not give rise to long-term settlement.

DIASPORA IN THE ERA OF WORLD CITIES

The contemporary diaspora reflects the rise of "world cities" (cf. Hall, 1966; Friedmann, 1986; Knox and Taylor, 1995; Sassen, 1994; Lo and Yeung, 1998) in China, and second wave diasporas from Hong Kong, Taiwan and Southeast Asia. While migrants from southern coastal China are still numerous, and informal migrants from Fujian have made headlines worldwide, contemporary migrants are just as, if not more, likely to be from China's major cities: Beijing, Shanghai, and Guangzhou. Migrants from Hong Kong especially increased in the run up to 1997, when Hong Kong was repatriated to China. Political economic dilemmas also contributed to the departure of Chinese from Malaysia, especially in the 1980s. In her study of New Zealand, Ip points to these conditions. Before the 1987 New Zealand policy changes on immigration, the overwhelming majority of the Chinese New Zealanders were Cantonese speakers from Guangdong Province. After 1987, the sources of Chinese immigrants became much more diverse, from Hong Kong, Taiwan, Malaysia, Singapore and other Southeast Asian countries, as well as from the People's Republic of China. Significantly, migrants from China to New Zealand in the last decade were more likely to be young urban intellectuals from metropolitan centers instead of from the historic source areas in rural south China. They also settled in the major metropolitan regions. In the early 1990s, 97 percent of the Chinese population lived in cities, over 90 percent in Auckland, Christchurch, and Wellington. Wu discusses similar patterns for Chinese settlement in Australia's capital cities and their suburbs. The characteristics of contemporary Chinese migration to the U.S.—which has the largest Chinese population outside Asia—also reflect changes in immigrant origins and patterns of urban settlement. Fan's study of post-1965 Chinese migrants to the U.S. indicates that greater numbers speak Mandarin and Formosan, and so are likely from northern China and Taiwan respectively. In addition, Chinese Vietnamese-language speakers among recent immigrants reflect an emerging source of Chinese immigrants from Vietnam. In the U.S. too, the settlement patterns of Chinese migrants show an overwhelming preference for urban regions: over 95 percent resided in urban areas, concentrated in Los Angeles, New York, and San Francisco, in addition to rapidly growing metropolitan areas like San Jose, suburban New Jersey, and Orange County.

The formation of urban Chinese communities worldwide and the mobility of diasporic populations is perhaps most powerfully symbolized by Hong Kong. The Chinese population of Hong Kong, with its population origins in the Lingnan region, in Guangdong and Fujian Provinces, epitomizes the distinctive patterns and processes of the historic diaspora. In addition, as a center of origins of second wave diasporas, Hong Kong also figures centrally in the contemporary diaspora of Chinese migration to and from world cities and metropolitan regions. Yet despite Hong Kong's contemporary centrality in the geography of diaspora, as Lin argues, local Hong Kong identity has been based in a sense of cultural marginality by comparison to China at large. As predominantly Cantonese speakers with a strong sense of being a historic migrant population on the periphery of the Chinese nation, a general perspective on Hong Kong identity reflects ideas about exclusion and the tradition of sojourning to other countries. Lin reasons that this marginal identity perspective among the southern Chinese accounts for strong attachments to native place in southern China rather than to the less known larger entity of "China." As a central place in both historic migrant flows and the sphere of contemporary Chinese transnationalism, the case of Hong Kong demonstrates how ideas about regional identity formation reflect both realities of migration and settlement, and symbolic cultural relations between places at different scales—Hong Kong, dialect regions of the south China coast, and China at large. On this basis we can also historicize changing identity formations in a preliminary sense. Historic ideas among the southern Chinese of Hong Kong have been maintained in association with transregional ties to the homeland region of the Chinese coastal provinces, whereas the places of contemporary identity formation, in an era of second wave diasporas, may more likely pivot around Hong Kong, Vancouver, San Francisco, London, and other world cities. Certainly too, some individuals maintain identity affiliations across a broad spectrum of place affiliations, from homeland village origins to residential and working experiences in multiple world cities.

Comparisons with conditions of Chinese settlement elsewhere in North America and the U.S., in addition to South America, underscore larger-scale patterns and processes of Chinese settlement on the world scale. In Canada too the Chinese population has increasingly concentrated in the largest cities and metropolitan regions. As Lai documents in his chapter, in 1941 nearly half of the Chinese settlement in Canada was in six major Chinatowns: Vancouver, Victoria, Toronto, Montreal, Calgary, and Winnipeg. By 1996, about 70 percent of the Chinese population were in Metro Toronto and Metro Vancouver, and 15 percent were in Montreal, Calgary and Edmonton. What is known about the Chinese in Latin America also brings us to focus on settlement in major cities, in Havana, Lima, Mexico City, and Panama City, as Kent demonstrates in his analysis. In the Caribbean basin, the Chinese population has declined through the twentieth century, while it has increased in Argentina, Brazil, and Peru. This change reflects the demise of the need for Chinese agricultural workers in island sugar cane economies, and the enhanced presence of Chinese mercantile and industrial interests in the larger urbanized economies of Latin America. Thus the increased urban predominance of Chinese settlement reflects transformations in regional economies and labor markets over the twentieth century.

Interest in the waxing and waning of Chinese settlement in "Chinatowns" frames the chapters by both Lai and Chang. In the case of the Honolulu Chinatown, Chang points out that it was never really a residential area solidly settled by Chinese: even in 1920, when the Chinese population was at its peak, the settlement composition of the Honolulu Chinatown was just over half Chinese. By 1990, its Chinese population had decreased to just over 20 percent, and the larger Chinese population in metropolitan Honolulu lived in diverse suburban areas, many of them upscale residential districts. Lai's focus on the rise, decline, and resurgence of Canadian Chinatowns also reflects transformations in regional economies and labor markets over the twentieth century, and speaks to more general processes of urban transformation worldwide. In Canada, Vancouver and Toronto have become the largest centers of Chinese settlement; these are also Canada's leading world cities. Like the city-regions of Toronto and Vancouver, at the heart of major metropolitan regions are primary and secondary world cities, cities that have emerged as central nodes of interconnected economic activity in the present era of the world economy. Many world cities have their origins as ports in mercantile trading economies and related speculative investment, from mining to railroads, and these economies typically drew on migrant labor. To fast-forward a century and more to the present era, these same nodes in the world economy have only continued to increasingly draw on the mobility of labor and capital. Where once "Chinatowns" were the distinctive areas of nonwhite immigrant settlement in nascent world cities, now world cities typically count several districts of peoples with different ethnic and country origins. Or in the case of Honolulu, the so-called Chinatown has functioned as an area of settlement for diverse ethnic groups. So the processes at work in historic "Chinatowns"—immigrant settlement, the formation of ethnic enclaves, and segmented labor markets—were precursors to conditions that are widespread in world cities today, conditions at the foundation of what we now regularly consider aspects of globalization.

As a result of these kinds of changes in major urban areas over the twentieth century, the reality of "Chinatown" in many world cities has become in part a historic concept: original Chinatowns have fallen into decline, only to be rehabilitated for commercial functions by tourism investment and cultural heritage movements. Lai especially documents this process in Canada, and Chang points to the role of the contemporary Chinatown in Honolulu as a tourist destination. In Singapore, after a remarkable postcolonial industrialization drive, which resulted in widespread modernization of the urban landscape, the state is actively engaged in revitalizing the original Chinatown for both cultural heritage and tourism purposes. In Malaysia too the Straits Chinese shophouses are being increasingly targeted by the state and private interests for commercial development, in some cases compelling longtime residents to move and spurring fragmentation of historic communities. As the reality of "Chinatown" as a concentration of Chinese migrants has shifted in importance, new commercial centers catering to Chinese populations have grown up in suburban areas. This transformation also characterizes Los Angeles, where the largest, most vibrant Chinese community is in the suburban city of Monterey Park, and New York City, in the case of Flushing, Queens, which is a new Chinatown on Long Island east of Manhattan. But the original Manhattan Chinatown remains distinctive for its continuing economic functions, including a garment industry, and in absorbing new migrants, especially from Fujian.

REGIONS AND IDENTITY FORMATION

If we understand the diaspora through geographies of regions, how might that bear on ways of thinking about diasporic processes? If region is foregrounded instead of nation-state, how might that suggest ways of resituating identity formation? The typical statistical measures of demographic analysis are based on the nation-state, but should that fact compel us to equate migrant populations with nation-state representations? Thinking about diasporic origins and destinations of settlement in terms of regional formations—the realities of dominant patterns of settlement—suggests downplaying the role of nation and nationalism as the prevailing geographical bases of identity formation. The idea of homeland as region of origin rather than nation-state maintains a sense of the possibilities of historic place attachment without the implications of competing nationalist loyalties that have characterized debates over identity in Chinese overseas communities, especially in the post–Second World War and postcolonial periods in Southeast Asia. Still, regions are only one scale of possible identity orientation. The territorial pivot of identity formation also shifts, from hometown to home province and nation in the contexts of migration, community formation, and distance from place of origin. These ways that diasporic identities are relatively fluid and hybrid are not ungrounded, but rather are shifting in their territorial attachments and place representations, among villages, cities, provinces, and nation-states, in the processes of diasporic mobility. While it has been common for the nation-state to view regionally based identity positions as either parochial or threatening to national interests, what is more interesting in the contemporary period of international mobility is how new regional identities intersect with national identities, other regional identities, homeland identities, and so forth (Cartier, 2001).

For Chinese overseas, the idea of region as homeland of origin both realistically and ideologically elides the national imaginary of China as the primary pivot of historic identity formation. The idea of the region of homeland origin, whether that region is south China or southern Fujian, affords

Chinese people outside China the opportunity to both claim their roots and maintain positions of citizenship and nation orientation in their resident countries. International migrants may also lay claim to diverse national identities, but it is important to consider how relations of scale bear on territorial associations of identity formation: at a large scale, far from one's homeland, it is common for the "host society" to ascribe national-scale identity markers to travelers, migrants, and people in immigrant communities. Among those communities themselves, by contrast, people are more likely to differentiate based on subnational and local-scale factors of association, from common provinces and cities of origin to hometowns and villages, and also common dialects and their regional dimensions. Assessing identity through perspectives on place and region, and in relation to national-scale interests, allows ways of seeing through to the geographical realities of individual and group identity formation.

The significance and potential of regionally based identity formations is underscored in Kong and Yeoh's assessment of changing state policy in Singapore. The state's mission to construct a uniform national identity has had the effect of eroding differences within the Chinese community identity by weakening markers of regionally based identities, especially by influencing language use. Promotion of English combined with the "speak Mandarin" campaigns diminished the use of regional dialects, one of the basic elements of subethnic identity formation among Chinese populations. Yet, in the state's ongoing project to emphasize "nation" above "community," it has also sought to reassert Chinese cultural identity, by supporting Chinese clan association ties, racially based self-help groups, the inscription of "Chineseness" in Chinatown, and in the explicit call to regionalize by building "Chinese networks" across the East Asia region. The Chinese community in Singapore has responded selectively and critically, sometimes apparently embracing such policies, in welcoming reconnections with their roots and ties, at other times, rejecting the state's constructions of "Chineseness," and at yet other times, renegotiating identity formation through new issues and discourses.

Interpreting identity formation for people with ties in both Taiwan and the mainland can be especially complex. Hsing's assessments of identity formation among entrepreneurs from Taiwan working in the mainland provide discerning perspectives that inform thinking about these geographical realities of identity formation. Her analysis maintains that shared group identities have historical and spatial dimensions that cannot be simply reduced to deterritorialized representations, and yet the multiple dimensions of identity, based on language, place of origin, gender and class, merge and intersect in sometimes apparently contradictory ways so that historic spatial conditions are complicated by such diverse axes of orientation. Such complex and potentially transformative identity formations challenge the monolithic forms of identity often ascribed to people in diaspora and those built by the state. But such circumstances do not necessarily undermine state-promoted identities; rather, understanding identity formation must be explored as a series of ongoing negotiations between the state and individuals at the local scale. In these ways, rather than trying to identify such a thing as a coherent "Chineseness," it is more realistic to assess multiple paths of identity formation as a dynamic at and between different levels of scale. The complications of Taiwan identity are obviously sensitive at the scale of the nation-state, as Williams discusses in his chapter about the historical and contemporary conditions bearing on identity formation in Taiwan. Tensions between "mainlanders" in Taiwan and "local Taiwanese" continue, and in the context of rising local identity movements in Taiwan among the Hakka and the Hoklo which play out distinctively in the political process.

The importance of the scale dimension in identity formation appears most explicitly in Leung's ideas about "home." Leung assesses how in diaspora, attachments to multiple places undermine notions that "home" should be equated with fixed and bounded territories, and especially with only the nation-state. Ideas and realities about multiple "homes" typically represent different geographical scales, from the household itself to hometowns, home states or provinces, and so forth, so that "homes" can be understood as intersections of social relationships at different spatial scales. Leung's research, based on interviews with Chinese migrants in Germany, in addition to that of Kong and Yeoh, and Hsing, point to possibilities for future research on geographical ideas and realities about identity formation in diaspora. In the way that cultural ideas about place are socially, politically, and economically constituted, people's ideas about themselves in relation to place must be discovered in local contexts and in relation to broader axes of spatial relations in state and society.

FUTURE DIASPORAS

Ultimately, and in considering directions for future research, it is critical to reconsider Skeldon's recognition that "transnational linkages of a Chinese diaspora may certainly have been no more, and were likely to have been less, than in European migratory flows." The countries of Southeast Asia essentially closed their doors to Chinese migration in the middle of the twentieth century with the emergence of the postcolonial state. In contrast, Australia, Canada, and the U.S. initiated legal Asian immigration again only in the middle of the 1960s. These conditions underscore how the settler societies of the U.S., Canada, and Australia became the principal destinations for new Chinese migrants by the 1970s. Moreover, the reality of the numbers of people at stake by comparison to European migratory flows, or any other migratory flow, points to important questions for conceptualizing diaspora studies. The Chinese diaspora has been understood to be distinctive for its size in shear numbers, the ubiquity of Chinese settlements in urban areas on the world scale, and the significance of Chinese capitalists in national and transnational economies; yet if European migrations and capital flows are even more significant on these terms, then on what basis do we calculate the importance of Chinese diaspora? Does some essential "Chineseness" define the field of study? In what ways is the field based on some common denominator of "Chineseness," and when is it simply based on race?

The idea of the commonality of "Chineseness," promoted by both Chinese and non-Chinese, has a long history (cf. Cohen, 1991; Tu, 1991; Wang, 1991; Chow, 1998). Discussions of constructions of Chineseness especially inform cultural studies; whereas some economic accounts of "Chinese capital" tend to leave what is "Chinese" unproblematized and so reify a priority of race above other factors of association. A central problematic is that these spheres, i.e., the cultural and the economic, are not entirely commensurate, but ideas about "Chineseness" sometimes move uncritically between them. The most uncritical studies of networked Chinese capital have assumed ideas about "Chineseness," but then in Malaysia, as my chapter critiques, the common paradigm of "networked Chinese" business organization does not define the role of the Chinese in the economy, since class alliances in the Malaysian economy have been more important factors of capital association than linkages maintained on the basis of race or ethnic group. The Malaysian case is distinctive for the size and political power of the Chinese elite in the country, but all places and regions have their social, political, and economic differences. Since, as Skeldon again cautions, the reality of the Chinese diaspora is not a single great wave of people, but is rather made up of many separate and distinct elements, on what other bases of conceptual organization besides "being Chinese" might diaspora studies be formulated? Accepting the realities of the global migration system means becoming aware of the differences among and within migrant groups, and working to theorize relations between contemporary economics, politics, and changing cultural formations.

In an era of poststructural theory and postmodern approaches in cultural studies, themes of place and space have become noticeably popular. While the explosion of interests on geographical subjects appears across the disciplines from economics to literary studies, it is not always clear why interest in geographical subjects has come to the fore. In many cases, the interest seems to be just a trend, and for some following the use of new postmodern language, the attention appears largely linguistic: we encounter this in the lively use of such words as "cartographies of . . . ," "mapping," "placing," etc., when the subject matter at stake may lack actual geographical concern. The new interest in place and space has origins though, which can be identified in the geographical realities and experiences of life and work under the contemporary conditions of the world economy. While the popular label for these conditions may be "globalization," from faster paced lifestyles to transnational capital networks and their concentrated effects in world cities and increasingly uneven wealth distribution, Harvey (1989) theorizes these conditions in "time-space compression." In this context, "rapidity" is the decrease in the turnover time of capital, which compels a faster pace of exchange in the economic sphere and ultimately diverse other arenas, from the workplace to the household. The increased mobility that results, including increased disruptions and relocations, from migrating for work to job loss, arguably leads to greater interest in achieving place stability—or at least interest in negotiating the new spatial complexities that have resulted in the process.

We might consider migration and diaspora studies in this broad context. How do regions of diaspora and their cultural histories figure in the geographies of time-space compression? In the early 1980s in Hong Kong the business-lunch landscape everywhere was distinguished by the world's greatest concentration of cellular phone subscribers, many using their new hand phones to maintain contact with factories in Shenzhen, before the conventional telephone lines were ubiquitously available and usable in Guangdong. Regional industrialists had effectively skipped over one level of infrastructure, from few stationary telephone lines to cellular technology, in the process of producing the most rapid growth rates, in Shenzhen, in recorded history. If "networks" are the hallmark of business and social organization in the contemporary era of globalization, it is because they are especially suited to the rapidity of information flow. But the cautionary conceptual response is, rather than becoming deterritorialized, corresponding geographies are more complex than ever before. "Flows" and "networks" signify a set of mobile, transcale spatial processes, including the experiences of migrants in diaspora; cultural forms and economic forces are a result of spatial processes and emplaced activities of diverse agents in multiple settings at different scales with discrepant histories. The historical layers of cultural, economic, and political practices that had to be laid down to produce the realities of the region in the Pearl River Delta are myriad and, practically speaking (in the demanding intensity of the present), apparently unaccountable. This is one reason why "flows," "networks" and "diaspora" have taken hold in both scholarly and popular discourses, for the ways in which they can be used to mark or stand in for complex spatial processes in the contemporary era. A next generation of diaspora studies increasingly focused on the realities of spatial processes and the meanings of place they influence will likely do even more to untangle these geographies.

REFERENCES

Cartier, Carolyn. 2001. *Globalizing South China,* Oxford: Blackwell.

Chow, Rey. 1998. "Introduction: On Chineseness As a Theoretical Problem," *Boundary 2,* 25(2): 1–24.

Cohen, Myron. 1991. "Being Chinese: The Peripheralization of Traditional Identity," *Daedalus,* 120(2): 113–134

Hall, Peter. 1966. *The World Cities,* New York: McGraw-Hill.

Harvey, David. 1989. *The Condition of Postmodernity: An Inquiry into the Origins of Cultural Change,* Oxford: Blackwell.

Friedmann, John. 1986. "The World City Hypothesis," *Development and Change,* 17(1): 69–83.

Knox, Paul and Peter Taylor, eds. 1995. *World Cities in a World System,* Cambridge: Cambridge University Press.

Lo, Fu-chen and Yue-man Yeung. 1998. *Globalization and the World of Large Cities,* Tokyo and New York: United Nations University Press.

Sassen, Saskia. 1994. *Cities in a World Economy,* Thousand Oaks: Pine Forge Press.

Tu, Wei-ming, ed. 1991. "The Living Tree: The Changing Meaning of Being Chinese Today," *Daedalus,* 120(2): 1–32

Wang, Gungwu, 1991. *The Chineseness of China: Selected Essays,* Hong Kong: Oxford University Press.

Index

agriculture, 118–19, 136, 167, 170–71, 293–94, 297, 303

Amoy, 80. *See also* Xiamen

anti-Chinese sentiment: in Australia, 367–69; in Canada, 313–16, 319–21; in Indonesia, 99–100; in Malaysia, 99; in Mexico, 120; in New Zealand, 340–41, 347, 353; in Thailand, 100, 104; in the United States, 264–65; in Vietnam, 105–8

Asian Americans, 262, 268–69, 279–80, 282–87

"Asian values", 199, 205–7

assimilation, 98, 103–4, 354

Association of Southeast Asian Nations, 81, 92n3

Australia, Chinese in and migration to, 9, 19, 27, 31, 33–34, 38, 55, 73–74

Baba Chinese, 61, 88

Bangkok, 20, 100, 103

Brazil, Chinese in and Chinese migration to, 117, 125, 128–30, 135

British Columbia, 26

Bukit China movement, 86, 89–91

business networks, 27–32, 58, 82–83, 104, 142, 222–29, 388–89

California, Chinese in and Chinese migration to, 269–78

Cambodia, Chinese in and Chinese migration to, 58, 60, 98

Canada, Chinese in and Chinese migration to, 9, 19, 22, 26, 33, 38, 73–74, 136, 146; Immigrant Investor Program, 27, 325–28

Canton, 20, 58, 80. *See also* Guangzhou

Cantonese, 20, 57, 144, 148–51, 150–55, 196, 264, 268, 303, 346–47

Caribbean, Chinese in and Chinese migration to, 52, 117–37

Changle, 22, 57, 59

Chaozhou, 20, 57, 150, 152, 154–55. *See also* Teochiu

China, 21–22, 29, 57, 166; mainland, 25, 31, 36–37, 166, 174–76

Chinatowns, 26, *83*, 106, 121, 130–33, 209–11, 273–74, 295–97, 302–5, 383–85

Chinese Americans, 261–62, 268–87, 315–17, 328–30

Chinese associations, 104, 133, 141, 302, 305–7, 317, 321, 349–51; clan, 204–8; *huiguan*, 141, 283; *tongxianghui*, 141

Chinese business conglomerates, 29
Chinese overseas, 12, *13–8,* 19–21, 28,
    35–37, 54–55, 59, 81, 143, 196;
    geographic distribution of, *13–8,* 19;
    population size of, 12, *13–8,* 19. *See
    also* overseas Chinese
"Chineseness", 37, 54, 62, 173, 205,
    211, 214–15, 225, 232n2, 353–55,
    388
Cholon, 106, 112n3
citizenship, 11–12, 33, 36, 61, 75, 81,
    99, 102–3, 250–51, 254n3, 254n5
Confucianism, 21, 40n9, 222, 232n3
Costa Rica, Chinese in and Chinese
    migration to, 127, 137
Cuba, Chinese in and Chinese migration
    to, 118, 126, 28, 130–32

dialect and speech groups, 54, *78–79,*
    150–55, 199–203. *See also*
    Cantonese, Hainanese, Hakka,
    Hokchia, Hokchiu, Hokkien, Hoklo,
    Kejia, Mandarin, Min, Shanghainese,
    Southern Fujian, Taishan, Wu
diaspora, 3–8, 22–23, 27–35, 37, 51–53,
    55, 57–58, 62–63, 73, 75, 92, 102,
    193–94, 237–49, 245n2; Chinese,
    4–5, 11–12, 19–23, 25, 27–28,
    30–31, 34, 37, 52–54, 56, 59, 61–63,
    89, 143, 216, 379–80, 388; diasporic
    consciousness, 32, 214; global, 6, 27;
    regions of, 380–87; Taiwanese,
    176–78; trade-based, 27–28

economy. *See* agriculture, business
    networks, Chinese business
    conglomerates, entrepreneurialism,
    migration, occupations, trade
education, 278–79, 298–79, 322,
    363–65
emigration, 2, 20, 53–55, 57, 73, 92,
    108
Enping, 57, *318*
entrepreneurialism, 27–32, 221–29

essentialism, 224–27
ethnic groups. *See* dialect and speech
    groups
ethnicity, 212–14, 216n9
Europe, 22, 52, 57

Fujian, 2, 9, 19–20, 22, 30, 57, 59, 61,
    76–77, 150, 152, 155, 268
Fuzhou, 22, 80

gender, 81, 249–52, 269, 300–301, 314,
    319, 341, 345
Germany, Chinese in and Chinese
    migration to, 237–38, 242–44
globalization, 4, 6–7, 19, 28, 30, 36, 52,
    75, 141–42, 156–57, 317, 389
Guangdong, 2, 19–20, 57, 59, 61,
    76–77, 118, 148–49, 268, 317, 346
Guangzhou, 80, 149, 346
guanxi, 29–31, 225–27
Guyana, 118, 122, 125–26, 135

Hainanese, 20, 57, 59, 196
Hakka, 20, 57–59, *85,* 118, 165–68,
    172, 178–79, 184, 196, 303. *See also*
    Kejia
Han (Chinese), 54
Hawaii, Chinese in and Chinese
    migration to, 59, 269, 272, 293–308
Hebei, 58
Heilongjiang, 58
Henan, 58
Hokchia, 57, 60
Hokchiu, 57
Hokkien, 20, 57, 59–61, 80, *85,* 196
Hoklo, 150, 152–55, 165–68, 172, 184
home, 34–35, 237–42, 246–54
homeland, 4, 7–8, 12, 32, 34–35, 37,
    51, 75; imagined, 8; region as,
    385–87
Hong Kong, 2, 9–10, 19–22, 27, 30–34,
    36–37, 56–58, 61–62, 84, 143–57,
    265–68
hostland, 4, 8, 12, 32–35

huaqiao, 39n7. *See also* overseas
Chinese

identity, 4, 6, 11–12, 32–33, 35–38,
52–54, 62, 75, 98, 143–44; Chinese,
36, 104–5, 205, 215; Chinese, in
Malaysia, 69, 86–88; Chinese, in
New Zealand, 353–55; Chinese, in
Southeast Asia, 36; Chinese
American, 283–84, 286–87;
diasporic, 36, 193, 253–54; ethnic,
212–14, 221–32; formation, 73,
75–76; "Hongkongese", 147–50;
national, 36–37, 53, 193, 197–99,
203–5, 213, 379, 385–87; native
place, 10, 144, 166, 168; place-
based, 36–37, 141–44, 148–49, 156;
regional, 385–87; spaces of, 98;
Taiwanese, 163–66, 183–86
immigration, 1, 2, 20, 57, 73, 92, 136,
145–50, 156, 195, 197, 262–68,
272, 287, 307, 311–33, 339–47,
359–66
Indonesia, Chinese in and Chinese
migration to, 9, 35, 54, 56, 69, 76,
90, 97, 99, 112n1, 2, 113n8

Jamaica, Chinese in and Chinese
migration to, 125
Japan: Chinese migration to, 74–75;
colonialism in Taiwan, 170–73;
imperialism in Thailand, 101

Kaiping, 57
Kejia, 150–53
Korea, Chinese in, 20
Kuala Lumpur, *83*

landscape, 87, 90–91; Chinese, 209–11;
cultural, 69; economic, 71–72; ethnic
and economic, 26; diasporic, 150–55;
urban, 36, 89
Latin America, Chinese in and Chinese
migration to, 37–38, 117–37

Lingnan, 148–49
Los Angeles, 22, 25–26, 271–78

Macau, 54, 57
Malay language, 199–200
Malaysia, Chinese in and Chinese
migration to, 69–92
Mandarin, 148, 152–54, 176, 200–204,
268
Melaka, Chinese in and Chinese
migration to, 76–77, 80–81, 89–90
Mexico, Chinese in and Chinese
migration to, 22, 117, 119, 133–34
migrants, 11–12, 20–22, 26, 28, 35
migration, 1–9, 51–54, 56–63, 75, 117,
167–68, 174–79, 181–83, 239;
container, 2; global, 3–4; informal, 9,
22–23, 39n1, 266; in-migration, 19;
internal, 178–79, 272–78, 362;
international, 2–4, 53, 55, 117–20,
155–56, 181–82; labor, 59, 80,
118–19, 195, 294, 297, 312–13;
"new", 61–62, 181–84, 346, 354–55,
359–75, 381–82; re-migration, 2, 8–9,
19, 34, 342; out-migration, 20, 299
migration theory, 2–4, 141–45, 239
Min, 165–66, 268
mobility, 1, 4, 29, 32, 37, 73, 75, 91,
141–43, 147–48, 156–57, 247–48,
382, 389

Nanhai, 58, 318
Nanyang, 20, 52, 70, 77. *See also*
Southeast Asia
New York, 269, 270–72
New York City, 22, 57, 271–73
New Zealand, Chinese in and Chinese
migration to, 9, 19, 33–34, 38, 73–74
Ningbo, 80
North America, 52, 59

occupations, 59, 176–77, 195, 279–83,
297–98, 312, 319, 322, 325–26, 330,
345

Orientalism, 63n, 240
overseas Chinese, 10, 52, 56, 120, 196.
    See also Chinese overseas

Panama, Chinese in and Chinese
    migration to, 120, 134–35
Panyu, 58, 318
Pearl River delta, 30, 32, 57–58, 76,
    264, 305
Peru, Chinese in and Chinese migration
    to, 117–22, 132–33, 135–36
Philippines, Chinese in and Chinese
    migration to, 20, 30, 61, 76
place, 4–11, 19, 25, 32, 36–38, 388;
    diasporic, 9, 12, 37; formation, 10; as
    home, 31, 34, 36, 241–42, 246–50,
    253; native, 10, 20–21, 28, 32, 34; of
    origin, 5–6, 9, 11, 19–20, 23, 25, 27,
    29, 54, 60, 63
Punti, 118, 165, 303

Quanzhou, 168

race and race relations, 262; Australia,
    363–70; Indonesia, 35; Malaysia,
    35, 82–87; and representations of
    race in Singapore, 193, 196, 198,
    204–6, 208–9, 215; and
    representations of race in the
    United States, 283–85
remittances, 6, 23, 31

San Francisco, 32, 272
Sanyi, 58, 118
Seattle, 271
Shandong, 20, 58
Shanghainese, 32, 61, 80, 151–55
Shantou, 20, 84–85
Shunde, 58, 318
Singapore, Chinese in and Chinese
    migration to, 21–22, 27, 30–31, 38,
    54, 59, 73, 76, 80–81, 84, 88–89,
    193–216

Siyi, 57–58, 152–53, 318, 346
smuggling, 22–23
"snakehead", 22, 266
social networks, 10–11, 20, 28
social exclusion, 109–12
sojourner, 52, 54–55, 60
South Africa, Chinese in and Chinese
    migration to, 52, 57, 80
South America. *See* Latin America
South China, 2, 4, 9, 57, 76–77, 80,
    148, 156, 380
Southeast Asia, Chinese in and Chinese
    migration to, 2, 9, 19, 28, 32, 36–38,
    52, 58–62, 69, 76–77, 80, 97–99,
    102, 109–12, 146, 380; and regional
    economy, 98–99
Southern Fujian, 228–29
space, 5–9, 11, 19, 37–38, 61, 245,
    388; global, 4, 7, 23; diasporic,
    7–9, 29, 239–40, 251; of places, 9,
    239; spatial distribution, 269–78,
    347–49; spatial interaction, 8, 12,
    19; spatial network, 8, 23; spatial
    process, 5, 37
Strait Settlements, 70, 80, 89, 380–81
suburbanization, 271, 273–78, 302,
    329–33, 348–49, 373
Surinam, Chinese in and Chinese
    migration to, 118–19, 122, 125
Sydney, 371–74

Taishan, 20, 57, 318
Taiwan, 2, 10, 19, 21–22, 26–27, 30–32,
    37, 51, 56–57, 61–62, 74–75, 222,
    224, 226–31, 265–68
Tanka, 150, 152
Teochiu, 20, 57–59, 61, 104, 196. *See
    also* Chaozhou
Thailand, Chinese in and Chinese
    migration to, 30, 38, 54, 58–60, 76,
    97–105, 110
Toronto, 22, 26–27
trade, 21, 80, 89, 180, 293

transmigration, 4–6, 8–11, 19–20, 23, 32–34, 36, 38
transnationalism, 4–7, 37–38, 141–42, 156–57
travel, 6, 23, 33–34, 37, 75
Trinidad and Tobago, Chinese in and Chinese migration to, 118–19, 122, 125–26, 128, 135

United Kindom, 56, 58
United States, Chinese in and Chinese migration to, 9, 19, 22, 33, 38, 56, 61, 73–74, 261–87
urbanization, 271–78, 302–4
Uruguay, Chinese in and Chinese migration to, 122

Vancouver, 22, 26–27, 35
Vietnam, Chinese in and Chinese migration to, 30, 76, 97, 105–13

Wenzhou, 57, 59
women. *See* gender
world cities, 381–85
Wu, 57

Xiamen, 80, 89
Xinhui, 57, *318*

Zhejiang, 22, 57–59, 61
Zheng He, 77, 90
Zhongshan, 58, 118, 294, 305–6, *318*
Zhujiang delta. *See* Pearl River delta

About The Editors and Contributors

EDITORS

Laurence J. C. Ma received his B.A. from National Taiwan University and Ph.D. from the University of Michigan. He is Professor Emeritus in the department of geography and planning of the University of Akron, and is now an independent scholar working in California. He is the author of *Commercial Development and Urban Change in Sung China, 960–1279* (Department of Geography, University of Michigan, 1971), *China: The Geography of Development and Modernization* (co-authored with Clifton W. Pannell, Edward Arnold, 1983), and co-editor of *The Environment, Chinese and American Views* (with Allen G. Noble, Methuen, 1981). He continues to publish widely on China's population and urban development.

Carolyn Cartier is associate professor of geography at the University of Southern California. Her research emphases are cultural and economic geography in South China and Malaysia. She is the author of *Globalizing South China* (Blackwell, 2001) and diverse articles on Asian landscapes and regional development, including a major review article on regional China in *Modern China* 28(1), 2002.

CONTRIBUTORS

Sen-dou Chang is professor of geography at the University of Hawaii. He has published numerous articles on China's urbanization, historical and contemporary, overseas Chinese, and China's population and environmental issues in such journals as *The Annals of the Association of American Geographers, Geographical Review* and *Cities*.

C. Cindy Fan is professor of geography and chair of the Asian American studies program at the University of California, Los Angeles. She has published widely on China's regional development, urban system and migration. Her works have appeared in *Annals of the Association of American Geographers, International Journal of Urban and Regional Research, International Migration Review, Professional Geographer, Environment and Planning A* and other major journals. Her current projects focus on migration and institutions, gender and marriage migration, and regional restructuring in China.

You-tien Hsing is associate professor of geography at the University of California, Berkeley. She is the author of *Making Capitalism in China: The Taiwan Connection* (Oxford University Press, 1998) and a number of articles on overseas Chinese capitalist networks and local politics in China. She is at present working on local-global politics of land development in China.

Manying Ip is senior lecturer in the school of Asian studies at the University of Auckland. Her books include *Dragons on the Long White Cloud: The Making of Chinese New Zealanders* (Tandem Press, 1996) and *Home Away from Home: Lifestories of Chinese Women in New Zealand* (New Women's Press, 1990).

Robert B. Kent is chair and professor of the department of geography and planning at the University of Akron. A leading geographer on Latin America, he has had extensive field experience and published widely on various aspects of Latin American countries.

Lily Kong is associate professor in the department of geography, National University of Singapore, and dean of the faculty of arts and social sciences. A social and cultural geographer, she has interests in religion, music, cultural policy, constructions of "nation," national identity, "nature" and environment in Southeast Asia, especially Singapore. She is the author of *Singapore: A Developmental City-State* (with Martin Perry and Brenda Yeoh, John Wiley, 1997), and co-editor of *The Naga Awakens: Growth and Change in Southeast Asia* (Times Academic Press, 1998, with Victor Savage and Warwick Neville), and *Globalisation and the Asia Pacific: Contested Territories* (with Kris Olds et al., Routledge, 1999).

David Chuenyan Lai is professor of geography at the University of Victoria. He has surveyed many Chinatowns in Canada and the United States and has published widely on overseas Chinese, including *Chinatowns: Towns within Cities in Canada* (University of British Columbia Press, 1988).

Maggi W. H. Leung teaches in the department of geography and resource management at the Chinese University of Hong Kong. She is completing her doctoral dissertation, "Making Homes in Transnational Space: An Inquiry into the Multiple Ways of Being Diaspora Chinese in Germany." Her research focuses on entrepreneurship, social identities, and ethnic networks among ethnic Chinese migrants in Germany.

George C. S. Lin is associate professor of geography at the University of Hong Kong. He is the author of *Red Capitalism in South China: Growth and Development of the Pearl River Delta* (University of British Columbia Press, 1997) and a large number of articles on economic development in South China and East Asia.

Jonathan Rigg is teacher in the department of geography, University of Durham. He has published extensively on Southeast Asia, especially Thailand. His books include *More than the Soil: Rural Change in Southeast Asia* (Prentice Hall, 2001), *Southeast Asia: The Human Landscape of Modernization and Development* (Routledge, 1997), *Southeast Asia: A Region in Transition* (Unwin Hyman, 1991), and *Counting the Costs: Economic Growth and Environmental Change in Thailand* (Institute of Southeast Asian Studies, 1995, editor).

Ronald Skeldon is professorial fellow in the School of African and Asian Studies at the University of Sussex. An authority on migration, he has taught in the department of geography and geology at the University of Hong Kong and the Institute for Population and Social Research, Mahidol University, Thailand. Among his books are *Migration and Development: A Global Perspective* (Longman, 1997) and *Population Mobility in Developing Countries: A Reinterpretation* (Belhaven, 1990). He is also the editor of *Reluctant Exiles? Migration from Hong Kong and the New Overseas Chinese* (M. E. Sharpe, 1994) and *Emigration from Hong Kong: Tendencies and Impact* (Chinese University of Hong Kong Press, 1995).

Jack F. Williams was for many years director of the Asian Studies Center at Michigan State University where he is currently professor of geography. He is an authority on Taiwan with extensive field experience and has published numerous studies about the island's economy, agriculture, environment and cities.

Chung-Tong Wu has been dean of the Faculty of the Built Environment at the University of New South Wales since 1996. Before that he held teaching positions at the University of Sydney and the University of Hawaii. Among his recent research projects are city and town design in Indonesia, Malaysia, Vietnam, Taiwan and China, comparative study of cross border development in Asia and Eastern Europe, and Asian migrants' views of multiculturalism in Australia. He has published extensively on Asian migrants in Australia.

Brenda Yeoh teaches social and historical geography at the National University of Singapore where she is also director of the Centre for Advanced Studies. She is the author of *Contesting Space: Power Relations and the Urban Built Environment in Colonial Singapore* (Oxford University Press, 1996), *Singapore: A Developmental City State* (co-authored with Martin Perry and Lily Kong, John Wiley, 1997), and co-editor of *Gender and Migration* (with Katie Willis, Edward Elgar, 2000).